Iran: Past, Present and Future

D0040384

Iran: Past, Present and Future

Aspen Institute/ Persepolis Symposium

**Edited by
Jane W. Jacqz**

Aspen Institute for Humanistic Studies

Library of Congress Cataloging in Publication Data
Main entry under title:

Iran—past, present, and future.

   "Held in Persepolis, Iran, in September 1975."
   Includes bibliographical references and index.
   1. Iran—Economic policy—Congresses.   2. Iran—
Economic conditions—Congresses.   3. Iran—Social policy
—Congresses.   4. Iran—Congresses.   I. Jacqz, Jane W.
II. Aspen Institute for Humanistic Studies.
HC475.I737   330.9′55   75-45315
ISBN 0-915436-10-8
ISBN 0-915436-09-4 pbk.

Preface

Iran has moved into the modern era—and assumed a central place in world affairs—with extraordinary speed. The rapidity of these events has outpaced the growth of knowledge about Iran. Many leaders from different societies have not been sufficiently familiar with the richness of Iran's cultural heritage, its traditional values, its current plans and aspirations. Fortunately, there is growing awareness of the need to obtain a deeper and broader understanding of Iran, which represents an interface between East and West in all of its dimensions.

The encouragement and support of Her Imperial Majesty The Shahbanou of Iran and a grant from the Pahlavi Foundation of Iran enabled the Aspen Institute for Humanistic Studies to organize the Aspen Institute/Persepolis Symposium. Its purpose was to bring about a better understanding of Iran—its past, its present and its future—and to widen the circle and deepen the thought of those who should be engaged in an ongoing dialogue with the people, ideas and institutions of that country. The Symposium was held in Persepolis, Iran in September 1975.

It was an occasion marked by a sense of history. More than 100 leaders from 14 countries met intensively for a week with over 50 leading Iranian Government officials, civil servants and scholars; enriched themselves through exposure to the cultural treasures of Persepolis, Shiraz, Isfahan and Tehran, and experienced the warmth of traditional Iranian hospitality.

Why did the Aspen Institute bring together the participants at Persepolis? The Institute is convinced that it is central to its objectives and its international mission to facilitate the opening up of dialogue among leaders of thought and of action on the critical human and social issues of our time. An assessment of how Iran can build a better future while preserving the best of its past is vital to this dialogue. Those outstanding participants who came to Persepolis from all over the world have helped to reinforce our conviction about the significance and usefulness of this process.

Discussion throughout the Symposium was full, open and frank. It covered many aspects of Iran's past; the vast range of opportunities and problems that characterize Iran today, including the central problems of how to preserve and adapt significant values from the past and how to discard those values that are impeding cultural and social development in a rapidly changing society; and, the implications of current plans in Iran for its future and the future of the world outside Iran. Throughout the sessions, Iranian participants responded openly to inquiries from the participants—a unique demonstration of candor and goodwill. For non-Iranians and Iranians alike, the Symposium was a significant learning experience; a dialogue that informed, stimulated and enriched; a communication that brought friendship and understanding.

The non-Iranian participants came to Persepolis from North America, Europe, Asia and Africa. They were a diverse group, representing the academic and scientific sectors, the business community, cultural institutions, jurisprudence, the media, government, and nonprofit organizations and private philanthropy. They returned from the Symposium with enormous respect for the range of talent and depth of commitment among the Iranian participants, many of them quite young, with firsthand experience of Iran's achievements in agriculture and industrial development; and with a sense of the richness and beauty of Iran's cultural history, a heritage that infuses all aspects of Iranian life. Non-Iranians and Iranians alike, through the Symposium experience, were stimulated to become more reflective about the problems of their societies and the interconnections between Iran, their countries and the collective world community.

Inevitably, this book has limitations. The sheer amount of printed space taken up by the formal papers prepared for the Symposium causes an imbalance. The brief summary of discussions does not adequately convey the extensive and frank dialogue at Persepolis. Those participants who had the benefit of historical lectures, briefings and trips to Persepolis, Isfahan, Shiraz and Tehran gained a much deeper appreciation for Persian culture and historic tradition, as well as a better understanding of Iran's view of its future. In brief, they came away with a more comprehensive sense of a nation in transition and the competing demands of economic, cultural and human development.

This first Symposium represented only a beginning. The dialogue should be carried on and extended.

Many possibilities of concrete action for strengthening understanding and communication between Iran and other countries and for cooperative efforts to help Iran achieve its economic and social goals emerged at the Symposium. Implementation of useful suggestions is being pursued through a variety of means. The Aspen Institute shares the goal expressed by Her Imperial Majesty at the opening session of the Symposium that concrete actions should follow from the papers and discussions. Indeed, "thought leading to action" is a goal of all Aspen Institute programs. We expect that the Symposium will lead to a wide range of future activities linking institutions around the world—including the Aspen Institute—with Iran, providing Iranians with new modes of outreach and new opportunities for international contact, enriching non-Iranians through their associations with Iran and uniting Iranians and non-Iranians alike in consideration of the major global problems that plague our increasingly interdependent world.

In closing, I would like to express the deep appreciation of Robert O. Anderson, Chairman of the Aspen Institute, and of the Institute's trustees to Her Imperial Majesty The Shahbanou of Iran, whose warm support and personal participation contributed enormously to the success of the Symposium. The vision of progress conveyed in Her Imperial Majesty's moving closing address typifies the finest expression of how development goals must be concerned with human beings and cultural values.

In addition, I would like to express the Institute's appreciation to Prime Minister Amir Abbas Hoveyda, to the many Iranian ministers and leaders who took precious time to be with the group, and to the co-chairmen of the Symposium, Messrs. Anderson and Majidi. Without the leadership, commitment and enormously hard and intelligent work of Manouchehr Ganji, the Symposium would not have been a success. Dr. Ganji was largely responsible for commissioning the papers, selecting the Iranian participants, supervising preparations and assuring that the Symposium would be conducted effectively in the warmest possible environment. A spontaneous tribute to his efforts at the end of the Symposium indicated our appreciation for what he did before we arrived, as well as for his lively contributions to the discussions.

I would also like to thank members of the Aspen Institute staff and others who contributed to the arrangements for the Symposium, including Moselle Kimbler and Jill Davis of the Aspen Institute and Forrest D. Murden and his colleagues. We are especially indebted to Jane W. Jacqz for her most skillful preparation of the Symposium report and for editing this volume.

Although no written summary can do justice to the Symposium's magnificent setting or the feelings of friendship that developed among participants, what follows is intended to bring the information discussed at the Symposium to a wider audience, summarizing the substance of the discussions and conveying a sense of participants' interests and concerns.

J. E. Slater
President
Aspen Institute for Humanistic Studies

February 1976

Table of Contents

In Lieu of an Introduction

In our attempt to write a suitable introduction that would give a sense of the symposium and the ideas and information presented there, we have come to the conclusion that in Daniel Yankelovich's concluding remarks we have a most eloquent statement, one that provides the reader with an intimate knowledge of what can be expected in this volume. We need only to add one point. We sincerely believe that if, in the process of the symposium and through this volume as one of its products, we have made possible a better understanding of the realities of Iran—its past, present and future—our efforts have been well rewarded.

Manouchehr Ganji and J. E. Slater

Statement by Daniel Yankelovich

There are many possible perspectives from which to sum up one's impressions of this remarkable week. It could be done from the standpoint of a Middle East expert, or an expert in economic planning, international trade, agriculture or oil; from a geopolitical point of view, or even from a professional conference point of view. From these varied perspectives, one might reach conclusions far different from my own, which are drawn from the perspective of the Aspen Institute for Humanistic Studies; that is, from the point of view of what is required to build a humane society and not just a rich, fast-growing industrial society.

From this standpoint, I will confess to you that by Tuesday night, after the first two days of meetings, I was not optimistic. We had heard many excellent papers on planning. They emphasized the crucial elements of economic development: the large-scale infusion of capital, thanks to the oil resource; plans for rapid development of the manufacturing sector leading to an export capability; the training of technicians and planners; and the quest for the all-important factor of technology transfer, etc.

I sensed that we were hearing not simply an economic plan, which is necessary and desirable, but an ideology of economic planning—a mystique that resolves all conflicts and difficulties in favor of rapid economic growth. At the heart of my concern lay the fear that even if the ambitious economic objectives could be reached, it would be at a tremendous human cost. I saw the specter of the dark and all-too-familiar side of too-rapid industrialization:

- A largely rural population uprooted from the countryside to generate urban sprawl in the cities;
- The emergence of a new economic/planning bureaucracy that would take on a life of its own;
- An urban elite growing more prosperous and materialistic while the mass of Iranians waited for an agonizingly slow "trickle-down";
- The breakup of families;
- The spread of delinquency, violence, crime and other symptoms of anomie and alienation;
- And then, inevitably, the inexorable rise of authoritarianism to contain the pressures, rather than the reverse process of gradually enhancing political freedom as Iran achieved emancipation from its ancient scourges of poverty, ignorance and disease.

During the course of our discussions there were many scattered warnings from the delegates—both Iranian and non-Iranian—about a too-exclusive emphasis on economic ideology:

- Mr. Farmanfarmian warned us to beware of economists bearing projections;
- Mr. Ajami warned us not to underestimate the Iranian farmer, observing that he was a survivor, skilled in the ways of outwitting bureaucracies;
- Mr. Farhat, and then Catherine Bateson, warned of the fragility of traditional Iranian life ways that might not bear the onslaught of materialism;
- Mr. Pesaran warned that the trickle-down theory would not work;
- Arjay Miller warned about trying to do too much too fast;
- Waldemar Nielsen warned about the temptations of authoritarianism in the pursuit of social discipline, a theme that reverberated throughout the meetings time and time again;
- For me personally, the most eloquent warning note came from Mr. Soedjatmoko, who asked: "How are we going to avoid the worst of all possible outcomes for the developing nations, which is to destroy life ways that have endured for centuries, without being able to deliver on the promise of a better material life?"

All of these warnings reinforced my own uneasiness about the hubris of economic planning, an uneasiness shared by many others, Iranian and non-Iranian.

Then came Wednesday's meeting, and with it a turning point—and a profound sense of relief. I began to see that these impressive, skillful, dedicated young Iranian planners were not ideologues of naive economic planning: they were fully aware of the dangers; they were struggling with them, and seeking to confront them head-on. And, instead of copying the institutions of the West, they were engaged in building new institutions appropriate to the special conditions of Iran.

I began to realize that the Iranians were determined not to permit economic development and modernization to destroy the goals of a humane society, but, on the contrary, were determined to make economic development serve these goals. Man does not live by bread alone, but without relief of poverty, disease and ignorance, a truly humane life is hardly possible.

Yet, to reconcile economic and social/humanistic objectives in a brief period of time is a task of heartbreaking difficulty. I think it may be useful, therefore, to list very briefly some six principal points of tension that exist between the economic and the social/humanistic objectives of Iran, because these can then serve as our common framework for understanding the dynamics of the process of reconciliation.

These six points of tension, which obviously apply to most societies undergoing rapid change, are:

1. The tension between being citizens and being subjects. Fulfilling the economic objective needs only malleable and passive sub-

jects mobilized to be responsive to the plan's requirements, while the humanistic side calls for active involvement by citizens who, as Mr. Ganji forcefully emphasized, participate in the political process because they know that their participation will count and will make a difference.

2.   The tension that surrounds income distribution. Paying attention only to economic development is likely to end up with the rich growing richer, while the poor have more babies. The humanistic side calls for a more equitable distribution of what there is to distribute.

3.   The tension over traditional values. Traditional values are often conservative and stand in the way of efficient execution of the economic plan. Yet, clearly, it is of the essence to ensure that a shallow materialism does not destroy the integrity of this rich, ancient and beautiful culture.

4.   The tension between economic efficiency and basic human needs. Optimizing the economics may call for bringing people to the jobs and depopulating the rural areas. Humanistic considerations call for efforts to minimize the impact of uprooting people's lives and for developing new methods of bringing jobs to people—even at the cost of some inefficiency.

5.   The tensions created by bureaucracy. Economic planning calls for "top-down" centralized planning and for setting priorities in accordance with rational economic considerations. Humanistic considerations call for rooting priorities in the felt needs of people.

6.   The tension between suppressing dissent and institutionalizing it. The most fundamental tension lies in the government's response to conflict and dissent, some of which is inevitable—and desirable. A humanistic society will develop institutionalized modes of channeling dissent that give the citizenry the opportunity to express confidence or lack of confidence in the leadership, while a planning bureaucracy will tend toward self-perpetuation, irrespective of its ability to meet people's needs and to gain their confidence.

Coping with these six foci of tension and finding a creative resolution to them is the never-ending challenge of a growing and vital society. Neither the Iranian nor the non-Iranian delegates pretend that this monumental task has been accomplished. The Iranians know that nothing worthwhile is ever created without risk.

What is enormously heartening to me is the depth of Iranian concern and determination not to ignore these gut issues. As I perceive it, this determination is rooted both in a compassionate concern for the Iranian people and in the practical pragmatic recognition that ignoring the humanistic side could create so much political chaos and destabilization as to betray the vision that inspires the entire effort.

John Gardner launched these meetings with a superb overview of the challenges ahead for all of us. As a fellow psychologist, I share with him his interest in those rare moments when institutions reach a peak of incandescent creativity and their efforts produce something new and vital for humankind.

All such moments of high creativity share certain common characteristics: the outstanding one is a fusion into a new unity of elements that previously appeared to be in opposition to one another. So it is with Iran's efforts to form a new unity out of the tensions between economic modernization and human needs.

Among nations, human history records relatively few acts of creativity that bring forth a new model of the good society appropriate to its time, place and circumstance. I feel we have had the rare privilege this week of catching a glimpse of such an act of creativity in the making— something new and unprecedented under the sun. Its significance for the emerging relationship between the developed and the developing nations cannot be overestimated.

I anticipated that I might see something of significance for Iran. I now feel that what Iran is seeking to accomplish holds great significance not only for Iran, but also for my own country and for all the countries of the world. For this gift of renewal, on behalf of all of us, I thank our Iranian hosts.

Iran: Past, Present and Future

1. Iran in the Modern World

Opening Address by Her Imperial Majesty The Shahbanou of Iran*

It is my pleasure to welcome you to Persepolis, the ancient capital of the Achaemenids, for the Aspen Institute/Persepolis Symposium. As you very well know, Persepolis at its height was the multifaceted center of the Persian Empire, the focal point of art, culture, economic and social development, and political innovations. It is therefore befitting that, on this day, we should inaugurate a symposium whose theme is "Iran: Past, Present and Future" under the shadow of this city's past greatness. For, if we are to connect Iran's past with Iran's present and future, there can be no better setting than these majestic ruins that lie silently at the foot of the Zagros Mountains, reminding us of the genius of the Iranian people, their history and the promise of their future. And if we are to visualize the Great Civilization that Iran is striving for, under the leadership of His Imperial Majesty The Shahanshah, then it is imperative that we immerse ourselves in the milieu that symbolizes the greatness of the past and reveals to us the animating light that has guided this country through the ages.

I would also like to reiterate, as I have done many times, how pleased I am to reinforce further by means of this symposium the strong bonds that have come to exist between Iran and the Aspen Institute for Humanistic Studies. It is no accident that this relationship, in a short span of time, has grown to the extent that we see today. For the Aspen Institute, at the very core of its philosophy and purpose, is an institute dedicated to research in value-oriented studies; that is, a type of research that places the human being on the center stage and that holds as its guiding theme that material well-being and technological innovation must enhance the creative instincts of the individual. And the Iran of today—a society undergoing rapid transition, traumatized by the conflicting winds of tradition and change, learning to cope with modernism, materialism and new technological processes, and attempting to maintain its cultural heritage—is a country where the ultimate aim of the Great Civilization is to provide a value-rich and creative environment, an environment where the individual will be able to express himself and to harness the material and technological processes for improving the quality of his life.

I have had the opportunity to look over many of the papers that will be presented by Iranian scholars to the symposium. While the topic

---

*The Aspen Institute/Persepolis Symposium opened on the morning of September 15 in a magnificent reception tent adjoining the ruins of Persepolis, the final and most eloquent expression of the culture of the ancient Near East. Participants were welcomed to the symposium by Her Imperial Majesty Farah Pahlavi The Shahbanou of Iran, who inaugurated the conference with this address.

"Iran: Past, Present and Future" is wide, the papers are of necessity much narrower in scope. Indeed, it would be impossible to discuss the multidisciplinary aspects of Iran's progress in its totality in the five days scheduled for the symposium. Yet I am sure that the main aspects of this overall experience in development and modernization will be isolated and discussed. It is my hope that the papers that will be presented to the symposium and the discussions that follow will better acquaint you and others concerned with the results of our endeavors toward the achievement of progress and social justice.

Ultimately, any gathering of this kind will be judged successful to the extent it lends itself toward a constructive dialogue. Man must share his problems and his experiences if he is to prevail in his struggle for a better world. To neglect the ultimate unity in man's problems and prospects is an invitation to his defeat. It is in the appreciation of this unity that we share with others the practice of our revolution and the experiences of our development.*

---

*Responding to Her Imperial Majesty, Robert O. Anderson, chairman of the Aspen Institute for Humanistic Studies and co-chairman of the Aspen Institute/Persepolis Symposium, expressed the hope that the symposium would permit focused discussion of various aspects of the Iranian experiment in rounded development, which represents, in many ways, the hopes and aspirations of all developing countries and in whose future the entire world has an enormous stake.

Social Change in the Modern World

Abdolmajid Majidi

The magnitude and timeliness of the subject that will preoccupy the attention of this symposium can certainly not be overlooked. For, at this particular juncture in history, Iran, along with only a handful of other countries, is in the midst of a uniquely challenging experience that is swiftly transforming the very structure of its economic, social, cultural and political life.

This is not to claim that the rest of the world is not simultaneously exposed to the inexorable mark of change. Indeed, one may be hard put to single out any society that is currently immune from social and economic changes of one degree or another. Even in the most industrialized and developed societies one is daily witnessing novel, and at times totally unexpected, developments that deeply affect his lifestyle, value orientation and socioeconomic structure. In fact, it is safe to assume that no society can long remain untouched by the incessant challenges of change in our era when the global diffusion of knowledge, technology and capital at an ever-increasing rate has become the most pronounced feature of international life.

After over a century of industrial and material progress that has paved the way for increasing individual and social well-being, the developed countries—whatever their sociopolitical systems—are still striving to improve their standard of life and reach higher levels of scientific and technological progress. The fulfillment of these dual objectives becomes nearly impossible in those countries where the political and administrative leaders are faced with a paucity of resources and a limited number of developmental possibilities. The resulting social and economic failures in such countries tend to complicate governmental functions, further increase the level of general discontent and often lead to violent upheavals—all of which can only delay and even fully halt the very process of socioeconomic development.

How long can the international community turn away from these facts and remain indifferent to the explosive nature of such a state of affairs? Must not the overriding universal objective be a high rate of socioeconomic development everywhere across the globe and not just in parts of it? And if this objective is truly accepted by all, can it be attained without full economic cooperation among all members of the international community, developed and developing, rich and poor?

Surely the divergence of views between the industrial and industrializing parts of the world—of which the current disagreements between the producers and consumers of raw materials are only one manifestation—leads us nowhere near that objective. Surely the wasteful and dangerous rivalries that still dominate the Great Power relations cannot but impede the holy struggle of millions, nay billions, of human beings for a better, a more decent life. And must not one regard such rivalries among great and powerful members of the international community—who indeed have many positive common interests—only as an evasion of their basic responsibilities?

Never in history has the human race been faced with greater perils than it is today: the perils of population explosion, of disastrous food and housing shortages, of inadequate health care and services, of illiteracy and low-quality education. These are all issues that must be dealt with in any discussion of the problems of development and developing societies.

Iran has, herself, fully come to grips with such issues and problems in the last decade. While availing herself of the valuable experience of other countries, both developed and developing, she has also broken new paths and devised unique national solutions for many of her social and economic problems—solutions that will be discussed in this symposium.

It may certainly be argued that we in Iran owe much of our developmental gains to our natural wealth. It must, however, be readily admitted that without a strong leadership, without a responsible administration and without a disciplined and orderly society—all of which have been the essential features of our society in the past decade and a half—we could not have taken advantage of our natural wealth and financial opportunities in the most rational and appropriate manner.

We have thus attempted not only to attain a steadily high rate of economic growth on as wide a basis as possible but also to accelerate the process of our sociopolitical development simultaneously. For we have come to believe that not merely by growth of production but by integrated, multifaceted and thereby self-sustaining development can our society truly aspire to a great future and reach for the lofty ideals that have beckoned mankind throughout the ages.

On these and other related achievements is based our firm belief that the future holds great promise for this land, that the benefits of our economic growth will be shared by all of our citizens and that economic and social justice must and shall be the hallmark of our society.

These are indeed the requisite conditions—in addition to financial possibilities—that must materialize for all developing societies. The international community as a whole cannot and must not abdicate its responsibility for the creation of these conditions.

The Modern World: General Perspectives

John Gardner

When Joe Slater asked me to give the opening speech at this conference, I protested that I knew little of Iran, and he said, "You will be the only person who is *not* talking about Iran. Your topic is the rest of the world." I asked what he meant by that and he said, "Oh, contemporary problems, trends, political and social currents—*you* know."

Obviously the assignment was impossible. The world in 31 pages. It's not a speech, it's an adventure in compression.

All that I say shall reflect two themes: interdependence and the renewal of institutions. And I address my remarks not just to the distinguished people in this room but to all people everywhere who worry about this troubled world.

We look at the world today with an awareness that an era is ending and something else is coming. We don't know what lies ahead. But we know that it will be a period in which problems become increasingly entangled with one another, and nations increasingly interdependent. Old sources of steadiness and continuity have disappeared, and we may have to live with instability for some time to come.

One characteristic of the great transitional periods is that old attitudes, customs and institutions live on despite their incapacity to serve new needs and realities. The new attitudes, customs and institutions must grow up amid the time-sanctioned clutter of the old.

New arrangements meet with resistance, for the very good reason that they threaten long-established ways of doing things. Established patterns are not easily changed, whether they are the ways of corporations or tribes, the prerogatives of a military bureaucracy in an industrial nation or an elite class in a developing nation.

The instinct of humans to stabilize their environment leads them to invest their institutions with a sense of permanence, of sacredness, of unchallengeable rightness. And this leads over the years to an institutional rigidity that is essentially anti-nature. Nature is tumultuous, moving, changing, always in flux. Things are being born, maturing, adapting, surviving, dying. One thing waxes, another wanes. There are cycles of growth and decay. Things ebb and flow.

Humans create organizations and societies to serve their shared purposes and then gradually rigidify those institutions as though in a vain attempt to shut out the tumult of nature. But nature wins. Eventually, in trying to shut out the great ebb and flow of life, organizations and societies smother themselves.

No society really enjoys the kind of transformations the unrolling future demands. In many of the problems a nation faces it can find a villain or external circumstance to be blamed and assaulted. But in matters of social change, the problem is all too often the villain within—within oneself, within one's society. Thus the critics among us who tell us precisely what our trouble is may be fiercely resented— because they tell us to rearrange things within ourselves (or our society) that we have no intention of rearranging.

We are really quite good at telling others how they should reshape their ways. It becomes more difficult when the nation involved is our own nation, when the social class is our own social class, when the power structure is the very one that gives us our privileges. Yet that is where renewal must begin—for every nation represented here today, and for all that are not, for the old societies that are also old nations, and for the old societies that find themselves functioning as new nations. We all have tasks of renewal.

It isn't just that we have problems to solve. We have problems that we can only solve together. Only together can we accomplish the tasks that will ensure the survival of the species and the planet.

I shall talk first about arms control, then economic matters, and will then make some general remarks about conflict and order.

Arms Control

The possibility of nuclear conflict outweighs all other dangers. In the question of nuclear arms control, the U.S. and the U.S.S.R. are living in the past. They seem wholly preoccupied with their wildly expensive rivalry, as though it was still the tidy, bipolar competition of yesterday. But it isn't. Debate over the effectiveness of détente is the ragged end of an old argument. The Cold War is over. Its fierce but clear-cut bipolar rivalry has been replaced by something infinitely more complicated, unpredictable and dangerous. It's a multipolar world. Proliferation is here. No one knows what additional nations will blast their way into the nuclear club tomorrow. Every day the possibility increases that accident or miscalculation will shatter the delicate balance of fear and readiness among the nuclear powers. Worse yet, unexampled destructive power will soon be available not only to extremist groups, with their berserk vindictiveness, but to warped or lunatic individuals. The next nuclear bomb detonated in anger will very likely be set off by a terrorist repre-senting no nation.

There is a strong tendency on the part of the Third and Fourth World countries to ignore the nuclear arms race. Yet all will suffer if radioactive dust envelops the globe in the wake of major conflict. All are suffering now as the arms race ravenously consumes scarce resources. And the rest of the world is affected by another consequence of Great Power rivalry: the U.S. and the Soviet Union, aware of the dangers of direct confrontation, are increasingly inclined to pursue their competition through intervention in the internal or external conflicts of smaller nations.

There are steps that the U.S. and the Soviet Union could take tomorrow to deescalate their deadly competition, but it is impossible to halt the arms race as long as no one really wants to. We must create a body of opinion, worldwide, that sees the dangers and demands that steps be taken to avert them. The Third and Fourth World countries can be helpful in that effort. We must all educate ourselves as to the processes by which international hostility escalates, and the things in our own natures, as individuals and as nations, that precipitate conflict. We should understand, for example, that the thing that will most surely contribute to everyone's national security is an international system capable of resolving conflict peaceably. We should understand that no nation can afford to leave national security policy solely in the hands of its military and defense bureaucracy, which must, by the nature of its commitment, imagine the worst and prepare for it. We must understand the ungovernable upward spiral of fear and suspicion that is generated when hostile nations confront one another. The myth of the U.S.-U.S.S.R. arms race is that each reacts to the other in a sort of Wimbledon symmetry; but the reality is more complex and frightening. Each reacts to what the other *might* do, or *might be capable* of doing. The reaction precedes the action. Both sides desperately need stabilization of the arms race, yet each is driven to seek a destabilizing superiority. In its nature the process is without limit.

Now the modest proliferation represented by the so-called "nuclear club" is swiftly giving way to the far greater proliferation that is inevitable with the commercial transfer of nuclear energy technology. It is said that there are already as many as 20 nations that can lay their hands on weapons-grade nuclear materials.

Unless we take a wholly new path, the moment of catastrophe is coming. The new path will have to be an internationally managed system for control of nuclear materials. Perhaps we will achieve such a system before catastrophe. Perhaps the catastrophe will have to come first. If we achieve it before catastrophe it will be an agreement freely arrived at, with minimum elements of coercion. After catastrophe, no doubt the solutions will be harsher. The nations of the world—all nations, not just the superpowers—could spare themselves great hardship by moving as rapidly as possible toward an ironclad, internationally managed agreement for supervision, inspection and control of all nuclear materials, including the production, transport and use thereof. What is most crucial is internationalization of the fuel cycle, the enriching of uranium, the reprocessing of plutonium and storage of the waste. We are at a histori-cally crucial moment in the spread of the technology. Internationalization could take place now with relatively little strain. With every year that passes, more nations will be deeply involved in activities that they will be most reluctant to internationalize.

There is an alternative, of course. We can put our heads down and await the disaster.

Poverty and the Developing Nations

Of the two billion people in the roughly 100 developing nations, about 40 percent, or 800 million, are barely surviving. Many aren't surviving. We all know the harsh facts of absolute poverty—mental and physical hand-icaps stemming from malnutrition and lack of medical care, handicaps that cripple for life, death at an early age.

Those in absolute poverty are found mainly in the rural areas, most of them living outside the monetary system. Educational opportunities are totally inadequate, illiteracy is almost universal. Population density is generally high and so are birth rates. Of course, poverty is not limited to the developing nations. It exists in many industrial nations, including the United States, and must be combated wherever found.

Hunger is a particularly serious problem. In most of the poverty areas it is not only a question of supply but of distribution. Even in good years many go hungry. Prices of food in the international market have made things worse. Since 1972, corn and wheat prices have more than doubled, rice has tripled. All the basic resources for food production—land, energy, water, fertilizer, seeds—have been either in short supply or very expensive.

While supplies dropped due to crop failures of recent years, de-mand continued its dizzying upward climb, pushed chiefly by popula-tion increases but also by excesses of consumption in the affluent na-tions. The latter is illustrated by the fact that a consumer in the low-income countries consumes about one pound of grain a day, directly, while in North America an individual consumes about five pounds a day, directly, or indirectly in meat, milk and eggs.

The most significant move to improve rural poverty and hunger will be to raise productivity on small subsistence farms in the food-deficit nations themselves. Japan and Taiwan have proved that the small farm can be productive.

But many of the measures required to improve small farm produc-tivity pose an internal challenge to the developing nations themselves. The elites within the developing nations have tended to favor urban constituencies and, in rural areas, to favor the large farmer—as happened in the United States. The supplying of credit, water, transportation and the like to the small farmer will require a sharp change in attitude on the part of elite segments of the population. Government food pricing policies often leave the farmer with little incentive.

In such internal power relations, as in population control and other matters, there is a point beyond which outsiders cannot help. Finally, all depends on the capacity of the developing nation itself to face its own problems, motivate its people and carry out necessary political reforms.

In many developing nations, unfortunately, the elite groups have shown little interest in taking the difficult steps to help their own poverty-stricken population. And if they show no interest, it's hard to stir interest in the industrial countries. But some developing nations have shown a heartening willingness to act, and we may hope that others will follow.

With all due credit to internal factors, help must also come from outside if the developing nations are to solve their problems. Robert McNamara has pointed out that without outside aid to the Fourth World nations, these nations will have negative growth rates per capita for the remainder of this decade, but that they could achieve a modest positive growth rate with very little additional help.

The past two or three years have brought a devastating combination of blows to poor nations. These nations have seen a loss of their export markets due to recession in the industrial nations, and inflated prices of almost everything they import. The rise in oil prices alone has more than outweighed the foreign aid they have received.

Meanwhile, the average share of the GNP that the developed countries allot to official development assistance has dropped from .52 percent in 1960 to .30 percent in 1973. The goal for such assistance during the second development decade was set at .7 percent of GNP, but the developed nations are far from achieving that figure. The United States, the Soviet Union, all of the industrial nations and the OPEC nations, should join hands in a development partnership that would meet the need.

Secretary Kissinger has proposed a $10 billion fund within the International Monetary Fund to be lent to the developing countries to protect their development programs against fluctuations in the international market.

Many experts are now seeking "automatic" means of raising development-assistance funds on an international basis. The most immediately discussed possibility would be to declare the deep sea bed an international "commons," with the resources drawn therefrom allocable to the poorer nations.

Those who manage programs of development assistance have learned much about the appropriate technology for such assistance. They have learned that the receiving nations must have a voice in formulating plans for assistance programs and that every program should build indigenous leadership and skills for the future. Unfortunately, donors of bilateral aid have not yet learned that development assistance programs should not be used as leverage to control the political or military policy of the receiving nation.

The United States bears a special responsibility for aid in meeting the food crisis. North America has a more dominant position with respect to the world's exportable food supplies than the Middle East does in oil. Since 1972, the U.S. has supplied 40 percent of the world export of food grains and oil seeds.

The target set by the World Food Conference was 10 million tons of food aid annually. As Secretary Kissinger pointed out, this fiscal year the U.S. food aid budget provides for almost 6 million tons of food grains— almost 60 percent of the world target. He also proposed a new International Fund for Agricultural Development.

Extremely important in solving some of the problems of the developing nations, particularly agricultural problems, is research and development of the sort most likely to be supplied by the industrial nations. New seed varieties are on the way. There is hope of developing cereals that fix atmospheric nitrogen as legumes do. There are new forms of agriculture—marine, bacterial, fungal, microalgal and so on.

Still another and immediately necessary form of outside assistance in agriculture is the creation of an internationally allocated system of food reserves in which nations would own their own reserves but act jointly to set policy. The reserves would not only build needed buffer stocks for crop failure years but would prevent sharp farm income declines in times of surplus.

Unfortunately, the solution to this as well as to a great many other problems is made more difficult by the presently somewhat troubled relations between the developing and the developed nations. The developing nations are demanding, with justification and with a new assertiveness, that world economic arrangements be reexamined and revised with a view to greater equity. But in seeking this, they must work collaboratively and in good spirit with the industrial nations, which have severe economic problems of their own.

Just as they must work with the industrial nations, so the industrial nations must work with them. That is the plain consequence of interdependence. The mutual need is going to become greater rather than less. It isn't just that the industrial nations need raw materials. With the extensive proliferation of nuclear weapons sure to come, a Third World wracked with hunger, tension and antagonism will be a threat to all, not least as fertile soil for the terrorists who may prove to be the most destabilizing element in our future—and by our future I mean the future of all nations, large and small.

Perhaps the most important single requirement is that the industrial countries show an open and good-spirited willingness to examine all charges of inequity and, where appropriate, to negotiate issues and the shape and functioning of institutions. Many of us were gratified by the positive tone of Secretary Kissinger's speech on September 1. We must all hope that it will be the prelude to constructive and forward-looking negotiations.

A final cautionary word on poverty. It would be brave but foolish to promise ourselves or others that we will abolish poverty. I don't say that casually; I have spent some of the ripest years of my life in that battle. What we must promise ourselves is that we will tackle with all the in-genuity and vigor at our command the conditions in which poverty oc-curs, the specifiable things that can be dealt with through pragmatic action, such as farm credit. We must try to understand the cultural web that so often seems to imprison the poorest of the poor and seek to unravel that web through health, education and other measures. We must work to alter the barriers of economic self-interest within a society that helps to keep the poor poor. And then we must pray for luck. I'm not trying to dampen anyone's enthusiasm. We can accomplish important things. If we go easy on the rhetoric and strike hard at the root causes, we will have earned the right to be taken seriously.

International Trade

Nowhere is the interdependence of all nations, developed or develop-ing, more evident than in international trade. No nation can have an autonomous economic policy any more. Nor can any nation treat its monetary, trade and investment policies as separate subjects.

The industrial countries have long maintained discriminatory tariff and nontariff barriers that favored the import of raw materials over man-ufactured goods from the developing countries. They must reduce these barriers, and there is apparently a willingness to do so. In the process they will have to provide adjustment assistance to their own workers who lose jobs in the process.

The industrial countries are poised between protectionism and liberalization. Ultimately, liberalization will prevail because the contem-porary world simply can't function with insurmountable barriers to the flow of trade—but the short-run hazards are considerable. The forces of protectionism are naturally strong in times of recession and unemploy-ment. But a number of the industrial nations have already agreed to trade preferences or duty-free entry for certain products of the developing nations; and it may be hoped that this trend toward preferential treatment will grow. To the extent that the developing nations can be helped to help themselves, so much the better for all. (Again, the developed nations will have to create programs to see their domestic labor force through the necessary adjustments.)

Another major problem in international trade is the need for stabilizing the market in commodities, which traditionally fluctuates greatly in price and volume; and this must be a priority for serious multilateral negotiations. The purpose would be to assure the producing nations steady prices and markets, and the consuming nations adequate supplies at reasonable cost.

In a world adequately sensitive to the requirements of stability, nations that export raw materials will not make sudden destabilizing moves such as the oil embargo of 1973, or the United States soybean embargo of the same year.

One cannot talk about raw materials without touching on the subject of conservation. The whole world must conserve energy and non-renewable resources. Nothing is more certain than the knowledge that in two more decades, at the most, we will have developed the art of recycling resources (chiefly minerals and water) to a level that cannot be imagined now. With respect to soil and forests and other renewable resources, we will rebuild as we use. But some natural resources, such as oil, coal and natural gas, are for the most part nonrecyclable and nonrenewable, so that the only means of their conservation are more efficient use and a reduction in consumption.

Today the waste of resources in the advanced countries, certainly in the United States, is phenomenal and inexcusable, and should be brought under some kind of discipline.

Transnational corporations are a powerful element in the energy field, as in other raw materials trade, and the stage is set for confrontation between them and the newly assertive developing nations. Given the nature of the transnational corporation, no single country can solve the problem they pose. What is needed is multilateral agreement on codes of conduct. The transnational corporation wants long-term assurance of the security of its investments and as much freedom as possible to do business without excessive regulation. The developing country wants foreign investment but also wants just recompense for its natural resources, no meddling in its internal affairs and a final say over what forms of business activity affect its national interest.

One of the most perplexing problems facing the world economy is the emergence in the postcolonial era of a multiplicity of small and medium-size nations that urgently require some kind of common market mechanisms for their economic survival—but it's not at all obvious how such mechanisms should work. There is no great point in the new nations creating such mechanisms among themselves, since some 80 percent of their trade is not with each other but with the developed nations. But if new nations establish common market ties with developed nations there arises the danger of a new, if more decorous, colonialism. An interesting third alternative might be a common market mechanism among a group of new nations and developed nations brought into being and supervised by the U.N.

Population

Recent U.N. estimates give somewhat lower projections of population growth, but there's small comfort in that. We're still going up at the daily rate of 200,000 more births than deaths a day and will have to endure heavy population growth for decades to come, with devastating consequences in human suffering and ecological overload. No matter how hard we work at controlling fertility from this point on, a world population of 6.5 billion by the year 2000 is almost inevitable (as against less than 4 billion today). Since we've had no experience with that level of world population, we can't know what it will do to living conditions, food requirements, consumption of raw materials and political balances. The "demographic investment," *i.e.,* the cost of resources that go to support added population, expressed as a percent of fixed capital formation, is 12.5 percent for the developed nations and 42.5 percent for the developing nations (73.2 percent for Bangladesh). The burden on a nation seeking economic growth is apparent. Because of the high fertility rates in the poorest countries, they might improve food production substantially and yet gain nothing—or even lose—in per capita food supply, so that the nutritional level will certainly not gain, and may drop.

There has been a certain amount of fruitless debate as to whether our concern over fertility rates should express itself in family planning programs or programs of education, health, nutrition and agricultural development. The only sensible answer is: Both. We don't know as much as we should about reducing fertility rates, but there is a good deal of evidence that they come down when the lowest income groups are lifted off the floor of absolute poverty and brought out of the utter darkness of malnutrition, ignorance and despair.

It is wrong to charge that the developing countries are making no effort with respect to population. Recent evidence indicates that 72 countries have made progress in reducing fertility. (But none of the nations identified by the U.N. as least developed showed a decrease.)

Ecology

The revolution in environmental awareness is surely one of the great landmarks in human history. Archaeologists now tell us that mankind has been destroying one or another part of the environment for the past 10,000 years. There is evidence that soil depletion, the exhaustion of water resources, deforestation, silted waterways and other consequences of environmental abuse occurred frequently in the ancient world—on the plains of the Indus River, in the lands of the ancient Maya and around the Mediterranean basin, for example. Plato expressed the view that the soil erosion so evident in the Greece of his time was caused by deforestation in earlier times. What is new is not environmental destruction itself but the scope and variety of the destruction and the extraordinary new awareness. We are now acutely conscious of the problems of the biosphere and the hazards to our life-support systems—the quality of our air, water and soil, the dangers to the upper atmosphere and to the climate, the effect of man-introduced chemicals on the natural environment (including us), the thoughtless use of nonrenewable resources and so on. We understand in new dimensions the wisdom of Francis Bacon's aphorism, "We can command nature only by obeying her."

Some say the developed nations want pollution control at whatever cost to economic growth and the developing nations want the reverse— economic growth at whatever cost. But that is an oversimplification. Sensible people in all nations are addressing themselves to the solutions that will permit ecologically sound economic activity. We must develop (and are developing) pollution-free technologies and technologies for the prevention of pollution. We are developing energy-efficient technologies and ecologically sound agricultural methods.

We must devise means of testing and screening the 1,000 new manmade chemicals that are introduced every year. We must learn to avoid the population overload that leads to unbearable stress on the environment. We must greatly advance the art of recycling.

It is not surprising that the environmental movement has been characterized at times by a strong antitechnology bias—but, ironically, much that we must do to be saved will require new technological ingenuities.

Conflict

I have spoken of nuclear conflict. Meanwhile, more conventional conflicts recur throughout the world—Southeast Asia, the Middle East, Cyprus, Angola—that might have been self-contained in the old days but are potentially catastrophic in the tinderbox of the nuclear age. It is apparent that we must devise new forms and processes to resolve conflict peaceably. After millennia of bloodshed, the goal seems unreachable, but until this century nobody really tried very hard.

Certainly it is only in the last 40 years that there has been a serious attempt to explore the nature of group conflict. With nuclear terrorism by small extremist groups a real possibility, it is no longer just a question of wars between nations. Research must concern itself with all sources of group conflict, including racial and religious prejudice. If the species is to survive, we must get ahead with the process of breaking down intolerance and xenophobia

The average person thinks of peace as something passive and uneventful—a happy vacuum. If we conceive of it in that fashion we shall never have it. We cannot abolish conflict, nor would we wish to. As a guide to a more mature conception of peace we need only point to the conditions within any free and lawful society, where the existence of conflict is accepted as a necessary and even desirable condition of social health. Conflict is not always an expression of the human impulse to violence. Sometimes it is a consequence of normal competition; sometimes it is the result of smoldering injustices that cry out for remedy. Any free and lawful society deliberately provides arrangements to make certain kinds of conflict possible, arrangements that encourage the existence of a "loyal opposition," that prevent economic monopoly, that foster freedom of expression, that empower those who have too long been powerless.

The whole history of law, and much of the history of government, has been an attempt to deal in a civil fashion with human conflict, to hold it within bounds and to resolve it peaceably within a framework of order. Thus is justice done and the peace preserved. If we do not blow ourselves up, we shall construct a peaceful world in much the same fashion—by painstakingly putting together the institutional arrangements that permit the ebb and flow of conflict and tension within a framework of order.

International Order

Today, not only nations but problems interrelate, and there is no way to proceed except through collaborative problem solving and joint management of agreed upon solutions. Yet foreign offices continue to play the old familiar zero-sum games—games of the strong, games of the weak. To be sure, international collaboration presents problems for each nation. Each has its distinctive economic objectives, its internal power structures and elites, and its long-nursed international grievances. But, finally, all must find their place in an international order.

To get from here to there will require some large changes. When Harlan Cleveland speaks of a "planetary bargain," he suggests an accurate sense of scale. And he understands very well the looseness and improvisation that must accompany such a bargain. He understands that one cannot think in terms of a grand compact that involves a carefully specified set of commitments on both sides covering everything from trade preferences to population controls, all wrapped up in one historic transaction. What we can and must have is:

- A recognition that both sides have very much to gain by cooperating, and very much to lose by not;
- A clear recognition of the major objectives of both sides;
- A good-faith willingness to negotiate;
- Early specific acts on both sides that demonstrate a constructive intent to resolve differences; and
- Collaborative creation of the institutions that must serve as the instruments and forums for joint action.

Agreement on some fronts may occur very rapidly. Other issues may prove intractable. We must move as rapidly as we can, when we can, where we can, and not be discouraged nor thrown off course by difficulties.

Most great changes that we accomplish *within* our own nations are changes within a well-established framework. On the international scene, we are trying to create the framework itself. That is the big goal: a framework of law, of custom, of attitude, of institutions within which a healthy interplay of competing interests and inevitable tensions can occur without escalating to violence.

It will not be wholly comfortable for anybody. The United States, accustomed to years of unthinking economic dominance among nations, will have to face the fact that the less-developed countries fully intend to demand a larger share of the world's wealth. The Soviet Union and China are going to have to give up the extraordinary secrecy and suspicion that cut them off from free give-and-take with other nations of this interdependent world. Some of the newly wealthy nations that have as yet shown little concern for the lowest income groups in their own countries are going to have to experience a change of heart.

The world won't be as loose as it once was, and this is due only in part to the fact that we can't afford lawless violence. We've learned from the biologists that a diminishing resource base leads a biological population to organize itself more tightly to exploit the narrowing base. Whether we like it or not, that is an element in our situation.

The first task is institution building. We need better institutional arrangements not only for all the tasks of conflict resolution but for monitoring the environment, negotiating and supervising international economic agreements, supervising food reserves, managing deep sea resources and so on.

States will continue to be the main actors but will align and realign in multiple ways on different issues. Transnational pressure groups—

nations producing a particular kind of commodity, or coastal nations, or manufacturing nations—will blur the old battle lines between individual nation-states.

The United Nations has performed valuable services and is the main base from which to do further institution building. The problems with the U.N. are several. First, its usefulness may be destroyed if Third World nations pursue deliberately destructive confrontation tactics in the General Assembly. This hazard might be eliminated if favorable action is taken on the recent recommendation of the U.N. Group of Experts, which urged a new decision-making process by negotiation and a search for consensus rather than by showdown votes in the General Assembly.

The second problem is that the U.N. has suffered increasingly from its own bureaucratic rigidities and organizational inadequacies. The recommendations of the Group of Experts just mentioned deserve serious consideration in this regard.

One of the most essential functions that can be performed by international institutions will be to gather and interpret the information on which forecasts may be made with respect to crucial questions of resource supply and demand. All our shared problem solving must begin with information gathering. It would greatly strengthen the U.N. if we were to give it major new information functions and the staff to perform those functions. Information gathering and forecasting will inevitably draw attention to the kind of policy analysis that will illuminate the choices ahead. The U.N. should also be equipped to do such analysis (though it should not be the only one doing it).

Values

In closing, let me say a word about values. No doubt the moral eclipse of our day is part of the problem. The confirmed pessimists among you may object to the hint of optimism in the word "eclipse," but you will have to bear with me. I count unrelenting pessimism as a failure of vitality—just as unrelenting optimism is a failure of sense. We must build on a moral base. But no nation wants its value system established by transnational agreement, so we start with a sense of limits. We must build on a few values shared among nations, leaving to individual nations broad freedom to pursue their own vision of the moral order.

Surely the senseless waste of life is a denial of all other values, so let us begin there. I would put it simply that the prime value on which we must build is preservation of the species and the planet. We've operated for centuries on the principle of self-preservation for the rich and the powerful, but that won't work any more. Now our fates are linked one with another; if we save ourselves, we will do it together. It would sound far more lofty if I were to say we build on the sanctity of life, but preservation of the species is just the commanding note that I want to strike. We want to save humankind, the endangered species, and Earth, the endangered planet.

The second value we can build on is justice. That may sound like an exceptionally abstract principle to place next to the powerfully moving value of preservation. But it is not without its capacity to move human beings. Of all the social values that humans have celebrated, none is more ancient and universal than justice. We know of few societies, ancient or modern, primitive or civilized, that have not had some concept of fair play. The hunger for justice reaches deep into the human psyche.

Next, I would list the worth of the individual, and I would include in that phrase the release of human potentialities, the enhancement of individual dignity, removal of the obstacles to individual growth and fulfillment. None of these is possible in a world of ignorance, hunger, disease, lack of opportunity—nor in a world of tyranny.

Finally, I would list a recognition and respect for our common humanity, a respect for those who are not of my village, tribe, nation, language, race or religion. One does get a little discouraged about the likelihood that such respect will prevail.

Our planet is but a speck of dust in the universe, and our life on it is but an instant in the long stretch of astrophysical time. Still, it is the only planet we have and our life on it holds great possibilities of beauty and dignity and meaning. Yet if it were asked of us how we spend our instant of time on our speck of dust, we would have to say, "We spend a good deal of it fighting one another and laying waste our earth."

Surely all of us here believe that we can do better. After all, every modern nation is a composite of earlier tribalisms and fierce regional loyalties, most of which have given way to national identity. With the new consciousness of our shared responsibility for our small planet— Spaceship Earth—it is not inconceivable that the same process might occur worldwide. In any case, it is only out of respect for our common humanity that we can create the sense of relatedness and mutuality that will prevent this riven, angry, frightened world from tearing itself to pieces.

Perhaps, in this ancient land, we can help begin the healing process.

Comments and Discussion

In the discussion that followed, various participants raised questions concerning points made by Messrs. Majidi and Gardner; others suggested additional points for discussion in subsequent sessions of the symposium.

Interdependence in Today's World

An Iranian suggested that there can be no interdependence between affluence and dire poverty and that, in general, the most affluent nations have to date been most responsible for creating "interdependence" in the sense that they have made other states depend on them. In his view, there will not be true interdependence until there is some common ground and acceptance of each other's rights and obligations. Similarly, it was said that application of the consensus principle, as proposed in Mr. Gardner's speech, should not lead to hegemony of the Big Three over the rest of the membership, as is more or less the case in the Security Council of the United Nations. Nations must regard each other as equal partners; deny themselves the prerogatives of forcing others to see things their way; stand ready to enjoy a little less and permit more to all; refrain from interfering in each other's domestic affairs; and acknowledge the sovereignty of others. In short, they must learn to live together. Other Iranian speakers observed that Iran believes in international economic interdependence and sees efforts "to put its own house in order" as contributing to this goal; that Iran's policy in regard to oil prices has been a natural way of rationalizing world consumption of oil; that the key to more equitable distribution of wealth between advanced and developing nations lies more in trade than in external aid; and that oil-producing countries, which were previously trade-deficit countries, have become more self-reliant, have raised their standards of living without external aid and have begun to constitute a new world market for industries and services. One speaker called for a new "framework" for the international institutions mentioned by Mr. Gardner—a global approach to world problems that will lead to the creation of jobs in poor countries and the establishment of fair prices for industrial exports by the advanced countries and for commodity exports by the developing countries. Past experience shows that if international institutions operate within a neutral framework, there is no contribution to development of the Third and Fourth Worlds.*

Others commenting on interdependence observed that the West is bringing new attitudes to the present world scene. It is no longer confident of its world mission, its technology, or even that its economic system provides a full, complete life for its citizens. The non-Western world has much to contribute to the wealthy nations' search for something broader, something new; it can take advantage of the West's new humility. In one participant's view, the cultural and philosophical dimension may be a better basis on which to build interdependence than are economic relationships. Young people especially doubt the West's ability to reshape the world; it was suggested that they see interdependence as a fact, not as a goal.

---

*The "Fourth World" refers to the 25 poorest nations of the world, the least developed states in the Third—or developing—World.

A new international economic order may require new internal economic orders, an American observed—steps by governments to assure that the rich help the poor at home. Some governments may need external help in seeing how to do this. Mr. Gardner concurred that adjustments within countries must come—including, for example, a reduction in American consumption of scarce resources—but he observed that these are difficult to achieve. The gravity of the situation is producing some action, however, and limited progress is being made.

The importance of focusing less on prescriptions—at which many governments are adept—and more on accomplishments was stressed by one American speaker, who called for the creation of constituencies that would give governments the "will and power" to make things happen.

The question of how little we know about tackling global problems was raised by an Asian participant, who observed that the directions in which knowledge expands are not the directions in which knowledge is most needed. Responding to a query about how the search for knowledge can be directed toward human goals, Mr. Gardner observed that too often academics work on matters that are 50 years ahead or 50 years behind, rather than close to the "moving edge" needed for decisions. New centers should be established around the world to deal with total problems and not merely component parts of interrelated situations. Minister Majidi suggested that greater cooperation is needed among government agencies and universities in planning and executing programs in developing countries. Specialized institutions should be formed within universities to propose possible new solutions for problems of development. But rapid educational expansion in many developing countries has strained administrative and teaching staffs. It may be possible to give more time to research, especially research relating to development, in the future.

The importance of transferring technology from the West was emphasized by several of the opening speakers, an Iranian observed, but Iran must also develop indigenous technology, including technology that will serve not only industry but agriculture. Another Iranian concurred that the dynamic forces required to develop needed technology lie within a society, that indigenous technology may be more important than imported technology and that modern (Western) technology has in part helped to destroy nature; he appealed to the West to cooperate in developing intermediate technology suited to the particular conditions of developing countries.

An important approach may be to see people as problem solvers and not merely as problem raisers, a European suggested. In his view, people have the potential for self-preservation. The quality of their participation is the most important factor in development—more important than institutions or education. People can be helped to develop values and realize their own goals. Women may be an undervalued natural resource, another participant suggested; if their contributions at home and to society were counted as productive labor, the measurements of gross national product (GNP) would be different.

The concluding Iranian speaker concurred with Mr. Gardner that ostensibly "the Cold War is over" but warned against accepting détente as "real"; although global nuclear war may be less likely today than at times in the past, local and regional conflicts abound, including the Middle East conflict in which the superpowers have played roles. Continuing competition between the Soviet Union and the United States is a factor affecting Iran's place in the world scene.

In his closing remarks, Robert O. Anderson, Chairman of the Aspen Institute for Humanistic Studies, expressed the hope that the symposium would help to bridge gaps in understanding and that it would explore the problem of how to achieve justice in a world characterized by inequality.

2. Iranian Development Experience

Developments in the Past 50 Years

The following is the first in a series of background papers specially prepared by Iranian officials for the Aspen Institute/Persepolis Symposium. Views expressed in this and all other background papers included in this report are those of the author or authors.

Iran: Past, Present and Future

Iran: Developments During the Last 50 Years

*Manouchehr Ganji and Abbas Milani**

History has had a turbulent and rapid tempo in Iran in the past century. To profoundly appreciate the present and predict the future, an understanding of the past is essential. The road from "backwardness" to modernization has indeed been a long one.

Disorder in Iran's economy began in the late 17th century. Before then, the country did not lag far behind the West in economic and social development.[1] During the Safavid period (beginning in the 15th century), a strong centralized government resulted in a flourishing economy with developing industrial techniques. Yet the stability and the prosperity that the Safavids provided was short-lived. The decline of the Empire began during the 17th century. The Afghani revolt in 1722 and the Afsharid period mark the beginning of the decline of the Iranian economy. The costly and devastating wars of this period had drained the economy, and famines had become a yearly fact of life. Transportation and travel were under the constant and serious threat of harassment and theft, since the authority of the central government did not extend far beyond major cities.[2]

The year 1779 saw the emergence of Agha muhammad-e-Qajar, the founder of the Qajar dynasty. The rule of this dynasty—lasting till 1925—was to become one of the bleakest periods in the history of Iran. In the words of a concerned European visitor, "The resources of the country [were] fruitlessly exhausted, its agriculture destroyed, its commerce embarrassed and obstructed, the roads infested with robbers, security to persons and property annihilated."[3] It was in the Qajar period that Iran became a virtual colony of England and Russia, and the decline evident in the Iranian economy only intensified.

The wars undertaken by the Qajar kings against Russia and Britain—usually instigated by either France, Britain or Russia—became a turning point in the history of that period. Of particular significance is the second war between Iran and Russia, in 1824. The concluding Turkamanchai treaty in 1828 signified the transformation of an independent, though corrupt, government to one becoming increasingly dependent

---

*The authors wish to express their gratitude to Mansour Farsad and Mahmoud Nilforoshan-Shahanshahi for their valuable assistance in gathering data for inclusion in the tables that appear in the appendix to this essay.

upon foreign powers. According to this treaty, two very large and prosperous provinces of Iran were enjoined by the Russians. Furthermore, the treaty granted extraterritorial jurisdiction over Russian subjects (capitulation rights), a most-favored-nation clause and a monopoly on shipping rights on the Caspian Sea for the Russians. It exacted heavy war reparations upon the Iranian Government, complete freedom for Russian citizens to conduct commercial business in Iran, reduction of tariff rates to a maximum of 5 percent and the elimination of any taxing power (by the Iranian government) over the profits and the properties of Russian citizens.

England, stubbornly unwilling to allow a one-sided increase in the power of Russians in Iran, asked for and received similar rights as granted to the Russians by Turkamanchai.

It is significant to note that colonial interests in Iran began as primarily political. Russia's increasing interest in having access to the Indian Ocean, to the resources of Southeast Asia in general and India in particular, and Britain's interest in keeping a "buffer state" between her sphere of influence and Russia were the original causes for these nations' interest in Iran. However, it did not take long for these two powers to establish near-absolute control of Iranian politics and the Iranian economy. As Morgan Shuster, the American adviser, observed, no decision could be made by the Iranian Government without the consent or the direction of at least one of the two powers.[4] The central government disposed of very little authority in the central cities and almost none in the outlying areas. Only the Russians and the British could provide protection for their commodities and their trade. What guaranteed a relatively easy accomplishment of the goals by foreign powers in Iran was the corruption and greed so characteristic of the Qajar court and Qajar courtiers. It has been suggested that the political implications of the then-existing colonial rivalry constituted a significant reason for the continuous, if only nominal, political independence of Iran in that period.

If political and economic dependence characterized the social reality of Qajar rule, stagnation and backwardness characterized its cultural aspects. More than 95 percent illiteracy, hand in hand with an absolutist clerical control of the few existing educational institutions, constituted a major obstacle to any serious development.

It was in such conditions of turmoil that the Iranian constitutional movement took shape in 1905. The constitutional movement was the collision of contending forces whose hitherto turbulent coexistence had created the conditions of social turmoil so characteristic of Iran at the turn of the century. If the French Revolution changed the basis of authority and legitimacy in much of Europe and in America, the constitutional movement attempted the same significant change in Iran. The autocratic, absolutist "patrimonial" authority was to give way to the rule and constraints of law and popular consent and popular participation. The constitutional movement promised political democracy and social equality. If it was unable to fulfill its promises immediately, it helped bring about a new social order that could provide the promised, and promise even more.

The constitutional movement also attempted to limit the power and the influence of foreign powers in Iran. Faced with the onslaught of the constitutional movement against their interests, Britain and Russia put aside their historic rivalry and conspired to sign the 1907 agreement, through which formal spheres of influence were designated for Russia and Britain.[5]

The Anglo-Russian Convention of August 31, 1907, ostensibly contrived by two powers "to defend the independence and integrity of Iran," divided Iran into two zones. The British zone consisted of the southwest corner of the country, including Sistan and most of the provinces of Kerman and Makran. The Russian zone consisted of the whole of northern Iran, including such major cities as Isfahan, Tehran, Tabriz Mashad, Rasht and Yazd. The area between the two zones, made up of parts of southern Iran and the Persian Gulf coastal area, was in the hands of the Iranian Government. In 1908, oil was discovered in Khuzestan, then part of the area nominally assigned to the Iranian central government. As Indian scholar Ramesh Sanghvi[6] states, the Anglo-Russian Convention "did not specify this as a third zone. . . . The reasons for this became clear in 1911. By an informal and unwritten arrangement, the two powers agreed to complete domination of the northern area by the Russians and the inclusion of this third zone into the British sphere of influence."[7]

The oil discovery at Masjed-Suleiman evoked further interest in Britain, leading to the formation of the Anglo-Persian Oil Company in London. The Abadan Refinery was built and Iranian oil began to flow to Europe before the outbreak of World War I.

Iran attempted unsuccessfully to seek justice from the same power that had sanctified the right of nations to self-determination at the Versailles Peace Conference of 1919. What Iran was asking for was the abrogation of the Anglo-Russian Convention of 1907 and the abolition of consular courts. As a consequence of British moves, the Iranian representatives were, however, not even allowed to plead their country's case.

The guns of the October Revolution in Russia were also to leave their impact on Iran. In the temporary lapse in Russia's interest in Iran, brought about as the consequence of the Revolution, Britain saw a golden opportunity to consolidate its control over the whole area of Iran. The most significant manifestation of this decision was to be seen in the terms of the so-called "Anglo-Persian Treaty" of 1919, imposed upon Iran by Britain. Under the terms of this treaty, effectively turning Iran into a British protectorate, the British government acquired for itself complete control over the Iranian army, and Iranian finance and trade. British military experts were to reorganize command and equip the Iranian armed forces at Iran's expense. British financial experts were to reorganize the revenues, customs and other sources of income, while British technical experts were to construct railways and other forms of transport, all at Iran's expense. In return for all this, as Sanghvi states, "Britain was to advance a loan, the terms of which were defined by a second 'agreement.' A sum of 2 million at 7 percent, redeemable in 20 years, was granted as the amount of this loan. A commission was to be appointed for the reorganization of the Iranian army in which Iranis were allowed to participate."[8]

There were implicit provisions in the treaty to the effect that Iran would not engage experts from any other country but Britain. Hence, an end should have been put to the services of the American, French, White Russian and other foreign experts. The "treaty" brought public protest from the United States Government.

The signing of this instrument by the then President of the State Council, Vossough-ed-Dowleh, brought widespread discontent with the government's policy of capitulation, which the Ahmad Shah was believed to be backing.[9]

Iranian nationalists showed much opposition to this agreement and to British plans for complete subjugation of Iran. As Peter Avery states, in September 1919, "Opposition in Iran had mounted sharply enough to cause the Shah great consternation."[10] The British were never able to fully implement the terms of the treaty.

After a brief period of conciliatory and peaceful gestures in which the Bolsheviks denounced the 1907 Anglo-Russian Convention and canceled Iranian debts to the Czarist government, the Bolsheviks suddenly landed troops at Bandar Pahlavi, the Iranian port on the Caspian Sea. They forced out British forces that were still occupying the area and moved southward, through Gilan, helping to form the Soviet Republic of Gilan[11] and providing assistance to the rebel forces operating Azaerbayjan. They also arranged for the creation of the Communist party of Iran as a section of the Communist International.

As Peter Avery states, "British help was not forthcoming to save Iran from invasion, in spite of British claims to be Iran's only legitimate protector." This was the death of the Treaty of 1910. Avery says, "Mr. Bonar Law read the extraordinary epitaph when, on 22nd May [1920], he said in the House of Commons that 'His Majesty's Government was under no obligation under the Anglo-Persian Treaty to defend Iran.'" Thus the final dismemberment of Iran appeared to be imminent. The inability of the constitutionalist forces to withstand pressures from the two powers, the intrigues of the corrupt Qajar court to maintain power and inability to exercise any independent control, led to many years of chaos-ridden dependency. The rule of a juvenile weakling as the last of the Qajar kings helped only to intensify the crisis.

During the state of a bankrupt, dependent economy and imperiled territorial integrity, the 1919 coup took place in Iran. Six years later, in 1925, the man who had played a determining role in bringing about the change was chosen the new monarch. In his 18 years in power, Reza Shah achieved a great deal toward the building of modern Iran. His first major accomplishment was to establish a strong centralized authority on the ruins of warlordism and to the detriment of future foreign intrigues in Iran. A modern army was set up acting as a significant lever of social change. Social chaos and social insecurity gave way to social order.

Reza Shah's enlightened historical vision enabled him to recognize the determining role governments were to play in the development scenarios of the Third World. During his reign, the central government played a very active role in all spheres of the Iranian economy, particularly in the development of industries. The extent of this industrializing effort was to include the ill-fated attempt to set up a steel industry in Iran, late in the 1930s, and the construction of the first trans-Iranian railroad, which brought a new vitality to the troubled economy. Along with the new railroad, major road construction projects were undertaken and financed by the government, creating a very essential, and hitherto nonexistent, transportation network.

Yet another historic step taken by Reza Shah was the sale of some government agricultural property (Khale-se)—traditionally a significant source of income for the extravaganzas of the Qajar court—to the peasants. In a sense, he championed the first land reform in Iran, on a minor scale.

On the cultural front, the efforts and the results were no less pervasive. Particular attention was paid to the field of education. The construction of the first university in Iran, in itself an act that left its impact on the very fabric of the future Iranian society; the sending of students abroad to acquire advanced technical skills; compulsory education along with the construction of many new schools; the forced separation of education from the influence of the clergy—all constituted aspects of the development on the education front. The first law directly dealing with the liberation of women from the oppressive traditions of obscurantist and obsolete religious bounds was put into effect with the personal initiative of Reza Shah.

While striving for economic and political independence constituted the bulwark of Iranian domestic politics in Reza Shah's period, Reza Shah also reflected the international posture of Iran at the time. He was a staunch nationalist and, as such, stood against any infringement upon the rights of Iran. His fierce struggle against Britain on two occasions (the oil agreement and the border question) signaled the emergence of a new Iran, unwilling to have its policies dictated by foreign governments and resolute in defending its rights.

The developing prosperity and the promised continuity of Reza Shah's rule were brought to a sudden halt as a consequence of the effects of World War II. In spite of repeated and definitive assurances by the Iranian government of her complete willingness to comply with the primarily strategic needs[12] of the Allied forces, the presence of some German technicians and advisers was used as a pretext for the occupation of Iran.[13] Reza Shah, unwilling to surrender sovereignty and yet unable to fight, was finally forced to abdicate and turn over the reins of government to his young son, Mohammad Reza Shah Pahlavi. For the duration of the war, the Allied command exercised virtually total control over the affairs of Iran.

The departure of Allied forces after the war and the continued military presence of Russia presented numerous problems for the new Iranian Government. A historical paradox was in the fact that a new government with a new leader was to perform monumental tasks and face monumental enemies. The Russian and the British Governments attempted to exploit this paradox, one to maintain a dying empire and the other to consolidate a new one. Soon, however, they realized how they had in fact underestimated the resolution of the Iranian people and the Iranian Government to preserve sovereignty and the willingness of international forces to assist this resolution. The implications of these struggles determined the turbulent character of the Iranian society in the period from 1945 to 1953.

If the Russian military presence was brought to an end through popular resistance in Iran and diplomatic pressures abroad, its political presence continued through the activities of the Tudeh Party of Iran. In the tradition of an effective "fifth column," this party maneuvered to implement the expansionist policies of Moscow in the era of the Cold War. Britain, on the other hand, intrigued to maintain a colonial monopoly of Iranian oil and to increase her influence in Iranian politics. The events of 1953 were the logical consequence and the unavoidable collision of the forces within the former power struggle that had shaped the crisis pattern of that period's history. It was a power struggle that ended in the restoration and continuation of legitimate monarchy.

A significant product of this period's history was the beginning of the process of the nationalization of Iranian oil. The signing of a new law and the conclusion of a new agreement marked the end of British monopoly and the beginning of a process that culminated in the complete nationalization of the oil industry, once again by a royal decree, in 1974.

The experiences of the 1940s and the early 1950s helped to shape the future pattern of Iranian politics and Iranian development. They showed how too formalistic a conception of pluralism in an underdeveloped country like old Iran can indeed create serious obstacles to the preservation of national sovereignty as well as to rapid social and economic development. To the leadership in possession of political and historical insight, they signaled the necessity for basic structural changes in the Iranian political and social landscape—changes that would result in a strong and dedicated leadership as well as in a more

Iran: Past, Present and Future

equitable distribution of social wealth and a more rapid rate of economic and social development.

The Iranian monarch used the 1953–61 period to consolidate power and make the necessary structural and superstructural preparations for the perceived necessary socioeconomic changes The development plans, adopted once again after their original collapse in 1948, were to become the spearhead in the systematization of the government's struggle for modernization. The Plan Organization, responsible for the adaptation and the implementation of these development plans, was henceforth to become a determining element in the Iranian economy and social scene.

Once power was consolidated and preparations were completed, the period of structural transformation began. The White Revolution, later to be called the Shah and People's Revolution of 1962, attempted and achieved a far-reaching transformation of the social, political and economic character of Iranian society. If modern Iran found its genesis in the essentially unfulfilled goals of the constitutional movement and its early development in Reza Shah's period, it found its maturity in the Shah and People's Revolution of 1962. As a developing consequence of this revolution, the very social structure of Iran was to change drastically, and, henceforth, change continuously.

From the time of its inception, our monarch declared the revolution to be an ongoing one with no dogma and but one commitment: the general welfare of the nation and the people. The social, political, economic and cultural implications (and requirements) of this general welfare would (and will) determine the cause and the character of this ongoing process.

By a royal decree, the six original principles of the revolution were put to a general referendum on January 20, 1962, and received popular approval. These principles were:

- Emancipation of the peasantry through a program of land reform and the abolition of the feudal landlord-peasant relationship;
- Fundamental reforms of obsolete election laws;
- Creation of an Education Corps to wipe out illiteracy;
- Sale of state-owned industries to the public to finance the land-reform program and agricultural development projects;
- Nationalization of the country's forests;
- Net profit-sharing programs for industrial workers.

Since 1962, eight new principles have been added, each aimed at curing some specific existing social problems or preventing possible future ones. The added principles are:

- Creation of a Health Corps;
- Creation of a Rural (Extension) Development Corps, Houses of Equity and Arbitration Councils;

- Emancipation of women;
- Administrative and educational reforms;
- Free education for all throughout the country;
- Free public health program throughout the country with emphasis on preventive medicine;
- Sale of 49 percent of the shares of industrial firms to the industrial workers, the farmers and the public;
- Consumer protection through price control.

As for the philosophy and thinking behind the Shah and People's Revolution, we cite excerpts from His Majesty The Shahanshah's book, *The White Revolution*:[14]

The distinguishing work of our revolution was that in accordance with humanitarian ideologies we were able to dispense equally amongst the whole population the rights that had been in the hands of a few. Thirteen centuries ago the Imam Ali wrote to Malek Ashtar, the Governor of Egypt, as follows: 'Mete out equal justice to all. Give preference to the will of the majority, as the dissatisfaction of many invalidates the satisfaction of a few, while the dissatisfaction of a few does not affect the satisfaction of many. This means that if the public supports you, the enmity of a few will be of no avail and, vice versa, the acquiescence of a few never justifies the disapproval of the public.' . . .

. . . if our nation wished to remain in the circle of dynamic, progressive and free nations of the world, it had no alternative but to alter the old and archaic order of society completely, and to build its future on a new order compatible with the vision and needs of the day.

I looked at Iranian society, recognizing its weaknesses, needs and potentialities; I studied the structure of other societies and saw how they had progressed; I analyzed the various philosophies and programs that had been advocated or implemented. The realization came to me that Iran needed a deep and fundamental revolution that could, at the same time, put an end to all the social inequalities and all the factors that caused injustice, tyranny and exploitation, and all aspects of reaction that impeded progress and kept our society backward.

In building a new society in place of the old one we had to find the way that was most beneficial for us and that would be in harmony with the Persian spirit and character, with the needs of our continent, our geography and history. Only then could we reach our goal rapidly, and our goal would be as great as that of any of the most advanced nations of today. . . .

The revolutionary aim I have presented to my people, and to which my people have responded with decisiveness and clarity, is that, God willing, I should utilize the present opportunity to construct a modern and progressive Iran on sound and strong foundations, so that my presence should no longer affect the destiny of the country. For inevitably I will go sooner or later, while Iran and its society will remain. It is therefore my duty to try to ensure during my lifetime that this society will become as prosperous and secure as possible.

Historically, social development and social change have always been opposed and obstructed by those interested in the preservation of the status quo rooted in, and deriving numerable benefits from, the fabric of the old society. The "privileged" who were economically, politically and socially disenfranchised as a result of the Shah and People's Revolution in many instances proved to be no exception to this historical tradition. They, too, used all they had at their disposal to bring to a halt an already irresistible process. Forming the original core of the opposition, the newly disenfranchised tried and often succeeded in allying themselves with the normal transitional opposition strata existing in Iranian society. The unavoidable errors usually accompanying any rapid social development—particularly those making structural changes—helped increase and consolidate the basis of this alliance. What characterizes a stable system and a rational revolution, however, is its ability to perceive and accept its mistakes and mobilize corrective efforts at its disposal to eliminate the perceived or existing problem. While the Shah and People's Revolution has made a concentrated effort to solicit constructive criticism, it has strongly opposed destructive violence or pessimism.

Iranian experience in development within the last decade shows that the existence of social discipline is an absolute precondition for the successful realization of all development plans. There is little hope for rapid and sustained development in a society that does not exercise a high degree of social discipline. It would be ideal if one could reach that condition through the personal volition of individual members of the society. Education and learning can and must play an important role in that regard. But that is a long-term process. In the short run, however, greater social discipline cannot be brought without properly enforced legislation and regulations.

The economic and political requisites of the new Iran cast by the Shah and People's Revolution forced many decisions in many far-reaching aspects of social policy. To give an indication of the extent and the dimensions of social and economic development in Iran in the past 50 years in general and in the past 14 years in particular, a number of tables have been provided as an appendix. Of particular significance is the effect the revolution was to have on Iran's oil policy. To accommodate the rising expenses of industrialization and development, particularly in light of increased prices brought up by inflationary conditions in industrial societies, increased oil revenues were sought. Furthermore, to ensure the stability of the volatile and strategically significant area of the Persian Gulf, itself becoming more urgent as a consequence of British departure from the area, a program to strengthen Iran's military capability was put into effect. Yet another significant consequence of the revolution, unfolding as late as 1974, can be seen in the creation of the National Resurgence (*Rastakhiz*) Party. To complement social and economic development with political participation was an imperative to ensure continuity and vigor in a profound sense. *Rastakhiz* was a significant step to eradicate vestiges of a dual society and dual development in favor of a truly modernizing one with a unified approach to development wherein participation by the "mass of the nation" in the decision-making process becomes the permanent political fact of life. Any development that depends solely on the exertions of the talents of a few of the elite is inherently fragile.

In dealing with this party—in fact, with any political phenomenon—attention must be paid to the context of its appearance. All too often, Western observers judge political phenomena in the developing world by ethnocentric models and criteria best suited to the peculiarities of Western society and Western political culture. In particular, in dealing with political parties, any deviation from the Western model is readily labeled as a deviation from democracy.

Political parties are the *means* to achieve political democracy and *not its end.* Leaving aside the arguments and the ambiguities surrounding the precise definition of the concept of democracy, it becomes evident that there is no party system or party structure that is, itself, a sufficient guarantee or indicator of political democracy. The only criterion for such a judgment must be the degree that the system invites, encourages and operationalizes mass participation and mass articulation of views and preferences. Hence, any judgment in its regard must be *substantive* rather than *formalistic.*

The visions of the future in Iran are indeed ambitious, and the obstacles are substantial. Yet the stakes are even higher. To fail in this vision is to miss a rare historical opportunity in which the many necessary elements for development have converged on a historical moment. To emerge victorious—as we must—is to ensure dynamic development and continued prosperity.

Appendix

Table 1
Gross National Product of Iran
at Current Prices
(billions of rials*)

Year	GNP
1959	283.9
1960	309.1
1961	319.6
1962	340.4
1963	360.3
1964	405.2
1965	456.4
1966	503.6
1967	556.5
1968	629.4
1969	704.2
1970	798.2
1971	979.1
1972	1,168.0
1973	1,745.3
1974	2,975.1

*69 rials = one U.S. dollar (as of December 1975).

Table 2
Percentage Breakdown of Total
Population of Iran

Year	Population	Urban	Rural
1900	9.8	21	79
1940	14.5	22	78
1956	18.9	31	69
1966	25.8	38	62
1972	31.1	43	57
1973	32.6	43	57
1974	33.3	44	56
1975	33.9	45	55

Source: Plan and Budget Organization.

Table 3
Age Groups of
Population of Iran, 1975

Age Groups	Percent
0–15	45.5
15–64	51.5
65 & up	3.0

Source: Plan and Budget Organization.

Iran: Past, Present and Future

Table 4
Educational Index of Iran

Year	Number of Institutions				Number of Students			
	Primary Schools	Secondary Schools	Technical Schools	Universities and Schools of Higher Learning	Primary Schools	Secondary Schools	Technical Schools	Universities and Schools of Higher Learning
1922	440	46	—	1	43,025	9,308	—	91
1932	1,186	156	—	3	141,103	13,120	—	602
1942	2,401	320	—	12	244,315	26,812	—	3,405
1947	3,209	314	—	18	386,266	37,866	—	6,257
1949	3,538	—	—	—	417,366	—	—	—
1950	8,612	308	—	—	756,683	44,585	—	3,624
1955	6,736	739	12	—	816,509	140,611	1,595	—
1960	9,809	1,183	83	—	1,436,169	281,928	9,348	—
1962	12,451	1,207	86	—	1,719,353	326,856	9,198	—
1965	15,135	1,559	109	78	2,181,633	493,735	15,224	29,683
1970	15,202	2,509	189	85	3,002,858	1,012,920	30,579	75,876
1972	15,902	2,925	277	118	2,862,596	942,523	56,795	98,377
1974	18,696	2,274	339	148	3,138,471	797,292	69,682	123,119

Table 5
Resume of Education Statistics

Year	Number of Ordinary Schools*	Primary School Pupils			Number of Teachers Employed by the Government			Number of Literacy Corps Teachers
		Literacy Corps	Boys	Girls	Men	Women	Total	
1947-48	3,224	—	28,459	95,873	—	—	13,145	—
1952-53	5,675	—	1,442,005	187,814	—	—	24,539	—
1957-58	7,750	—	1,553,546	326,604	—	—	34,924	—
1961-62	10,852	—	542,979	506,532	—	—	46,772	—
1962-63	12,451	82,091	694,099	558,102	35,674	18,500	54,174	2,460
1963-64	13,302	105,995	1,048,022	602,395	39,390	20,952	60,342	3,216
1964-65	15,657	228,497	1,161,251	665,605	41,607	24,686	66,293	7,344
1965-66	15,135	365,813	1,238,806	739,628	41,442	27,465	68,907	17,795
1966-67	14,740	252,638	1,365,128	824,536	41,051	30,230	71,281	7,974
1967-68	15,439	269,437	1,897,204	947,900	43,373	33,200	76,573	7,901
1968-69	15,556	292,970	2,006,202	1,039,900	44,699	36,373	81,072	8,873
1969-70	15,776	321,239	1,134,396	1,134,396	46,621	38,603	85,224	10,050
1970-71	15,200	412,792	2,208,930	1,206,720	44,426	42,370	86,796	16,099
1971-72	15,348	427,239	2,084,956	1,145,924	40,178	42,850	83,028	16,302
1972-73	15,902	482,932	2,217,095	1,228,433	41,920	44,674	86,594	20,088
1973-74	18,648	507,950	2,348,304	1,298,117	46,838	48,747	95,585	20,161

*Excluding the Literacy Corps School.

Iran: Past, Present and Future

Table 6
Secondary School Student-Teacher Statistics

Year	Number of Secondary Schools	Number of Students			Number of Secondary School Teachers		
		Girls	Boys	Total	Girls	Boys	Total
1947–48	283	7,870	28,461	36,331	—	—	2,302
1952–53	465	21,053	80,087	101,140	—	—	4,236
1957–58	963	48,531	139,211	187,742	—	—	7,841
1962–63	1,207	98,383	228,473	326,856	3,223	11,315	14,538
1966–67	1,682	185,291	394,425	579,716	5,255	16,012	21,267
1970–71	2,509	334,757	678,163	1,012,920	7,134	19,878	27,012

Table 7
Number of Pupils in Literacy Campaign
Classes for Adults

Year	Literacy Campaign Classes		Literacy Corps Classes		Army and Gendarmerie Classes	Police and Prison Classes	Total
	Women	Men	Women	Men			
	1	2	3	4	5	6	7
1956	59,750	171,951	—	—	17,907	17,093	266,701
1961	54,986	176,202	—	—	124,720	15,300	410,978
1967	172,054	215,972	4,500	62,000	69,476	—	484,232
1971	28,394	34,155	9,011	20,324	142,446	—	234,330
1974	54,970	54,970	31,228	95,077	79,893	696	261,864

Note: Reasons for the downward curve in number of pupils in the Literacy Campaign Classes for Adults can be summarized in three items:

1. Men and Women of *retirement age* who attended classes reached the limits of their learning capacity and dropped out of the program.

2. Over an 18-year period the program encouraged the *active-age* population who were illiterate to attend, and a large number of these people reached an acceptable literacy level. A multiplier factor where those who had learned to read and write also taught other illiterates reduced the numbers attending official classes.

3. A very broad youth-education program reduced the number of potentially illiterate adults. This becomes an important factor when one realizes that about 50 percent of total population is under 20 years of age.

Iran: Past, Present and Future

Table 8
Ownership of Agricultural Land

Types of Ownership Before Land Reform	Percent of Rural Areas
The whole village belonging to one person	23.4
Part of the village belonging to one person	10.9
Partial ownership	41.9
Royal land holdings	2.0
Endowed properties	1.8
Public domain	3.6
Combination	15.2
Other	1.2

Note: After implementing the three phases of the land reform (the first phase: dividing the large estates; the second phase: sale, long-term lease or crop-sharing option; the third phase: dividing the land rented to tenant farmers), over seven million hectares of land were divided among 2,300,000 heads of farmer families. This figure does not include the mechanized farms.

Table 9
Share of Economic Activities
in Gross Domestic Products

	1970	(percent) 1971	1972	1973	1974
Agriculture	19.9	16.5	16.5	12.3	9.4
National Oil	18.7	20.0	27.0	40.8	50.6
Industries and Mines	22.3	22.8	20.1	17.6	14.4
Services	39.1	40.7	36.4	29.3	25.6
Gross Domestic Products	100.0	100.0	100.0	100.0	100.0

Source: Bank Markazi Iran.

Table 10
Production of Electricity
(millions of kilowatt hours)

Year	Production
1967	4,298
1968	5,008
1969	5,539
1970	6,758
1971	8,106
1972	9,553
1973	12,093
1974	14,022

Source: Ministry of Power.

Table 11
Value of Iranian Imports and Exports
(millions of dollars)

Year	Imports	Exports
1963	513.5	128.2
1964	742.3	153.1
1965	898.5	180.8
1966	963.7	157.5
1967	1,190.3	181.8
1968	1,389.2	216.9
1969	1,542.7	244.7
1970	1,676.6	272.6
1971	2,060.9	334.6
1972	2,570.1	439.8
1973	3,737.2	634.7
1974	6,615.5	610.0

Source: *Foreign Trade Statistics of Iran.*

Table 12
Geographical Distribution of Iran's 1969-74 Imports
(millions of dollars)

	1969	1970	1971	1972	1973	1974
Common Market Countries	732.1	769.9	920.0	1,144.1	1,627.1	2,514.3
United States	209.7	217.4	293.0	428.2	487.3	1,225.3
United Kingdom						
Japan	166.4	201.0	275.7	359.5	548.5	1,006.8
Socialist Countries Party Clearing Agreements	178.6	207.3	232.9	153.7	329.0	418.9
ECAFE Member Countries*	84.8	94.1	121.4	129.7	180.7	364.8
Turkey and Pakistan	9.8	9.9	11.2	19.3	33.1	79.0
Other Countries	161.3	176.8	206.7	335.9	531.4	906.4
Total	1,542.7	1,676.6	2,060.9	2,570.4	3,737.1	6,615.5

Source: *Foreign Trade Statistics of Iran.*

*Excludes Japan and Pakistan.

Table 13
Geographical Distribution of Iran's Exports*
(millions of dollars)

	1969	1970	1971	1972	1973	1974
Common Market Countries	62.2	70.4	89.8	106.5	211.5	174.8
United States	25.4	24.2	27.8	41.5	54.8	46.1
Japan	9.3	12.3	12.7	12.9	43.1	31.6
Socialist Countries Party to Clearing Agreements	96.2	100.3	106.5	151.4	152.6	167.5
ECAFE Member Countries**	6.6	9.2	21.6	22.1	34.1	21.9
Turkey and Pakistan	1.4	1.7	0.8	0.8	1.7	4.0
Other Countries	43.6	54.5	75.4	104.6	136.9	164.1
Total	244.7	272.6	334.6	439.8	634.7	610.0

Source: *Foreign Trade Statistics of Iran.*

*Excludes export of oil and gas.

**Excludes Japan and Pakistan.

Iran: Past, Present and Future

Table 14
Percentage of Value of Exports
In Gross National Product of Iran
At Current Prices*
(billions of rials**)

Year	Gross National Product (1)	Exports (2)	(2) as Percent of (1)
1959	283.9	7.8	2.7
1960	309.1	8.5	2.7
1961	319.6	9.7	3.0
1962	340.4	8.7	2.6
1963	360.3	9.7	2.7
1964	405.2	11.6	2.9
1965	456.4	13.7	3.0
1966	503.6	13.3	2.6
1967	556.5	13.8	2.5
1968	629.4	16.5	2.6
1969	704.2	18.6	2.6
1970	798.2	21.1	2.6
1971	979.1	26.2	2.7
1972	1,168.0	34.2	2.9
1973	1,745.3	42.5	2.4
1974	2,975.1	41.5	1.4

Source: Bank Markazi Iran.

*Excluding oil and gas.

**69 rials = one U.S. dollar (as of December 1975).

Table 15
Share of Iran's Oil Production in Middle East,
OPEC Member Countries and the World
(percent)

Year	Middle East	OPEC Member Countries*	World
1966	22.7	14.8	6.4
1967	26.1	16.5	7.3
1968	25.4	16.0	7.3
1969	27.3	16.6	8.0
1970	27.7	17.3	8.3
1971	28.1	18.1	9.4
1972	28.4	19.1	9.6
1973	28.0	19.3	10.3
1974	28.0	19.6	10.6

Source: *British Petroleum Statistical Yearbook.*

*Share of Iran from total production of OPEC member countries has been calculated on the basis of the number of its members during each year.

Footnotes

1. In numerous articles and books, Professors Lambton and Keddie have subjected this period's history to very competent scrutiny and analysis.

2. Fraser, James, *A Historical Journey through Persia in 1804–09,* London, 1812.

3. Fraser, James, *Historical and Descriptive Account of Persia,* New York, 1833, p. 401.

4. Shuster, W. Morgan, *The Strangling of Persia,* New York, 1920.

5. Ramazani, Rouhollah, *The Foreign Policy of Iran: A Developing Nation in World Affairs, 1900–1941,* Charlottesville, 1966.

6. Sanghvi, Ramesh, *Aryamehr: The Shah of Iran* (London: Transorient, 1968), p. 8.

7. Sanghvi, Ramesh, *Aryamehr: The Shah of Iran* (London: Transorient, 1968), p. 8.

8. *Ibid.,* p. 16.

9. This treaty was never ratified by the Irani Parliament. It never reached the Majlis. That is because the Majlis was not in existence at this time, because the government had not held new elections since 1915. The fourth Majlis, which came into existence through corrupt elections at the hand of Vossough-ed-Dowleh, also did not get a chance to ratify it.

10. Avery, Peter, *Modern Iran* (London: Ernest Benn Limited, 1965), p. 207.

Iran: Past, Present and Future

11. Evidence of this close relationship between the Soviet Republic of Gilan and the Russians can be seen in the following telegram sent on June 25, 1920 by Kuchik Khan, the Soviet "ally," to Lenin: "Bearing in mind the establishment of brotherly union and full unanimity between us, we expect from the free Russian nation the assistance that may prove indispensable for the stabilization of the Persian S.S.R." Quoted in Fatemi, Nasrollah; *Diplomatic History of Persia, 1917–1923,* New York, 1932.

12. The significance of the strategic position of Iran was such that the Allied command referred to Iran as "the bridge to victory."

13. At 4 A.M. on Monday, August 23, 1941, the Russian ambassador, Alexy Tchernikh, and British minister, Sir Rearder Bullard, delivered to Irani Prime Minister Mansur the statement of decision to send military forces into Iran. Later that morning, Allied troops attacked Iran from the north and the south and eight Axis ships were seized on the Persian Gulf. Iran's appeal to the United States to help preserve sovereignty was left essentially unanswered.

14. His Imperial Majesty Mohammad Reza Pahlavi Aryamehr The Shahanshah of Iran, *The White Revolution,* pp.3 , 14, 24.

Development of Iran: A Statistical Note

Firouz Tofigh

During the last several decades, social and economic development in Iran has been very fast, and during recent years this growth has accelerated. In this essay we do not intend to cover all topics* related to this growth but we will limit ourselves to the most meaningful ones. As far as possible, the reference period will be the last 50 years, but it goes without saying that for many topics the period necessarily will be shorter because adequate statistics are lacking.

Population

During the first quarter of the 20th century, the increase or decrease in the population of Iran was related to natural or climatological conditions affecting crops and animal production. Since that time, the population has grown steadily, first slowly and later very rapidly. In 1925 the population of Iran was about 10 million. It is over 33 million now.

The rate of natural increase of the population during the decade 1910–20 was six per thousand. Later, during the 1940s, it reached 14 per thousand and is currently 30 per thousand. The latest survey in this respect indicates that the natural rate of increase of the population is 24 per thousand in urban areas and 35 per thousand in rural areas in Iran.** (See Table 16 in the appendix to this essay.)

Urbanization

The rate of urbanization in Iran has been very rapid. For the more distant past we do not have reliable figures. In 1871 the urban population of Iran

---

*Those interested in additional growth-related topics can refer to the Statistical Year Book.

**It is worth noting that the natural growth rate in urban areas is declining coincidentally with a drastic cut in fertility during the last few years. If the trend continues, along with rapid urbanization, it will lead to a decrease in population growth.

was estimated to be 2 million, *i.e.,* about 26 percent of the total population. The 1956 population census, the first such census in Iran, provided better estimates of the urban-rural distribution. During that year the cities were estimated to include six million inhabitants, *i.e.,* 31 percent of the total population. The next census, for 1966, showed that the urban population was about 9.8 million, *i.e.,* 38 percent of the total population. In 1971, the urban population was estimated to be about 12.4 million, *i.e.,* 41 percent of the total population, and currently it is estimated to be about 14.7 million, *i.e.,* 44 percent of the total population. The urban population has increased about 5 percent a year since 1966.

Despite rapid urbanization, the dispersion of population in Iran is very high. The capital city of Tehran, which is 6.6 times as large as the next city, includes 11 percent of the population of the country. Of the 67,000 localities in Iran, the 14 largest cities have 23 percent of the population. At the other extreme, 13,000 localities, each having a population of less than 25 persons, *i.e.,* about five households, have only 5 percent of the total population. The policy of the government is to reduce the dispersion through the creation of service centers in rural areas. (See Table 17.)

Labor Force and Manpower

In a country where the growth of the population is 3 percent a year, the equilibrium of the labor market is of prime importance. Fortunately, rapid economic growth in Iran has prevented unemployment from becoming a problem of any magnitude. In fact, in some cases, especially in the case of skilled labor, there are shortages. Nevertheless, in the long run, the problem will be a serious one.

The active population of Iran has increased in a parallel manner to the total population, but at a slower pace. From 3.3 million in 1921, it has reached 9.4 million in 1975, an increase of 2.8 times, while during the same period the population has increased 3.4 times. The difference is explained partly by a change in the age structure of the population and partly by a drastic increase in school enrollment rates for the younger population and in retirement rates for elderly people. Consequently, the ratio of the active population to the total population has decreased from 34 percent in the early 1920s to 28 percent now.

The unemployment rate for the years for which we have figures— from 1956 to 1971—has rather regularly decreased, so that in 1971 the figure is an insignificant 2.2 percent. (See Table 18.)

The participation rate of females in the labor force in Iran is very low. Only 12 percent of women 10 years or older are active. The male participation rate is 73 percent for the same age span, and the overall average is 43 percent.

The absolute size of the agricultural labor force has remained quite stable. As a consequence, the proportion this sector accounts for has decreased from 56 percent in 1966 to 47 percent in 1971. The labor force in the industrial and service sectors has followed a reverse trend. The share of the industrial sector has increased from 20 percent in 1966 to some 28 percent in 1971, and in the same period the service sector has increased from 24 percent to over 25 percent of the labor force.

Education and Literacy

During the last 50 years, Iranian society has evolved from one in which illiteracy dominated to one in which the ability to read and to write is becoming predominant. Only 20 years ago, 8 out of 100 females were literate. At the present time, the proportion is 30 percent (in urban areas 48 percent). In the case of the male population, the percentage of literates two decades ago was 22 percent, while it is now 56 percent (in urban areas 77 percent).

The main effort was carried out in terms of formal education; *i.e.*, primary, secondary and university. Half a century ago there were only 440 primary schools, 46 secondary schools and two institutions of higher education in Iran. Currently there are some 19,000 primary schools (29,000 if we include the education corps), 3,700 guidance schools, 2,300 secondary schools, 339 vocational schools and close to 150 institutions of higher education. Over the past 50 years, school enrollment at the primary level has increased by 84 times and at the secondary school level by 120 times. The rate of growth at the university level during the last decade was about 17 percent a year. (See Tables 19, 20 and 21.)

National Income

The regular computation of national accounts was started in 1959, so it is difficult to make any comparison before that date. For the decade and a half for which we have the accounts, the picture is as follows:

The total gross national product quadrupled between 1959 and 1973 at constant prices. The annual rate of growth of the GNP of about 5 percent during the early 1960s rose to over 10 percent during the remaining part of the decade. Recently, primarily due to increasing oil revenues, the growth rate has exceeded 30 percent a year. The increase in capital formation averaged about 2 percent annually during 1959–63, reached 18 percent a year during 1964–68 and then climbed in the 1970s to close to 70 percent a year. The investment ratio is currently 22 to 25 percent.

The total gross national product of Iran during 1973 was estimated to be $26 billion; *i.e.*, about $800 per capita. The current figure is estimated to be over $1,300 per capita. (See Table 22.)

Industry

Industrial growth during the latter part of the period under study has been considerable. Despite the lack of reliable and/or comparable data, one can safely say that the number of large industrial establishments since the early 1940s has increased more than tenfold: 500 in 1941 as against some 6,000 in 1972. Industrial value added has increased by 10 percent a year since 1959 and by 17 percent since 1966. Considering that industrial employment during recent years has grown 5 percent annually, this indicates not only a very rapid increase in industrial productivity but also the propensity of Iranian entrepreneurs to invest more and more in capital-intensive activities.

An interesting feature of industrial growth in Iran is the change in the pattern of employment and production. Between 1956 and 1972 industrial employment in food and textiles decreased from 77 percent to 57 percent of the total, while during the same period the share of metal and machinery has gone up from 5 percent to 20 percent. (See Tables 23 and 24.)

Agriculture

The most important change during the period under consideration is the land reform of the early 1960s. In 1960, *i.e.*, before land reform, only 26 percent of the land was cultivated or sown by the proprietors. In 1972, *i.e.*, after land reform, the proportion was 78 percent. The total value added in the agricultural sector in 1973 is 235 billion rials* (139 billion at constant prices) as compared with 85 billion in 1959. However, agricultural output has not kept up with the growing demand for food in Iran due to population growth and the increase in per capita income. Just an example: in 1933 the production of wheat was 1.4 million metric tons; in 1972 it was 4.4 million, and yet 0.8 million tons were imported during the same year. (See Table 25.)

---

*69 rials = one U.S. dollar (as of December 1975).

Foreign Trade

In the period between 1920 and 1950, the imports, and also to a lesser extent the exports, of Iran had an erratic pattern. They fluctuated from one year to the next without showing much of a trend. But since that period, both imports and exports increased steadily. Imports in 1973 increased by 42 times compared with 1921. During the same period total exports increased by over 80 times.

Oil has steadily increased its share of Iranian exports and is currently about 90 percent of the total despite a very rapid increase in non-oil exports. In fact, the growth rate of Iranian non-oil exports, except for the year 1974, has been over 26 percent a year during the 1970s. (See Table 26.)

Table 16
Evolution of Population in Iran

Year	Total Population (millions)	Percent Urban
1921	9,707	26
1941	12,833	—
1951	16,237	—
1956	18,955	31
1966	25,040	38
1971	30,020	41
1974	33,375	44
1975	33,900	45

Table 17
The Distribution of Population of Iran, 1966

Size of Locality	Number	Population	Percent of Total Population	Cumulative Percentage
1 million Persons and More	1	2,720	10.9	10.9
500,000 to 1 million	—			
250,000 to 500,000	5	1,780	7.1	18.0
100,000 to 250,000	8	1,170	4.7	22.7
50,000 to 100,000	15	1,070	4.3	27.0
25,000 to 50,000	30	1,080	4.3	31.3
10,000 to 25,000	72	1,100	4.4	35.7
5,000 to 10,000	119	800	3.2	38.9
2,500 to 5,000	308	1,020	4.1	43.0
1,000 to 2,500	2,087	3,010	12.0	55.0
500 to 1,000	5,314	3,640	14.5	69.5
250 to 500	10,415	3,660	14.6	84.1
100 to 250	16,936	2,780	11.1	95.2
50 to 100	10,528	770	3.1	98.3
25 to 50	7,884	290	1.2	99.5
Less than 25	12,966	150	0.6	100.0
Total	66,688	25,040	100.0	

Iran: Past, Present and Future

Table 18
Labor Force in Iran
(thousands)

Description	1921	1941	1956	1966	1970	1972	1975
Total Population	9,707	12,833	18,955	25,789	30,020	30,820	33,375
Population over 10 Years of Age	6,992	9,244	12,784	17,045	19,877	20,435	22,613
Inactive Population	3,664	4,899	6,717	9,199	11,200	11,583	13,235
Active Population	3,328	4,345	6,067	7,846	8,677	8,852	9,378
Employed	—	—	5,908	7,546	8,471	8,656	—
Unemployed	—	—	159	300	206	196	—
Percent of Active Population to Total	34.3	33.9	32.0	30.4	28.9	28.7	28.1
Percent Active Population 10+	47.6	47.0	47.5	46.0	43.7	43.3	41.5
Percent Employed/Active	—	—	97.4	96.2	97.6	97.8	—
Percent Employed/Total Population	—	—	31.2	29.3	28.2	28.1	—

Table 19
Literacy Rate
(6 years and over)

Year	F	Iran M	Percent of Total Literacy	F	Urban M	Percent of Total Literacy
1956	8	22	15	22	46	35
1966	18	40	29	39	62	50
1968	21	45	33	44	67	56
1971	26	48	37	48	69	59
1975*	(30)	(56)	(43)	(55)	(77)	(66)

*Estimated.

Table 20
Educational Institutions

Year	Primary	Guidance	Secondary	Vocational	Higher Education
1923	440	—	46	—	2
1931	1,048	—	156	7	2
1941	2,336	—	351	41	8
1956	6,736		739	12	19
1961	9,809	—	11,836	83	27
1966	15,135*	—	1,554	109	48
1971	15,202	—	2,509	189	113
1974	18,696	3,728	2,314	339	148

*Since 1962, education corps, tribal and special classes have added to the total. In 1966 there were 11,133 Education Corps, 448 tribal and 14 special schools.

Table 21
School Enrollment
(thousands)

Year	Primary	Guidance	Secondary	Vocational
1923	43		9	
1931	126		11	1
1941	287		28	3
1956	817		140	2
1961	1,436		282	9
1966	2,182		494	15
1971	3,003		1,013	31
1974	3,138	907,368	747	—

Table 22
GNP and Investment GNP
Gross National Product Capital Formation
(billions of rials*)

Year	GNP		Capital Formation	
	1959 Prices	Current	1959 Prices	Current
1959	284	284	53	53
1966	462	504	88	90
1969	622	704	132	156
1973	1,143	1,745	257	396

*69 rials = one U.S. dollar (as of December 1975).

Table 23
Large Industrial Establishments
in Urban Centers of Iran

	1941	1956	1961	1966	1971	1972
Alimentary Materials Industries	108	249	315		1,090	1,141
Textile and Clothing Industries	118	120	222		1,775	1,802
Wood Industries	26	32	71		196	204
Paper Industries, Printing Distribution	143	43	67		180	196
Chemical Industries, Oil, Coal, Plastic	54	78	97		302	307
Non-metallic Mineral Industries	9	57	180		958	998
Basic Metal Industries		17	34		76	88
Manufacture and Repair of Equipment and Tools	23	83	180		830	834
Miscellaneous Industries	1	15	25		80	81
Total	482*	694	1,191	3,661	5,487	5,651

*Not including 236 agriculture-oriented establishments.

Table 24
Distribution of the Industrial Labor Force
According to Branches of Activity

	1941	1956	1961	1971	1972
Food and Beverage	16.1	26.4	21.6	19.4	20.1
Textile and Apparel	68.6	50.6	49.0	39.5	36.5
Wood and Furniture	1.3	1.5	2.1	1.7	1.8
Paper and Printing	1.6	2.6	2.7	2.7	2.7
Chemical and Pharmaceutical	7.8	6.0	6.8	8.5	7.4
Construction	3.3	7.3	9.6	9.8	10.9
Metal	n.d.	.8	1.5	2.2	3.1
Machinery	1.2	4.4	6.2	15.6	16.9
Miscellaneous	.0	.5	.6	.5	.5
Total	100.0	100.0	100.0	100.0	100.0

Iran: Past, Present and Future

Table 25
Land Tenure Before and After
Land Reform
(percent)

	1960 (Before)	1972 (After)
Owner	26	78
Rented	7	15
Partly Owned and Partly Rented	3	5
Other	64	2

Table 26
Foreign Trade
(millions of rials*)

Year	Import	Export Total	Export (Percent Oil)
1921	610	502	64
1931	631	1,736	59
1941	791	1,837	55
1951	7,405	11,233	61
1961	47,171	66,045	85
1971	157,658	202,270	87
1973	253,190	418,840	90
1974	448,075	—	—

*69 rials = one U.S. dollar (as of December 1975).

Comments and Discussion

Discussion at the second session of the Aspen Institute/Persepolis Symposium focused on the Iranian development experience during the past 50 years. In his initial remarks, Mr. Tofigh stressed that Iranian society is changing very rapidly; that population, urbanization, education and literacy, GNP and industry have all experienced tremendous growth. There have also been important qualitative changes, especially as a result of land reform. Although many changes represent clear gains, some also signal warnings that development may carry liabilities as well as assets. In his own presentation, Dr. Ganji added that rapid social changes in Iran—including land reform, the emancipation of women and the forced sales of company shares to industrial workers—have created many satisfied groups and, as was to be expected, some dissatisfied ones, with the result that there has not been complete unanimity of response.

Question of "Social Discipline"

An American commented on the turbulent political conditions of Iran's distant and more recent past and on Dr. Ganji's conclusion that the "existence of social discipline is an absolute precondition for the successful realization of all development plans." He wondered what forms of social discipline were judged desirable and what kinds of actions were considered lacking in social discipline. A European added that social discipline is obviously a key factor in Iranian development. Observing that social discipline is relatively easy to achieve in countries where literacy has long been eliminated, where the value system subordinates individuals' needs to the needs of society and where individuals see themselves as part of society, he asked whether this kind of value—a sort of "productivity orientation"—is characteristic of Iran today.

Dr. Ganji and various Iranians offered these comments in response:

1. The meaning of "social discipline" insofar as public officials are concerned is that laws and regulations may not be manipulated on the basis of an individual's social, economic or political status and that, therefore, all Iranian citizens must, in fact, be equal before the law. It means that the political system's reward structure must be based upon individual competence and achievements. It cannot allow for the misuse of official or political power or misuse of public funds for the benefit of any one person or group of persons. Insofar as citizens' obligations are concerned, it entails understanding and application of corollary obligations that go together with the exercise of each individual's rights and freedoms. Social discipline as perceived by Iranians is, in fact, intended to ensure that the fruits of development are distributed in such a way as to bridge the gap between the rich and the poor. Iranians' understanding of social discipline is precisely that mechanism and condition, prevailing in Iran today, which aims at ensuring such a necessary redistribution. Criteria for judging social discipline, its necessity and its legitimacy must correspond to the peculiarities and necessities of the country con-

cerned. The political values that lie behind Western criteria for judging social discipline are suited to the sociopolitical, cultural and historic fabric of Western society and are not necessarily universally applicable or meaningful.

2. Iran's past experience has shown that national sovereignty and national stability are prerequisites to effective national development. Iran has achieved its present stage of development only by exercising social discipline; this does not mean abolition of freedom of expression, of participation in the political process or of fair trials. Iran's record of accomplishment in the economic and social spheres is the achievement of an indulgent leadership accepted by the people. Land reform did not come about because of the people or the parliament, composed as it was of landholders; it resulted from a royal decree, approved by a popular referendum. What has been accomplished in Iran is not in the interests of a particular group but in the interests of the nation, and social discipline has been instrumental in preventing small groups from impeding progress. Social discipline implies that once a law is enacted (including, for example, the land reform program, the emancipation of women and the sale of shares of industrial firms to workers, farmers and the public), particular groups cannot oppose, delay or block its implementation.

3. There are always some dissatisfied elements in countries undergoing rapid social change. Students at Tehran University, for example, where approximately half the student population is now drawn from the lower farmer and worker classes, are demanding more; some feel that their "rights" to a degree have been jeopardized by the government's efforts to improve standards of education. Discipline is needed in education, in work, in implementation of development plans and in the administration of justice and law. One's rights should be respected and guaranteed as long as the exercise of these rights does not hamper the exercise of the rights of others.

Conventional wisdom decrees that change must come from within and cannot be imposed, a European observed, but Iran is successfully imposing social discipline; this experience may hold lessons not only for the Third World but also for advanced nations like Great Britain. Lack of political will and political courage, combined with social permissiveness, has been a major cause of social disorders in the West, an Iranian added, warning that Iran must avoid importing bankrupt ideas and institutions from the West or East, along with the good.

The Economic Outlook

Economic Growth and Development in Iran

M. Ali Fekrat

I propose to provide a concise and systematic review of Iran's recent economic development. To this end, I shall first outline the conceptual framework of my thoughts and then proceed with my main analysis.

Analytical Framework

Iran's economic development could best be studied by accounting for intersectoral flows and intrasectoral changes. This approach not only suits the inherent structural characteristics of the Iranian economy but it is also consistent with the widely accepted view that the analysis of economic interactions among sectors offers the most promising path for the study of the developmental process.

Accordingly, the Iranian economy could be thought of as comprising three distinct sectors interlocked by a continuous intersectoral flow of resources. These sectors are the oil sector, the modern sector (manufacturing and services) and the indigenous agricultural sector. The interaction among these three sectors generates the main spark that sets in motion ripples that result in growth and development. In simple terms, the oil sector provides the capital needed for the growth of the other two sectors but does not receive any substantial return flow of resources from either the modern or the indigenous sector. By contributing the capital needed for the growth of the rest of the economy during the critical stages preceding full maturity, the oil sector obviates perhaps the most pressing constraint that has traditionally inhibited the growth of other less-developed countries.

The modern sector (manufacturing and services) draws on the oil sector for capital and on the indigenous sector for labor and raw materials to achieve growth, but sells its output mainly to the latter in addition to satisfying its own needs. As the growth of the modern sector continues and gathers momentum, it will begin to generate its own capital requirements and consequently will draw on the oil sector, not so much for capital but as a source of raw material and energy. Gradually, the once capital-producing, export-oriented oil sector will turn into an appendage of the rest of the economy and then slowly drift toward extinction as oil reserves are depleted. By then, the combined capacity of the modern-cum-indigenous sectors should have attained such self-sufficiency levels as to provide not only for their own capital needs but also for the acquisition of energy hitherto supplied by the oil sector.

The indigenous agricultural sector uses the products originating in the oil sector and the modern sector, but at the same time it loses labor only to the latter. This inevitably leads to the shrinkage of the indigenous sector relative to the other sectors, which should also ideally be accompanied by increases in productivity so that the burgeoning demand of the expanding population can be met without diverting scarce resources needed by the modern sector for its optimal growth.[1]

Growth: Aggregative and Sectoral

Now let us briefly review Iran's economic growth, first in aggregate terms and then by sectors. During the 1962–72 decade, real gross national product (GNP) increased by an average rate of 11 percent a year. For 1973 and 1974, increases in GNP were, of course, exceptionally higher (nearly 50 percent in 1973 at current prices) because of the spectacular rise in oil income.[2] Private consumption during the decade rose by over 7 percent a year, public consumption by about 20 percent and gross domestic investment by upwards of 15 percent. These trends have continued more or less unchanged as the government has moved into center stage in leading the economy and in providing expanded social and economic services. Consequently, the proportion of private consumption in domestic product has declined, while that of public consumption and gross investment (both private and public) has increased. Meanwhile, there has been a general trend away from public investment in infrastructure and toward major industries. This suggests that the role of government as a pacesetter and entrepreneur has taken a more active and innovative turn with far-reaching repercussions for the direction and content of Iran's development for some time to come.

Paralleling these shifts have been changes in the sources of finance. Public sector savings have, of course, almost always been the main source of finance for domestic investment activity. However, toward the latter part of the 1960s, increases in public sector investment were not matched by increases in public sector savings—owing to large consumption expenditure outlays—with the result that foreign borrowings were substantially increased. But this trend unexpectedly came to a halt in 1971 as oil revenues began to rise sharply as a result of successful negotiations between oil companies and OPEC countries. Oil income has thus been an important contributing factor to public sector savings and hence to the critical and pace-setting investments made by the public sector.

An inevitable by-product of this sort of relationship between public sector savings and investment is the injection of excessive liquidity into the economic system. This was bound to give rise to immense inflationary pressures, especially when infrastructural bottlenecks (*e.g.,* inadequate port facilities) made it virtually impossible to fight inflation by simply relaxing foreign trade barriers for a quick increase in the supply of goods on the market.[3] Both imports and exports have nevertheless reached unprecedented levels in recent years.

During most of the 1960s, economic development in Iran was accompanied by remarkable price stability, partly because of the existence of underutilized capacity due to the recession of the late 1950s and early 1960s, and partly because of the magnitude of oil income itself. But as the former began to shrink and the latter grew in quantum jumps, inflationary pressures were intensified. While the annual average change in the consumer price index during the period 1969–71 was only 3.5 percent, it had accelerated to 6.3 percent in 1972 and 11.2 percent in 1973.[4] Moreover, with excessive liquidity pumped into the system, the task of monetary policy as a counterinflationary weapon becomes extremely complex such that resort has instead to be made to selective and direct control measures in an effort to keep price rises within manageable proportions.[5]

Inflation worsens the distribution of income. Even though a wide variety of heroic schemes (*e.g.*, land reform) has been initiated to distribute the benefits of development geographically and by socioeconomic group, income distribution remains fairly skewed. Roughly, on the basis of 1971 data, more than half of all households in Iran could be classified as "poor"—with annual expenditures of under $800—and only 4 percent as "rich"—with annual expenditures of over $3,000—and the remainder as "middle income." There are, however, certain qualifications. First, there is very little absolute poverty in Iran in the sense of households having to forgo minimum dietary, clothing and shelter needs. Secondly, many of the distributive measures that have been implemented are, in fact, a redistribution of wealth, or rights to income and benefits. Until these measures have had time to bring about a noticeable change in the pattern of household income and expenditure, inflation, if unchecked, may partially nullify the redistributive effects of measures aimed at reducing income disparities.[6] They will, nevertheless, have the effect of uplifting the basic living standards and welfare of the majority of Iranis.

Oil Sector

Iran is the second largest crude oil producer in the Middle East and the fourth largest in the world. While oil income has for years been the largest single source of funds for the government and foreign exchange, its importance in recent years has dramatically increased as a result of sharp increases in oil prices and production.[7]

Crude oil production in 1974 topped 2.2 billion barrels—up from 2.1 billion in 1973 and 1.8 billion in 1972. Crude production first exceeded the 1-billion barrel mark in 1968 and then doubled in about five years. Production for 1975 will reportedly be lower due to the ongoing recession in the major consuming countries.

More important, however, have been changes in the oil terms of trade. During the 1960s, posted prices (*i.e.,* tax reference prices) of Iranian crude oil remained more or less unchanged. A small increase in the posted price of heavy crude occurred late in 1970, but starting with the Tehran agreement between OPEC and the oil companies early in 1971, posted prices of Iranian light crude were raised to $2.17 per barrel (from $1.79) and then to $5.34 in October 1973, and then finally the big jump to $11.87 in January 1974.[8]

The outcome of all this has, of course, been a dramatic increase in Iran's oil income: about $20 billion in 1974—up from $5 billion in 1973 and only $2.5 billion in 1972. Income for 1975 is expected to decline and, on the basis of the output during the first quarter of the year, may be as much as $4 billion less than the 1974 income—nonetheless a hefty $15 to 16 billion.

To demonstrate the significance of the oil sector as a source of capital for the rest of the economy, let us use the data given in Iran's revised Fifth Development Plan (1973–78), submitted to the parliament in the winter of 1974. Total fixed investments envisaged in the plan are nearly $70 billion, approximately two-thirds of which are public and the remaining one-third private. Public outlays (investment plus current expenditures and other payments) during the plan are expected to amount to about $123 billion, about 80 percent of which are expected to come from oil revenues.[9] In other words, oil revenues not only cover the entire public sector investment outlay during the plan period but also contribute significantly toward current expenditures (social, economic, defense). Thus, the importance of the oil sector as a source of funds goes far beyond the provision of long-term capital: it is by all yardsticks the lifeblood of the whole development effort.

Modern Sector

If the oil sector can be described as the lifeblood of the development effort, then the modern sector (manufacturing and services) has certainly been the engine of growth. The capital provided by the oil sector is put to use together with other factors of production (labor being supplied by the indigenous sector) to produce the wide range of consumer and capital goods in which the economy either possesses or is likely to possess a competitive advantage. Since the mix of capital and labor in this sector is such that capital is relatively more abundant, capital-intensive industries and methods of production could be employed without the usual concern about their adverse employment repercussions. Indeed, Iran's experience in this regard has demonstrated that economic development would generate sufficient employment to wipe out any surplus labor that might have existed prior to the start of development—an experience that contradicts the prevailing wisdom that industrialization creates little employment.

To provide a better perspective, in 1963 there were very few of what may be described as "large" industrial establishments, and most of the 3,500 or so large establishments consisted of workshops that employed 10 to 25 workers. Of a total population of about 23 million and an approximate urban labor force of more than 2 million, less than half a million were employed in urban industries. In 1972, there were close to 6,000 large industrial establishments and some 220,000 small ones. Included in the large establishments were at least 95 factories employing more than 500 workers and 34 with 7,000 or more persons. During 1969–72, employment in the 400 largest establishments rose by 20 percent, output by 57 percent and average productivity by 25 percent. Iran's total labor force currently stands at about 9.5 million—up from 7.9 million a decade earlier. Of this total, some 60 percent are engaged in industry and services. Manufacturing and mining alone employ over 2 million persons, while the "services" sector employs about 3.5 million. The rates of growth in employment in both of these sectors during the past decade have been significantly higher than those of the population in general and the labor force in particular, implying that they have been the focal point of employment and growth during the past decade.

Performance in the modern sector could perhaps be better gauged by examining output data. In 1973, value added in manufacturing grew by about 18 percent in real terms—up from an annual rate of about 14 percent during the Fourth Development Plan period (1968–72). Almost all the industries—consumer-durable and nondurable goods, intermediate inputs and the capital goods subsector—grew more rapidly during the Fourth Development Plan, reflecting a relatively small base and the entry into production of units producing tractors, buses, machine tools, telecommunications equipment, petrochemicals, and others. In basic metals, the Aryamehr steel mill in Isfahan began production during the Fourth Development Plan, using domestic iron ore and coal. Also, the Arak aluminum and machine tool plants and Tabriz tractor factory came into operation.

The establishment of these highly capital-intensive industries during the Fourth Development Plan marked an important advance in Iran's industrialization efforts. For they led Iran into a process of "backward integration," into deepening the manufacturing process and internalizing industrial activity. This process has quickened as Iran has entered into the production of electric motors, tractors, forklift trucks, compressors, boilers, sophisticated metals, into shipbuilding, and even nuclear energy.

Other related sectors and especially services, too, have registered impressive gains. Installed capacity for power generation, transport, telecommunications, banking and insurance, housing, education, health and welfare services, have all been considerably expanded, even though progress in many of them (*e.g.*, housing and telecommunications) has been less than satisfactory. These problem areas have been singled out for special attention under the present development plan, and available evidence indicates that concerted effort is being mounted to overcome these hurdles.

Indigenous Sector

The indigenous sector comprises the rural agricultural sector. This sector's basic interaction with the other two sectors would be to experience an inflow of capital from the oil sector and perhaps an outflow of labor to the modern sector. This should allow the indigenous sector to modernize and mechanize and expand output and productivity even though it may be losing labor to the modern sector (at least in the sense of not proportionately gaining from the increase in population and the labor force).

In considering sectoral interactions, we must note a significant difference that exists between the modern sector and the indigenous sector. Whereas in the case of the former we start at a small base (or in some instances, a nonexistent base), in the case of the latter we, in fact, have a large and already established sector to contend with. This preexisting condition has a far-reaching influence on sectoral interactions and the performance of the various sectors. To be sure, a preexisting condition may impede the absorption of capital by the indigenous sector or make its effective utilization difficult and unprofitable. These problems, of course, do not exist with the same severity when a sector is to be started from scratch where most of the relevant factors could be transplanted or copied. Not so in the case of an indigenous sector, where preexisting structural factors make such a transformation difficult and time-consuming.

These and other factors (including water shortage and climatic conditions) have restrained the full development of the agricultural sector. Although it still employs some 40 percent of the labor force, agriculture contributes only about 10 to 12 percent to the gross domestic value added—down from 26 percent in 1963. The sector's growth averaged only about 4 percent a year during 1962–72 (about 6 percent in 1973). During 1968–73, the output of wheat practically stagnated, while that of barley actually declined. The output of rice, cotton, sugarbeets, oil seeds and tea increased. The widening gap between demand and domestic output has, in turn, caused substantial increases in imports.

Of the total 8 million to 9 million hectares of land cropped annually, less than half is irrigated. The large dams built so far have had only a marginal impact because of a lack of complementary distribution systems. Thus, even though capital investment in agriculture has increased (at an average annual rate of about 23 percent during 1967–72), many other constraints such as inadequacy of extension services, credit facilities and improved seeds and fertilizer have hindered the development of this sector.

To remedy the problems inherent in the preexisting conditions, development efforts in agriculture have been focused on changing the structural framework of agricultural production by creating new institutions and renovating, improving and expanding old ones. Consequently, performance in agriculture should not be gauged solely in terms of output but also in terms of achievements in correcting and remedying old conditions. Of paramount importance here is the sweeping land reform, initiated in 1962 and implemented in three phases, which by 1974 had resulted in redistributing 17,000 villages covering 8 million hectares and 2.3 million rural families, one-third of whom were landless peasants prior to the land reform program. Also important have been the establishment of rural cooperatives and supporting financial institutions, agricultural corporations and a host of other rural development programs, including a vigorous anti-illiteracy campaign, that have as their goal a complete revitalization of Iran's indigenous rural sector.

Toward a Welfare State

The ultimate objective of any economic development is, of course, to maximize society's aggregate welfare. This, in turn, involves adequate measures to ensure that the benefits of development are shared by the citizenry and that everyone has sufficient opportunity to participate in the development to the maximum of his or her potential.

Iran's answer to this challenge is contained in what has come to be known as The Shah and People's Revolution—a peaceful program of radical socioeconomic reforms aimed at maximizing social welfare and distributing the fruits of development as widely as possible. This includes, in addition to land reform and literacy campaigns already mentioned, sale of government factories by the private sector, workers' participation in company profits, health and rural reconstruction campaigns, reform of electoral laws, judicial reform, nationalization of water and forests, urban development and educational and administration reforms. Important strides have been taken to implement these broad reform schemes. The nation's youth have been deployed, in lieu of their military service, to teach basic literacy to the peasantry and promote practical skills as well as sanitary standards. This is perhaps the lowest-cost but most effective method of tackling a staggering problem. Many industrial workers have come to share in the results of their efforts by sharing in the profits of their enterprises; electoral laws have been amended to ensure justice and equality of sexes; village courts have been set up to process innumerable minor litigation problems; concerted efforts for judicious water utilization and for reforestation and afforestation have been launched; the nation's educational system has been reoriented to become responsive to emerging needs while elementary education has become free for all; and a determined effort is currently underway to decentralize the government bureaucracy and to simplify and streamline the operations.

Detailed schemes are too numerous to review here. Suffice it to say that together these reforms basically constitute a coherent whole and a general framework within which equality of opportunity, equity and justice may be achieved for the largest number of people as quickly as possible.

Footnotes

1. For a formal development of this approach, see Jahangir Amuzegar and M. Ali Fekrat, *Iran: Economic Development Under Dualistic Conditions* (Chicago: University of Chicago Press, 1971).

2. It must be noted that 1973 and 1974 increases in GNP have deliberately been excluded from the computation of long-term growth trends of the economy, mainly because they represent exceptional, one-time increments in the national income.

3. Although increasing imports may prove effective in temporarily containing inflationary pressures, it may have exactly the opposite effect in the long run. By raising the level of consumption and future expectations, capital formation and capacity creation may suffer, thereby giving rise to an imbalance between aggregate supply and demand—an imbalance that may have to be rectified by either a general rise in the level of prices or a forced reduction in aggregate demand.

4. Price indices for Iran may understate actual price movements insofar as they use official prices in the computation of indices instead of actual market prices.

5. It is interesting to note that in October 1973 the Government of Iran instituted a comprehensive price control program by establishing a Price Intelligence Center and a High Council on Prices. These were later overhauled and streamlined to cope with a deteriorating price situation.

6. In the last two months, a *new* principle was added to the tenets of the Shah and People's Revolution. That principle deals with "consumer protection through price control." In this short period of time, countrywide price control measures have succeeded in lowering the prices of most consumer goods to those which prevailed nine months ago.

7. The bulk of production and exploration activities in Iran is carried out under a 20-year agreement (effective March 21, 1973) between the National Iranian Oil Company (NIOC) and a consortium of international oil companies. NIOC exercises full ownership and operational control, furnishes fixed capital and has first call on crude oil for domestic use and stated export. The consortium companies carry out production and exploration activities through their nonprofit subsidiary in Iran, the Iranian Oil Service Company (IOSCO) and purchase crude from NIOC through their trading companies. Iranian Government revenues are derived from payments by the trading companies.

8. Posted prices as a system for determining the government "take" are being dismantled in favor of unitary pricing under which the price of Iranian crude is determined on the basis of the average government "take" for the Persian Gulf market crude (*i.e.,* Saudi Arabian light) with adjustments for gravity and other relevant factors.

9. Should oil revenues fall short of the projected amounts for the entire plan period, expenditures will then be adjusted accordingly. So far foreign-aid outlays have been cut to only "vitally important cases," low-priority programs have been trimmed, and belt-tightening advisories have been put into effect. However, policies, guidelines, goals and priorities have been left intact.

Iran's Basic Macroeconomic Problems: A 20-Year Horizon

F. Vakil

During the period 1962–72, Iran experienced a period of relative price stability accompanied by a substantial rate of economic growth. The rate of growth of GNP, in current prices for the period 1962–67, was approximately 10.3 percent per annum, while its counterpart for 1967–72 was about 16.4 percent per annum. The GNP deflator grew almost imperceptibly during the first period at the rate of 0.6 percent per annum, while the comparative figure for the second period was somewhat higher at 3.4 percent per annum.[1]

While inflation did not seem to be a major concern during that decade, growth was a primary consideration. Much of the efforts of the government were concentrated on obtaining the financial resources with which to implement the development plans and with which to stimulate the performance of the private sector. This was accomplished through relatively careful usage of oil revenues and foreign loans, as well as domestic loans through the existing banking system. Foreign exchange was relatively scarce, and thus Iran's international credit-worthiness did not permit significant capital inflows likely to create inflationary pressures. Moreover, oil revenues did not show any dramatic increases until late in the decade under consideration; that is, until 1971, and even then there was no way of predicting the dramatic changes in the international oil prices that were to take place late in 1973.

Tables 27 and 28 (for all tables, see the appendix following this essay) show the relevant GNP, growth and price data for the period 1959–70.[2] Indeed, a cursory look at these tables suggests that the period in question was relatively free of inflationary pressures while growth was deemed substantial from 1964 onward. There are two distinct phases evident during this period. These are Phase I (1959–63), characterized by a relatively lower rate of growth and a practically nonexistent inflation; and Phase II (1964–70), characterized by a high rate of growth and minimal inflation.

By the end of 1973 the Tehran agreements, whereby the Organization of Petroleum Exporting Countries (OPEC) unilaterally increased the price of oil, thus resulting in a government "take" of approximately $7 per barrel as opposed to the $1.85 pre-agreement rate, radically changed the economic picture of Iran. This was further enhanced by additional increases in the government take to approximately $10.21 per barrel for Iranian oil in 1974. Tables 29 and 30 reveal the recent performance of the Iranian economy in the light of the new international oil conditions.

This is in line with the notion that oil revenues may well be a mixed blessing, depending on the size of the annual liquidity injections relative to the availability of complementary factors of production. Indeed, these revenues are on the one hand "like the blood of the economy, carrying badly needed investment resources to particular areas for purposes of expanding productive capacity; and on the other they are capable of producing an excessive liquidity situation, if capital resources become suddenly out of line with other complementary factors of production (such as skilled labor, technology, organizational skills, natural resources or general infrastructure services)."[3] This duality renders the planning task all the more difficult under conditions of financial surplus, since it requires a shift of emphasis in the planning circles, from an allocation of resources according to the real scarce factor or a combination of them.

The Iranian experience with economic and social development is most likely to represent a very novel case in the annals of developing countries' histories. It is novel on the one hand because it represents one of the few instances of very rapid sustained growth in the postwar period prior to the OPEC successes of 1973; and it is novel on the other hand because, among the OPEC countries, Iran is extremely well placed in terms of absorptive capacity, national and human resources, as well as in terms of an already existing and vital economic élan, to take advantage of the recent developments in the international oil market. The *sine qua non*s of success are there.

Yet many problems remain, especially if our time horizon is stretched beyond the near term to the 20–year span suggested as the yardstick for analysis in this research effort. Against the backdrop of macroeconomic data presented above, and designed to bring us up to date on the broad performance of the Iranian economy from 1959 to the present, it is the purpose of this essay to isolate and analyze some of the major macroeconomic problems likely to face Iran in the next 20 years. While many such problems exist, for the sake of brevity and clarity only four will be dealt with here. These are: (1) the role of oil revenues in Iran's long-term development process; (2) inflation as a short-term loss of resources with longer-term consequences; (3) the urban-rural income gap; and, (4) the strategy of export promotion as a "no-choice policy" for Iran's long-term development strategy.

The Role of Oil Revenues

Aggregate Supply Role

There is no question that the oil sector has played a major role in the growth performance of the Iranian economy over the last 20 years. Indeed, on the aggregate supply side of national accounts, the growth in the value added of the oil and gas sector has been a main contributor to the growth of GDP and GNP. Table 31 indicates the absolute contribution of the oil and gas sector in billion rials of current and constant 1972 prices as well as the relative share of the oil and gas sector in current and constant GNP. The data clearly indicate that over the period 1959–74, the share of the oil sector in GNP has risen on a sustained basis from 9.7 percent in 1959 to 47.8 percent in 1974. This suggests that the rate of growth of the oil sector has been consistently higher than the national average. Thus, in Phase I (1959–63), the gains in the oil sector's contribution to GNP are appreciably slow; in Phase II (1964–70), these gains show a distinct acceleration; and in Phase III (1971–present), due to the OPEC achievements of 1973, the contribution of the oil sector to aggregate supply is seen to reach major proportions.

Aggregate Demand Role

In any given time period, aggregate supply must equal aggregate demand. Thus, the oil and gas sector's absolute contribution to aggregate supply must translate itself into a contribution to aggregate demand, that is, in addition to consumption, investment and import expenditures. Because oil revenues accrue centrally to the government's coffers, it is clear that a major portion of these revenues will translate themselves into government consumption and government investment expenditures, although through multiplier effects, credit availability and liquidity injections, there are less direct impacts on the private consumption and private investment expediture components of aggregate demand. The oil sector is seen to drive both the public and private sectors and its impact is more important, in the short and medium run, on the former than the latter.

The primary vehicle of transfer from oil revenue to government expenditure is the government budget, which is itself composed of two basic components: (1) current expenditures for the running of government agencies and the meeting of expenditures arising out of public services (*e.g.*, defense, justice, health, education, welfare, etc.)[4] and (2) developing expenditures for the purpose of planning the economic and social development of the country through a public investment allocation process between the sectors in Five Year Plan intervals. Once allocated and expended, these oil-financed development expenditures contribute to the expansion of the economy's productive capacity. Indeed, it must be pointed out that much of the successful performance of the agricultural, industrial and mining and services sectors are due to the transfer of resources to them from the oil sector, a situation made possible by the special relationship enjoyed by oil in the international market.[5] The term "black gold" has often been used in this context, in that oil revenues represent an easy source of savings and of foreign exchange readily convertible to capital via imports. There is no need here to use often painful fiscal and monetary tools for curtailing consumption in order to increase the share of investment in GNP.[6] Quite the contrary, oil revenues on the scale presently available in Iran permit the pursuance of a growth-with-welfare policy, thus bypassing the traditional conflicts of growth versus welfare, of consumption versus investment and, to an extent, of the conflict between meeting the needs of the present and the future generations.

Yet while the benefits of oil to oil-producing countries are clear, there are risks to be taken into account. The most obvious are (1) since an oil-dependent growth process requires an ever-increasing level of oil revenues in order to sustain its growth momentum, what will happen when the oil revenue trend begins to taper off and then decline?;[7] (2) "The dependence of fiscal authorities on oil as an easily accessible source of revenue may tend to retard a smooth and gradual development of a tax base sufficiently broad to be closely interwoven with the mainstream of domestic economic activity. . . . The obvious danger implied by such a reliance is the incongruity that may emerge in the long run between the feeble capability of the fiscal apparatus to generate sufficient revenues and the requirements of a developing economy for such public income";[8] and (3) an easy source of access to foreign exchange now may encourage production to meet local demand rather than to meet export targets designed with an eye to developing an international comparative advantage in the industrial and services sector. There are few doubts that the long-term development of the Iranian economy is eventually dependent on the building of a non-oil export sector capable of meeting the future import requirements. Present availabilities of foreign exchange should not cloud the planners' foresight with respect to future possibilities and future requirements.

Future Oil Scenarios

With the advent of higher oil prices, it was initially thought that the Iranian economy would be incapable of domestically absorbing a jump in oil revenues from its $5-billion level of 1973 to its $20-billion level of 1974. Based on an econometric model for the Iranian economy developed in the Plan and Budget Organization,[9] it was thought best to look at the planning task as a decision concerning the division of annual oil revenues between that portion which could be domestically absorbed and that portion which should be invested abroad in interest-bearing securities, until such time as the local economy could grow large enough to absorb not only the annual oil revenue inflow but also the additional funds required to maintain its forward momentum. Through a system of national savings, managed by a portfolio management approach at the national level and taking into account the country's needs[10] (somewhat akin to the present portfolio management activities now undertaken by investment bankers and securities counselors for individuals), model results indicated that the easy process of oil-induced growth could be extended out in time, as excess funds[11] are put aside in the initial years for purposes of earning interest abroad, until such time as local absorptive capacity determines their repatriation. Indeed, when a comparison was made between the two alternative approaches, that is, (1) "spend the oil revenues as they accrue" or (2) "pace the spending of oil revenues according to absorptive capacity," it was found that the latter approach avoided the forecasted downturn in the Iranian economy associated with the peaking and tapering off of oil revenues in and around 1980;[12] extended the protective financial umbrella of oil-based resources out in time to, say, 1987, as well as the "normalization" point of the economy away from oil-induced growth to a growth process dependent on more traditional sources of capital formation;[13] smoothed out Iran's growth path, avoiding on the one hand large jumps in the initial years of oil revenues' upsurge, as well as significant drops associated with steep declines; avoided excessive inflationary pressures in the initial years; tried to cushion the anticipated balance-of-payments crisis that will face the Iranian economy when oil revenues taper off drastically; and allowed the accumulation of a wealth stock abroad on which the economy could draw in difficult times.[14]

While these conclusions were based on early 1974 estimates of the future, it became clear with the passage of time that oil income earning scenarios could vary drastically with the vagaries of world supply and demand conditions for oil.[15] The adjustment points mentioned above clearly must be resituated and reevaluated in each scenario. Table 32 presents three alternative oil scenarios with a best-guess estimate of anticipated gas revenues for the period 1973–92. The total figures for the 20-year period vary from a low of $311.9 to a high of $527.9 billion or a difference of 70 percent if the base is taken as the low figure.

It seems reasonable to suggest that the differences are wide enough to cover most eventualities. Yet in terms of the impact on the economy, not only the absolute total is important, but also the distribution over time, as it is this distribution that will determine the adjustment or "normalization" point. On a "pay-as-you-go" basis, the "normalization" point, as seen from this point in time, for Scenario 1 will be in 1977–78, for Scenario 2 as early as 1975–76, and for Scenario 3 as late as 1985–86. On a spending policy basis, these estimates turn out to be beyond 1992 for Scenarios 1 and 3 and in the late 1980s for Scenario 2.[16]

What seems clear is that oil plays a crucial role in the future growth momentum of the Iranian economy; that this economy is highly dependent on the absolute value of total oil receipts in any period as well as its annual distribution pattern over that period; that, given the limitation on total reserves, at some time in the future oil revenues will decline and therefore cause major structural adjustments in the economy which we have called "normalization"; that it is to the benefit of the society to pace the domestic spending of oil revenues according to absorptive capacity because, among other things, such a policy extends "normalization" out in time; that based on a planned spending policy," "normalization" can be avoided until the period 1987–95, depending on the oil scenario most likely to materialize, and that, based on a "pay-as-you-go" basis, "normalization" will occur much sooner, say some time during the period 1979–87, again depending on which oil scenario materializes.[17]

From the experience of the year 1974, it seems that there are strong forces working against the accumulation of a surplus and for increased spending, and therefore against the putting together of a spending policy. Among these we may note (1) the rise in the price of imported goods; (2) the tendency of planners to concentrate on financial bottlenecks alone and thus allocate resources as if capital were the constraining factor; and (3) the reluctance of Western industrialized countries to accept equity investments in their industries. Indeed, the available evidence for 1974 and early 1975 suggests very much lower financial surpluses than originally estimated. This in turn means that, based on our present best guesses for the future, "normalization" in the Iranian economy should begin to take place sometime in the period 1979–86.

Inflation

While it is difficult to predict long-run inflation rates, the evidence of the last few years carries certain implications for the longer-term development of the Iranian economy. As noted earlier, the period 1959–70 was characterized by rapid growth with minimal inflation. This can readily be seen in the data on the GNP deflator and its rate of increase shown in Table 28. By contrast, the period 1971–74, as shown in Table 30, was characterized by an accelerating inflation rate that stood at 2.17 percent in 1970 and at 19.8 percent in 1974. A comparison of the rate of increase in oil revenues in Table 29 and of the rate of increase in the GNP deflator in Table 30 suggests a correlation between inflation rates and liquidity injections associated with increases in the oil revenue levels. This in turn implies that in the latter period the Iranian economy had advanced beyond its absorptive capacity in the sense of finding the complementary factors of production (such as human skills, natural resources and infrastructure) to be put to work alongside the new financial resources. Thus, it seems clear that any tendency for oil revenue injections to go beyond a certain level—that level being the annual absorption capacity—can only lead to higher inflationary pressures, with little or no corresponding increase in output resulting from the spending of financial resources over and above that level defined by absorptive capacity.

Needless to say, the overspending of financial resources, in the face of nonfinancial bottlenecks, represents a loss in real resources with intertemporal implications. To begin with, it sets in motion a set of inflationary pressures in the near term that may be difficult to halt without drastic restrictive measures. This is corroborated by the cumulative aspects of inflation, as the implicitly taxed group in the society attempt to recover their loss of purchasing power. It must not be forgotten that inflation has redistributive effects that, if severe enough, can act to break the social fabric. Secondly, the amount of real resources lost—real in the sense that they represent exported barrels of oil—are resources that could have been used in the future to expand productive capacity at such a time when the relationship between annual financial inflow and annual absorptive capacity would permit it. When used in the present, these resources are simply dissipated in the form of higher prices.

The evidence for Iran in the period 1971–74 suggests a tendency to try to do too much in too short a time, a problem that is seen to affect most developing countries with a genuine desire to improve the welfare of their populations. This has resulted in a double-digit inflation with consequent losses in real resources for the future. The problem has been aggravated by the unusual international inflation rates observed in 1973–74. Yet it would be a mistake to suggest that the high rates of domestic inflation are due purely to international factors. On the contrary, most studies on the subject indicate no more than a 25 percent contribution of international inflation to domestic inflation, thus leaving a substantial portion to be accounted for by domestic factors.

Fortunately, the Iranian Government has become aware of the problem and is presently (1975) conducting a seemingly successful anti-inflation campaign. This is likely to lead to a more careful use of oil income in the future, in line with the gradually expanding absorptive capacity, and to avoid the dissipation of real resources through international inflationary pressures. One can therefore expect, with a little optimism, that the present inflationary trend can be reversed gradually through the fiscal mechanism without reverting to an austerity program. Nothing could be more disastrous to the long-term development of the Iranian economy, in terms of both the losses of real financial resources through higher prices and the imbalances resulting from drastic changes in the relative price structure, than the acceleration of the present inflation into a galloping inflation.

The Urban-Rural Gap

Evidence from the Past

Because of data scarcity and inconsistency, one way to measure the urban-rural income gap is to proxy the relative welfare positions by comparing private urban consumption expenditures per capita to private rural consumption expenditures per capita. This has been done in Table 33 for the period 1959–73 in constant 1972 prices. A cursory look at the data indicates that the urban-rural gap has widened substantially from the early 1960s to the mid-1970s. Indeed, the gap ratio is seen to drop from 2.13 in 1959 to a low of 1.91 in 1965 and then to rise significantly to a peak of 3.21 in 1972. One can hypothesize that these observations are in line with the concept of a dual economy in which the modern urban sector "takes off" and the backward rural sector stagnates, relatively speaking.[18]

The Distribution Problem

It is widely noted in the development literature, by Simon Kuznets among others, that income distribution tends to widen in the initial stages of growth, then to stabilize as the economy develops and finally to narrow as the industrialization process begins to engulf the whole economy.[19] It seems clear, from a comparison of the data shown in Table 33 and in Tables 27 and 29, that the rate of growth of the Iranian economy accelerated significantly from 1964 onward and that this period corresponds more or less with the beginning of a sustained deterioration of the gap ratio. Indeed, as the economy began to grow, the intersectoral distribution of income between urban and rural areas significantly widened.

While the problem seems to have been most generally stated by Kuznets' empirical generalization, the situation in oil-producing countries is aggravated by the large influxes of oil-based financial resources. As can be noted from a comparison of Tables 33 and 29 for the pertinent years 1970–74, there seems to be a correlation between the very rapid rise in oil revenues and the deterioration of the gap ratio. This is not to say that a causal objective relationship exists, but rather to suggest that the probable pattern of spending these revenues has been in favor of the urban areas as opposed to the rural areas. Indeed, the availability of financial resources encourages allocations toward urban-based, capital-intensive industrial services and infrastructure-building activities with little spillover benefits for the rural sector. It is not surprising, then, that the data in Table 33 indicate such a rapid deterioration in the gap ratio.

Iran: Past, Present and Future

Given the oil scenarios of Table 32, it is to be noted that the gap ratio is likely to deteriorate much further in the near and intermediate term, before the corrective forces spoken of by Kuznets begin to take effect. Preliminary estimates of the gap ratio, assuming continuation of basic trends and no introduction of policies designed to mitigate the urban-rural gap, suggest peak values in the area of 8.0 to 12.0 before equilibrium begins to be restored. Worth mentioning also is the fact that this worsening of the gap ratio occurs in the relatively medium term, that is, when the Iranian economy seems most well off in terms of oil revenues and substantially prior to "normalization."[20] When policy variables are introduced in the model runs, the expected peak gap ratios are lowered substantially to a range of 5.0 to 7.0.[21]

While one cannot place a great reliance on the absolute predicted values of the gap ratio, one can nevertheless fairly safely conclude that the urban-rural gap will get worse before it gets better. A do-nothing approach to urban-rural disparities does not bring about a self-adjusting mechanism, and therefore there is a great need to develop policy alternatives to deal with this particular aspect of the distribution problem. Yet many policy suggestions, such as rural industrialization, are on shaky empirical grounds, in that there are no examples, in the annals of developing countries' experiences, with massive efforts in these directions. Nevertheless, with its newly available financial resources, the Iranian Government is in a particularly well-placed position to begin to implement those policies needed to reduce the gap ratio, and to engage in innovative designs of policy packages intended to bring nonagricultural employment to the rural areas.[22] Among those that have been mentioned are rural industrialization, where light agriculturally oriented industries are located in the rural areas close to their source of raw materials, and the creation of service malls designed to render public and private services to a large number of villages usually dispersed over a unified area.

Export Promotion

The Role of Non-Oil Exports

A basic task in the longer-term planning process in the Iranian economy is to lessen the country's dependence on oil as a basic earner of foreign exchange and as a motor of the growth process. This is in line with the concept that a developed economy is diversified and capable of self-sustained growth based on an internal generation of savings. For this to become a reality within the context of the Iranian situation, it is necessary to develop a non-oil export sector capable of replacing the foreign exchange-earning capability of the oil sector within a defined time horizon.

Much of the eventual success of the Iranian experience, and of oil-producing countries in general, will be based on the success or failure of this "replacement" policy. Given that oil revenues contribute to an ever-increasing productive capacity of the non-oil sector, this ever-larger industrial machine also requires an ever-increasing import bill to support it. This observation is supported by an empirical observation of OECD countries where no industrialized country is capable of meeting the needs of its own very diversified industrial machines, and, even if some were, they would have to operate in direct conflict with the concepts of comparative advantage and economic efficiency. Rather than autarky, industrialization brings increasing trade requirements. Thus, it is to be expected that, with oil revenues tapering off over the next 20 years, the Iranian economy will suffer severe shortages of foreign exchange unless the non-oil export sector can grow significantly enough to fill this anticipated foreign exchange gap.

Yet the problem of export promotion is more complicated than the problem of simple gap filling. This is because, in order to develop a comparative advantage in the industrial and services sectors, it is necessary to become an internationally competitive producer.[23] This is a very complicated task requiring the proper mix of protection policies, skills development, managerial training, technology transfer and research and development strategies. Moreover, the strategy of export promotion is further constrained by the very high demand levels of the domestic market relative to domestic production levels, and the inherent tendencies of entrepreneurs to satisfy local demand before considering export possibilities.

While these observations point to the difficulties involved in solving the export promotion problem, they do not in any way diminish the importance of serious preplanning to overcome the inherent difficulties of developing comparative advantage situations. One must not forget that Iran will eventually give up its easy source of foreign exchange earnings and that the nation must prepare itself gradually, starting even now, for the eventual transition.

Evidence from the Past

Before looking at the future, it is necessary to look at the past behavior of non-oil exports. Table 34 presents data on total imports and non-oil exports of goods and services, their respective annual rate of growth, as well as the ratio of non-oil exports to total imports. The latter indicates to what degree the non-oil exports are capable of covering the import bill. From Table 34, it is clear that non-oil exports cover at most only 20 percent of the total import bill on the average in the period 1959–73. Moreover, the time trend in the coverage ratio seems to be on the downside throughout the period covered, a situation that must be reversed if the export promotion policy is ever to be successful.

When a closer look is taken at the composition of exports shown in Table 34, services excluded, it becomes clear that up to now Iran has depended solely on traditional non-oil exports. That is, most of these data include exports of cotton, carpets, dried fruits, nuts, etc., rather than the industrial goods necessary for implementing a successful export promotion policy. In other words, the surface has barely been scratched. Of course, high on the priority lists are steel and petrochemical industries, to be implemented during the Fifth and Sixth Development Plans, and aimed not only at the local but also at the foreign market.[24] Nevertheless, export promotion, even though recognized as a basic problem over the next 20 years, has not gained the required momentum to achieve the very high targets aimed at in the very short time available. The data in Table 34 seem to support the above observation.

Future Targets

If we assume that 1992 GNP in current prices, based on alternative oil scenarios and policy recommendations, will fall anywhere between 14,000 and 20,000 billion rials,[25] and if we further assume that import requirements will be in the 20 percent–25 percent range, then the level of non-oil exports required to cover the import bills will be in the range of 2,800–4,000 billion rials for the 20 percent figure, and 3,500–5,000 billion rials for the 25 percent figure. Given the present level of 67.6 billion rials in 1973, the required annual rate of growth to reach the 2,800 billion rials figure in 1992 is about 20 percent. For the upper figure of 5,000 billion rials, the corresponding annual rate of growth in non-oil exports is about 26 percent.

While this does not compare unfavorably with the non-oil export growth performance of about 18 percent per annum during the period 1963–73 as shown in Table 34, one must bear in mind the difficulty of keeping up such a sustained pace of growth over a 20-year period. In other words, the target does not seem way out of reach in terms of the numbers shown in Table 34, but it is one thing to set targets and quite another to achieve them. Suffice it to say that such a program of non-oil export development is quite crucial to the long-run development of the Iranian economy, especially if one considers the finality of oil revenues.

But one must remember that, while the non-oil export growth of the period 1963–73 was achieved mainly in the traditional exports area, the growth to come according to the above preliminary calculations will have to be in an arena of international competition. It is clear that preparations and planning must be begun in this area right away.[26]

Summary and Conclusions

This essay has attempted to show that, given the very exciting and successful performance of the Iranian economy during the last decade, Iran was in a particularly well-placed position to take full advantage (in a domestic sense) of the higher oil revenues accruing as a result of OPEC successes in the 1973 Tehran agreements. Yet the emphasis was to caution against unguarded optimism by pointing out, at the macro level, those areas that seem to be major problem areas within our specified time horizon. These were:

1. In order to achieve its longer-term development objectives, Iran will have to lessen the economy's dependence on oil revenue injections in a planned fashion, because, like it or not, the finality of oil reserves (85 billion barrels) means that sometime between now and 1992, depending on the oil scenario that materializes, oil revenues will taper off and decline rapidly. The "normalization" process will have to take place and the period of easy oil-induced growth will be over. While the timing of this "normalization" process depends on the surplus accumulation in the initial years, as well as on the pattern of oil revenue distribution over time, it seems already evident from the experience of the year 1974 with high oil revenues that this surplus will not be forthcoming in the initially expected amounts. Thus the "normalization" of the economy is seen to begin sooner rather than later.

2. Inflation in the near term, such as the one that has been gradually developing in Iran since 1974 under the push of higher oil revenues and of international inflationary pressures, is bound to affect the longer-term development path, especially if controls fail to prevent the present inflation from assuming galloping proportions. This is because the present inflation causes a loss in real resources (barrels of oil), resources that could be used for future productive capacity expansion, and because it causes imbalances in the relative price structure with possible negative impacts on consumer and investor confidence.

3. Generally, the process of rapid growth leads to a widening of the income distribution. In this Iran is no exception, as shown by the rise of the gap ratio in Table 33 over the period 1959–73. Because oil revenues accrue basically to urban areas, it is quite likely that, based on present patterns, the urban-rural gap will worsen before it gets better, especially

Iran: Past, Present and Future

in the face of the upsurge in oil prices. In order to remedy the situation, the planning task will of necessity require innovative policy packages, before the magnitude of the urban-rural gap strains the social fabric.

4. The promotion of non-oil exports, derived from the industrial and services sectors, is seen as the key to the success of the longer-term Iranian development effort. This is because on the one hand, Iran faces the industrialization process with increasing import requirements, while on the other, a situation of eventually declining oil revenues. The guarantee of foreign exchange availability no longer being there, it becomes essential to plan now for the development of an internationally competitive non-oil export sector capable of replacing oil as a main earner of foreign exchange. Yet the preliminary forecasts of 20 percent to 26 percent annual growth of non-oil exports until 1992 reflect by no means an easy task. This is especially so when one considers that this policy requires the development of an international comparative advantage.

In concluding, one must add that the process of economic and social development is fraught with conflicts—conflicts between the present and the future, between the rich and the poor, between the traditional and the modern, between the urban and rural, etc. The task of guiding the ship of state through this transitional period is by no means simple. It requires a constant vigil against problems that arise and against imbalances that can abort a very carefully balanced "takeoff." The problems spoken of throughout this essay were isolated as some of the more important illustrations of things to be seriously tackled over the next 20 years. Fortunately, if Iran's experience in the last 10 to 15 years with economic development is any indication, these problems will be surmounted through awareness, good leadership and good planning. Indeed, research efforts and policy experimentations are well under way in all the areas mentioned above. Suffice it to say that since the awareness exists among the policymakers and the planners, the solutions will be found.

Table 27
GNP in Current and Constant 1972 Prices and Oil Revenues
(billions of rials)

Year	GNP (Current)	Annual Rate of Growth (percent)	GNP (1972 Prices)	Annual Rate of Growth (percent)	Oil Revenues	Annual Rate of Growth (percent)
1959	283.9	—	387.8	5.3	19.4	—
1960	309.1	8.9	408.5	3.2	21.4	10.3
1961	319.6	3.4	421.6	5.1	21.8	1.9
1962	340.4	6.5	442.9	5.6	25.7	17.9
1963	360.3	5.8	467.9	9.7	29.1	13.2
1964	405.2	12.5	513.1	11.1	35.0	20.3
1965	456.4	12.6	570.2	10.6	38.6	10.8
1966	503.6	10.3	630.9	11.3	45.6	18.1
1967	556.5	10.5	701.9	19.8	56.4	23.7
1968	629.4	13.1	777.9	9.2	64.0	13.5
1969	704.2	11.9	849.2	11.0	72.9	13.8
1970	798.2	13.3	942.2		87.2	19.6

Table 28
Variations in the GNP Deflator and Its Rate of Increase[27]

Year	GNP Deflator	Rate of Increase in GNP Deflator (percent)
1959	73.2	—
1960	75.7	3.41
1961	75.8	1.13
1962	76.9	1.45
1963	77.0	0.13
1964	79.0	2.59
1965	80.0	1.26
1966	79.8	-0.25
1967	79.3	-0.63
1968	80.9	2.10
1969	82.9	2.47
1970	84.7	2.17

Table 29
GNP in Current and Constant 1972 Prices and Oil Revenues [28]
(billions of rials)

Year	GNP (Current)	Annual Rate of Growth (percent)	GNP (1972 Prices)	Annual Rate of Growth (percent)	Oil Revenues	Annual Rate of Growth (percent)
1971	962.7	20.6	1,036.3	10.1	152.1	74.4
1972	1,183.1	22.9	1,183.1	14.2	182.9	20.2
1973	1,763.3	49.0	1,587.3	34.2	477.5	161.1
1974	3,020.4	71.3	2,270.0	43.0	1,297.4	171.7

Table 30
Variations in the GNP Deflator and Its Rate of Increase [29]

Year	GNP Deflator	Rate of Increase in GNP Deflator (percent)
1971	92.9	9.68
1972	100.0	7.64
1973	111.1	11.11
1974	133.1	19.80

Iran: Past, Present and Future

Table 31
Value Added in Oil and Gas in Current and Constant 1972 Prices[30]
(billions of rials)

Year	GNP (Current)	Value Added Oil and Gas	Ratio 3 = 2/1 (percent)	GNP (1972 Prices)	Value Added Oil and Gas	Ratio 6 = 5/4 (percent)
	(1)	(2)	(3)	(4)	(5)	(6)
1959	283.9	27.7	9.7	387.8	28.1	7.2
1960	309.1	30.1	9.7	408.5	32.1	7.9
1961	319.6	33.7	10.5	421.6	38.2	9.1
1962	340.4	38.4	11.3	442.9	45.1	10.2
1963	360.3	40.6	11.3	467.9	48.1	10.3
1964	465.2	46.4	11.5	513.1	63.8	12.4
1965	456.4	52.4	11.5	570.2	70.5	12.4
1966	503.6	60.8	12.1	630.9	84.8	13.4
1967	556.5	71.4	12.8	701.9	101.8	14.5
1968	629.4	82.7	13.1	777.9	119.8	15.4
1969	704.2	95.3	13.5	849.2	141.4	16.7
1970	798.2	114.3	14.3	942.2	168.2	17.8
1971	962.7	178.8	18.6	1,036.3	202.1	19.5
1972	1,183.1	216.4	18.3	1,183.1	216.4	18.3
1973	1,763.3	579.6	32.9	1,587.3	514.6	32.4
1974	3,020.4	1,443.0	47.8	2,270.0	1,046.1	46.1

Table 32
Oil Revenue Scenarios and Gas Revenues [31]
(billions of rials)

Year	Oil Revenue Scenario 1	Oil Revenue Scenario 2	Oil Revenue Scenario 3	Gas Revenue
1973	477.5	477.5	477.5	—
1974	1,297.4	1,297.4	1,297.4	12.7
1975	1,563.3	1,303.2	1,592.7	12.8
1976	1,733.4	1,176.6	1,660.7	13.6
1977	1,902.8	1,061.2	1,822.5	103.6
1978	1,897.3	957.4	1,819.1	115.5
1979	1,884.8	955.3	1,814.4	127.5
1980	1,874.6	952.2	1,810.1	243.3
1981	1,852.5	1,050.3	1,846.8	245.9
1982	1,838.0	1,157.5	1,940.0	250.3
1983	1,859.3	1,154.9	1,995.1	253.4
1984	1,883.9	1,152.8	2,053.9	256.4
1985	1,555.6	1,148.7	2,112.6	259.6
1986	1,271.0	1,148.4	2,173.2	262.6
1987	1,016.3	1,143.6	2,237.0	265.7
1988	792.0	1,086.6	2,114.1	268.8
1989	713.2	1,031.9	1,997.2	271.8
1990	467.7	980.9	1,798.0	275.0
1991	307.9	931.4	1,617.9	278.0
1992	154.4	884.9	1,455.5	281.2
Total	26,341.6	21,052.7	35,635.7	3,797.7
Billions of dollars	$390.2	$311.9	$527.9	$57.1

Table 33

Ratio of Urban Private Consumptive Expenditures Per Capita to
Rural Private Consumptive Expenditures Per Capita for Iran in Constant 1972 Prices[32]

Year	Urban Consumptive Expenditures	Urban Population	Ratio 3 = 1/2	Rural Consumptive Expenditures	Rural Population	Ratio 6 = 4/5	Gap Ratio 7 = 3/6
	(1)	(2)	(3)	(4)	(5)	(6)	(7)
1959	145.4	6,972	20,855	139.0	14,199	9,789	2.13
1960	153.1	7,330	20,887	148.0	14,446	10,245	2.04
1961	154.9	7,703	20,109	148.8	14,695	10,126	1.99
1962	167.1	8,091	20,652	150.2	14,947	10,049	2.06
1963	175.2	8,495	20,623	153.6	15,201	10,104	2.04
1964	187.9	8,915	21,077	168.8	15,458	10,920	1.93
1965	197.2	9,353	21,084	173.8	15,716	11,059	1.91
1966	233.2	9,808	23,776	183.3	15,977	11,473	2.07
1967	254.6	10,282	24,762	194.9	16,240	12,001	2.06
1968	295.5	10,775	27,424	207.9	16,505	12,596	2.18
1969	320.9	11,287	28,430	219.7	16,772	13,099	2.17
1970	370.0	11,820	31,303	225.2	17,041	13,215	2.37
1971	392.6	12,375	31,725	199.5	17,311	11,524	2.75
1972	455.7	12,951	35,186	192.9	17,583	10,971	3.21
1973	491.3	13,550	36,258	205.0	17,856	11,481	3.16

Table 34
Ratio of Non-Oil Exports to Total Imports of Goods and Services at Current Prices[33]
(billions of rials)

Year	Total Imports	Annual Rate of Growth (percent)	Non-Oil Exports, Goods and Services	Annual Rate of Growth (percent)	Ratio Non-Oil Exports/Imports
1959	48.2	—	10.7	—	0.22
1960	49.7	3.1	10.2	-4.9	0.21
1961	47.8	-4.0	10.8	5.9	0.23
1962	43.6	-9.6	10.5	-2.9	0.24
1963	41.8	-4.3	11.4	8.6	0.27
1964	59.8	43.1	13.1	14.9	0.22
1965	69.5	16.2	15.9	21.4	0.23
1966	81.5	17.3	14.7	-8.2	0.18
1967	101.1	24.0	16.9	15.0	0.17
1968	120.4	19.1	20.7	22.5	0.17
1969	139.6	15.9	22.5	8.7	0.16
1970	158.4	13.5	26.1	16.0	0.16
1971	200.8	26.8	37.2	65.3	0.19
1972	254.5	26.7	48.0	29.0	0.19
1973	348.2	36.8	67.6	40.8	0.19

Footnotes

1. "A Twenty-Year Macroeconomic Perspective for Iran 1972–1992," *Planometrics and General Economy Bureau*, Plan and Budget Organization, Tehran, Iran, 1974, p. 4.

2. The data for these tables were obtained from: Bank Markazi Iran, *National Income of Iran: 1959–1971*, Tehran, Iran, 1973, pp. 1, 32.

3. Firouz Vakil, *Determining Iran's Financial Surplus 1973–1992: Some Management Concepts*, The Institute for International Political and Economic Studies, Tehran Papers No. 2, Tehran, Iran, June 1975, p. 6.

4. Jahangir Amuzegar and M. Ali Fekrat, *Iran: Economic Development under Dualistic Conditions* (Chicago: University of Chicago Press, 1971), p. 33.

5. Firouz Vakil, *op. cit.*, p. 4.

6. Jahangir Amuzegar and M. Ali Fekrat, *op. cit.*, p. 57.

7. It is clear that oil revenues equal number of barrels produced times government take per barrel. Iran's production time pattern will obviously be a function of world supply and demand, the resulting price per barrel, the development needs, the internal consumption and intermediate requirements and the availability of sufficient oil reserves for export. Since reserves are not unlimited, sooner or later oil revenues will

taper off and decline. This will necessitate an adjustment process in the economy entwined around what one could call the "normalization of the Iranian economy" away from the relatively easy process of oil-induced growth to a growth mechanism much more dependent on traditional forms of saving. The planning task is to predict and be prepared.

8. *Ibid.*, p. 57.

9. See "A Twenty-Year Macroeconomic Perspective for Iran 1972–1992," *op. cit.*, pp. 24–33.

10. This question has been dealt with in some detail in: Firouz Vakil, *Determining Iran's Financial Surplus 1973–1992: Some Management Concepts, op. cit.*, pp. 36–46.

11. By excess funds are meant government financial revenues of a size well beyond the absorptive capacity of the economy in the year in which the revenues accrue.

12. Note that the timing of this downturn, by virtue of the oil revenue injection dependence for growth of the Iranian economy, is a function of the predicted future patterns of oil revenues. Depending on future world demand and supply considerations, this point may be closer or further in time from the present. The 1980 date mentioned in the text assumes that the old consortium production plans are implemented. It also assumes that government take per barrel increases steadily to $10 per barrel by 1980 and then remains stable until 1992 (the end of the 20-year horizon of the initial study).

13. The year 1987 was based on initial estimates in the PBO study. Note that seven years of grace, from 1980 to 1987, can be extremely important in terms of the additional productive capacity that can be created before the easy source of savings dries up.

14. "A Twenty-Year Macroeconomic Perspective for Iran 1972–1992," *op. cit.*, p. 67.

15. Indeed, projected oil revenues for Iran in 1975 are estimated to be below those of 1974, say $18 billion as opposed to last year's $20 billion figure. See Eric Pace, "Iran is Borrowing Cash Despite Oil Revenues," *International Herald Tribune*, August 16–17, 1975, p. 5.

16. Firouz Vakil, *op. cit.*, pp. 32–34.

17. It is assumed here that the "pay-as-you-go" Scenario 2 is least likely to materialize.

18. "A Twenty-Year Macroeconomic Perspective for Iran 1972–1992," *op. cit.*, p. 57.

19. Simon Kuznets, "Economic Growth and Income Inequality," *American Economic Review*, March 1955, pp. 1–28.

20. "A Revision in the Twenty-year Macroeconomic Perspective for Iran According to Revised Oil Scenarios," *Planometrics and General Economy Bureau*, Plan and Budget Organization, Tehran, Iran, June, 1975, pp. 50–52.

21. *Ibid.*, pp. 53–55.

22. Because of the low growth potential of the agricultural sector, the only feasible way to effect rapid income increases is through the location of light industries and service centers in the rural areas.

23. Iran is not likely to produce agricultural goods in large enough quantities to make its exports an important component in the future foreign exchange gap filling process. This is clearly stated in B. Baldini, "The Quantitative Analysis of the Perspective Study of Agricultural Development for Iran," *Food and Agriculture Organization of the United Nations*, Rome, 1975. This paper was presented at the joint Iran/FAO Workshop on Agricultural Sector Planning in Tehran, May 7–18, 1975. One is therefore left with the industrial and services sectors to contend with.

24. Plan and Budget Organization, *Iran's Fifth Development Plan 1973–1978: Revised, A Summary*, The Imperial Government of Iran, Tehran, Iran, January, 1975, pp 142–144.

25. "A Revision in the Twenty-Year Macroeconomic Perspective for Iran According to Revised Oil Scenarios," *op. cit.*, pp. 50–55.

26. As a suggestion, it might be worth considering a policy of forced exports, whereby at least 10 percent of all industrial production (as a target) would be sold abroad, even if local demand requirements necessitated additional imports to fill the gap left by the 10 percent target. The reasoning is that export promotion requires brand-name acceptance as well as certain marketing operations that need to begin as soon as possible in order to achieve the longer-term targets.

27. Firouz Vakil, *Determining Iran's Financial Surplus 1973–1992: Some Management Concepts*, The Institute for International Political and Economic Studies, Tehran Papers No. 2, Tehran, Iran, June 1975, p. 6.

28. Data on GNP, current and constant for the period 1971–74 are provided by Bank Markazi Iran, Statistical Department. Oil revenue data for the period 1971–73 are also given by Bank Markazi, while the 1974 estimate was obtained from the Budget Division of the Plan and Budget Organization.

29. Firouz Vakil, *op. cit.*, p. 10.

30. The data for the period 1959–72 were obtained from the Statistical Research Unit of the Planometrics and General Economy Bureau, Plan and Budget Organization. The data for the period 1973–74 were obtained from the Statistical Department of Bank Markazi Iran.

31. This table was obtained from Firouz Vakil, *op. cit.*, p. 24. Scenario 1 is a moderate scenario somewhat akin to previous consortium production plans with moderate price increases. Scenario 2 is a pessimistic scenario with both production and price falling in the middle period, as world economies are assumed to be incapable of absorbing world oil outputs. Scenario 3 is an optimistic scenario with moderate production increases and large price increases. Note that all scenarios are constrained by reserve availabilities, now estimated at around 85 billion barrels and including primary, secondary and tertiary recovery techniques. Therefore, in all scenarios oil income must decrease after a certain period.

32. The data for this table were obtained from the Statistical Research Unit of the Planometrics and General Economy Bureau, Plan and Budget Organization and Bank Markazi Iran, *op. cit.*, Table 54.

33. The data for Table 34 were provided by the Statistical Research Unit of the Planometrics and General Economy Bureau, Plan and Budget Organization, Tehran, Iran.

Strategies of Industrial Development in Iran

F. Najmabadi

The first real attempt to industrialize Iran was made prior to World War II, during the reign of Reza Shah the Great, when a number of light and consumer goods industries were created. In 1940, Iran had already embarked on the construction of its first integrated steel mill sited at Karaj near Tehran, but the war, unfortunately, brought these serious efforts to a complete stop. It was not until the late 1950s, after a period of virtual stagnation in industrial activities, that industrial investment started anew, supported by fairly extensive government investment in infrastructural facilities, as well as in some consumer goods and building material industries, and fueled by the incentives provided by the government for the private sector.

However, the true and dynamic growth in industrialization came after the advent of Iran's Shah and People's Revolution, when under the wise guidance and enlightened leadership of H.I.M. Aryamehr The Shahanshah of Iran, a new socioeconomic framework was created, leading to massive investment by both the public and the private sectors.

The new socioeconomic framework emphasized, *inter alia*, rapid industrialization and the building up of a diversified and self-sustaining industrial base in order to broaden the base of the economy, increase employment opportunities and improve the standard of living of the people and the general welfare of the society as a whole. Toward this end, policies were devised to encourage the private sector to set up industrial units through appropriate fiscal, monetary and trade incentives, while the government played an active role in the enlargement of infrastructural facilities and the establishment of capacities in the basic industries. The basic policy framework included encouragement of foreign investment in Iranian industry so as to ensure adequate inflow of modern technology and know-how.

As a result, the industry and mining sector in the past decade has been the main instrument through which the government has successfully built up the overall economy of the country. The annual rate of growth in industry has been increasing very rapidly, from 5 percent per annum in 1962 to over 20 percent per annum in 1974. In the same period, the share of industrial production in the gross national product increased from 11.7 percent to about 17 percent. Employment in this sector increased from 1.3 million persons in 1962 to more than 2 million in 1974, while productivity, expressed as value added per employed person, increased by 10 percent per year in the same interval. This remarkable growth in industry induced rapid development in other sectors.

Permit me to trace back some of the basic policies and strategies that have helped shape our industrial development in the past, leading up to the present situation. I shall then discuss the manner in which our policies are developing for the future.

The Emergence of Private Sector Enterprises

Generally speaking, investment by the government has played a very important role in the industrialization process in Iran. In the earlier part of this century, when our first attempts at industrialization were made, sugar refineries, textile mills, cement and a few other consumer goods industries constituted the bulk of industrial units. Even as late as the 1950s and the early 1960s, government investment dominated the manufacturing sector as shown in Table 35.

Table 35
Capital Investment in Industry and Mines

Period (year)	(1) Private	(2) Government	(3) Total	(2) to (3) (percent)
Third Plan	(30.5)	(34.5)	(65.0)	(53.1)
Fourth Plan	(183.6)	(116.4)	(300.0)	(38.8)
(1968)	22.7	16.6	39.3	42.2
(1969)	31.7	22.3	54.0	41.3
(1970)	36.2	28.5	64.7	44.0
(1971)	46.6	25.8	72.4	35.6
(1972)	46.4	23.2	69.6	33.3
Fifth Plan (Projected)	(507.0)	(339.0)	(846.0)	(40.1)
(1973)	57.0	23.4	80.4	29.1
(1974)	109.0	54.6	163.6	33.3

A major change in the investment picture and the involvement of private capital in industry came about in the 1960s when the private sector invested heavily in new plants and equipment. The government also started divesting its holdings in the consumer goods industries through the sale of its shares to the private sector. Simultaneously, government investment was redirected toward large-scale units such as integrated steel mills and other metal smelting, petrochemicals, heavy engineering, machine tools, tractors, pulp and paper and electronics.

Iran: Past, Present and Future

The government only invested in industries when private invest-ment was not forthcoming because of inadequate return on investment even though the social gains might well have been substantial, or when the private sector could not easily afford the cost of technology. Another condition for government investment was when the project involved the utilization of natural resources. Furthermore, the government invested in industries that were a strong force for regional development and employment policy, or when the stabilization of prices was high on the list of government priorities.

In actual practice, quite a number of the units thus created by the government during the previous and the present (1968–77) Five Year Development Plans have already been transformed into government/ private sector joint ventures leading to a more diverse and consequently efficient utilization of the investment.

It should be indicated here that such industries as oil, steel and copper smelting will remain totally in the government domain, with the private sector in some instances allowed or even encouraged to partici-pate in the downstream operations.

Licensing

One of the major instruments employed during the initial stages of Iran's industrialization effort was licensing. It was practiced very rigorously as a means of directing and maximizing the use of limited resources as well as ensuring the orderly implementation of industrial planning for the various sectors. It was further used as a lever for regional development, increased integration and local manufacturing and for the guidance and control of foreign investment. During the early part of the 1960s, the main objective of the licensing system, working in combination with numerous incentives, was to encourage the private sector to invest in manufactur-ing activities primarily for the production of durable and nondurable consumer goods and later on for the production of intermediate and capital goods. It was designed to ensure that technical, managerial and financial capabilities of the firms to whom licenses were granted would be able to provide a reasonable assurance of their success. This system was complemented on the government side by a comprehensive and promotional list of sector studies indicating the areas of desired invest-ment plus a thorough evaluation of the feasibility studies.

As a practical matter, the license would entitle the holder to receive all other permits connected with infrastructural facilities such as water, electricity, etc., at advantageous industrial rates, as well as financing from industrial development banks.

Over the course of years, as industry developed, it became evident that the objective of the licensing system had to be progressively modified in line with Iran's national needs and priorities. Thus, toward the end of the 1960s the revised industrial policy called for a shift from import-substituting consumer goods to intermediate and capital goods, a competitive framework was established. The framework ended excessive protection and minimum economic size for new plants and halted unnecessary fragmentation. It fostered the optimum utilization of national resources and regional diversification, and gave impetus to a strong drive toward export promotion. Licensing was therefore utilized very effectively.

An important facet of licensing was its strong promotional character in instances where the government considered the creation of a particular industry to be necessary in order to meet an essential need.

Financing of Industrial Projects

Prior to 1957, most new industrial projects began with the entrepreneur investing his savings, supported by some fixed-investment loan facilities from a fund set up by the government and credit facilities, mostly in the form of working capital, by the existing commercial banks. In 1957 the government established the ICB (Industrial Credit Bank), and two years later another institution called IMDBI (Industrial and Mining Development Bank of Iran) was created as a private bank charged with the task of promoting private industrial development. A few years later, in response to an immediate need, a fund, known as the Industrial Guarantee Fund, was established for the express aim of assisting the small-scale industries.

All these three lending institutions, though of comparatively different character, were strongly supported by the government with the provision of soft credits as well as guarantees for their borrowings from the international financial institutions.

In 1973, in order to strengthen further the industrial financing network, another specialized industrial bank, called DIBI (Development and Investment Bank of Iran), was established in the private sector, augmenting the capability of the system in meeting the ever-increasing demand generated through the increased pace of industrial development.

These institutions have been instrumental in supporting the bulk of new industrial investment in the last decade, and their dynamic approach, managerial acumen and experience, coupled with foresight and vision, have immensely assisted the government in the realization of its industrial targets and, at times, have been helpful in the formulation of new industrial policies. They have also performed admirably as a catalyst in joint venture projects with foreign investors and have been very effectively involved in the much wider concept of enlarging the shareholding base in industry.*

Taxation

Iran's taxation system is heavily geared to the promotion and expansion of the industrial sector. The income tax law provides for an effective battery of tax incentives in conformity with the general government policy of rapid industrialization. Here an attempt will be made to enumerate a few of the major provisions of the law.

1. Company profits are generally exempted from taxation for five years, provided that they are located at least 120 kilometers from Tehran.

2. Exemptions apply not only to company profits but also to the shareholders' personal tax liability on dividends.

3. Losses incurred in any one year can be carried over a number of years and recouped from subsequent profits.

4. Profits reinvested in new facilities or derived from the export earnings of the business are exempted from taxation. In line with the efforts made toward deconcentration of the Tehran area, plants that are moved completely from this region and relocated in other regions of Iran are entitled to receive tax exemptions up to 12 years.

In general, these tax incentives, which are designed to meet various policy measures, have greatly assisted the establishment of new industries around the country, as testified to by the overwhelmingly larger investments made in the provinces during the previous and the present Five Year Development Plan periods.

Trade Policy

Since the beginning of the Third Development Plan (1963–68), Iran's trade policy has been geared to the following basic objectives: to provide the Iranian economy with its basic needs for commodities, intermediate goods, parts and components, capital goods and generally manufactured articles; to act as a vehicle for rapid industrial develop-

---

*A review of the major lending institutions to industry would be incomplete without making a special reference to Bank Melli Iran and the Agricultural Development Bank, the former representing the single largest institution providing the bulk of working capital to industry as well as some fixed-assets financing and the latter being primarily involved in the establishment of agroindustrial projects.

ment in order to strengthen the manufacturing and producing capability of the national economy; and to promote exports from Iran, especially in the field of manufactured articles. Trade policy has, therefore, been used as one of the strongest motivating forces behind Iran's quest for industrialization by providing the necessary protection to infant industries. Iran has not only used the general tariff structure as a means of protecting those industries but it has also utilized its capability to revise the export-import regulations annually in order to increase or decrease the commercial benefit tax (which is levied over and above the general customs tariff) and to exercise, where deemed essential, quantitative control over the importation of some manufactured articles to the benefit of indigenous industry.

Consumer Protection and Price Control

From the early days of Iran's struggle toward industrialization, the problem of consumer protection has been high on the list of government priorities. The establishment of the Iran Standard and Industrial Research Institute (ISIRI) was a move not only toward the setting up of quality standards for various manufactured articles but also an attempt to improve quality through research in industrial processes and practices. Though originally not compulsory, many industrial enterprises have volunteered to apply the Standards Seal to their products, and in such instances a very rigorous system is applied by the Institute to ensure that the articles actually comply in every respect with the quality standards. In recent years, a law has been passed that entitles the Institute to require the compulsory adherence to the national standards on various grounds, especially those connected with consumer safety.

As for price control, it must be borne in mind that at the early stages of any developing country's industrialization (and there are many examples to illustrate this), owing to the limited size of the internal market and the planner's preoccupation with the minimum economic scale, the emergence of monopolistic or oligopolistic practices is to a certain extent inevitable. Although the policy for creating a competitive atmosphere has been pursued with vigor, the government has found it necessary in the past and in the present to take steps to prevent the abuse of monopoly power and to protect the consumer with some form of price control. Up to the middle of 1973, the number of items for which prices were established was rather small, but, as a result of an antiprofiteering drive by the government during the period when the world and the Iranian economy experienced a high inflationary tendency, a large number of articles came under price control measures, and the practice is being continued up to the present time.

Foreign Investment

The value of and the need for foreign investment and technical know-how has been recognized by the government since the middle of the 1950s, and the law for the attraction and protection of foreign investment dates back to 1955. According to this law, all the rights, exemption and facilities accorded to domestic capital and private production enterprises shall apply also to foreign capital and firms. Subject to the formalities as provided in the law, original capital, profits and dividends may be repatriated in the same currency as the original investment, and the Central Bank is required to make the necessary foreign exchange available.

Iran's desire to attract foreign capital does not in practice mean that any project under any set of conditions may be accepted. In fact, the proposed projects receive very detailed scrutiny not only to determine their conformity with the basic industrial policies and criteria, but also for their general contribution to the economic and industrial development of the country. The government is determined to use foreign investment as (1) a vehicle for increased reliance on indigenous material and human resources, (2) the export of industrial goods, (3) the training of Iranian personnel at all levels, (4) the transfer of know-how and technology leading to the creation of research and development capability in Iran and, in some instances, for (5) the transfer of managerial ability. Under no circumstances has Iran allowed long-term foreign domination of any important field of industrial activity, the basic principles being that the association must retain an essentially Iranian character and must be of real benefit to the Iranian economy.

Up to now some 193 joint ventures have been set up with firms from 18 countries, and the interest shown by foreign investors has been rapidly increasing in recent years.

Present

I referred in my opening remarks to a "success story." Allow me to cite first of all certain figures illustrating the growth in value added, industrial employment and the shift in the pattern of production as shown in Tables 36 and 37.

These figures, I hope, have given you some idea of what Iran has achieved during a comparatively short period of time, indicating not only the progressive diversification into some basic intermediate, component and capital goods industries but also the degree of integration achieved.

Table 36
Employment and Value Added in Industry*

Period (year)	Value Added		Employment (thousands)
	Actual	Planned	
Third Plan	(12.7)	(10.0)	(1329)
Fourth Plan	(15.2)	(12.8)	(1742)
(1968)	13.4	—	1,399
(1969)	15.6	—	1,468
(1970)	12.6	—	1,543
(1971)	17.5	—	1,580
(1972)	18.5	—	1,742
Fifth Plan	21-22**	18.0	(2,500)
(1973)	18.0	—	1,872
(1974)	22	—	2,013

*Average annual growth.
**Estimated.

As an example, Iran's automotive industry can now look to indigenous production of a sizeable part of its components, such as engines, batteries, radiators, shock absorbers, filters, rings and fenders, windshields and side-window glass, tires, ball bearings, spark plugs, springs, all its interior upholstery, and a whole host of other components. Other projects under implementation or discussion will soon provide practically all the other components, such as the piston, the electrical parts, forged parts and the transmission.

Future

Having discussed the strategies of the past and the present, I would like to talk briefly about the future.

In starting this discussion, it is fair to say at the outset that industrial policies to be implemented in the future will be essentially the continuation of what Iran has been practicing up until now. In fact, it might be noted here that stability in our policy measures, coupled with clarity of approach, has been one of the major contributory factors to Iran's achievements. Nevertheless some of the policy measures envisaged for

Table 37
Manufacturing Weights by Sector
(percent)

	Beginning of 3rd Development Plan	Beginning of 4th Development Plan	Beginning of 5th Development Plan	1973-74
Food	33.4	39.9	32.0	31.9
Beverage (alcoholic and nonalcoholic)	1.4	0.8	0.8	0.8
Textiles	25.6	19.6	17.0	16.6
Wearing Apparel	6.4	10.7	10.9	11.0
Wood and Furniture	3.3	2.2	2.2	2.1
Paper and Cardboard	0.5	0.8	1.2	1.2
Leather	2.5	1.2	1.1	1.0
Rubber	1.0	1.3	1.2	1.2
Chemicals	4.6	3.9	6.1	6.2
Nonmetallic Minerals	6.8	4.1	4.5	4.6
Basic Metals	0.8	1.7	4.7	4.9
Metal Products	7.8	4.4	4.6	4.6
Nonelectrical Machinery	0.1	0.7	1.5	1.7
Electrical Machinery	.5	3.1	4.0	4.1
Motor Vehicles	4.4	4.6	7.5	7.6
Others	0.9	1.0	0.7	0.5

the future are intended to shape our industry in such a manner as to enable it to continue contributing substantially to the growth of GNP and to place Iran firmly among the industrialized countries.

While continuing to trade with industrialized countries of the world for the supply of up-to-date machinery and equipment and also industrial raw materials, intermediates and components, Iran will progressively widen and strengthen its industrial base by expanding metal smelting, machinery and equipment manufacturing and electrical, electronics, chemical, petrochemical and automotive industries. These industries, which will constitute the thrust areas, will complement our efforts to produce practically all of Iran's needs for durable and nondurable consumer goods and building materials.

In establishing the growth areas of the future, Iran will make use of its comparative advantages, which are based on indigenous natural resources, namely, mineral and hydrocarbon resources. Thus, in the years to come, the iron and steel and petrochemical industries shall emerge as forerunners of Iran's industrial development. Toward the end of the Sixth Development Plan (1982), the capacity for steel production will exceed 15 million tons and will utilize the new direct-reduction technique as well as the conventional BOF (Basic Oxygen Furnace) technology. In the field of petrochemicals, Iran will gradually appear as a large exporter of basic petrochemical building blocks as well as a substantial exporter of intermediates, final products and fertilizers. The energy-intensive industries such as aluminum, ferroalloys and others will play an increasing part not only in meeting our own requirements but also in feeding our export markets. Copper and other nonferrous metals and their products will also join the scene and provide a wider base for our industry. As far as machinery and equipment and electrical and electronic industries are concerned, Iran will progressively widen industrial effort in the immediate future, while, by 1980, Iran's automotive industry will be essentially integrated.

The foregoing discussion indicates that Iran is determined to enter into practically all main industrial sectors so as to meet the major part of its requirements with the possibility of export playing a major role in our industrialization. With the degree of dependence that the present and future projects will have on indigenous resources, and in view of their nature and linkage, the value added in industry will continue its rapid and constant growth in the years to come.

We may now turn to discuss the question of location. Tehran and Isfahan have traditionally formed the nuclei of our industrial cities, but policy in recent years has been to establish industries in what has been termed the "poles of development." There are a number of industrial poles already established, but we have now reached a juncture where the question of regional development will have to be tackled in the general context of optimum utilization of resources, such as land and water. Owing to the constraints created by water availability and the need to allocate this precious resource for agricultural activities in suitable areas, and the further need for a balanced countrywide regional development, industrial cities are now being set up in various parts of the country close to existing large urban centers. From an investment point of view, the creation of these industrial cities makes more economical use of infrastructural services and allows a more orderly, long-term development of the various regions.

In the selection of these locations, the following criteria have been taken into consideration:

- To introduce industries in areas with good ecological condi-

tions, i.e., good climate, availability of sufficient water and vegetation, high residential and recreational value;
- To introduce a closer coordination between the development of existing urban centers and the location of new industrial cities using industrial development as an instrument of active urban planning;
- To minimize the risk of environmental pollution.

It should be noted that the identification of industries to be established in each city will be affected by other factors, such as the proximity to markets, raw materials, etc. Insofar as raw material-based industries—for example, metal smelting or pulp and paper—are concerned, their location may well fall outside the industrial city areas. Again, as the result of the limits on water availability in the interior of the country, export-oriented industrial activity will be created in and around the port cities, where desalinated water will be available from the nuclear desalination units. In all areas of the country, industry will be required to use water very sparingly and to install recycling facilities for maximum utilization of the existing resources.

The foregoing approach does not mean that all industrial activities will be concentrated in these cities; rather, strong emphasis is being placed on the creation of industrial employment at rural and small township levels. In these locations, a considerable number of small-scale industries will be placed and, in fact, smaller workshops and factories could act as feeder industries for a number of activities in the large urban centers. In other words, wherever the nature and the size of industry permits, the work will be taken to the labor site rather than the reverse. It is hoped that many urbanization problems may thus be avoided.

In order to strengthen further the mixed nature of Iran's industrial economy and to create conditions for full and effective private sector involvement, the government will continue to limit its own industrial activities to areas mentioned before and will encourage the private sector to enter into new areas of endeavor. There are already a sizable number of projects that are being implemented by the private sector, either alone or with government minority shareholding for the production of capital goods and component and petrochemical intermediates. In general, policy, as indicated in the Fifth Development Plan, is to confine government investments to basic industries such as steel, copper, petroleum and others that are especially significant from the point of view of national defense and public welfare.

Along with this definition of the private sector's area of activity, the recent move toward liberalizing the licensing system will be pursued without hesitation. As the size of our market and economy has grown with long strides, it has become evident that the need for strict licensing in many sectors, especially consumer goods and some durable consumer goods industries, has become redundant. In these areas the act of licensing has become more of a formality and is being used largely in order to bestow upon the license holder the privileges as provided in other laws and regulations such as the income tax act.

There are, however, two exceptions to the above general rules.

The Tehran area, and one or two other industrial centers, are jealously guarded against the creation of new and large expansions of the existing industries in a move to contain the employment and, thereby, the population growth in these regions. The problem of Tehran and its upper capacity for population growth, I believe, is well known to most of us and does not need elaboration, but it is the government's policy to provide extra incentives in various forms for the establishment of industries in the provinces, should the present incentives prove to be insufficient.

Insofar as new industries producing intermediate, component and capital goods are concerned, the policy is to use licensing as a means of ensuring the minimum economic size, avoiding unnecessary fragmentation. The rigorous application of licensing to these multimillion-dollar projects further ensures the economic use of established capacity leading to decreased cost of production along with rapid expansion. The government is, of course, intent on avoiding monopoly situations. As a matter of policy it not only encourages the establishment of a number of indigenous competitors but reduces the protection given to the industry as each sector achieves more maturity. At the moment, a scheme linking protection with national content and a sliding annual scale of protection is being studied for future implementation.

Lest I should leave you with the impression that the government provides automatic protection, it should be emphasized here that Iran has followed its industrialization course mainly through "backward integration," and the backup industries have been set up only when the volume of production of an intermediate or component justified its establishment. By this mechanism we have avoided to a very great extent the kind of dilemmas in which many developing countries find themselves having too many producing units in a sector where fragmentation can be disruptive and the scale of production is of the essence. The automotive industries of a number of countries, which started long before Iran's did, are a prime example of this dilemma. Perhaps Iran has been fortunate in not having to introduce too onerous a national content in its industrial planning, being satisfied with an orderly but constant improvement in this area.

An important facet of this backward linkage has been Iran's attempt to make use of the best technologies and know-how in creating these industries, and in many projects of this nature, joint ventures have been set up with foreign firms. Iran will continue its policy of encouraging foreign investment in industry as we also enlarge our industrial investment base abroad. Our basic aims in attracting foreign investment, as discussed before, are to introduce the most up-to-date technology together with organizational and managerial know-how, and gain access to international markets and the full utilization of foreign investors' training facilities. Iran's investment abroad and foreign investment in Iran within the established criteria are destined to play increasingly important roles in future development.

The introduction of the latest techniques of production to our industrial system will bring with it an ability to maintain a reasonably high-quality standard, thereby protecting the consumer. In this area, the increased attention given to vocational training and skill, together with constant vigilance exercised by the government through the ISIRI (Iran Standard and Industrial Research Institute) and the creation of a more competitive atmosphere—especially by exposing our industry to outside competition—will have a decidedly beneficial result. This is all the more important because the export of Iranian industrial goods will have to play the major role in providing for us much needed foreign exchange in the future, and we must make significant inroads in the international market year by year. In this context we are determined to make full use of our comparative advantage in energy and some raw material areas, plus the capability of our managerial and labor force, together with our geographical location.

In the previous discussion, the question of training was duly stressed. Unlike the fears expressed three years ago about the capital-intensive nature of our industry, Iran is now facing a situation where we are experiencing a noticeable shortage of skilled labor, leading to large turnover in some industries with all its attendant problems. It is, therefore, essential that the comparative nonavailability of the labor force not act as a brake in this otherwise fast-moving area. The need for a massive program of training by both the government and the private sector cannot be overemphasized if Iran is to achieve its targets. Furthermore, with the income distribution effect of increased industrial activity and its direct bearing on much needed productive employment, measures must be introduced to step up the qualitative and quantitative aspects of labor training. Since the addition to the existing industrial labor force will have to come mainly from the rural areas, coordinated and decentralized programs of basic training must start at the rural level. Furthermore, greater emphasis should be placed on paid on-the-job training. Above all, coordinated manpower development planning is needed to prepare the work force requirements of industry for specific levels and types of skill.

Two areas that have been accorded and will continue to receive special attention are the handicraft and small-scale industries of Iran. For both these sectors, specialized government agencies have been set up with the express task of guiding and rendering technical, financial, marketing and management assistance. With its very rich and varied heritage of handicraft work, of which you may witness some excellent samples in the city of Shiraz, Iran intends not only to retain the traditional excellence of its artistic value in workmanship design and form but to utilize this capability for increased income and added employment.

Up to now we have discussed the effects of industrial policies on employment. I would now like to dwell for a few moments on another strategy that is aimed at providing a wider participation in the industrial and economic prosperity of Iran by a much larger portion of our population.

Historically, the ownership in Iran's industrial enterprises was characterized by large shareholdings of family groups, though at times some shares were held also by industrial banks and other small shareholders. In some isolated cases, the companies had distributed a small part of their holdings to their staff.

In the middle of the 1960s, the industrial banks, in line with government policy, embarked on a program of widening the shareholding base of industry. Their efforts were concentrated mainly on new enterprises. As a result, a fair number of public corporations were set up in accordance with the new commercial code, taking advantage of the tax incentives provided in the income tax act, and a few companies had their shares also listed on the stock exchange.

In spite of these measures, by the beginning of the 1970s the bulk of the shareholding in industrial enterprises was still in the hands of family groups. It was at this juncture that, in order to further widen the base of shareholding, specifically as a vehicle for the creation of greater motivation in the work force of industrial enterprises, His Imperial Majesty Aryamehr The Shahanshah advised the business community to divest itself voluntarily of between one-third and 49 percent of their shares, first to their own workers and staff and subsequently to other workers, farmers and the public at large. Up to the beginning of this year, some 39 companies were at different stages of implementing this program, at which time His Imperial Majesty issued an edict ordering the government to speed up this process. As a result, a law was passed, setting up the legal, institutional and financial framework for the implementation of the edict. In conformity with the continuous nature of Iran's revolution and as an instrument of expanded social justice, larger participation of Iranian people in the results of industrial progress, and further democratization of Iran's industrial system, it was subsequently proclaimed by His Imperial Majesty that this program constituted the 13th Principle of Iran's revolution and thus became one of the most important pillars of Iran's revolutionary program.

From a socioeconomic point of view, the program has far-reaching implications in that not only will it lead to a more equitable distribution of income but it also aims at a degree of participation that would create a totally new atmosphere in Iran's labor-relations scene, leading to a more stable and logical course in Iran's industrialization efforts.

This program, with all its ramifications, constitutes one of our major strategies for the coming years on a continuing basis. The initial plan calls for a 45 percent share distribution by 320 large companies during a period of three years. Another important feature of this law is the provision for 99 percent of government shareholding in some industries to be offered for public participation during the same period, once more indicating the desire on the part of the government to limit its own involvement in industry to only a few of the basic areas.

Along with this new development there is a strong and welcome sign that a new managerial class is emerging on the industrial scene, indicating a gradual shift from the owner-managers to professional managers. The valuable efforts of IMI (Industrial Management Institute) for many years and the recent appearance of ICMS (Iran Center for Management Studies) on the management-development and training scene have been instrumental in creating a cadre of trained managers that is finding increasingly more acceptance in the industrial system. Not only is government heavily dependent on these new sources for filling its own managerial positions, but the private sector is now showing increasing interest in this direction, attracting an ever-growing number of trained managers to head its expanding operations.

From a policy point of view, two programs will be pursued diligently by the government. First, the strengthening of the existing management training institutions and, if necessary, the creation of new ones; and, second, the establishment of incentives and credit facilities so that progressively more industries are established by the emerging young and dynamic managerial class.

Having just touched on the question of incentives and credit facilities, I should note that past and present policies will be vigorously followed in the future, with their more intensive application as an instrument of regional development and industrial integration policy. In addition to the support given by the government to specialized industrial lending institutions, the recent creation of three regional development banks, the imminent establishment of investment corporations, the strengthening of the stock exchange, the floating of industrial bonds and a host of other measures are all intended to create a dynamic capital market, thereby mobilizing other resources for faster industrial development.

Another area that demands our careful and constant attention is the field of technology. Hitherto, Iran has been essentially the recipient of technology from outside with indigenous capability claiming only a small share of the market. Originally this technology transfer included such areas as plant design and construction, product designs and blueprints and production technology, all geared to physical production activity. Although the past approach proved indispensable to industrial development in Iran, it has been recognized for some time that this substantial dependence would not meet the ultimate aims of Iran's industrialization drive. The creation of industrial and management consultancy services and engineering capability began on an expanded scale some years ago. Institutions such as the Iran Standard and Industrial Research Institute, Technolog, Technicon and other joint venture engineering and industrial-contracting companies, have all helped to augment the indigenous engineering and technological capability. But Iran is far from having reached a comfortable position in this respect, and much ground needs to be covered in the future. The policy is to develop a wide spectrum of technological ability in as short a time as possible, and for this purpose the government has taken a strong lead. Through its wholly owned IDRO (Industrial Development and Renovation Organization) it has embarked on the creation of a series of establishments for effective technology development and has directed the private sector to take up more involvement in research and development activity. For this purpose, the industrial concerns will be required to invest progressively in research and development, and the government is prepared to provide the necessary tax incentives.

At the moment, the problem of indigenous research and technology development is being tackled from all sides, and institutional framework at the national level is being created whereby research and development institutes, each dealing with a specific scientific and industrial sector, may operate under the general guidance and umbrella of a national body.

In short, our industrial strategy is heavily geared and totally committed to the promotion of indigenous technology development, because a real claim to being an industrialized society can be made only when Iran possesses a sufficiently large and independent technological base leading to innovation and creativity.

A discussion of Iran's industrialization strategy would be incomplete without expressing to you our total preoccupation with the problem of environment, both inside the industrial units as well as the countrywide ecological system. Iran is particularly fortunate in this respect because not only is there an increasing awareness of environmental questions, but we are determined to avoid the problems facing other industrialized countries and to learn from their experiences. We have made it a special requirement for all industries to incorporate such anti-pollution devices as are necessary to keep the air, water and the land within specified safe limits of pollution. In certain instances, there are serious cost and investment considerations, and the government is seriously considering some form of relief in hardship cases, coupled with the required incentives. In order to contain the problem more effectively, the establishment of industrial cities in suitable locations and sufficiently distant from urban areas will play an important role. The extensive and increasing use of natural gas as fuel will also help remove soot and smoke and other noxious gases and odors from industrial sites. As far as

Iran: Past, Present and Future

working environments are concerned, the policy calls for measures to be introduced to create better and more pleasant working conditions.

You may have noticed that throughout this essay there has been a singular absence of any reference to the mining sector. This was done purposely because not only is the mining field a completely separate area of activity meriting a totally independent treatment, but many of the policy issues must be discussed in the context of the exhaustibility of mineral resources. It can, however, be stated that the mining sector is receiving and will receive a great deal of attention for many reasons, one of which is its ability to provide the industry with the necessary mineral base, thereby creating a fully national industry.

Comments and Discussion

The general economic outlook, with reference to Iran's economic growth and development and its basic economic problems— present and anticipated—was the main subject of discussion on the second day of the symposium. Points made in plenary and workshop discussions are summarized below.

In "Economic Growth and Development in Iran," Mr. Fekrat stressed Iran's strong rate of development in the past 15 years, with GNP rising at 11 percent a year in the period 1962–72 (and 50 percent in 1973–74, owing to the oil price rise). Although development during most of the 1960s was accompanied by remarkable price stability, the large increase in oil revenues has not brought inflationary pressures. The rate of inflation has grown from 3.1 percent in 1969–71 to 6.1 percent in 1972 and 11 percent in 1973. Dr. Fekrat emphasized that oil revenues are the lifeblood of the development plan. The modern sector has been the engine of growth, with the traditional (agricultural) sector registering much less impressive gains, although there have been some sweeping achievements. The Shah and People's Revolution seeks sweeping economic and social reforms aimed at improving the lot of the people.

In "Iran's Basic Macroeconomic Problems: A 20-Year Horizon," Dr. Vakil observed first that Iran's oil reserves—estimated at 85 billion barrels—are finite. Yet, as the economy expands, ever-increasing oil reserves will be needed to maintain economic growth. Iran will have to move away from "easy sources" of savings to more difficult sources; this is the process of normalization. Although it is difficult to predict future oil prices, rates of production and other factors, Iran probably has a 20-year period in which to operate fairly smoothly. A second problem relates to the distribution of income between urban and rural areas. The gap is widening—an inevitable development in a situation of rapid growth—with the problem being exacerbated by the centralization of oil revenues. Government policymakers are seeking innovative ways of redressing inequalities, but various possible methods are still untested. Dr. Vakil suggested that Iran's third major problem is to develop non-oil exports to replace oil. (An estimated $50 billion in export revenues will be needed within 20 years.) These non-oil exports must be competitive in world markets. Fourth is the problem of inflation, which reduces the value of oil revenues, although Dr. Vakil described this as a short-term problem.

In "Strategies of Industrial Development in Iran," F. Najmabadi observed that industrial growth has increased from 5 percent a year in 1962 to more than 20 percent in 1974. The share of industrial production in the GNP has also increased in that period, from 11.7 percent to 17 percent. Mr. Najmabadi noted that government investment has played a very important role in industrialization but that the role of the private sector has been growing steadily since the 1960s when government began selling shares in the consumer goods industries to the private sector. Mr. Najmabadi commented on various government strategies aimed at furthering industry: licensing, used as a tool to direct and optimize limited resources, to further industrial planning for various sectors, to spur regional development and to stimulate production of consumer, intermediate and capital goods; financing industrial projects; taxation, heavily geared to promotion of the industrial sector; trade policy, aimed at protecting infant industries; consumer protection and price controls; and foreign investment. Mr. Najmabadi also summarized plans for the future, including emphasis on developing industries based on Iran's mineral and hydrocarbon resources—iron, steel and petrochemical industries; developing new industrial cities in various parts of Iran near urban centers; encouraging the private sector to enter into new areas; modifying some licensing policies; new worker training programs, etc. Mr. Najmabadi commented also on the government's policy that companies should voluntarily sell between one-third and 49 percent of their shares to workers and the public. This may contribute to more equitable distribution of income, worker participation in industry and, it is hoped, the emergence of a new managerial class. Mr Najmabadi concluded by noting that the problem of indigenous research and technology is being tackled from all sides.

Major Issues in Development Growth

Symposium discussion focused initially on five points: (1) the relation between Iran's military expenditures and economic growth; (2) income distribution; (3) the implications of development for human rights; (4) whether Iran's development goals may be too ambitious; and (5) the future role of exports in Iran's economy.

In response to an American's questions about the proportion of GNP spent on defense, the rationale for defense policies and Iran's nuclear plans, several Iranians indicated first that Iran's expenditures on defense—29 percent of the national budget—include expenditures for a wide range of activities, including food procurement operations, vocational training programs, production of means of transport and deployment of youth in service programs, which would not normally be regarded as defense spending, and that the percentage of GNP spent on defense—under 14 percent—is not exaggerated and is significantly lower than expenditures for defense by some other Middle Eastern countries. Second, it was suggested that Iran's long history of invasion and intervention by others shows the need for an effective defense

---

*See Table 69.

program; that Iran has long been undefended despite border problems with some neighbors; that Iran, together with other neighboring countries, must protect the Persian Gulf and sea lanes to the Indian Ocean, thus preventing a power vacuum that could give the West an excuse for intervention; and that Iran needs sufficient force to "buy time" in which to mobilize world public opinion, if invaded—enough deterrent force to give a "bloody nose" to aggressors. This has become even more important since Viet Nam, which showed that America cannot be relied on to defend Iran. Third, a speaker observed that Iran has ratified the Nuclear Non-Proliferation Treaty (NPT) and seeks a nuclear-free zone in the region. But if another Middle Eastern country acquires nuclear weapons, Iran would have to reappraise this policy. (Iran's defense policy was discussed at greater length in the sessions on Iran's role in world affairs. See section 5, "Iran in World Affairs.")

Responding to a participant's observation that societies must achieve more equitable income distribution internally before there can be more equitable distribution among rich and poor nations, an Iranian observed that economic development does not lead promptly to equity. In fact, the more rapid the growth the greater the strain on the social fabric. The question is not how to achieve equity rapidly but how to ease stress while seeking longer-term goals. Second, he observed, inequities within nations will be reduced provided a new international economic order is instituted to allow a more equitable distribution the world over. Increased foreign revenues will enable poor countries to reduce their internal inequities. A number of Iranian participants remarked that they were fully aware of the experience of some Latin American and other countries, which shows that a high growth strategy based on maldistribution of income and a poor network of social services is not conducive to sustained growth. They believed that a strategy of development based on income disparity prevents the nation concerned from realizing the full potential of its citizens' capacities and capabilities. Iran's strategy of development, in their view, is not of that nature and has become increasingly socially oriented in the past fourteen years.

A European stated that inequity goes with development (but pointed out that "unequal" societies may achieve development). In his view, it is important to think about how to create the resources that will be needed twenty years from now in what clearly will be a dual society. Dual societies do not lend themselves to capital accumulation. Iran's large modern sector tends to consume a lot and will be experienced in consumption twenty years hence. But twenty years from now the modern sector will not be producing so much and will be unable to transfer resources to the poorer sector. The government may also have fewer resources and will transfer less to the poorer sector. Twenty years from now social discipline will become very important. In the speaker's view, Iran should seek to promote a society capable of sustaining development, investment and growth, a society that will be able in the future to transfer resources to the poorer sector.

Another participant observed that economic development involves social and political development as well as economics, the distribution of goods and services as well as their production, and human rights as well as social discipline and military might. Responding to this observation and previous comments on defense expenditures and income distribution, an American observed that a purely Western, libertarian approach is not feasible in countries undergoing rapid development; somewhere on the spectrum between pluralism and control there is an optimum solution. In each country's experience there are tradeoffs, and each government pays certain prices for the exercise of control. The costs and benefits of controls should be studied, with each country resolving this question on its own terms in light of its stage of development, culture, experience and possible tradeoffs.

Views differed on the question of whether Iran's development goals are too ambitious, with an American participant suggesting that Iran's very rapid growth may be increasing inflation, disturbing economic balance, increasing expectations that cannot be met later on and harming humanistic values; he warned that if growth is too rapid now, it will be difficult to taper off later. An Iranian official commented on this point (also discussed at length later in the symposium) that Iran's future revenues from oil and gas—now only 10 percent of oil revenues—will probably be far greater than what was suggested in symposium discussion. In his view, oil and gas revenues will be sufficient to ensure a continuing high rate of economic growth for many years to come.

Another Iranian suggested that the future of Iran depends on manufactured exports and warned that Iran cannot convert its raw materials to goods for export without transfers of technology from the West. Too little has been done in this regard. The gap between rich and poor nations will never be bridged until the developing countries acquire needed skills and training. Another Iranian concurred that, with infusions of technology, Iran may be able to produce goods for export. But it will be unable to sell these unless foreign tariff barriers are removed. Iran is seeking a new world trade pattern, including removal of European Economic Community (EEC) preferences favoring some developing countries and not others. An American suggested that hope for Iran's future lies in the development of an integrated economy, with consumption at home and exports abroad absorbing overproduction.

Concluding speakers on the question of whether the government is exercising controls to prevent overproduction and/or wasted human and financial resources indicated that Iran is keenly aware of the need for coordination, which it achieves mainly through the planning mechanism. The effectiveness of coordination in public sector planning has been demonstrated, but better coordination may be needed between the public and private sectors. This will take time to achieve.

Workshop Discussion

Iran's general economic outlook was further discussed at a workshop session, where these main points were made.

1. Various speakers identified factors that would indicate cause for optimism about Iran's future, including the fact that Iran has no balance-of-payment problems, does not lack capital and can concentrate on the character of its growth. It was observed that Iran's economic upsurge preceded the huge increase in oil revenues; oil is important but it has not been alone in contributing to growth. At the same time, new oil fields and gas fields, as well as deposits of other minerals, are being discovered all the time; future revenues from these sources may be very great. The con-

cluding speaker on this point predicted that the West's demand for oil would recover and that the Middle East would become the new industrial bloc of coming decades.

2. Factors that may have other effects on the future were also identified. Among these were:

Inflation. Inflation is now at a relatively high rate, partly because the money supply has increased rapidly without corresponding price increases owing to government controls. (A speaker suggested that investments abroad are one means of building up foreign reserves to spend after bottlenecks limiting purchases of goods are removed; foreign investments also give Iran access to Western technology.)

Rising popular expectations. Economic projections don't take into account the possible need for greater expenditures to carry out possible new political and social reforms in addition to the principles enunciated in The Shah and People's Revolution. It is relatively easy to identify problems and determine policies but harder to implement them, and pressures may build up in the form of people's demands.

The problem of waste through corruption. The possible need for laws on "briber and bribed" disclosure, which have proved effective in the United States, was mentioned; audits, annual reports, affidavits on bids and other devices can also help to reduce the problem of waste through corruption.

The "cash flow" problem. One speaker noted that export prices have risen only 22 percent compared with increases of 44 percent in import prices and suggested that monitoring be extended to import prices. Second, the pricing system of the Organization of Petroleum Exporting Countries, in his view, is unresponsive to world market demand; consumer resistance can lead to a drop in the purchases of Middle Eastern oil and to reduced income from oil revenues; Iran does not have sufficient foreign exchange to compensate for significant drops in oil revenues.

Depleted reserves. Conversely, it was suggested, increased world demand for Iranian oil could lead to much more rapid depletion of Iran's reserves than predicted.

Rising military expenditures. If Iran's defense budget rises, this will consume an increasing share of national resources and could spell problems if oil revenues stabilize or decline.

Changing conditions abroad. The rest of the world is not static, one participant warned. Large economic and political blocs may be forming and Iran may become relatively isolated.

3. In considering prescriptions for the future, various participants stressed the need for:

Formation of a new world economic order involving a greater flow of resources and technology to the oil-producing states;

Realistic planning for development of an economy with fiscal and foreign exchange elements independent of oil reserves;

An expanded export program with products that can compete effectively in world markets;

Development of a trade area in the Middle East and an expanded internal domestic market;

The buildup of handicrafts and small industries;

Greater attention to the development of the private sector; conversion of human resources from "bureaucrats" and "planners" to "managers" and "entrepreneurs"; and

Revision and broadening of the tax system to develop income apart from oil revenues.

An Iranian speaker also observed that Iran may have to adapt to a "slowed growth rate"—as Japan has done—if the international situation leads to a lower level of oil production and reduced revenues from oil.

Agricultural and Rural Development in Iran

Agrarian Reform, Modernization of Peasants and Agricultural Development in Iran

Ismail Ajami

While the contribution of agriculture to economic and social development is fairly well recognized,[1] the problem of modernizing traditional agriculture has remained a highly controversial issue. Although the decline of agriculture in terms of agricultural population and labor force, and of agriculture's share in GNP in the course of development is one of the best established empirical generalizations in economics,[2] the significance of interdependence between the agricultural and nonagricultural sectors and the dynamic role of the peasantry in transitional societies should not be overlooked. In this context, J. W. Mellor discusses the three primary objectives of agricultural development as: (1) to provide food and raw materials for an expanding population with rising purchasing power; (2) to provide capital for economic transformation;

and (3) to provide a direct increase in rural welfare.[3] Additional contributions to development from the agricultural sector are the labor force for the expanding industrial sector and a market for the output of consumption goods and production supplies from the expanding industrial sector.

Ohkawa and many others have stressed the important role Japanese agriculture played in financing investment in infrastructure and industry and in providing funds for the expansion of education.[4] In more general terms, Kuznets has emphasized that "one of the crucial problems of modern economic growth is how to extract from the product of agriculture a surplus for the financing of capital formation necessary for industrial growth without, at the same time, blighting the growth of agriculture, under conditions where no easy surplus is available in the country."[5]

The usual view that there should be a net flow of capital from agriculture to industry in the earlier stages of development has recently been challenged. Ruttan and Ishikawa, in particular, have argued that because of the rapid growth of demand for food, resulting from high rates of population increase, it is likely that the agriculture sector may require a net flow of capital from the industrial sector.[6] There also has been a reaction against the earlier views with respect to the existence of redundant labor in agriculture. In fact, recent years have witnessed increasing attention to the problems of unemployment in urban areas.

The Significance of Agricultural Development in Iran

The growing interdependence between agricultural and industrial sectors, and the problem of accelerating farm production, are of special concern in Iran today. While Iran is experiencing an unprecedented growth in its national income—mainly through a rapid rate of industrial development averaging over 14 percent per year and through a substantial increase in oil revenues—agriculture has been a lagging sector growing between two and three percent per annum during the last decade. Increases in population (an estimated three percent per year), coupled with a rapid growth in personal expendable incomes, are currently leading to an overall growth in demand for agricultural products in Iran of 8 to 10 percent. The present high growth rates in demand for food and fiber, which seem likely to continue for some time, could lead to mounting inflation in food prices and/or import bills.

Iran's population is still predominantly rural, with 56 percent of the population living in villages. Although the proportion of rural population is declining, the absolute number is increasing and is projected to rise from the currently estimated 18 million to about 20 million by the mid-

1980s. Agriculture remains the major sector in terms of labor force, employing some 40 percent of the working population but contributing only 16 percent to the GNP. It is also a fact that a considerably higher proportion of the poor live in rural areas. Therefore, a more equitable distribution of income, a self-sustaining rural development and an increase in living standards require a more rapid modernization of the agrarian sector. Productivity increase in agriculture is also a significant precondition that underlies not only rural advance but also urban advance. A crucial dilemma facing the Iranian economy stems from industrial overproduction at comparatively high prices and agricultural underproduction. Thus, creation of a more favorable interaction between agriculture and industry is deemed necessary to partly solve said dilemma.

Finally, the significance of agriculture in the present situation of our country does not end with its economic dimensions. We may note that the social significance of the peasantry on the path to modernization is supported by several studies of the last decade. These studies substantiate the broad sociological generalization that the specific ways in which peasants are transformed define for many subsequent decades the political, social and economic characteristics of a postpeasant society.[7]

Thus, for economic and sociopolitical reasons, and human considerations, the importance of agricultural development in Iran needs no argument. The real questions are what to do and how to do it. Part of the answer lies in a deeper understanding of the great variety of physical land and water resources, institutional changes in land tenure and production structures as a result of the implementation of the land reform program of 1962, the culture and personality of the peasant farmers and adaptation and domestication of modern technology.

The present study underscores a theoretical framework that incorporates changes in institutional structure, technological structure and values, motivation and behavior of the farmers as functionally interrelated elements in agricultural transformation. Within this context, an attempt is made to provide an analysis of the traditional agrarian structure, including resources, cultivation processes, a land tenure system, the organization of traditional group farming, output and employment. This is followed by a discussion of the implementation of the land reform program of 1962 and its sociopolitical and economic implications. Finally, an effort will be made to demonstrate the dynamic role of the peasant farmer's response to new economic opportunities in the process of agricultural development.* This will be undertaken by comparing the indi-

---

*The problems of resource management, production structures and investment requirements are discussed in Dr. Reza Doroudian, "Modernization of Rural Economy in Iran."

ces of agricultural productivity and innovativeness for two groups of peasant farmers—one receiving water from a new irrigation dam since 1970, the other depending on traditional sources of water supply in a sample of six villages in Fars.

Theoretical Framework

A major difficulty in discussing theories of agricultural development is that two authors writing on the subject seldom mean the same thing by the phrases "agricultural development" or "transformation of traditional agriculture." Although the term "transforming" may connote a cultural or institutional or a purely technological transformation, Professor Schultz prefers to define a transformation as one that is in response to new economic opportunities. He maintains that the sources of the new economic opportunities are predominantly improvements in the state of the productive arts.[8] Johnston and Mellor's delineation of three phases in the process of agricultural development underscores the structural transformation that has occurred mostly through technological change and innovation.[9] Mosher views agricultural development as a complex system involving multiple changes in all facets of agriculture, particularly underscoring efficiency in public administrative machinery and the role of education, research and extension.[10]

Barraclough maintains that agricultural development makes sense only if it is understood as a part of national development: development is conceived and measured in national terms. Therefore, any strategy to affect its rate must work through national power structures or at least be tolerated by them.[11] A similar notion is expressed by Dantwala in his analysis of India's problems with subsistence agriculture. After examining three commonly prescribed measures—reform of agrarian structure, provision of adequate credit and guaranteed minimum support prices—he finds that none of them offers a solution to the problem of transformation of the Indian subsistence agriculture unless the general problems of underdevelopment are also attacked.[12]

A fairly comprehensive attempt that integrates all these diverse ideas into an interdisciplinary framework is that of Robinson.[13] The basic assumptions underlying his theory of general interdependence of economic development involve four different areas: those referring to the (1) technical structure, (2) institutional structure, (3) aggregate preference structure and (4) mechanism of interdependence, or the "articulation" of the system.

An effort will be made here to adjust Robinson's scheme to the problems of agricultural development. The technical structure in agriculture can be thought of as a production function or set of such functions relating outputs to inputs. It is a description of the state of human knowledge or technology effectively applied to the problems of agricultural production. The institutional structure refers to the social and political institutional system in which the agricultural sector operates. In this context, the system of land tenure, production structure, credit and marketing are of special interest. The aggregate preference structure refers to the social, cultural and political value system that influences the choices of goods and services in the economy. In this respect, the attitude, motivation and behavior of the peasant farmers, affecting the very basis of what is to be produced as well as those in the bureaucracy, power elite and economic institutions, play significant roles in modernizing traditional agriculture. Articulation can be thought of as the interdependence between agricultural and nonagricultural sectors as well as the flow of information, knowledge and communication.

While the role of technological innovation and the interdependence of agricultural and nonagricultural sectors in the modernization of traditional agriculture are fairly well established,[14] the potential contributions of agrarian reform and of attitudes, motivation and behavior of peasant farmers are highly controversial issues. For example, concerning the relation of land reform to development, Warriner observes, "No conclusion emerges which would suggest that agrarian reform is a condition of development . . . so the best way of demonstrating the nature of the relationship between structure and growth is to look for empirical investigations of the belief that reform can *aid* development, rather than try to prove that it *must* do so in terms of general theory or historical analogy."[15]

However, one certain conclusion emerges from historical research—that agrarian reforms do liberate the peasants. If this liberation is not to be frustrated, the potential conflict between sociopolitical and economic objectives of agrarian reform has to be reconciled. It may be noted that revolutionary governments can carry through reforms that genuinely abolish the old defective structure, but in many cases they are not able to replace it with something more productive. It should be emphasized that redistribution or transfer of large holdings to peasants does not provide the panacea to the complex problems of transforming traditional agriculture. Such transformation is not simply a question of land redistribution, or a question of the scale of farming operation; it depends on the capacity to invest, and the ability to adapt to changing market conditions, new methods and new inputs. Furthermore, it depends on the response of the farming community and whether the new production structures to evolve are capable of channeling the gains to farmers.[16]

Finally, the question of the impact of land reform on production and on the scale of farming depends on the type of prereform systems of land ownership and production in a given country. To bring out the main contrasts in the effect of reform on scale of production, Warriner has distinguished three types of landownership: Asian tenancy, latifundia and plantation.[17]

Social attitudes, motivation and behavior, as discussed in the preceding theoretical framework, are an essential part of modernization of traditional agrarian structure. These human dimensions, while contributing to growth, can also be fostered by it, that is to say, in a process of agricultural development, subsistence peasants can turn into farmers, and large estate owners can become developers.

However, one very important aspect of such changes is the question of whether or not peasants in traditional agriculture significantly respond to opportunities that are made available by changes in market conditions. The degree of peasant response to innovations and prices has been a point of major controversy. Near one end of the spectrum of viewpoints are Boeke, Dalton, Lewis, Olson and others, who suggest that cultural and institutional restraints limit to insignificance any price response.[18] Near the other end of this spectrum of viewpoints (in addition to Schultz and Mellor) are Bauer, Dantwala, Yamey and others, who maintain that peasants in traditional agriculture respond quickly, normally and efficiently to market incentives.[19]

Accumulating evidence concerning the responsiveness of small-scale farmers to economic incentives, especially the advent of "green revolution," underscores the importance of innovations in agricultural modernization. Being highly dividable and neutral to scale, high-yielding varieties of crops can be readily incorporated into existing systems of small-scale agriculture. Furthermore, this type of intensification of agricultural production can make a notable contribution to the problem of absorbing a rapidly growing labor force into productive employment.[20]

The problem of conceptual confusion on paths of modernization of traditional agriculture is aggravated by a gap between the power elites and the peasants in many developing countries. Little effective upward or downward communication occurs between these two groups. Too often, the needs, the aspirations and the capabilities of the peasants are not adequately communicated to their governments and thus are not reflected in the centrally planned development program.[21] In some countries, the bureaucracy is the only means of communication the political elites have with the masses of the peasantry.

Within the bureaucracy, however, those who plan and manage the agricultural development programs are likely to have little understanding of the realities of the peasant production and sociocultural processes in the village communities. A common notion prevalent in the bureaucracies of many developing countries assumes little differentiation in the socioeconomic structure of the peasantry. This assumption is often coupled with a stereotype—"tradition-bound peasant farmers"—lacking achievement motivation, managerial capabilities and desire for change and innovation in farming. Thus, there seems to be a general tendency among the bureaucracy and the urban intelligentsia to greatly underrate the peasant farmer's entrepreneurial capacities, his aspirations for improving his subsistence living and his potential dynamism in social change.[22]

The Prereform Agrarian Structure

In studying the Iranian agrarian structure, one encounters a great number of difficulties. The size of the country, the great variety of natural and socioeconomic conditions, the coexistence of nomadic and sedentary communities and repeated foreign invasions have combined to produce a diverse and highly complicated system of land tenure and social organization of production. Furthermore, quantitative information on the development of the agricultural sector is notably scarce and of poor reliability.

Essentially, Iran's traditional mode of peasant farming remained unchanged until the beginning of the present century. Like other parts of the Middle East, most of Iran suffers from a severe shortage of water, yet government expenditures on irrigation schemes were negligible until well after World War I.[23] Along with the neglect of irrigation, the complete indifference to the improvement of agricultural techniques, the very high cost of transport, the system of land tenure, the vulnerability of the villages to nomadic pillaging and the arbitrary rule of state and provincial governments over the peasantry were all obstacles to the development of agriculture and the improvement of the living conditions of the peasants.

The dominant settlement pattern—the village—not only provided the organizational framework, the labor force for production, including the construction and maintenance of irrigation networks (in particular, the qanats), but also supplied sufficient numbers to resist both natural and human predators.

The traditional distribution of village settlements was strongly influenced by the availability of water. From early times, government policy has encouraged such agglomerations because of the relative ease with which they could be dealt for purposes of tax assessment and the collection of revenues. The village farmland was normally divided into "ploughlands" called juft, meaning the amount of land a yoke of oxen could cultivate. For equality of cultivation rights, each cultivator would have several strips of land of varying quality scattered throughout different parts of the village domain. The village provided the basic framework in which the majority of socioeconomic and political transactions took place. The isolated farmstead remained the exception.[24]

Prior to the land reform of 1962, about 15.5 million of Iran's population, 65 percent of the total, lived in some 55,000 villages.* Half of Iran's total land area of 164.8 million hectares is uncultivable, with towns, villages, roads and surface water together making up another 25 percent and forest land a further 12 percent. Of the remaining 22 million hectares of potentially productive land, 7 million are cultivated (3 million being irrigated), 5 million are left fallow, 7 million are used as pastures and 3 million are not utilized.[25] It appears that the above division of land usage has remained much the same throughout the 20th century, with the exception that the area of land under cultivation has recently increased.

Two-thirds of the cultivated land is planted in wheat and barley. These two grains account for 45 percent of the total value of farm production. Rice, cotton, sugar beets, tobacco and fruits are the other main crops. Production of the five major crops, as estimated by Bharier, for the period 1925–69 is given in Table 38.[26]

Apart from substantial increases in tea and sugar beet production and the changes brought about through attempts at opium control, the structure of agricultural production has remained basically unaltered. For the most part, the amounts shown in Table 38 were sufficient to meet domestic consumption needs. However, in recent years, as a result of high rates of population growth and rapid increases in per capita income, some imports have been required to meet the rising demand for agricultural products. It is estimated that agricultural imports, largely food items, grew at an average annual rate of 9 to 10 percent between 1958 and 1972, from 4.9 billion rials to 20.9 billion rials.

However, throughout the period 1900–70, as Bharier observes, the agricultural sector, comprising farming, stock breeding, forestry and fishing, was the largest contributor to GNP, though in proportionate terms this contribution declined over time. In the first quarter of the century, it is probable that agriculture made up 80 to 90 percent of GNP, and from 1926 to 1950 about 50 percent. By 1959, the contribution had fallen to 33 percent, and it further declined to 23 percent by 1968. The distribution of gross value added within the sector during the 1960s shows that forestry and fishing together constituted only about 1 percent, stock breeding 40 percent and farming 50 percent. In earlier decades, it is likely that the percentage for stock breeding was somewhat higher. Agriculture also employed the largest proportion of the country's workers during the period—at the beginning of the century 90 percent, 85 percent in 1930, 75 percent in 1946, 56 percent in 1956 and 46 percent in 1966.[27]

Before the land reform of 1962, agricultural productivity was very low due to many factors, the most important of which were primitive

---

*The number of villages in Iran is estimated at between 49,000 and 65,000. The figure 55,000 is based on the operations of the second phase of land reform.

Table 38
Production of Various Crops
(annual averages over five-year periods, in 000 metric tons*)

Crop	1925-29	1930-34	1935-39	1940-44	1945-49	1950-54	1955-59	1960-64	1965-69
Wheat	1,120[1]	1,400[1]	1,870[4]	1,400[3]	1,880[4]	2,160[3]	2,700[5]	2,720[5]	3,330[3]
Barley	580[1]	630[1]	790[4]	600[3]	860[5]	810[3]	960[5]	820[5]	1,020[3]
Rice	270[1]	420[1]	390[4]	350[4]	430[5]	450[5]	450[5]	610[5]	880[3]
Cotton (raw)	20[5]	20[4]	38[5]	23[5]	19[5]	41[5]	140[5]	240[4]	370[3]
Tobacco	7**	11[1]	15[4]	14[3]	14[5]	15[2]	12[5]	11[4]	24[3]

*Superior figures indicate the number of years for which statistics were available.
**Estimated.

Note: Reliability poor for all periods.

Sources: Various, including League of Nations, United Nations and Iranian Government publications.

farming practices, absentee landlordism with sharecropping predominant and a low level of capital formation in agriculture. As an illustration, wheat yield was 1.2 tons, rice 2 tons, cotton 1 ton and sugar beets 15 tons per hectare of irrigated land in 1960.[28] The lowest yields were often found to be on holdings farmed under permanent sharecropping arrangements in certain regions of the country.

The high concentration of land ownership in the majority of cases, along with the large share of the crops extracted by the landlords, had perpetuated a very inequitable distribution of agricultural income. The vast majority of the tenants lived at or near subsistence level while they were almost always indebted to their landlords or village moneylenders. The tenants, for the most part, had no permanent right to the land they cultivated, as the landlords had the power to periodically redistribute holdings at will. In some areas, landlords levied dues in addition to a share of the crop, and the tenant was also subject to perform certain personal services. In short, the Iranian tenants lived in poverty, ignorance and continual insecurity.

The four broad categories of land ownership consisted of public domain lands (state lands), crown lands, *waqf* lands (land endowed for religious and public purposes) and private land holdings. Land records were fragmentary and a cadastral survey did not exist. However, of the 51,300 villages enumerated in the 1956 census, the public domain lands accounted for 10 percent, the crown lands for about 4 percent, the *waqf* lands for about 10 percent and private holding for the remaining 76 percent.[29] Generally speaking, large-scale absentee landlords held about 50 percent of the cultivated land of the country. The large holdings were let in small subunits to tenants who farmed the lands on the basis of sharecropping or fixed rental arrangements. The share of crops accruing to the respective landlords was either collected directly by his agents or through intermediaries who sublet to the tenants.

A major characteristic of large-scale landlordism, which is known in Iran as *arbabi*, was that the tenure, production and supporting services structures were all fused into one highly centralized hierarchical system controlled by the owners of the large estates. Iranian landlords not only let their holdings to the tenants but in almost all cases also provided water and often seed. In many cases, the landowners used to advance credit to their tenants and facilitate the marketing of their products. Under the *arbabi* system, the sharecroppers would cultivate the land individually or collectively.

In collective or group farming, the landowner (*malik*) gives cultivation rights (*nasaq*) to the sharecropper (*ra'iyat*), but the individual cultivation rights become effective only when the tenants assume the farming responsibility as a group. These farming groups are known in different parts of the country as *boneh, sahra, harasseh,* etc. The tenants in each group would pool their landholdings and tools for joint cultivation while still retaining their individual rights to their landholdings. The *boneh* over centuries has evolved as a complex social organization for agricultural production with distinct cultivation and water rights, and a semistructured farm management.[30]

The development of group farming in Iran seems to be the result of two major conditions. First, the irrigation system requires teamwork in the utilization of the village water resources, in particular, the digging and maintenance of the *qanats*, the main underground water channels. Second, the imperatives of the management of the large estates by absentee landowners encouraged group farming in order to run the large estates and deal with sharecroppers with relative ease. This form of production structure has especially developed in the dry areas of the country, including the central, eastern and southern regions.

Because a major constraint to land use in Iran is rainfall, irrigation has been of vital significance in the development of agriculture. A multitude of methods for the utilization of surface and ground water supplies have been applied. In particular, ground water is traditionally exploited by *qanats*, which bring water from the foothills to the cultivated area through a series of gently sloping tunnels dug in loose, alluvial sediments. When the *qanat* is completed, no power source other than gravity is needed to maintain the flow of water. The length of a *qanat* may vary considerably from less than 1 kilometer extending to 40 or 50 kilometers. It is estimated that nearly one-third of the irrigated area of Iran is watered by 37,500 *qanats*. *Qanat* construction by traditional technology is highly labor-intensive, taking many years and requiring both a large amount of investment capital and high maintenance costs.[31] In addition, its uncontrolled flow results in a waste of water when irrigation is not required. However, the adaptation of modern technology to *qanat* construction and maintenance deserves serious study.

Prior to 1962, the three main types of land tenure consisted of sharecropping *Mozareh,* fixed rental in cash or in kind *(Ejarei)* and owner-operated farms *(Melki).* As Table 39 shows, the predominant type of tenure was sharecropping, which applied to approximately 54 percent of the total agricultural land of the country.

In the sharecropping system, the rental share usually depended on who supplied the five traditional production inputs—land, water, seed, oxen and labor—as well as on the type of crop grown, local traditions and quality of the soil. Generally speaking, one-fifth of the crop was allocated to each of the mentioned five basic inputs, but there were so many variations in the practice of dividing the crops between the landlords and the tenants that no general rule applicable to the different regions of the country existed. The landlord's share ranged from 20 to 80 percent of the crop. For cash crops, such as cotton and sugar beets, the landlord's share amounted to about half the crop, whereas for wheat and barley, the landlords usually received two-thirds of the produce.

Table 39
Number and Area of all Holdings by Type of Tenure, 1960

Type of Tenure	Number of Holdings		Area (hectares)	
	'000	Percent	'000	Percent
Mozareh	814	34.2	6,222	54.8
Ejarei	235	10.0	844	7.4
Melki	624	26.2	2,976	26.2
Holdings Operated under More Than One Tenure Form	201	8.4	1,315	11.6
Holdings Without Land	508	21.2	—	—
Total	2,384	100.0	11,357	100.0

Source: First National Census of Agriculture, October 1960, Tehran.

The tenure arrangements on public domain lands, *waqf* lands and crown lands did not differ greatly from those on large private holdings. In other words, regardless of the form of ownership, the lands were let in small holdings to the tenants, and rents were collected directly or through agents of the landowners.

The whole fabric of socioeconomic life of the Iranian village was governed and determined by the nature of the landlord-tenant relationship. The villages were, in practice, owned, ruled and often made an object of commercial bargaining, without the knowledge—to say nothing of the consent—of their inhabitants. The government's sphere of influence in village public life was generally weak. Since many of the landlords exploited their tenants with the sole purpose of getting labor and the land rent out of them, there had developed in many areas a deep-rooted sense of mistrust between the landlord and the tenant.

Before the recent land reform, the two major changes in traditional agrarian structure were commercialization and tractorization of agriculture. Commercialization emerged in the early 1930s as a result of rising demand for cash crops and exports, and advanced at a slow pace. Tractorization of agriculture developed mainly because of the government policy of agricultural modernization, which focused mostly on farm mechanization without institutional changes. As an illustration, a law granting substantial credit at low interest rates to farmers (mainly landowners) for the purchase of agricultural machinery was passed by the Iranian Parliament in 1956. The implementation of this law and the allocation of substantial funds out of the reevaluation of Iranian currency rates in 1958 to agricultural investors contributed to the expansion of mechanization. It is difficult to estimate the total area of mechanized estates. However, implementation of the first stage of land reform revealed that some 1,100 villages were exempted from redistribution because the land was cultivated with hired workers and agricultural machinery. This figure represents about two percent of the total number of villages in Iran. The other indicator of development of farm mechanization is the extent of mechanical power that was used on under 10 percent of landholdings, with about four percent being fully mechanized by 1960.[32]

It seems, therefore, that mechanized farming developed to some extent along with subsistence agriculture in the prereform period. However, there is little systematic research on various types of production structures that existed before 1962. This author has made an effort to differentiate various types of agricultural production structures on the basis of four factors: land tenure, size of production unit, degree of mechanization and relation of the rural family toward the farm. The preliminary results of this study revealed that five different types of agricultural production structure coexisted in Iran before the recent land reform. These types were (1) peasant subsistence holdings, (2) small-scale owners' holdings, (3) large traditional estates, (4) large-scale capitalist farms and (5) entrepreneurial tenant farms.[33]

Socioeconomic and Political Implications of Land Reform

Before the radical land reform law of 1962, some attempts to reform the land-tenure structure and to improve the conditions of the tenants had been made. Transfer of ownership of land to the tenants began in 1927 when some of the state lands (Khalesse) in the provinces of Khoozestan and Sistan were redistributed to the local farmers. In 1951, the Shah began his reform by redistributing the crown lands to the tenants. As a result, some 507 villages covering an area of 199,628 hectares were transferred to 42,203 tenant households by 1961.[34] The government proceeded with the distribution of the state lands in 1958, and by 1963, when the transfer of the state lands came under the comprehensive land reform law, some 157 villages had been transferred to 8,366 tenants.

In April 1960, the first comprehensive land reform law was passed by the Iranian Parliament, 50 to 60 percent of whose members were drawn from the landowning class.[35] This law provided for the redistribution of all private holdings in excess of 400 hectares of irrigated or 800 hectares of unirrigated land. But the law had so many loopholes and qualifications that its enforcement was made wholly impracticable.

In 1961, a broad analysis of the social conditions by the monarch indicated the prevailing need for a drastic change in the socioeconomic structure commensurate with the requirements of a rapidly changing society. Among these changes was the amendment of the 1960 land reform law by a cabinet decree that was approved by the Council of Ministers on January 9, 1962. This decree, which was initially enacted in the form of an amendment and which was later approved by the Iranian Parliament, is recognized as the "original land reform law." According to this law, all estates in excess of one village or parts of villages equivalent to one village (sheshdang) were to be transferred to the occupying tenants. "Mechanized estates," i.e., lands cultivated by agricultural machinery and wage labor, gardens and tea orchards, were exempted from redistribution. Under the provisions of this law, the ownership of land was granted to the tenants in conditional title in proportion to the land previously held by them. This pattern of land ownership is known in Iran as Mosha. The enforcement of the original law is generally referred to as "the first stage of the Iranian land reform program."

The objectives of the land reform program in its early conception were stated in general terms as abolition of the existing landlord-tenant relations, emancipation of the peasants, promotion of democracy and development of agriculture. The economic aspect was not neglected, but development was not the primary aim. Generally speaking, the political objective of land reform loomed larger than any economic goal because it seemed to be necessary to carry out a reform that would lessen the power of the landowners before any economic and social progress could be made.[36] As the reform program got underway, its aims became more clearly formulated. The economic objective was to increase agricultural production by generating economic incentives among the tenants through the transfer of land ownership. Also connected with this objective was the provision of financial and technical assistance through an expanding cooperative network and agricultural extension services. Politically, the reform program was aimed at enlarging the scope of political consciousness and participation among the rural population. The social objectives included a more equitable distribution of agricultural income and improvement of the living conditions in the villages. On the whole, the basic strategy of land reform in its early years was directed toward development of a self-reliant and independent peasant proprietorship system.

The transfer of ownership of absentee landowners that was implemented in three states took more than a decade.[37] While the first phase of the reform sought to solve the problem of large land ownership, once this was initiated, the next issue, improving tenancy situations, became a matter of concern. However, in practice, the enforcement of the second stage did not produce the expected results, and the third phase of the reform was launched to eliminate all forms of land tenancy.

Iran: Past, Present and Future

Three major factors seem to have contributed to the rapid implementation of the Iranian land reform program, namely; (1) the adaptability of the program; (2) the political will; and (3) the phasing in of the reform measures.

1. *Adaptability.* The land reform law of 1962 was prepared with utmost consideration for the existing agrarian situation of the country. It was not an imitation or adoption of the best reform laws designed for other countries. It was strategically planned for the purpose of preventing evasion, and was meant to work. The fixing of one village as the ceiling of land ownership, rather than adopting the standard practice of a fixed area of land, in the first stage of the reform program can be cited as an example of the cultural adaptability of the program. Furthermore, the reform procedures were designed to depend less on the decisions of government officials, especially regional officials who might have been influenced by the landowners.

2. *Political will.* The government, under the leadership of His Majesty, gave the land reform program top policy priority. Encountering strong opposition from the landlords, the government mobilized its executive power at all levels, engaged in very active propaganda work and stimulated the tenants to gain ownership of the land they were cultivating. The peasants' genuine interest and their active participation in the land reform movement, coupled with the government decision to allocate fairly adequate amounts of funds for the compensation of the landlords, are among the significant factors that contributed to the rapid implementation of the reform measures.*

3. *Phasing the program.* Both the legislative and enforcement measures of the land reform program were carried out by a process of trial and error. At the outset, the original law was approved and was immediately put into force without any reference to future plans. However, in the process of implementation, the need for some amendments was felt. As a result, the second phase of land reform was introduced and was later ameliorated by the third stage.

A major question that is often raised both by students of agrarian reform and by the layman is: To what extent has Iranian land reform been successful? The precise effects are difficult to estimate because of insufficient data, potential tendencies for value judgment and numerous legislative enactments. However, there is little doubt that, in terms of its sociopolitical objectives, the reform has been successful, resulting in the transfer of land to the tenants and in the breakup of the power base of the landlords. It also contributed to a rapid expansion of rural cooperative societies. These societies, in addition to supplying credits and some

---

*By 1971, the government's payments to landowners for their lands amounted to about $130 million.

new farm inputs to the new farm owners, have created a potential mechanism for active participation by peasant farmers in economic and political processes.

One major result of the past decade of land reform has been the rapid expansion of peasant proprietorship. Assuming that all owner-operated holdings with less than 10 hectares of land fall in this category, we may estimate that by 1974, about 60 percent of agricultural families farmed some 44 percent of the total cultivated land of the country. Comparing these figures with those of the prereform era, we note that the number of peasant farm owners has more than tripled, while the area of land operated by them has quadrupled. In addition to small tenants, sharecroppers who are doing well, *i.e.*, those cultivating holdings over 10 hectares, were also granted ownership of the land. It is estimated that this group currently farms some 15 to 20 percent of the cultivated land. On the whole, it could be said that under the three phases of the land reform program, between 40 and 50 percent of the cultivated land was transferred to some 70 percent of Iran's rural population.[38]

As to the achievement of the economic objectives of land reform, no definitive statement can be made before answering two basic questions. The first question rests on the new types of land tenure and farming structure that replaced the old ones. The second question deals with the postreform variation in the level of agricultural production. At present, valid conclusions are not forthcoming in answer to these questions for three reasons. First, there exists some uncertainty as to the desired pattern of tenure to be developed in the country; second, the efforts to reorganize the farming structure are still in an early experimental stage; and third, any attempt to determine the effects of the reform on agricultural production is handicapped by the shortage of reliable statistical information on physical output. An effort to estimate the production impact of land reform on major crops was made by this author by comparing the production of wheat, rice, cotton and sugar beets for the six years after the land reform with that for the three years preceding the reform. The results of this study indicated that the production of these crops increased by 7, 20, 13 and 120 percent respectively.[39] It could be said that the level of agricultural production did not fall after the land reform as many critics of the reform expected; in fact, a slow rate of growth has been maintained. However, it should not be forgotten in this respect that some additional land was newly brought under cultivation and some was improved by irrigation. Increased mechanization also played a part in the growth of production. The production increase pertains not just to the tenant sector mainly affected by the land reform, but to all agricultural holdings.

On the whole, the economic results of land reform for the peasants have been generally favorable. Lambton observes that in almost all the villages divided under the first stage, the peasants said they were better off and that indebtedness had been greatly reduced. In many villages, there was evidence of increased cultivation and also better cultivation. Higher incomes were being used chiefly in building new houses.[40] However, the economic impact of the second and third stages is more complicated to evaluate, particularly in those villages where the landlords did not aid the repair of *qanats,* or damaged the village water supplies by sinking deep wells, or tried to uphold the old patterns of economic and power dominance by maintaining a relatively larger portion of the more fertile soil of the village farmlands.[41]

In short, land reform in Iran stimulated circulation of a number of sociopolitical and economic currents with diversified and often contradictory implications. Economically, the reform measures have been shifting between radical tenure changes and more moderate ones in an effort to strike a balance between land transfers and maintenance of agricultural production levels. A number of efforts are being made to reorganize the traditional farming system through creation of rural cooperatives, farm corporations, production cooperatives and agribusiness.

Sociopolitically, the reform impact tends to take a multidirectional course: a rising expectation among the peasantry for a higher standard of living, a demand among the peasants for a more dynamic role in national life and a change in their value system. In particular, the peasant's horizon, which was traditionally limited to the safeguards of his kinsmen and his village, seems to have broadened into a growing identification with the nation and its affairs. An unintended consequence of the land reform program leading to a greater social polarization in village communities developed as a result of transferring ownership of the lands exclusively to the sharecroppers *(Nassaghdar).* Although this policy was based on a practical consideration to prevent further fragmentation of small peasant holdings, the problem of farm laborers *(Khushneshin),* who constitute some 25 percent of the rural population in Iran and who have been deprived of the advantages of the land reform program, deserves serious research and public action.

The reform impact on societal structure could be described as having hastened the circulation of power elites in the modernization process. However, the exact nature and extent of this elite circulation remains to be studied. There are certain tendencies suggesting that the landlord elite of the past, with its monopolistic powers in the socioeconomic and political life of the nation, is tending to be replaced by an industrial elite, who appear to harbor certain similar characteristics. The implications of this trend may not be conducive to a balanced development.*

---

*To avoid this tendency to turn into a monopolistic power in the hands of an industrial elite, recently proclaimed principles of the Shah and People's Revolution have called for a wide participation of workers, farmers and the general public in the holding of equity capital belonging to major corporations and for consumer protection against abusive power of the industrialists—in the form of government price control measures.

Peasant Farmers' Response to New Opportunities

The theoretical framework adopted in this study, as discussed earlier, perceives modernization of traditional agriculture as a complex multidimensional process. A significant element in this process is the manner in which farmers respond to new economic opportunities. In this context, we may note that rationality, efficiency, achievement motivation and other personality traits that contribute to modernization are not necessarily limited to urban population. As Inkeles and Smith observe, ". . . certain universal patterns of response persist in the face of variability in culture content. These transcultural similarities in the psychic properties of individuals provide the basis for a common response to common stimuli. On these grounds we concluded that men, from a very different culture, might nevertheless respond in basically the same way to certain relatively standard institutions and interpersonal patterns introduced by economic development and sociopolitical modernization."[42]

The main contention of this section is that Iranian peasant farmers are not overwhelmingly "tradition-bound"; rather, they respond to institutional and infrastructural changes fairly rationally. As a case in point, the response of a sample of farmers to a new water supply source (an irrigation dam) is studied. The measures of this response are captured through the change in proportion of farmland brought under cultivation, productivity per hectare and agricultural innovativeness. These indices are compared for two groups of peasant farmers—one receiving water from the new dam irrigation channels since 1970 (experimental villages), the other depending on traditional sources of irrigation, *i.e., qanats* and springs (controlled villages). These two sets of villages are located in close vicinity in the Marv Dasht plain.

The Setting

The data for this part of our study were obtained by field work and interviewing the heads of all the households enumerated in the summer of 1974 in a sample of six villages. In addition, detailed interviews were conducted with the heads of traditional group farming units *(Harraseh)* on their land use, production and distribution functions. These villages were located in two rural districts 20 to 50 kilometers northwest of the city of Shiraz. Three of the villages, the "experimental" ones, were selected from some 65 villages that have recently been watered by a newly built dam and that were surveyed during 1969–70. This larger survey was

undertaken by the author to measure the socioeconomic and technological impact of the new dam on the surrounding rural communities. The
other three villages were selected as "controlled villages" from a
neighboring region that was not included in the new irrigation scheme.

In general, farming and keeping livestock is the main occupation of
85 percent of the heads of households interviewed, yet some 15 percent
of household heads are engaged in nonagricultural occupations such as
storekeepers, truck drivers, construction workers, etc. Wheat, barley, rice
and sugar beets are the main crops. While wheat and rice are used
largely for household consumption, sugar beets and oil seeds make up
the peasants' main cash crops. The sample villages are not, generally
speaking, subsistence peasant economies, isolated from rural and town
markets. The villagers are engaged, to a considerable extent, in commercial transactions with the rural town of Marv Dasht (present population estimated about 35,000). They are also engaged in the exchange of
goods with nomadic groups when the latter are migrating to their winter
or summer quarters.

The population of the largest village was 500, while the smallest
one had a population of 107 in the summer of 1974. The average population of the six villages in our sample was around 310 people who were
living in 52 households. The mean number of persons living in each
household was 5.9. Approximately 68 percent of the heads of households are cultivators or peasant farm owners, while some 32 percent are
farm and nonfarm laborers who, with a small number of storekeepers and
village artisans, constitute the landless rural class, known in Iran as
Khoosh-neshin. The ownership of land of these villages was transferred
exclusively to the sharecroppers under the second phase of the land
reform program. According to the regulations of this phase, village lands
were divided between the landowners and their respective sharecroppers in the same proportion as crops had been divided between them
under the existing crop-sharing arrangements. Thus, as a result of the
implementation of land reform in the six villages, the sharecroppers, in
general, were granted the ownership of 40 percent of the cultivated lands
while the landowners maintained their ownership over the remaining 60
percent of the village farmlands.

In the three "experimental" villages where land and water are relatively more abundant, the peasant farmers were given, on the average,
9.2 hectares of cultivated land. In the agricultural year 1972–73, these
farmers, on an average, brought about some 7.2 hectares of their land,
approximately 80 percent, under cultivation, while leaving two hectares,
the remaining 20 percent, fallow. Wheat covered 4.2, rice 1.7, barley .9,
sugar beets, oil seeds and alfalfa together some .2 hectares. In the two
years since these farmers have had access to water from the new dam
irrigation structures, they have reduced their fallow lands from 32 to 20
percent and their dry farming from 1 to .3 percent, whereas they have

increased the area under rice cultivation from .03 hectares to 2.3 hectares*, and have begun the cultivation of alfalfa on some .02 hectares of their holdings. However, they have reduced cultivation of sugar beets and oil seeds by 74 percent and 71 percent, respectively. The mean net income of the peasant farmer household in "experimental" villages from farming is calculated at $3,067, and $340 from livestock, totaling $3,407 for the year 1972–73. Thus, the per capita income in these three villages is estimated around $577.

The peasant farmers in the three "controlled" villages were granted ownership of an average 5.9 hectares of cultivated land. In the agricultural year of 1972–73, each of these peasants farmed, on an average, some 4.2 hectares, 71 percent of his holdings, leaving the remaining 1.7 hectares, 29 percent, fallow. The main irrigation sources of these villages are *qanat* and spring water. Due to water shortage, there is little rice cultivation in these villages. In 1972–73, the cultivation of irrigated wheat and irrigated and nonirrigated barley covered some 2.9 hectares, sugar beets, 1 hectare, alfalfa, .15 hectares and other cash crops, .2 hectares. The mean net income of the peasant farmer household in the "controlled" villages from farming is calculated to be about $830, and from livestock about $430, totaling some $1,260 in 1972–73. The per capita income in these three villages is, thus, around $213.

Generally speaking, yields per hectare are fairly higher in the "experimental" villages than in the "controlled" ones. As an illustration, yields of irrigated wheat and sugar beets in the former are 2.3 tons and 25 tons per hectare, respectively, as compared with 1.5 tons and 23.5 tons, respectively, in the latter.

The Data

The total number of all households residing in the six villages covered in the present study was 313 at the time of our interview in the summer of 1974. A total of 235 interview schedules, representing 75 percent of all the households in the sample villages, was completed. This figure consisted of 158 peasant farmers and 72 *Khoosh-neshin.* The data reported in Table 40 relates to the subsample of peasant farmers. Since information on items relating to agricultural productivity and innovativeness was not adequately reported for 64 farmers, the number of our subsample was reduced to 94. Out of these, 54 farmers belong to the three "experimental" villages and the remaining 40 to the three "controlled" villages.

*The very substantial increase in area under rice cultivation has not been due only to more water available to peasants but also to a 100 percent rise in the price of rice in Iran in the last four years.

An index of agricultural innovativeness composed of four items—variety of wheat cultivated, alfalfa cultivation, oil seed cultivation and treatment of diseased livestock by veterinarians—was constructed. Productivity per hectare was calculated as the average market value of total farm production divided by area under cultivation in 1972–73 (See Table 40).

The data in Table 40 reveal that new infrastructures such as dam water supply are obviously creating a substantial difference in agricultural productivity and land use. We may note that among the crucial factors conducive to agricultural development are the increase in productivity per units of lands, expansion of acreage under cultivation and agricultural innovation. According to Table 40, on all three counts the peasant farmers have reacted favorably and rather quickly to the new source of water supply.

It is obvious that differences in productivity per hectare could result from a number of factors, including quality of soil and other such physical characteristics. While keeping these in mind, the data in Table 40 show a substantial difference in agricultural innovativeness between the two groups. Comparing the data on agricultural productivity and acreage under cultivation for the period before the construction of the new dam with those given in Table 40 for the three "experimental" villages,[42] one could easily argue that the higher level of agricultural innovativeness in 1972–73 is closely associated with the peasant farmers responding efficiently to the dam water supply.

In short, the preceding analysis suggests that traditional Iranian farmers respond fairly efficiently to new economic opportunities. This implies that agricultural modernization in Iran could be accelerated by peasant farmers, provided that essential new inputs, research and extension education, adaptation and domestication of modern technology, favorable price incentives, adequate infrastructures—particularly water supply, credit and marketing facilities—are made available to farmers. In this context, we may note that development of indigenous cooperative associations, security of land titles and social mobilization of the peasant farmers, reorganization of colleges of agriculture—particularly their admission policies and curriculum—and above all, restructuring of agricultural planning and administrative organization resulting in greater decentralization and local participation, are essential elements in an efficient strategy of agricultural transformation.

Conclusions and Implications

In the preceding sections, the significance of agricultural development in Iran, the major traits of the prereform agrarian structure, socioeco-

Table 40

Agriculture-Related Statistics for Three "Experimental" and
Three "Controlled" Villages in Fars, 1972-73

Type of Village	Number of Farmers	Farm Size (hectares)	Net Farm Income (rials)	Mean Productivity per Hectare (rials)	Percent under Cultivation	Innovativeness Score
"Experimental" Villages	54	10.6	201,950	26,040	76	3.2*
"Controlled" Villages	40	5.2	67,070	17,534	70	2.2

*Differences between the means of agricultural innovativeness scores are statistically significant at 0.005 level.

nomic and political implications of land reform, peasant farmers' response to new opportunities and the need to treat modernization of traditional agriculture as a complex multidimensional process, were discussed. The analysis indicated (1) the physical, cultural and organizational diversity and complexity of the Iranian agrarian structure; (2) the impact of land reform on mobilization of the peasantry, circulation in certain segments of power elites and a more flexible and egalitarian tenure structure; and (3) a fairly efficient response of peasant farmers to institutional and infrastructural changes.

The implications of this study underscore the significance of indigenous sociocultural potentialities and the entrepreneurial skills of small- and medium-scale farmers for agricultural development in Iran. While the role of modern science and technology is well recognized, our underlying assumption is that agricultural development does not necessarily imply the application of Western technology, production and management styles. Our primary emphasis is placed on the belief that modern technology, especially that which is mechanical in nature, should be adjusted, tailored and adapted to the agrarian structure in Iran. This suggests a strategy for modernization of agriculture through transformation of traditional farming structure rather than through displacing it by capital-intensive, large-scale technology.

There are certain potentialities for such a strategy within the Iranian agrarian structure. The adaption and utilization of modern technology to *qanat* construction, which taps underground water sources from the foothills to the cultivated area through a series of gently sloping tunnels without input of mechanical energy, deserves serious consideration. This should contribute to the preservation of energy in the exploitation of underground water. The existence of traditional group farming *(Boneh)* offers potentialities for development of production cooperatives on a voluntary basis. The group farming structure could be rather easily reorganized into fairly efficient medium-size production organizations because, under the land reform law, the ownership of land was granted to the tenants in conditional title in proportion to the land previously held.

Finally, it should be emphasized that the enormous diversity of climatic, physical and social conditions, as discussed earlier, demands a variety of alternative strategies to agricultural modernization. However, there are certain issues that have to be considered regardless of the type of strategy adopted. These include: (1) a fair profit on agricultural investment relatively comparable to that in the industrial sector; (2) a consideration of peasant farmers' characteristics, which suggest that the farmer is partly a "petit capitalist," partly worker and partly an entrepreneur in his own right; (3) the tendency toward bureaucratization of agriculture, which could hinder development of individual initiative and popular participation; and (4) the apparent uncertainty in the minds of some new peasant farmers as well as among a certain number of middle-size farm operators over the security of the title to their land. These issues call for systematic and objective research to provide guidelines for reconstruction and modernization of Iranian agriculture.

Footnotes

1. See especially B. F. Johnston, "Agriculture and Structural Transformation in Developing Countries: A Survey of Research," *Journal of Economic Literature,* 8 (1970), pp. 339–341.

2. S. Kuznets, "Quantitative Aspects of the Economic Growth of Nations, II. Industrial Distribution of National Product and Labor Force," *Economic Development and Cultural Change,* 5 (1957).

3. J. W. Mellor, *The Economics of Agricultural Development* (Ithaca, NY: Cornell University Press, 1966), pp. 129–131.

4. Ohkawa and H. Rosonsky, "The Role of Agriculture in Modern Japanese Economic Development," *Economic Development and Cultural Change,* 9 (1960), pp. 43–67.

5. As quoted in B. Johnston, "Agriculture and Structural Transformation in Developing Countries," *op. cit.,* p. 383.

6. Ruttan, "Two Sector Models and Development Policy," in C. R. Wharton, Jr. (ed.), *Subsistence Agriculture and Economic Development* (Chicago: Aldine Publishing Co., 1969), pp. 353–359.

7. T. Shanin (ed.), *Peasants and Peasant Societies* (Middlesex, England: Penguin Books, 1971), pp. 238–261. See also B. Moore, Jr., *Social Origins of Dictatorship and Democracy: Lord and Peasant in the Making of the Modern World* (Boston: Beacon Press, 1967), pp. 413–484.

8. T. W. Schultz, *Transforming Traditional Agriculture,* (New Haven: Yale University Press, 1964).

9. B. F. Johnston and J. W. Mellor, "The Nature of Agricultural Contribution to Economic Development," *Food Research Institute Studies,* I (1960), pp. 335–336.

10. A. T. Mosher, "Agricultural Development", in J. P. Leagans and C. P. Loomis (eds.), *Behavioral Change in Agriculture* (Ithaca, NY: Cornell University Press, 1971), pp. 12–27.

11. S. L. Barraclough, "Response," in J. P. Leagans and C. P. Loomis (eds.), *Behavioral Change in Agriculture,* (Ithaca, NY: Cornell University Press, 1971), pp. 51–74.

12. M. L. Dantwala, "The Problems of a Subsistence Farm Economy: The Indian Case," in C. R. Wharton, Jr. (ed.), *Subsistence Agriculture and Economic Development* (Chicago: Aldine Publishing Co., 1969), pp. 383–386.

13. S. Robinson, "Theories of Economic Growth and Development: Methodology and Content," *Economic Development and Cultural Change,* 21 (1972), pp. 54–68.

14. J. W. Mellor, *The Economics of Agricultural Development, op. cit.*

15. D. Warriner, *Land Reform in Principle and Practice* (Oxford, England: Clarendon Press, 1961), pp. 372–385.

16. *Ibid.,* p. 389.

17. *Ibid.,* p. 45.

18. J. R. Behrman, "Supply Response and the Modernization of Peasant Agriculture: A Study of Four Major Annual Crops in Thailand," presented at the *International Congress of Orientalists,* Ann Arbor, Michigan, August 17, 1967.

19. *Ibid.*

20. B. F. Johnston, "Agriculture and Structural Transformation in Developing Countries," *op. cit.,* pp. 381–383.

21. E. Rogers and L. Svenning, *Modernization Among Peasants: The Impact of Communication* (New York: Holt, Rinehart and Winston, Inc., 1969), pp. 362–363.

22. R. Schickele, *Agrarian Revolution and Economic Progress: A Primer for Development* (New York: Praeger, 1968), p. 113.

23. C. Issawi (ed.), *The Economic History of Iran, 1800–1914* (Chicago: The University of Chicago Press, 1971).

24. See especially A. K. S. Lambton, *Landlord and Peasant In Persia* (London: Clarendon Press, 1953).

25. Plan Organization, "The Fourth Five-Year Development Plan of Iran," Tehran, 1968.

26. J. Bharier, *Economic Development in Iran,1900–1970* (London: Oxford University Press, 1971), p. 134.

27. *Ibid.*, p. 132.

28. Ministry of Interior, Department of Public Statistics, *The First National Census of Agriculture* (Tehran, 1960).

29. A. Dehbod, "Land Ownership and Use in Iran", *CENTO Symposium on Rural Development,* Tehran, 1960.

30. See especially J. Safi-Nejad, *Boneh: The Group Farming Systems Before Land Reform* (Tehran: Toos Publisher, 1974). In Persian. See also I. Ajami, *Sheshdangi: A Study in Village Life in Iran* (Shiraz: Pahlavi University Press, 1969). In Persian.

31. English has calculated the construction cost of Javadieh *qanat* in the Kirman basin to be $11,000 per kilometer. The construction of this *qanat* of 3 kilometers, which began in 1941, took over 17 years. It provides sufficient water to irrigate less than one-half acre of land every 24 hours. See P. W. English, *City and Village in Iran: Settlement and Economy in the Irman Basin* (Madison: The University of Wisconsin Press, 1966), pp. 138–140.

32. The First National Census of Agriculture, 1960.

33. I. Ajami, "Transformation of Agricultural Production Structures in Iran—Before and After Land Reform," a paper presented at the *FAO Inter-Regional Seminar on New Forms and Organization of Agricultural Production,* Berlin, May 20–30, 1974. See also A. Ashraf, "The Socio-Economic Characteristics of Agricultural Production Systems in Iran," a paper prepared for the *Center for Research and Training in Regional Planning*, Tehran, 1974. In Persian.

34. A. Dehbod, *op. cit.,* p. 5.

35. Z. Shajyee, *The Majlis Deputies in Twenty-One Sessions* (Tehran: Institute of Social Studies and Research, 1965). In Persian.

36. D. Warriner, *Land Reform in Principle and Practice, op. cit.,* pp. 109–139.

37. See especially A. K. S. Lambton, *The Persian Land Reform, 1962–1966* (Oxford, England: Clarendon Press, 1969). See also I. Ajami, "Land Reform and Modernization of Farming Structure in Iran," *Oxford Agrarian Studies*, 2 (1974), pp. 1–12.

38. Estimates based on various figures published by different government agencies and international organizations.

39. Ajami, "Land Reform and Modernization of the Farming Structure in Iran," *op. cit.*, pp. 7–8.

40. A. K. S. Lambton, *The Persian Land Reform, 1962*–1966, op. cit.

41. See especially N. R. Keddie, "The Iranian Village Before and After Land Reform," *The Journal of Contemporary History,* 3 (1968), pp. 69–91.

42. A. Inkeles and D. H. Smith, *Becoming Modern: Individual Change in Six Developing Countries* (Cambridge, MA: Harvard University Press, 1974), p. 12.

43. See I. Ajami, J. Sadeghi, *et al.,* "Socio-Economic Impact of Daryush Dam—A Survey of Sample Villages Before the Dam Irrigation Water Supply," Department of National Development and Sociology, Pahlavi University, 1973. In Persian.

Modernization of Rural Economy in Iran

R. Doroudian

Before the agrarian reform, Iran's agricultural sector was relatively stagnant. Its total production fluctuated at around 87 billion rials during a period of three to five years before the reform. The landlords enjoying the highest possible standard of living had no motivation for investment. Neither did they show any interest in benefiting from the heavy investments contributed by the government through dam construction or by complementary investments required for irrigation network. At the same time, the peasants, lacking know-how and financial resources, had no incentive to put up more work for increasing the yield per hectare. Thus, a sluggish production, combined with maldistribution of income in the rural sector, were detrimental to both the economic and social stability of the nation.

The primary objectives of the Iranian agrarian reform should therefore be explained in terms of (1) creation of economic motivation for achieving a high growth rate in production and (2) improving the wealth and income distribution in the rural sector as a social aim. Thus, about 2.5 million farmer peasants became owner-cultivators under the land reform program. Altogether, they cultivate about 7 million hectares of land, including rain-fed and irrigated. The immediate problem after land reform was how to fill the financial and managerial gap created by the disappearance of the landlords. Under the new pattern of ownership, 2.5 million small family farms, with an average ownership of 2.8 hectares, were created. The new owner-cultivator found the motive to work harder, as every extra kilogram of production meant an improved standard of living for him and his family. As a result, the total value of agricultural production, which before the land reform was fluctuating at around 85 to 87 billion rials, increased by 53 percent during a 10-year period after the reform. There is still a considerable margin of yield improvement that can be achieved through greater effort in land fertility and more efficiency in water utilization under the individual family production system. Beyond this margin, however, there is little to be achieved without large-scale programs for small farm consolidation, water-use rationing and marketing improvement. The important fact in Iran's agriculture is that water is the most scarce resource and any major step in rationalization of its use would require large-scale projects for land consolidation, land leveling, modern irrigation systems and, above all, a new management responsible for such large-scale operations. Four different models to solve these problems have been adopted and put into operation alongside the implementation of land reform. These are:

1. Rural Cooperative Societies
2. Agribusiness
3. Farm Corporations
4. Production Cooperatives

To complete the list of all existing types of ownership and cultivation, we should mention also the large privately owned farms that were not subject to land reform because of their modern method of cultivation.

1. Rural Cooperative Societies

At the start of the land reform program priority was given to the establishment of rural cooperative societies as an instrument for organizing small farmers. The major functions of these societies have been (1) to provide credit facilities at relatively low rates of interest—for this purpose, the Agricultural Credit Bank was changed to the Agricultural Cooperative Bank, (2) to construct local and regional warehouses for storing and distributing consumer goods, agricultural inputs and agricultural products, and (3) to purchase the surplus production of the cooperative members for sale in major wholesale markets in order to protect them from excessively unfair dealings with middlemen.

Initially about 8,400 rural cooperative societies were organized, but later on it was recognized that the financial and technical services of the government could best be channeled through a smaller number of societies. Thus, 8,400 societies were consolidated into about 2,800 larger societies that joined in more than 130 rural cooperative unions. Today, out of 3.4 million farmers, 2.5 million are members of rural cooperatives. They own about 7 out of 15.3 million hectares of arable land, of which about 30 percent is irrigated and about 70 percent is rain-fed.

The amount of credit extended to cooperative societies increased from 1.4 billion rials in 1964 to 19.2 billion rials in 1974. In the meantime, 300 cooperative warehouses with a total capacity of over 120,000 tons have been built. In 1973, cooperative unions could market about 2 billion rials of agricultural produce belonging to rural cooperative members. At the same time, they supplied about 6.5 billion rials of consumer goods through rural cooperative stores at prices equal to those in the cities. From the point of view of production technique, the cooperative societies are continuing to operate with labor-intensive methods under family management.

2. Agribusiness

The second model is agribusiness, which was adopted as a solution for water and soil management in arable lands under new dams. Generally speaking, the lands under the dams or groups of wells, which can be developed through a modern irrigation system, have been defined as "agricultural poles of development." In view of the large amounts of investment made in controlling and regulating water resources, the government policy has been to make sure that such resources are used with maximum efficiency. Given the existing physical and topographical characteristics of lands in Iran, the construction of any modern irrigation system would require heavy investments in land leveling and drainage. This factor, besides the fact that greater yield per hectare would require heavier investments in mechanization, in fertilizer, disease control, etc., had originally led the government to conclude that major steps should be taken to consolidate small farms into large and economic units where such modern techniques can be applied more comprehensively under a new government or private management. According to this policy, in all areas recognized as an "agricultural pole of development," the government prepared a general master plan for development, including the production pattern. Small farms had to sell their lands to the government for land consolidation, land-leveling and construction of irrigation canals. Afterward, the government would either rent the land to private agribusiness companies or would organize state companies for its exploitation. The objective of the Fifth Development Plan has been to organize such companies in an estimated area of 300,000 hectares. As a matter of fact, the areas already allocated to private or state agribusiness are mostly characterized by a relatively low population/land ratio. In addition to capital intensity and a high level of technology in utilization of land and water as a scarce resource, these companies are expected also to make investments in processing industries related to their agricultural production, taking advantage of their large scale of production. Examples of this type are agro-industrial complexes established for milk and meat production. The emphasis being on capital, technology and management, this model has presented a wide scope for attraction of foreign investors in Iran's agriculture. Presently, a number of American agribusiness firms are operating in Khuzestan under Mohammad Reza Shah Dam.

3. Farm Corporations

The concept of the farm corporation model is based again on large-scale consolidation of lands and exploitation of land and water with intermediary or high-level technologies, depending on the type of production and the availability of manpower. In contrast to agribusiness, the small farmers are not required in this model to sell their lands. The land consolidation is realized by asking the farmers to exchange their titles to lands for shares in the corporation. According to legal procedures, a farm corporation can be established only after the majority of owner-cultivators in rural societies vote for joining the corporation. Afterward, the amount of shares to be issued to a member of the corporation would be measured on the basis of the value of his land. The operation and management of these corporations are similar to industrial corporations, the only difference being that the managers, technicians and accountants are recruited and paid by government. Besides, the government finances freely their investments in modern irrigation, drainage, road building and other village infrastructures and technical training, providing also cheap loans for investments in mechanization, construction of warehouses, machinery sheds, housing and current operating expenses on the basis of approved annual plans of operation. The basic investment activities financed by government through the management of farm corporations include surveying, soil and water studies, land leveling, construction of irrigation canals, building of service roads, mechanization and implementation of advanced farming techniques and marketing of agricultural products. The appointed managers of farm corporations are not only concerned with development of new land and water resources, increasing production and income of the farmers; they are also involved in the physical and environmental improvement of village communities, construction of schools, clinics, child-care centers, cultural houses and other social activities. As such, the farm corporation projects operate as fully integrated development packages under unified management. Compared to the rural cooperative society model, this approach requires much heavier government involvement in terms of capital and technical manpower. Consequently, rapid rates of growth in production and income of shareholders as well as change in the social environment have been achieved. These corporations have been able to increase their total cultivated land by 28 percent. Besides, they have achieved considerable increases in the yield per hectare for different products, e.g., 69 percent for wheat, 40 percent for sugar beets, 184 percent for sunflowers, 80 percent for cotton, 225 percent for vegetables and over 200 percent for corn. So far, 21 small industrial units have been established and about 50 new units are under study. As a result of these, the shareholders' income has increased on the average of over six times in the case of corporations with five to six years of activity and over four times in the case of corporations with only three years of activity. Accordingly, in the six-year-old corporations, the family income has increased from $410 to over $2,700.

So far, about 65 farm corporations have been established, with a coverage of 525 villages and farm units consisting of about 180,000 hectares. A total of 140 corporations are planned by the end of 1977. The major limiting factor for increasing the number of farm corporations beyond this target figure is the manpower on the medium and high levels of management.

4. Production Cooperatives

The production cooperative model is conceptually a variant of the farm corporation model in terms of its objectives, methods of cultivation and scope of government involvement. It differs only in view of farmer's right of ownership. In contrast with the farm corporation, in a production cooperative the farmer retains his title to the land he owns. Presently there are 24 production cooperatives, with a coverage of 126 villages and farm units consisting of about 37,000 hectares . A total of 60 production cooperatives are planned by the end of 1977.

Evaluation of Different Models

The performance of the aforementioned models should be evaluated in terms of broad objectives and constraints under Iranian agricultural and socioeconomic conditions. The salient features of different models in this context are as follows.

1. Production techniques have changed little under the rural cooperative societies that cover small, labor-intensive farms. This institution has, however, contributed to increasing the net income of farmers through lowering their cost for loan capital and also raising their gross income through ensuring a higher price for their marketed produce. In addition, the supply of agricultural inputs as well as basic consumer goods in the cooperative stores at prices equal to urban areas has helped the farmers to realize a more decent standard of living. From the point of view of productivity, small farms presently organized under the RCC system still have a large scope to be achieved.

2. The other three models, *i.e.*, agribusiness, the farm corporation and the production cooperative, are competitive approaches to small-farm consolidation and the use of advanced techniques in production and marketing. The major difference is, however, the way each of these models tackles the social aspects of the rural society, *i.e.*, the problem of the individual farmer. In agribusiness, the consolidation of small farms is

accompanied by a transfer of land from the small farmer to a large private and/or state-owned firm. The employment problem created by the dislocation of some of the small farmers who become landless should be tackled through provision of other agricultural or nonagricultural jobs to be supplied by government. The magnitude of the employment problem depends, of course, on the proportion of the land available to each farmer and the degree of capital intensity applied by the agribusiness firm. In the farm corporation and production cooperative models, however, there appears to be no problem of manpower dislocation, as the same number of owners may remain on the land as shareholders or cooperative members to benefit from advantages of large mechanized farming. In addition, a package program for rural development is also followed in villages covered by farm corporations and production cooperatives. Given all these advantages, a substantial increase in the number and coverage of the agribusiness and farm corporation/production cooperatives has been hampered because of a number of constraints which include:

- Inadequacy of high-quality managers. This problem is more pronounced in the case of agribusiness characterized by a more ambitious level of technology as compared with farm corporations or production cooperatives;
- The lack of experts and contractors to build new irrigation canals and facilities to maintain machinery or to do other technical jobs in a large farm;
- The lack of detailed soil specifications.

The core of the problem is that agricultural development should not be looked at solely as a problem of resource development to be solved only through physical consolidation of lands and more rational use of water. Analysis of the experiences gained during the last five years shows that it is the development of human resources in the agricultural and rural sector that accounts for any considerable gain in productivity. Small farms around Isfahan and Lake Reza ijeh have been able to demonstrate high levels of performance as a result of the individual farmer's know-how and hard work. The conclusion one should draw from this analysis is that no universal solution can be adopted. Major variables, such as the regional distribution of land and manpower resources, the type of culture and the crop pattern, the level of managerial know-how and the state of land and water resource development in each region and subregion, should be considered as determinants of an appropriate model. Regionally, models of agribusiness and the farm corporation/production cooperative can be applied in Khuzestan and Dasht-e-Mogan, where the land-labor ratio is relatively high. Farm corporation and production cooperative models can be applied with no problem in Khorasan, Central Zagros, Southern Zagros, south coastal areas and parts of the northwest and northeast, where the land-labor ratio is medium and cooperation of the rural population under a capable management would lead to fuller utilization of water and soil resources, guaranteeing at the same time higher income for the majority of the rural people. The same argument applies more vividly to the southern arid zone, *i.e.*, Kerman, Sistan and Baluchestan, where, in addition to a difficult climatological situation, the land-labor ratio is very small—except for subregions like Jiroft, where efficient private large farms are already developed. However, in areas like Isfahan, Yazd, Caspian and parts of the northwest, where the land-labor ratio is smallest while already highly sophisticated farming is practiced by small individual farmers, no rapid transition to either of the consolidation approaches is feasible from the socioeconomic points of view.

The manpower needs dictated by the expansion of the three consolidation models would set specific target figures for agricultural training institutions during the coming decades. Meanwhile, however, some interim solutions have to be devised. One measure of considerable impact would be to let the managers and agronomists working in farm corporations/production cooperatives step out of their farming units, leaving the daily operations to the elite of the community. They can then function as regional development planners, extension service agents and supervisors in an area three or four times larger than their present farming units. The existing farm corporations and production cooperatives can further be used partly as centers for on-the-job training of farmers in adjacent village communities.

Future Agricultural and Rural Development

During the next 20 years, Iran is going to face one of the most formidable challenges of its economic history in the field of agriculture and rural development. Iran's population is estimated to rise to about 53 million by 1992, 31 million of which will be urban and 22 million will be rural. Thus, we have to expect a total increase of 20 million in population, at least 16 million of which will be in the urban areas. To provide this increasing population with a fairly improved diet consisting of 2,800 calories and 85 grams of protein, we have to increase agricultural production by over six times for meat and eggs, by over 10 times for vegetables, by over three times for fruits and over two times for starchy foodstuff.* Of course, we can allow for a margin of our food needs to be imported. But the recent

---

*See Table 4.12, page 4.18, National Cropping Plan, Interim Report, Volume 1, Bookers and Hunting. (March 1975).

world food crisis warns us to be cautious about undue dependence on imports. Besides, the increasing population and income in the developing world will accentuate the pressure on the international supply of foodstuffs during the next 20 years. In former times, the only problem bothering the countries with great dependence on food imports was the pressure exerted on their balance of payments. In future, the problem will be mainly that of access to a secured supply in the world market. Thus, our most important challenge during the next one or two decades would be how to expand the available resources and how to maximize the efficiency of soil and water use. The basic policies and programs envisaged by the government to meet the agricultural objectives include:

- Development of irrigated agriculture. Recent studies indicate that water resources amount to 84 billion cubic meters as compared to previous estimates of only 52 billion cubic meters. Accordingly, it is foreseen that 2.7 million hectares of improved irrigated land, including 1.4 million hectares of newly irrigated land, could be available by 1992.
- Making the most efficient use of water and land through high standards of competence in agricultural technology, which must rely on research , know-how and able management. The consolidation of small holdings under the production cooperative system and technical support and promotion of larger private farms will constitute the organizational backbone of Iran's agriculture. The farm corporations and production cooperatives are planned to increase to 200 units, covering a total of 600,000 hectares by the end of 1977. Another 600,000 hectares are to be covered under this system during the Sixth Development Plan period.
- Promotion of managerial and technical training for the agricultural sector in a more decentralized system based on regional specialization and with a view to the above-mentioned physical targets.
- Streamlining of agricultural marketing and further emphasis on price support policies, and implementing of a crop insurance program.

Commensurate with the modernization of agriculture, a total restructuring of the rural setup will be needed. Presently, 18.5 million rural dwellers are living in over 66,000 village communities. Of this, roughly 14 million are living in 18,000 villages with a population over 250; the remaining 4.5 million live in 48,000 villages with a population under 250. The wide dispersion of villages, together with their small population size, has always made it very cumbersome and costly to provide them all with adequate road and communications facilities and other social services. Besides, given the present rural structure, there is little scope for development of local contractors and technical service capabilities by the private sector. Thus the concept of rural service centers was adopted in the Fifth Development Plan. Accordingly, about 1,200 rural service centers are to be set up in areas satisfying the following criteria:

- An upward population trend during the past five or ten years;
- A high level of agricultural and livestock production;
- The existence of facilities for the establishment or development of local administrative organizations;
- The existence of transportation, banking and shopping services or the availability of land for the establishment of such services; and
- A central geographic position making it a suitable base for providing services to other villages in the area. As is evident from these criteria, the rural service centers are to be located in areas that have already shown their viability. In addition, the villages in relatively remote or relatively poor regions have to be serviced independently; the priority and scope of such services being established, of course, on the basis of their population and production levels. The ultimate aim is to induce people in the small and remote villages to migrate to larger communities that will be developed gradually into agricultural towns equipped with all basic facilities and services.

It is therefore very important to be highly selective in choosing locations for rural service centers. This process should be coordinated with plans for water and soil resources. The aim is to prepare and implement agricultural development and rural reconstruction projects in a package development program for all areas with agricultural growth potential.

A recently passed law called "Agricultural Development in Agricultural Poles" provides for establishment of Agricultural Development Authorities in every major agricultural region. These authorities are expected to prepare integrated rural development programs to be carried out, with their help, through farm corporations, production cooperatives or other large private firms. The authorities also will take the responsibility to construct all infrastructural facilities and provide all agricultural and technical services, training and marketing either directly or through contracts with private contractors and institutions. According to this law, the legal and executive power of three ministries—the Ministry of Agriculture, the Ministry of Cooperatives and Rural Affairs and the Ministry of Energy—will be delegated to regional Agricultural Development Authorities. In the center, an Agricultural Development Council, consisting of four ministers, will coordinate and supervise regional plans and programs. The new organizational setup, it is believed, will start a new thrust at modernizing Iran's agricultural and rural life, following the implementation of land reform. An important feature of this law, in contrast with previous agribusiness regulations, is that it provides the farmers of the selected "poles" with the choice of either organizing themselves in the form of farm corporations/production cooperatives or any other form ensuring a farm size no less than 20 hectares, or selling out their lands to the government, which would in turn create farming units of the agribusiness type. The emphasis, as noted, is laid on resource management objectives with policies aiming at the maximum possible degree of self-sufficiency in basic foods.

A related objective declared by His Imperial Majesty The Shahanshah Aryamehr is that rural income and standard of living reach as nearly as possible that of the urban population. This latter objective could simultaneously be achieved with the first one if the average size of the farm ownership was sufficient.

Presently, however, the average farmer is living on about 2.8 hectares of land, which cannot provide him with a fair standard of living even with the highest level of technology and management. Given the highest possible level of technology, and assuming 60 percent of the income of the rural population to be earned from off-farm activities, a minimum average ownership of 12 hectares would be needed in order to achieve a rural per capita income close to the urban by 1992. This implies, with a view to land and water constraint, a 65 percent reduction in the number of existing owner-cultivators through a deliberate scheme stimulating small holders to sell out their lands to more efficient farmers and to find jobs in other sectors. Without such a drastic rise in the rural per capita income, no major improvement in rural housing and environment or level of education and health can be sustained. This emphasis on income policy does not preclude the government's carrying out interim social programs. The transfer of redundant farmers to other jobs would require the creation of new orientation and training courses and placement activities for rural people on a very large scale. The establishment of polytechnic schools and technical training centers to substitute for the existing general schools has to receive top priority in our education system during the coming decades.

Investment Requirement

As noted from the above, the development of agriculture may not be planned separately from the development of the rural community, and both of these rely heavily on human resource development in the rural sector. The main solutions for the problem of the gap between rural and urban sectors have to be found in the transfer of the redundant labor force from agricultural to nonagricultural jobs; the modernization of agriculture; and the development of viable agricultural towns. These objectives require heavy investments and a great deal of organizational and social mobilization work. The Fifth Development Plan has earmarked, out of public resources, over $3.7 billion for agriculture, plus over $2 billion for irrigation facilities and rural reconstruction, and $255 million for rural electrification. Private investment in agriculture is estimated to be about 1 billion. Sizable amounts are also included for rural education and health under respective chapters. Accordingly, it is planned that all primary-school-age children in the rural areas will attend schools by the end of the Fifth Plan. It will, however, take another three consecutive five-year plans, with a multiple of such investments in the rural sector, before the standard of living of the rural person can reach anywhere near that of the urban counterpart. This would be in addition to a much greater investment to be made in nonagricultural sectors in order to create job opportunities for the three-quarters of the rural labor force. According to a tentative perspective plan, Iran's per capita GNP is expected to rise to about $4,600 by 1992. With a 1.2-million agricultural labor force and an agricultural sector GNP of $8 billion * in 1992, the income of the farmers will reach $6,800 or about $1,900** per head. Even with an urban-rural income ratio of 1.4:1, an additional income of $1,800 has to be generated for the same man through off-farm jobs. The required fixed investment for the generation of this level of income for a 1.2-million labor force would be about $23 billion.† In addition, the fixed investment needed to create job opportunities for the 3.2 million†† redundant rural laborers during the next three plans would be in the area of $155 billion. Thus, an average annual investment of $12 billion will have to be made outside agriculture during the next three plan periods, just for the sake of reducing the number of people depending on agriculture and in order to diversify the rural sources of income.

The housing conditions in the rural sector have to be improved in coordination with rural income growth. To reconstruct 80 percent of the existing substandard houses through 1992, about 3.5 million houses, at a total cost of no less than $21 billion, have to be built during this period.

The above-mentioned figures provide just a partial picture of the future investment requirements for rural development in Iran, as they do not cover investment in education, health care, environment, culture, roads, electricity and other infrastructural facilities. This partial analysis

---

*As foreseen in National Cropping Plan, Interim Report, Volume 3, p.X.10.

**On the basis of a dependency ratio of 3.5:1 defined as the total number of family members divided by the number of working members.

†On the basis of an incremental capital output ratio of 3:1.

††About one million new members of the labor force are to enter the market during this period.

can help only to illustrate the order of magnitude of the resources Iran needs to mobilize during the next decades in order to face the rural challenge, along with the other challenges of economic, social and technological progress.

Iran's agrarian reform started with a political decision taken by His Imperial Majesty The Shahanshah Aryamehr and supported by the people. The original aim of land reform was to secure a fair distribution of wealth and income in the rural sector. At the end of the land distribution program on January 1972, His Imperial Majesty declared a new phase characterized by land consolidation under a cooperative system, aiming at increasing its productivity. In several statements made at later occasions, H.I.M. has declared that in the new phase Iran's primary objective will be to bring about an equilibrium between the level of income in the rural and urban sectors through an increase in agricultural productivity and an expansion of nonagricultural job opportunities. This objective is undoubtedly beyond the scope of the conventional agrarian reform programs. It more appropriately fits within the framework of a more general program to be called "rural reform," implying change in the social and economic structure as well as change in the living conditions of the rural society, along a line asymptotical to the urban. The most important components of this program will consist of a new education and training policy specially designed for rural reform, reduction of the number of people depending on agriculture and consolidation of smaller farm units into larger ones and small villages into towns equipped with all basic facilities. The implementation of this program puts a high demand on the financial and manpower resources of the country with a complete reorganization of the relevant administrative setup during the next two decades.

Comments and Discussion

Discussion at a plenary session and workshop dealt with various issues raised by Ismail Ajami and R. Doroudian. In "Agrarian Reform, Modernization of Peasants and Agricultural Development in Iran," Mr. Ajami commented on the growing interdependence of the agricultural and nonagricultural sectors; the need to accelerate farm production; and the importance of furthering agricultural development for many reasons—not just economic ones. He discussed theories of agricultural development and the types of agricultural production structures existing in Iran before the land reform program.

   Mr. Doroudian introduced "Modernization of Rural Economy in Iran" with comments on the objectives of the land reform program—to create economic motivation for increased agricultural production and to improve income distribution in the rural sector—and on models created to fill financial and management gaps created by the disappearance of the landlords, including rural and cooperative societies, agribusiness, farm corporations and production cooperatives. Mr. Doroudian briefly evaluated the performances of these different structures and concluded by outlining the government's agricultural objectives in the next 20 years, including modernization of agriculture and massive restructuring of the rural areas.

Responding to a European's questions about plans to develop a self-sufficient "rural elite" as a means of retaining talented people in the agricultural sector, Mr. Doroudian and his colleagues observed that shifting some industry to rural areas will create new types of jobs and that creating a rural elite, essential to bridging the gap between rural areas and cities, may be achieved through such means as rural education, political participation by peasant farmers, agrarian reform leading to the deposition of some old elites and the development of new elites (especially through giving rural youth opportunities for higher education), and the organization of agricultural cooperatives that give peasants a role in management and decision making.

Priority Given to Agricultural Development

In the workshop session on agricultural development, a European participant suggested that the changing world food situation may make "urban bias" outdated; agricultural development may no longer be ignored in favor of industrial development. If the Iranian government recognizes the changing, *i.e.,* growing, role of agriculture, it may want to increase its investments in agriculture, possibly including investment in expensive new technology like desalination plants. Another European concurred that maximum effort is needed in Iran to further agricultural development—an effort equal to that being made for industrial growth. Iranians responding to these views affirmed that Iranian agriculture has been revolutionized in 15 years, with much accomplished, especially as a result of land reform, which has produced social change and incentives to agricultural production, and that the government's Fifth Development Plan gives the agricultural sector much higher priority than previous plans, with substantial allocations for social/economic development in rural areas. (An Iranian noted with respect to desalination programs that these would not be feasible now but might be possible a decade hence.) Although the government recognizes the need for even greater efforts in the agricultural sector, the problems are vast: three-quarters of Iran's villages have fewer than 250 inhabitants, *i.e.,* about 40 families, and are widely spread out and difficult to reach.

Agricultural Production Strategies

An Iranian emphasized the need for a "framework," an overall strategy for increasing agricultural production that treats modernization of agriculture with reference to other major problems including the world food, energy, population and environment crises. All are interrelated; for example, new technologies useful for increasing agricultural production may need to be reviewed in light of their energy requirements. In the speaker's view there are four related issues bearing on agricultural production: (1) economies of scale, *i.e.,* the desirable size of farms; (2) the role of incentives and social institutions; (3) the role and types of technology; and (4) attitudes toward agriculture and the value orientation of the political elite, who may have an "urban bias." Consideration of these factors in an integrated way may lead to a production strategy. Another Iranian concurred that the government must form a master strategy taking into account all relevant factors, including population, consumption, land and water resources, land policy and other factors. A national cropping plan is due shortly, which will set some regional goals.

A European responded that emphasis should be given first to the land—the capital asset—involving people who know the land and, second, to minimizing imports and developing import substitutes. In his view there are obvious benefits to large-scale farming but operations may suffer if the scale becomes too large and people who lack knowledge are involved in planning.

Other relevant views on the question of scale included the view expressed by several Iranians and non-Iranians that the size of Iran's farms must be increased, through such means as the farm corporations and production cooperatives. An American attributed the vast agricultural output of the United States and

Australia/New Zealand to economies of scale, along with superior organization and a free market; he urged rapid modernization of Iranian agriculture and applauded the government for encouraging both large- and small-scale farming. (An Iranian noted that the farms remaining in private hands after land reform were large-scale mechanized farms practicing modern techniques.)

The question of whether farm corporations and production cooperatives are effective was raised by one participant who noted that agricultural cooperatives in socialist states are often managed by people with urban backgrounds who have theoretical knowledge of farm production but lack agricultural experience; in the Soviet Union, individual farmers are three and a half times more productive than agricultural cooperatives. He emphasized the need for local management of farm corporations and agricultural cooperatives rather than direction from the center. Farmers who know what they are doing should play the major role. An Iranian observed on this point that work in the farm corporations and production cooperatives is divided among groups of farmers so that each participating group knows its responsibilities and how to achieve them. A participant also warned that some kinds of mechanization not only require huge amounts of capital but may force farmers beyond their capability for operating, maintaining and repairing equipment. Technology, including complicated machinery, should not be beyond the capacity of farmers to handle.

Agricultural Trade and Pricing Policies

Major subjects for discussion were the related questions of prices paid farmers for agricultural products, market prices for food products and Iran's food imports.

An Iranian participant indicated that the agricultural sector has grown only 3 percent, about the same rate as the population growth. He attributed this in part to the government's policy of keeping prices, including food prices, constant for the lowest income groups. Incentives for farmers have been weakened.

Several speakers observed that farmers may warrant protection in the form of government subsidies; that farmers are not adequately compensated for what are, in fact, highly skilled jobs; that government subsidies to farmers may be a way of absorbing monetary surpluses currently contributing to a high rate of inflation; and that increased prices might stimulate increased agricultural productivity.

Various spokesmen replied that price policy is recognized by the government as being an essential tool for furthering agricultural production. Although there is no real overall price policy as yet, minimum prices have been established for some commodities, including wheat, barley, soybeans, milk and meat. The minimum price for wheat rose from 7 to 10 rials last year; the price of rice was also increased. One official expressed reservations about increasing prices further at this time: such a rise might stimulate only a small group of commercial farmers, leaving out a majority of farmers with little marketable surplus. Other means, such as input subsidy, soft loans, marketing facilities and promotion, should receive more emphasis now. Another participant suggested that if the government were to subsidize one kind of product, this might affect others; a policy is needed, but prices for products must be related within some overall framework.

The relatively low rate of agricultural production has led to extensive food imports, an Iranian speaker observed. (Other factors identified by participants as contributing to the need for food imports include the rise in population and a much higher rate of increase in consumption resulting from greatly increased per capita income, as compared with the maximum possible growth in agricultural production.) Several participants indicated that Iran is now importing about 30 percent of its food (although a planning official estimated that Iran may become 80 percent self-sufficient in the intermediate future). The government is paying high prices for food imports but subsidizing these so that the prices to consumers are low, *i.e.,* it has bought wheat abroad at 15 rials and is selling this to consumers at 7.5 rials. Some participants expressed alarm that Iran is becoming dependent on food imports and hoped that increased agricultural production could be achieved and the present trend reversed.

Government Aid to Farmers in Lieu of Subsidies

The government is pursuing an integrated approach to rural development, it was observed, and has provided many types of assistance to farmers short of direct subsidies. These have included substantial aid in the form of (1) fertilizer, purchased abroad at high prices but sold to the farmer at low cost; (2) seeds; (3) pesticides and disease control programs; (4) animal hygiene and vaccination programs; (5) subsidies to pay farm managers in the case of large-scale farms; (6) extension services; (7) large-scale irrigation programs; (8) credit; (9) subsidies for mechanization; and (10) grants-in-aid for infrastructure projects. The government has also supported Literacy Corps projects in rural areas, made huge investments in dams and irrigation and subsidized supplies of consumer goods, like sugar and tea, in remote areas so that their prices are comparable to city prices despite the added cost of transport.

Government policies with respect to farm credit were discussed by one speaker, who noted that outright grants or a combination of grants and loans are made available to farmers for such undertakings as (1) feasibility studies and land development; (2) construction of on-farm irrigation and drainage networks; (3) land leveling; (4) well digging; (5) rural and forest industries; (6) service companies; and (7) importing and transporting livestock from abroad.

The wide range of government programs aimed at furthering rural development and stimulating agricultural production was applauded by various participants.

Distribution Mechanisms and Problems

Problems in distribution were identified as one factor adversely affecting agricultural production, including both heavy profit making—up to 50 percent—by middlemen, who purchase, store and distribute agricultural products, and the shortage of warehouses at some seasons, which dampens prices. Steps are being taken by some farmers, however, to form marketing cooperatives that will own small warehouses on a regional basis. (The government provides larger warehouses.) American farm experience, where farmers have banded together to build their own storage and distribution facilities, at savings of 50 percent, was mentioned as a possible model for Iran.

Extent of Farmer Political Activity

Several participants asked about who represents farmers' interests and whether farmers may organize lobbies or pressure groups to obtain higher prices for agricultural products. An Iranian suggested that farmers have relatively little influence on central decision making. Two ministries represent farm interests, but the extent to which they are successful depends somewhat on support from other agencies.

The anticipated emigration of people from rural areas (see section to follow) and unequal concentration of population for greater effectiveness may lead to some radicalization of farmers, it was suggested; *i.e.,* they may become more aware of what they lack. Conversely, a European held, a peasantry that actually owns land is generally a very stabilizing political force. The experiences of countries like Bolivia, Iraq and Spain suggest that, after land reforms, peasants have swung to the center and resisted leftist movements.

Income Distribution

Government policies favoring industry may be helping to increase the gap between a privileged urban bourgeoisie and the rural population, it was suggested. Certainly the rising per capita income of some citizens is in sharp contrast to the situation of peasants, most of whom are outside the market and monetary systems. An Iranian acknowledged that the gap between rich and poor will widen for a while but suggested that it will close later as development takes hold.

Emigration from Rural Areas

Various Iranian officials acknowledged that there is a steady movement of population from rural areas to cities, partly because all steps taken by the government have not been enough to supply a high standard of living for farmers. But this migration is desirable, in the view of several, who affirmed that the agricultural sector, despite population shifts, is still overpopulated and that Iran needs a much more rapid transfer of population from rural to urban areas than has occurred in such countries as Italy. An Iranian indicated that there would not be problems of unemployment in the cities, currently short of labor for services and industries, but some problems will arise in providing needed training and education for displaced persons in order to qualify them for urban employment. The government is already seeking technical assistance from Great Britain and the United States with short-term training programs.

3. Human Resources Development in Iran

Human Resources Development

Human Resources Development: Problems and Prospects

F. Aminzadeh

The development and utilization of human resources have emerged as one of the most important aspects of Iran's development strategy during the 1970s. Over the last decade, the tempo of development has steadily gained momentum. The growth rate of the economy tripled between 1962–63 and 1972–73 from a little over 5 percent to almost 15 percent. National income more than doubled during the 1960s and, with the implementation of the Fifth Development Plan, it is expected to increase more than threefold in five years. Under the impact of this rapid acceleration in the growth of the economy, the human resources sector in Iran is facing both quantitative and qualitative problems of unprecedented magnitude. On the one hand, the demand for labor—in particular, skilled, professional and highly trained manpower—has outstripped the traditional sources of supply. On the other hand, the qualitative changes in the structure of the economy and rising incomes are altering the attitudes and expectations of the people. It is imperative to ensure that the ambitious social and economic goals that the nation has set for itself are supported and carried forward efficiently and expeditiously by its manpower resources. This is by no means an easy task, particularly during a period of dynamic and continuous change. In this context it is important that the issues in human resource development be frequently reviewed and policy measures devised to harmonize the demands of this sector with other elements in the strategy of development.

Human Resources Development—An Overview, 1956–72

In 1956, Iran's population was estimated to be about 19 million with an age structure heavily weighted in favor of younger age groups and with a built-in potential for accelerated growth. The birth rate was high, around 50 per thousand, and the death rate declined. By 1966 it had reached 17.8 per thousand while the birth rate remained at the fairly high level of 48. Population increased at an average annual rate of about 3 percent. This high rate of growth further accentuated the young age structure of the population and lowered its rate of participation in economic activity. The literacy level of the population was low but it increased appreciably during the decade 1956–66, from 15.4 percent to 29.4 percent. There was a steady trend in urbanization, the share of urban population increasing from 31.4 to 38.5 percent. These demographic parameters are summarized in Table 41 (see the appendix to this essay).

This broad demographic picture simplifies the situation to a great extent but provides many points of interest. Of the latter, a few are of particular relevance in today's context. First, the birth rate remained relatively stagnant during the intercensual period while the death rate declined. This, together with the young age structure of the population, strengthened the probability of continued rapid growth, for it was apparent that not only will the size of successive future cohorts of reproductive age be larger but the rate of natural increase would also accelerate as the gap between birth rate and death rate widens. Second, neither the age structure nor the resultant low participation could be regarded as unfavorable in the short-term in the prevailing economic situation, which was one of slow growth. Third, although literacy levels were rising, which was a matter for satisfaction, their overall impact on the educational status of the population was relatively slow. By 1966, just over half a million persons had had more than four years of secondary school. Finally, while urbanization was taking place under a deliberate policy of industrialization and infrastructure development, its implications for human resource development were not fully apparent.

In order to construct a comparable picture for 1972, it is necessary to rely on the results of various household surveys conducted in the country in the intervening period.[1] The results of these surveys need to be interpreted with caution as they do not necessarily reflect the actual variation in the characteristics under study because of differences in scope, coverage, concepts and definitions, as well as in methodology. Moreover, estimates obtained from these different surveys often seem to imply substantial sampling errors; the final picture, therefore, has to be constructed with the help of assumptions drawn from a variety of other sources. The demographic parameters for 1972 presented in Table 42 reflect these limitations. (All tables are in the appendix to this essay.)

Over the fairly long period from 1956 to 1972, some significant trends can be discerned in these characteristics. The dissimilarity in the rate of decline of the crude birth rate and death rate is one item of policy significance. During the 16-year period, the birth rate fell by 14.6 percent while the death rate fell by almost 40 percent. It may be observed that during 1956–66, the comparable figures were 11 percent and 24.7 percent. This widening gap between the rates of decline implies that much greater effort would need to be made to induce a fall in birth rates in future years in order to stabilize the rate of population growth within reasonable limits. Although there was a slight shift in the age structure in favor of the working-age group, 15–64, the overall, as well as male, participation rates declined. This can be attributed largely to the impact of the expansion of educational facilities and increased retention of children in the school system.

It is important to note that the level of female participation was maintained. There was a steady improvement on the educational side, and by and large the imbalance between educational output and manpower demand remained qualitative. Urbanization also maintained a steady pace but was gradually moving toward a critical level.

The period was marked by a phenomenal expansion of the educational system at all levels. School enrollments increased more than threefold between 1959 and 1972, while vocational and technical school enrollments increased sevenfold. In the field of higher education, there was more than a threefold increase in enrollments (see Table 43). The quantitative expansion was accompanied by various structural and qualitative reforms. The deficiencies of education in terms of quantity and quality were often discussed, and a vigorous program for matching education with economic and social requirements was launched in the early 1970s.

The overall labor supply situation during this period was one of surplus. In 1956, the size of the labor force was 6.066 million, with 2.6 percent unemployment. By 1966, the labor force had increased to 7.584 million with 9.6 percent unemployment. However, if the seasonally unemployed are included among the employed in accordance with the international definition, the unemployment rate falls to 3.7 percent. It is noteworthy that by 1972 even this low rate of unemployment was reduced further. The only evidence of unemployment that is available comes from the household survey of the Ministry of Labor for December 1972–January 1973. The estimate is on the order of 88,000, or 1.15 percent of the survey labor force. Such a low magnitude of unemployment must be regarded as marginal.

However, underemployment continued to be a feature of the labor supply situation, particularly in the rural sector. In 1966, 11 percent of the employed population was reported to be working 28 hours per week or less. By 1972, this had been reduced to 2.2 percent, but the proportion working below 36 hours per week remained almost unchanged between the two years.

The distribution of employment by broad sectors of economic activity showed some distinctive trends (see Table 44). There was a steady decline in the share of agriculture in the employment pattern. In the decade 1956–66, this took place in favor largely of industrial employment, but in the subsequent period employment in the service sector apparently increased faster. This shift in the employment pattern was largely a consequence of a deliberate policy of industrialization and urban orientation.

It was natural that this policy made more demands on technical, managerial and production workers, who increased in response (see Table 45). Some unemployment among the educated was reported both in 1966 and 1972, but in both cases it was negligible in proportion to the total labor force.

This brief overview of the human resources situation in the period 1956–72 conceals many complexities. However, for the present purpose it is not necessary to enter into a rigorous technical discussion of the data or their interpretation. Suffice it to say that it was substantially a period of continued labor surplus even as the processes of industrialization and urbanization were going apace. The balance between manpower demand and supply appeared to be tilted in favor of supply. For most categories of high-level manpower, supply and demand appeared to be matched in the latter part of the 1960s in quantitative terms.

Fifth Development Plan: The Changing Context

In part, this apparent balance was a result of rapid educational expansion. In part, it could be attributed to the continuation of a fairly large traditional sector in the economy where the process of technological change had not yet made a deep enough impact. It would also be true to say that, at least partly, the native ability and inventiveness of Iran's labor force was able to cope with the rate of change and meet both the qualitative and the quantitative challenge of the developing economic situation.

What could not be foreseen sufficiently clearly was that the momentum of development was reaching a critical level, particularly under the persistent push from industrialization, urbanization and modernization. The Fifth Development Plan provided the framework for self-generating growth, substantially changed the economic context and aimed at economic and social objectives hitherto considered beyond reach.

The broad magnitudes for the human resources sector in the Fifth Plan may be summarized as follows: The growth of population and labor force was estimated to continue more or less at the same rate as in the preceding plan period. However, the importance of a more urgent and concerted effort in the field of family planning became clearer, particularly in the context of the social objectives of more equitable income distribution, greater access to education and health facilities and widened base for social security. Only a small change was anticipated in the age structure, but the rate of growth of the economically active population was estimated to increase.[2]

However, on the demand side, it seemed clear that the nature and magnitude of planned investment would create significantly more employment opportunities than the supply lines could meet (see Table 47).

It was not only in the overall labor supply that a shortfall developed. Indeed, this would not be so serious by itself. What is more important from a manpower viewpoint is that shortages are estimated to arise in a wide variety of professional, managerial, technical and skilled occupations (see Table 48).

It may be observed here that these estimates rest on several assumptions and, depending on the pace of development and the realization of physical and financial targets, they could undergo considerable modification during the remainder of the plan period. However, they indicate very clearly both the direction and the magnitude of the change in the human resources sector.

It was natural, therefore, to set for the educational system the short-term objective of meeting quickly as large a share of the anticipated demand for trained manpower as possible. As shown in Table 49, this would involve a doubling of enrollments at the elementary level, a 46 percent increase at the secondary level, and a 160 percent increase in higher education. This expansion of education and training programs is expected to meet a very substantial proportion of the additional manpower requirements. Nevertheless, as the table shows, significant shortfalls could develop in critical categories. The policy implication of this is not difficult to comprehend. On the one hand, it is necessary to make a vigorous effort to increase the overall supply of labor in the economy. On the other hand, ad hoc arrangements need to be made to meet urgent manpower needs until such time as they can be indigenously satisfied.

The Emerging Problems

It is in this quantitative context that the problems in the human resources sector should be viewed. The first two years of the Fifth Plan are over, and some experience has already been gained in dealing with these problems.

It has already been mentioned that one of the most important aspects of human resource development in Iran is that of matching demand and supply. This has assumed a great deal of urgency in the context of accelerated development. Moreover, it is apparent that there can be no return to a labor surplus situation in the foreseeable future. In the long run, the increased supply of additional workers to the economy can be generated by manipulating the factors that govern the participation of women in economic activity. Women have traditionally played a minor role in the economy and their participation rates in the labor force have been low. This situation would undoubtedly undergo a change with greater urbanization and spread of education. However, the main question human resource planners have to answer is whether the rate of change can be accelerated to close the gap between the overall demand and supply of labor. There are many social and institutional factors that need to be overcome, particularly in the rural sector.

Two basic approaches to which attention is being given at present are (1) identification of factors that will induce the seasonal female workers in agriculture to become full-time workers, and (2) identification of jobs where male labor can be replaced by female labor in the urban sector. Policy packages can be developed around these once the initial research effort is completed and the required programs can be developed for providing training or price-wage incentives.

A change of approach and emphasis is similarly needed in the field of education and training.

Accelerated skill development programs for professional, managerial and technical personnel can help improve productivity and, in the short-term, bridge to some extent the quantitative gap by qualitative upgrading. A few such programs have been organized and their experience has been encouraging. However, in order to make a greater impact, the change has to permeate all educational institutions from the university to the vocational school. The private sector must also play a much greater role in organizing intensive training and career development programs. In the industrial sector, it may be necessary to organize upgrading training in every shop floor that has the required capacity and facilities simply because the building of institutions and training of teachers and instructors takes time. The training gap to be filled is enormous and the efforts required would therefore have to be both extensive and intensive. A resource that can be used with greater advantage in this regard is the know-how available in collaborative enterprises with foreign companies.

A similar resource is available in the Iranian professionals studying and working abroad. In 1973–74, more than 20,000 Iranian students were abroad following various courses of advanced study. In addition, several thousand professional personnel were reported to be working abroad. The knowledge and experience of these personnel would prove to be invaluable in the country's development if they could be attracted back to serve here even for limited periods. Several efforts have been made toward this end. Mention may be made of a recent exercise in which a list of 457 doctors working abroad and willing to return was compiled and circulated to prospective employers. There is a clear need to widen this effort and initiate a comprehensive program for attracting back technical, professional and scientific personnel studying and working abroad. The first steps in this direction should be an in-depth review of the existing situation, the systematic collection of information on these personnel and establishing contacts between them and prospective employers.

In the short term, some use of foreign labor is unavoidable in a shortage situation. This aspect has been receiving continuing attention since 1970.[3] During 1974–75, about 7,000 work permits were issued to foreign workers. Recently, government-to-government agreements have been signed for bringing qualified professional and technical personnel into Iran to fill specific positions. There are several aspects here that need to be carefully considered. First, the decision to permit foreign workers to take employment in the country presupposes a full knowledge of the employment market for the particular skill as well as the availabilities in the region. This involves continuous effort at investigation, inspection and decision making. Second, the social aspects of importing into the country large numbers of foreign workers from different countries and in different categories are important. Third, the organizational arrangements required for this purpose should be adequate in view of the magnitude and nature of work involved. Much experience has been gained in this regard over the last few years. It seems appropriate to review the situation from time to time and adjust the various policy elements in accordance with changing needs. It is important to emphasize that in the course of time the manpower shortage would be made good by locally available personnel. The basic manpower policy of the country seeks to ensure this. It is, therefore, necessary to be selective in approach and to identify priority sectors and categories in which employment of foreign workers needs to be encouraged.

The rapid growth of the economy is bringing about changes in the structure of employment. Between 1956 and 1966, the share of wage earners in the economy rose from 45.6 percent to 48.1 percent. The absolute numbers increased by more than 725,000. The data for 1972 are not strictly comparable, but it seems certain that the increase of employment in manufacturing, construction and service sectors has accelerated the growth of wage-earning categories. This tendency would be further strengthened in the near future. The growth of wage earners in the economy would raise important problems for wage-price policy, savings and consumption, and above all the need for training. Moreover, as an essential aspect of modernization, it would require greater commitment of the work force to industrial discipline and changes in technology. In such a situation, the role of the farmer, the agricultural worker or the self-employed entrepreneur could become relatively depressed. From a human resources point of view, this should be avoided. The experience of several other countries shows that in a period of transition from predominantly agrarian to industrial society, it is necessary to support the self-employed in order to avoid disruptions in the economy arising out of rapid change, at least until such time as the industrial work force matures. A further change can be anticipated from the faster growth of service sector employment in the 1980s. With increasing levels of income and changes in the pattern of consumption, the nature and level of services to be provided by the economy should undergo changes, and these in turn would raise training and productivity problems of a different type. The managerial, supervisory and other specialized skills that this shift requires would involve a fair transformation of present attitudes and practices. Many of these changes can be foreseen, and preparatory steps can be taken on the human resources side to smooth the process of adaptation.

The movement of the economy from a labor surplus to a labor shortage position has widened the entire opportunity structure of the work force. There is evidence of greater turnover in skilled and professional categories. And as the demand for trained personnel rises, an accentuation of these trends can be anticipated. The problem of matching opportunities and expectations could thus arise very early in this process. Three factors would contribute to this trend: rapid increase in wages, continuing shortage of skills and the transmitting of these pressures to educational and training institutions. Minimum wages have increased by more than 50 percent over the last two years. The wages of skilled workers are going up still faster, and, in addition, workers participate in the profits of the enterprises where they are working. There is also a trend toward concentration of income groups in the income bracket of between 60,000 and 120,000 rials per year. It is natural that with the support given to farm-gate prices, agricultural incomes are also rising. These rising incomes are in turn changing the expectation levels of the young labor force entrant, particularly with the premium currently attached to his skill. It is inevitable that the wage push would alter the traditional social structures, even as the relative status of different occupations changes with industrial growth and related financial incentives. Social mobility can be fostered through these changes and with increasing education. It can be foreseen that these changes would in the early years favor blue-collar employment, while in the latter years the emphasis will shift to white-collar employment. There will also be qualitative shifts in the nature of work along with these changes.

Outlook for the Future

It is difficult to capture all the various qualitative dimensions of human resource development and utilization into one narrative. It is relatively easier to forecast the quantitative aspects. A perspective of the manpower and employment situation over the 20-year period 1972–92 has been developed with the help of available data. These reflect some of the shifts mentioned earlier. The forecast is summarized in Table 50. That forecast is provisional at present. It will be revised from time to time as more data and information become available. It is hoped that rolling forecasts will be developed in the future to keep the manpower situation under continuing review.

Under the massive increases in manufacturing and service sector employment indicated in this forecast, the primary need would be to increase the adaptability of the labor force to change—change in technology, industrial organization, urban discipline and change in attitudes and practices to those of a modernized economy. This, in turn, would involve continuous adjustment in the education and training system—adjustment not only in numbers, which are relatively easy to manipulate, but also in courses and curricula, training methodology and in creating an environment for rapid absorption of new knowledge and techniques. It will be necessary for the system to foresee the new demands arising years hence and prepare itself to meet the manpower challenge—not lag behind change, as was the experience in the recent past. A bold forward view would be needed because the production of trained personnel with the right skills, in right numbers at the right time, takes enormous effort and time. And time is of the essence in today's human resource dynamics.

It is evident that in this endeavor the responsibility for research, investigation and planning must be shared between planners as well as users of manpower. The organizational arrangements in various governmental agencies for manpower planning would need to be further strengthened. The private sector would also have to play an active role in human resource development. A much greater effort would necessarily be required to coordinate the activities in this field. It would soon become imperative to bring together all the diverse elements of the manpower policy into a coherent national statement of objectives, policies and programs.

A human resource development strategy cannot be viewed in isolation. It must form an integral part of the overall framework of national social and economic development and should buttress the larger goals that this framework implies, implicitly and explicitly. This consideration has dominated the reasoning underlying the presentation made above. There are many gaps in the data that have to be bridged.

Much more groundwork must be completed to ensure greater manpower preparedness in the future. It is essential that human resource planning become a continuous concern of all major governmental, as well as private sector, agencies.

Table 41
Demographic Parameters

	1956	1966
Total Population (millions)	19.1	26.1
Vital Statistics (per thousand)		
Crude Birth Rate	48.50	46.48
Crude Death Rate	22.2	17.8
Age Structure (percent)		
Below 15 years	42.0	46.0
15-64 years	54.0	50.0
Over 65 years	4.0	4.0
Literacy Rate (percent of population 7 years and over)		
Total	15.4	29.4
Male	22.4	40.1
Female	8.0	17.9
Share of Urban Population (percent)	31.4	38.5
Economically Active Population (percent of population 10 years and over)		
Total	47.5	46.1
Male	83.9	77.4
Female	9.2	12.6

Note: For both census years, adjusted population estimates have been used. The crude birth rate and death rate are also estimates. Data on the economically active population for the two censuses are not strictly comparable because of change in the reference period.

Table 42
Demographic Parameters, 1972

Total Population (million)	31.045
Vital Statistics (per thousand)	
Crude Birth Rate	42.7
Crude Death Rate	43.4
Age Structure (percent)	
Below 15 years	45.5
15-64 years	51.5
Over 65 years	3.0
Literacy Rate (percent of population 7 years and over)	
Total	36.9
Male	47.7
Female	25.5
Share of Urban Population (percent)	42.8
Economically Active Population (percent of population 10 years and over)	
Total	42.5
Male	67.8
Female	12.5

Table 43
Growth of Educational System

	1959		1972	
	Number of Institutions	Enroll-ment	Number of Institutions	Enroll-ment
Elementary Education (primary and orientation)	9,289	1,327	18,030	3,534
Secondary Education	1,163	253	2,425	617
Vocational and Technical Education	91	8	277	57
Teacher Training	55	4	88	26
Higher Education	—	23	—	74

Note: Enrollments are in thousands. The data for 1959 are taken from the Statistical Abstract for 1968 while those for 1972 have been taken from Educational Statistics Department of Coordination for Educational Planning, Ministry of Education, 1974.

Table 44
Sectoral Distribution of Employment
(percent)

	1956	1966	1972
Agriculture	56.3	46.2	39.8
Industry	20.1	27.1	29.4
Services	23.6	26.7	30.8

Note: 1972 figures are estimated.

Table 45
Occupational Pattern of Employment
(percent)

	1956	1966	1972
Professional, Technical and Related Workers	1.6	2.9	3.5
Administrative, Managerial and Clerical Workers	3.1	3.0	4.3
Sales Workers	5.8	7.1	8.5
Service Workers	7.7	7.2	6.3
Agricultural Workers	55.6	47.1	48.5
Production Workers	22.6	29.0	28.7
Workers Not Elsewhere Classified	3.6	3.7	0.2
Total	100.0	100.0	100.0

Iran: Past, Present and Future

Table 46
Demographic Parameters, 1977-78

Total Population ('000)	35,922
Net Addition During Fifth Plan ('000)	4,877
Vital Statistics (per thousand)[4]	
Crude Birth Rate	42,7
Crude Death Rate	13,4
Age Structure (percent)	
Below 15 years	45,2
15-64 years	51,8
Over 65 years	3,0
Economically Active Population (percent 10 years and over)	
Total	42.2
Male	69.1
Female	14.1
Net Addition to Labor Force (1973-77) ('000)	1.391

Table 47
Distribution of New Employment Opportunities During the Fifth Development Plan by Sectors[5]

Sector	Number of New Jobs	Percentage of Total
Agriculture	129,600	6.1
Industry and Mining	846,000	40.0
Oil and Gas	12,500	0.6
Water and Electricity	44,000	2.2
Construction	528,000	25.0
Services	551,900	26.1
Total	2,112,000	100.0
Net Addition to Labor Force	1,390,800	—

Table 48
Manpower Supply and Demand
During the Fifth Development Plan by Major Occupations [6]
('000)

Category	Demand	Supply
Engineers	36.4	20.3
Medical Personnel	44.1	21.5
Educational Personnel	287.4	230.0
Other Personnel	279.5	266.0
Technicians	116.6	75.0
Skilled and Semiskilled Workers	810.0	250.0
Unskilled Workers	538.0	528.0
Total	2,112.0	1,390.8

Table 49
Educational Enrollments in the Fifth Development Plan
('000)

Elementary Education (primary and orientation)	7,170
Secondary Education	904
Vocational and Technical Education	560
Higher Education	190

Note: Includes the annual capacity of vocational training centers for skilled and semiskilled workers as well as all technical training carried out by various ministries and teacher training for primary schools.

Table 50
Human Resources Perspective

	1972	1982	1992
I. Population			
Total Population ('000)	31,045	41,469	53,532
Active Population ('000)	8,851	12,002	16,449
General Activity Rate (percent)	28.5	28.9	30.6
II. Employment by Sectors ('000)			
Agriculture	3,535 (39.8)	3,100 (25.6)	2,800 (17.2)
Industry and Mining	1,789 (20.1)	3,355 (27.8)	4,746 (29.1)
Oil	50 (0.6)	75 (0.6)	75 (0.5)
Construction	699 (7.9)	1,034 (8.5)	1,262 (7.7)
Utilities	80 (0.9)	92 (0.8)	152 (1.0)
Services	2,730 (30.7)	4,447 (36.7)	7,243 (44.5)
III. Employment by Occupations ('000) (percent)			
Skilled and Technical Workers	408 (4.6)	842 (7.0)	1,448 (8.9)
Managers and High-Level Administrators	18 (0.2)	121 (1.0)	407 (2.5)
Clerical Workers	230 (2.6)	423 (3.5)	928 (5.7)
Sales Workers	701 (7.9)	1,173 (9.7)	1,953 (12.0)
Agricultural Workers	3,526 (39.7)	3,074 (25.4)	2,767 (17.0)
Miners and Resource-Exploitation Workers	20 (0.2)	116 (1.0)	325 (2.0)
Transport Workers	977 (11.1)	1,392 (11.5)	1,628 (10.0)
Production and Professional Workers	1,768 (19.9)	3,389 (28.0)	4,883 (30.0)
Specialized Service Workers	1,235 (13.9)	1,573 (13.0)	1,939 (11.9)

Note: The table has been compiled on the basis of exercises completed in 1973, the results of which have been summarized in the two papers mentioned in Note 2. Both the population and labor-force estimates are based on Assumption I of PBO-Shorter projections.

Footnotes

1. There are two principal series of surveys, the current population survey, conducted annually by the Statistical Center of Iran, and the household sample survey, conducted by the General Department of Statistics of the Ministry of Labor.

2. A considerable amount of technical groundwork was completed in preparation for the Fifth Plan. Among the important papers are (1) "Iran's Population: Past, Present and Future," and (2) "Perspective of Manpower and Employment Planning, Iran (1972–1992)," Population and Manpower Bureau, Plan and Budget Organization, Tehran, 1973.

3. Regulations concerning the issuance of official work permits were approved in November 1970.

4. These are average rates for 1971–76 used for projecting the population.

5. Iran's *Fifth Development Plan, 1973–1978* (Revised), Plan and Budget Organization, January 1975, Table 6, page 73.

6. *Iran's Fifth Development Plan, op. cit.*, Table 47, p. 76.

Comments and Discussion

In "Human Resources Development: Problems and Prospects," F. Aminzadeh stressed the importance given to the development and utilization of human resources in Iran's development strategy. He described Iran's population, with reference to such factors as age, literacy, geographic location and productivity; the remarkable expansion of the educational system at all levels, including threefold to sevenfold increases in enrollment at different levels; employment, by sector and type of job; the framework provided by the Fifth Development Plan for self-generating growth; and problems currently affecting the development and use of human resources.

Academic and Nonformal Education in Iran

At the workshop on human resources, it was noted that Iran's revolution requires education and training as a base. The first eight years of formal schooling have been made obligatory and are free; after that, education is free for those students who promise to serve their country on conclusion of their studies (at prevailing salaries) for a number of years equal to their years of free education after the eighth grade.

The role of higher education is to provide trained manpower for the Iranian labor market, in the view of one participant. Another observed that developing higher education for Iranians in Iran is obviously a key part of economic and social growth. Yet there was some feeling that, despite the growth of higher education opportunities, some higher education may not be totally relevant. It was suggested that, generally speaking, educational standards and curricula at Iranian universities and schools of "higher studies" are not so "high" or relevant to the needs of Iran today and tomorrow as they should be. In addition, they are educating too many students, proportionally, in literary and nontechnical fields and training too many for white-collar work and urban life styles. The lack of sufficient emphasis on technical and vocational training was criticized by several. The mania of some students for degrees, regardless of content, was also criticized. Non-Iranians emphasized that higher education cannot be expected to carry the whole burden of preparing people to participate in the development process. "The university," said one, "is not the principal vehicle of development education."

There was agreement that not all educational institutions in Iran are equal in quality. However, a few Iranian participants stressed, it may be more important in the early stages of development to emphasize quantity of higher education and professional training over very high quality. As one put it, "I would rather have a number of mediocre managers than one excellent manager."

There was agreement, too, that the crust of highly qualified people is still thin in Iran and that the best qualified Iranians are often "overworked" or "overemployed." The latter is not necessarily bad, however, since a good professor may do better to use nonteaching time in some development-related function rather than in irrelevant or unimportant research.

The question was raised of whether Iran should develop advanced research institutions like Rockefeller University. Some participants felt no need to copy the West in this respect, but others suggested that the special needs of development, e.g., research on how to derive edible proteins from hydrocarbons, may not be emphasized sufficiently in advanced countries, thus warranting study in Iran.

A brief exchange on legal education emphasized the value

of training laymen to handle legal responsibilities, especially since 95 percent of local adjudication in Iran was said to be handled by lay magistrates.

It was also observed that, in addition to formal schooling, new thrusts include the use of factories as training institutions, new drives for vocational education and informal education, including the use of radio and TV. At a subsequent session on a communications strategy for Iran, it was reported that one of three Iranian TV channels provides informational and educational programs. National Iranian Radio and Television (NIRT) priorities include using broadcasting for general training and education initially; for programs aimed at the sixth, seventh and eighth grades subsequently; and for news and entertainment in a later phase. Receiving sets have been provided by the government to schools and village cultural centers.

Influx of Educated Youth to Cities

A dilemma identified by several participants is that educated young people in Iran, as in other developing societies, tend to leave the villages where their skills are needed. (This was attributed partly to a tendency to import culture from abroad through TV and other means rather than emphasize indigenous culture, which might help to make rural life more attractive.) The more government planners do to develop education in rural areas, the more they contribute to the departure for cities of educated youth seeking full-time employment or higher education. Ironically, mobile training centers, bringing skills training to the villages, themselves promote mobility.

The Problem of Overseas Training

How to assure the return to Iran, and productive use, of students trained abroad was discussed at length. (An estimated 35,000 Iranian students are currently studying abroad, including 18,000 in the United States.) Although graduates in many disciplines return, an estimated 70 percent of foreign-trained doctors remain abroad, especially doctors trained in the United States. This is one reason for the new emphasis on training paramedicals. Rapid development of large corps of primary health care personnel to serve at the village level is receiving much attention in Iran.

It was not felt that foreign-trained students remain abroad for fear of social discipline at home; many obtain interesting jobs, earn good salaries and marry abroad. The government is trying to tie scholarship aid, at levels of $250 to $400 a month, to commitments to return and work in Iran. Other steps include special recruitment drives involving offers of employment and conveying the sense that there is a relevant place for trained people in Iran's development boom. These are now resulting in the return of approximately 3,000 foreign-trained graduates a year. Too often, however, Western-trained students on return see themselves only as managers and specialists, not workers, and are unwilling to leave Tehran or other major cities with amenities and good schools for their children.

At the special session on education that followed (see following section) several participants expressed the view that Iran is no longer experiencing a "brain drain" problem, as before, insofar as Europe and the United States are concerned, owing to the attractiveness of economic and professional opportunities in Iran today.

Special Session on Education

A number of similar points were made at a special optional session on education that considered, first, the relationship between education, on the one hand, and social development and modernization, on the other. Three topics were suggested as specially relevant: (1) primary education, especially as it relates to the eradication of illiteracy and educating the mass of the people; (2) the relationship between secondary education and higher education, including questions of access and selectivity; and (3) available and potential alternatives at the post-secondary level to the traditional university and the development and testing of innovation within the system.

As in the workshop, participants recognized that Iranian educational opportunities have been greatly expanded at all levels in the past decade and that strong efforts have been made to reach a broader segment of the population with all levels of education. But some problems were identified by Iranian participants, including:

- *The need to make higher education more relevant to people's needs.* The training of rural primary health personnel at Pahlavi University was cited as a constructive development in this regard; another approach to training, termed "sandwich education," involving alternate periods of formal education and practical experience, is under study.
- *Shortages of qualified university professors and other professionals,* coupled with maldistribution of highly qualified people between urban areas, especially Tehran, and lesser cities and rural areas. In addition to more than 11,000 Iranian doctors, Iran employs approximately 3,000 physicians from other developing countries on short-term contracts and still depends on many expatriate faculty.
- *The need to spread qualified teachers and educational administrators very thin* in order to meet the demands of an expanded educational system; this is especially a problem at the elementary and secondary levels, since a very high proportion of the population is under 15, and in rural areas, where villages are often too small to sustain a school; mobile schools, the institution of busing systems and functional literacy programs are being attempted to help meet this problem.
- *A widespread decline of standards.* Factors contributing to lowered standards may include the rapid expansion of education and resulting strains on qualified personnel, the "depressing effect" of government-established minimal standards and too slavish copying of external models without sufficient attention to methodology or the need for adaptation to serve new conditions.

Non-Iranian participants in the session emphasized the importance of flexibility and adaptability, of not being tied down by traditional patterns and rigidities, of developing multiple and varied options to serve varied talents and needs. The difficulty in conferring legitimacy on such alternatives was also recognized, but it was hoped that the extent to which the Iranian educational system seems to be in flux might help obviate this problem, *i.e.,* reduce the overvaluation of traditional programs and the social status they have tended to confer. The opportunities for rural and adult education latent in television and other new technology were mentioned as potentially useful.

A brief but strong plea was also made for development on an international basis of a methodology for talking about educational development that would better identify and interrelate critical elements, including the political and social environment, the educational purpose and mission within the environment, the process of admission and recruitment as related to the foregoing, the nature and relation of curricula, the structure of the system and its relationship to government, and its definition of social purpose.

The co-chairman closed the session with a warning against too great reliance on imported capsule solutions, designed for quick results, and with an endorsement of an educational internationalism in which Third World experience has an important place.

The Role of Women in Iranian Development

Dynamics of Women's Condition in Iran

Mamideh Sedghi and Amad Ashraf

The purpose of this essay is to provide a historical and structural analysis of the changing societal status of women in contemporary Iran. The key structural elements to be examined are the roles assigned to women by the sociocultural elements and economic and political institutions. The concrete relationship of these structures may shed some light on the role of women in a society. As regards Iranian women, the main assumption will be that the modernization of Iran has changed the position of women in the society. Modernization is defined as the processes of change in the polity and social structure that have accompanied Westernism and reformism in the country. This will be tested through an examination of the role of religion and family on the position of women, their place in the economy and the system of production and their participation and attitudes in politics.

Women, Tradition, and Sexuality

Any analysis of women's condition must take into account the concrete cultural context within which they are inserted. It is the role of culture in molding and influencing social relations that significantly forms attitudes, beliefs and norms of a society. Islamic culture within the Iranian social setting has been the determining influence in the creation of an environment in which the role of male domination has been tightly interwoven in social relations.

Islamic history bears the marks of its Arabian origin; cultural values and social norms determining the social status of women in Islamic societies can be traced back to the pre-Islamic practices of ancient Arabian tribes. The burial of unwanted girl children at birth was being practiced and women were barred from holding important positions in public affairs. With the advent of Islam, the Great Prophet Mohammed introduced fundamental and profound changes in tribal practices concerning the status of women. Among the most revolutionary instructions of the Mohammedan Golden Age were abandonment of the tradition of women's burial after birth; allowance of women's participation in public affairs (prominent women like Ayesheh, Zaynab and Fatemeh performed important roles); granting of private property rights to women (British women were given such rights in the 1930s); upgrading maternity status; and setting up rules and regulations concerning marriage and divorce, in order to protect women's social and economic rights.

In the later Islamic era, however, some of the initial revolutionary attitudes and measures were reversed. The traditional view of women's nature is a case in point. Women were considered as "erotic creatures [who were] continually giving trouble to men. . . "[1] As it is expressed in an Iranian novel, women were "imperfect" among the created beings and, "in consequence, capricious and of ill repute, regarding this world and the next for the sake of a moment's desire. . . . "[2] They were, therefore, advised to "lower" their gaze and be modest and "to display of their adornment only that which is apparent, and to draw their veils over their bosoms, and not to reveal their adornment. . . . "[3] This denigrating and dark view of women's nature served a twofold function in social relations. First, it deteriorated women's position both socially and psychologically. Second, it created a situation in which men granted themselves the authority to objectify women as instruments of fulfilling their sexual desires. The maintenance of this taboo is dependent upon the organization of family promoted through marriage. Marriage as a process of transference of authority from father to the husband over the woman reinforces male domination.

According to the traditional Islamic view, marriage, as a common core of the contract, "shows traces of having developed out of the pur-

Iran: Past, Present and Future

chase of the bride; bridegroom concludes the contract with the legal guardian (*wali*) of the bride and he undertakes to pay the nuptial gift (*mahr, sadak*); not to the *wali* as was customary in the pre-Islamic period, but to the wife herself."[4] Thus, marriage is analogous to a commercial transaction in which the woman is the object to transaction to be exchanged for the *mahr*.

In this respect, while women were given private property rights, they were *privatized* as property. This was accomplished through the institution of marriage, which caused the female to be considered the "property of her husband, who, having in fact paid for her, regards himself as entitled exclusively to her services."[5] This privatization of women into the men's world might better be demonstrated by the following passage:

> Women, like jewels, are admired and sought after, but should be protected and guarded lest they be stolen. They are property, valuable property, but really not persons, and must not take upon themselves the prerogative of persons who are, after all, exclusively male.[6]

In all, in spite of its profound teachings of respect for women, particularly mothers, the traditional Islamic culture established the rule of male domination and superiority. While the granting of private property rights to women was introduced, women became privatized as sexual objects and property. To further maintain its rule, male domination was institutionalized through various provisions of marriage, and, finally, the position of women was greatly lowered by giving the absolute and arbitrary right of divorce to men.

Women and Legal Change

The confinement of women by the traditional cultural barriers remained intact until the beginning of the 20th century when Iran underwent an intense period of Westernization and modernization. Among the various historic measures that have been adopted in Iran's modern history to liberate Iranian women from traditional restrictive practices, four are of particular significance. The first is the 1935 decree that banned the wearing of a veil (*chador*), which thus literally opened up new vistas to the Iranian women. The second is the granting of suffrage to women in 1963, as well as the right to run for, and be elected to, the national legislative bodies and to provincial and local elective councils all across the country. The third is the promulgation of the 1967 Family Protection Law (FPL).[7] The fourth is an amendment to the Constitution granting regentship to Shahbanou Farah in 1967. These and other radical measures have paved the way to changing the image of women in Iranian society and to their greater participation in the developmental processes of the past half century.

Important steps in changing women's status are some of the new provisions of the Iranian Civil Codes (CC). Thus, Article 1041 of the CC sets out an age limitation for marriage to prevent the traditional arbitrariness of the father's (or *wali*'s) will in arranging marriages for daughters regardless of their young age. Currently, the minimum age for marriage is 15 for girls and 18 for boys. In exceptional cases, the law provides lower ages for marriage: 13 for girls and 15 for boys. Nevertheless, by 1971, nearly one percent of the total married female population was between 10 and 14, with a higher frequency in the rural areas than urban sections.[8] This may be an indication that the age limitation laws are more effective in the urban than rural areas where about 55 percent of the population resides.

Another measure to change the position of women has been the attempt to discourage polygamy, under the FPL, by requiring men to obtain written permission for their subsequent marriages. The granting of this permission is not, however, prohibited by law. Moreover, contrary to the earlier provisions of the Civil Codes, which required women to have their husband's permission to obtain employment, the FPL grants women the right of employment.

The fourth type of reform under the FPL concerns matters of divorce. According to the law, all divorces must be decided by the Family Protection Courts. Men must have valid reasons when petitioning for divorce. Women have equal rights in submitting requests for divorce. The impact of this measure on divorce rates has been significant. In 1971, out of the total of 18,000 divorces that were concluded, according to the FPL, 15,000 took place in cities and 3,000 in villages.[9] If other factors are held constant, the higher rate of divorce in cities may be explained not necessarily in terms of a higher liberated consciousness of women in cities, but perhaps by the greater suitability of these laws to urban areas than to the countryside.

Women, Production and Education

The preceding discussion was an attempt to analyze the place of women within a specific sociocultural context. As such, it is only one determinant of the women's condition in a society. Associated with this element is women's role in production, an extension of their alienated and objectified position connected with their sociocultural role and the so-called "natural" role in reproduction.

Looking specifically at the Iranian situation, it may be noted that while the per capita income increased from $200 in the early 1960s to $1,500 in the mid-1970s, female employment rose from 9.2 percent of the total population in 1956 to 11 percent in 1971.[10] The employment of women was highest in industry, agriculture and services[11] in 1971. Thus, 51.1 percent of the total female population was employed in industry, 29.8 percent in agriculture and 16.4 percent in services. In urban areas, the employment of women is mostly centered around services, totaling 53 percent. In rural areas, the employment of women is highest in industry, totaling 55.8 percent in 1971.

With regard to the distribution of the three major types of occupation, a distinction must be made between machine industry and manual industry, because most women engaged in the latter do weaving and carpeting and earn very little income. There are, however, many women in rural areas who carry more then half the burden of agricultural work but are not independent wage earners.[12] This group of women is excluded from official statistics and is categorized as an "economically inactive population."[13] Their economic activities consist of agricultural work, gathering of products, cleaning of grains, picking up and cleaning of fruits, milking and making dairy products, planting rice, tea, making baskets, carpets, spinning, knitting, feeding animals and making bread, combined with housework for the family.[14] Interestingly, "inactive women" seem to be more active than "active women," defined as wage earners who make up the categories of the employed labor force in industry, agriculture and services. It makes little difference whether women's employment is categorized as "active" or "inactive." It is true that there has been an increase in the female labor force, yet, compared with men, the economically active population of women numbers much less[15]—an indication of the unequal status of women. Moreover, the bulk of working women are in either difficult or low-paying jobs and are thus relegated to a relatively low position in the society.

The noteworthy point in the aforementioned analysis is the increasing trend of women's economic activity in the urban areas, for it is the urban sector that is most substantially influenced by the impact of modernization, both at the sociocultural and economic levels. Therefore, for the purpose of this study, differential female activity rates and their trends must rest on the urban indicators as the most relevant tools. In this connection, it may also be noted that the societies of the Middle East display one of the lowest female activity rates compared with countries located in comparable regions of the world. Thus, the average urban female activity rate in these societies is approximately only five percent, whereas that of Latin America and Asia exceeds 25 percent.

In Iran, the general female activity rate in urban areas has increased from 9 percent in the early 1960s to 13 percent in the early 1970s[16] and is expected to almost double to 25 percent by 1992. Nevertheless, the explanation of differential urban female activity rates in these three economically comparable regions of the world—the Middle East, Southeast Asia and Latin America—cannot be made only in terms of levels of economic development, particularly in view of the fact that the structure of the labor force in these regions does not show significant differences. Thus, it may be assumed that similar states of economic development in given societies do not necessarily entail similar rates of female participation in production.

This is not, however, to minimize the importance of economic development in terms of its overall impact on the expansion, availability and market utilization of women's role in production. Participation of women in nonagricultural, out-of-home economic activities is related, to a great extent, to the accessibility of employment at the labor market and availability of womanpower in society. The accessibility of employment and availability of womanpower depend on several economic as well as sociocultural factors. The economic variables, such as level of economic growth and structure of labor force, influence mainly the accessibility of employment, whereas sociocultural variables, such as expansion of education, family structure, system of social control and role of women in reproduction and family, influence the availability of women in the labor market. For the image of woman and her societal role are related to the set of normative order and the machinery of social control. Nevertheless, although these sociocultural variables are of the utmost significance in the explanation of the existing differential employment rates, their importance should not be overestimated in the analysis of the prospective trends.

Moreover, the dynamics of economic development and the subsequent changes in the structure of the labor force in the long run lead to an increase in the employment rate within the female labor force, particularly in those countries that have initially had a very low womanpower-participation rate. Such a trend is especially likely to occur in a number of societies, such as Iran, as a result of the acceleration of demand for labor and the subsequent shortage of manpower, even in the unskilled categories.

Economic development, industrialization and urbanization, social mobilization, accelerated rate of educational participation, particularly among the hitherto neglected women, and the ever-widening use of mass media, especially radio and television, are all major factors that, in the coming decades, will not only affect women's role in family and society but will also expand the rate of women's participation in production. And yet such indices of economic development will not provide adequate clues to the causes of the existing differential womanpower participation rate. Neither can they provide the most significant manipulative variables for the increase of women's participation in developmental activities.

One must therefore look elsewhere for such variables, and the most likely area for the purposes of this paper is the field of general education. Luckily, the trend in the past few years has been toward a diminishing illiteracy rate, but there is still a wide gap in the increasing rate of literacy between men and women. In general, the national statistics[17] show that there is an increasing rate of literacy—17.5 percent for women (1956–71), reaching 25.5 percent in 1971; 25.3 percent for men (1956–71), reaching 47.7 percent in 1971. These data indicate that the literacy rate for men is 22.2 percent higher than that for women. The same survey demonstrates that the rate of change in literacy is 2.9 percent greater for urban women than for urban men (1956–71), with 48.1 percent of the urban women being literate in 1971. In rural areas, however, the rates of change are much more in favor of men, making 13.9 percent increase in the literacy of men over women (1956–71), with only 8.3 percent of the rural women being literate in 1971.

In the area of education-specific activity in 1972, female education-specific activity rates were as follows: primary education, 2 percent; secondary education, 12 percent; and tertiary education, 49 percent.[18] The significance of this single variable would be appreciated by noting that the female education-specific activity rate for the women with secondary and tertiary education at the 25-to-29 age group was 37.3 percent and 70 percent, respectively.[19]

In a single decade, from academic year 1961–62 to academic year 1971–72, the average annual growth rate of female students at the different educational levels was: 13 percent for primary schools; 30 percent for high schools; 88 percent for technical and vocational schools; 76 percent for teacher-training schools; and 65 percent for institutions of higher education.[20] It is expected that by the early 1990s, the female participation rate will reach 100 percent at primary schools; 95 percent at guidance schools; 90 percent at secondary schools; and about 10 percent at the institutions of higher education.

In terms of the distribution of female labor force in white-collar and professional positions, the following figures may be of particular interest. Of almost 195,000 women in these occupations, 45 percent are in teaching—including 1 percent in professorial positions—44 percent in clerical and administrative jobs, 10 percent in paramedical professions, only half a percent in the medical profession and only 38 practicing female lawyers.[21] There are also a few female judges and diplomats as well as a number of female members of various urban arbitration councils; rural houses of equity; and provincial, district and city councils. In all, in spite of the increasing role of women's participation in production and the trend in the past few years toward a diminishing illiteracy rate, there is still a wide gap in the literacy rates of men and women, particularly in the rural areas. However, it is in light of the accelerated growth of female educational participation that one may confidently expect that the female economic activity rate would double by the end of the Eighth Development Plan in 1992, reaching a 25 percent plateau.

Women and Politics

Thus far, it has been maintained that the concrete relationship of sociocultural and economic elements makes up the structures of women's condition. Another important element to complete the total analysis of women's condition is their role in political affairs. The substructures of this political indicator ought to focus on the location of women's power in the community's power structure and on their multiple political roles, such as voter, candidate for office, elected representative, public official and associational functionary.

Looking at these elements from a historical perspective, a number of significant changes can be observed in the political role of Iranian women. To begin with, the franchise section of the early 20th-century Iranian constitution, Article 10, places women in the same category as criminals and insane people, in that:

> Those deprived of the right to vote shall consist of all females, minors and those under guardians; fraudulent bankrupts, beggars and those who earn their living in a disreputable way; murderers, thieves and other criminals. . . .[23]

This situation was intact until 1963. In that year, women received voting rights. Following this period, toward the end of 1963, of the total of 197 members[23] elected to the Majlis (the National Consultative Assembly), six were women and, of the total of 60 senators, two were women. In comparison, in the present Majlis (terminating in September 1975), of the total of 270 members, 18 are women and, of the 60 senators, two are women. In the recent election, of the total of 97 female candidates of the Rastakhiz Party, two females ran for the Senate and 95 for the Majlis. Of the total number of these candidates, 21 were elected: one female for the Senate and 20 for the Majlis.[24] Thus, as compared with the 1971 elections, recent electoral politics witnessed a decrease of one female senator and an increase of two female deputies in the Majlis. It may be interesting to note that, up to now, there has been only one female minister, who has been replaced, and no woman prime minister.

Iran: Past, Present and Future

The above discussion indicates that, despite the growth of women's consciousness in political affairs, their political participation still lags greatly behind that of men. Especially, given the fact that women comprise one-half of the total population, the rate of their political participation, both as voters and high public office-holders, is quite low. In general, it appears that women's rate of progress is much higher in attaining higher education than participating in economic and political activities, respectively. This means that modernization trends have not yet provided a direct relationship between educational, political and economic variables. Consequently, considerable efforts must be made to highlight women's interest and participation in political affairs as they rapidly obtain a higher place in educational institutions.

Outlook

In the preceding discussion, an attempt was made to review and analyze some of the forces that have historically shaped the socioeconomic and political conditions of women in Iran. It was noted that, despite the significant gains in the rates of female economic activity rate and educational participation, and despite the increasing involvement of women in Iran's developmental processes, the overall participation of Iranian women in all facets of social life must be accelerated considerably. An additional element that has helped to further our understanding of this traditional society is the theme of male domination which, similar to other civilizations, runs throughout Iranian history: women, like Rousseau's citizens, were born free but were everywhere in chains. The post-Islamic culture paid homage to this paradox, and the 20th-century reforms upheld it.

Footnotes

1. Vern Bullough (ed.), *The Subordinate Sex: A History of Attitudes Toward Women* (Maryland: Penguin Books, Inc.), p. 137.

2. Robert Surieu, *Sarv-e' Naz (An Essay on Love and the Representation of Erotic Themes in Ancient Iran)*, trans. by James Hogarth (Geneva: Nagel Publishers, 1967), p. 65, as it appeared in *Ibid.*, p. 145.

3. Koran, IV, trans. by M. Pickthall (New York: New American Library, 1953), as it appears in Vern Bullough (ed.), *op. cit.*, pp. 137–138.

4. Joseph Shacht, *An Introduction to Islamic Law* (Oxford, England: Clarendon Press, 1964), p. 93.

5. Reuben Levy, *The Social Structure of Islam* (England: Cambridge University Press, 1957), p. 93.

6. Bullough, *op. cit.*, p. 149.

7. *Ketabe Semarē Barresiē Natayegē Egraiē Ghanunē Hemayatē Khanevadeh (The Book of the Investigating Seminar on the Effects of the Family Protection Laws)* (Tehran: Women's Organization, 1972).

8. General Department of Civil Registration (Tehran) as appeared in *Selected Statistics* (Tehran: Plan and Budget Organization, Statistical Center of Iran, 1972–73), p. 14.

9. *Degargunihayē Egtemaiē va Eghtesadi yē Zanan ē Iran (Social and Economic Changes of Iranian Women)* (Tehran: The Plan and Budget Organization, The Statistical Center of Iran, 1974), pp. 12–13.

10. Statistical Center of Iran, as appeared in *Selected Statistics*, *op. cit.*, p. 16.

11. *Degargunihayē Egtemaiē*, *op. cit.*, pp. 76–78.

12. Ruth F. Woodsmall, *Women in the Near East* (Washington: The Middle East Institute, 1969), p. 71.

13. *Selected Statistics*, *op. cit., p. 15.*

14. *Degargunihayē Egtemaiē*, *op. cit.*, p. 54.

15. *Selected Statistics*, *op. cit.*, p. 15.

16. *Manpower Statistics* (Tehran: Statistical Center of Iran and Bureau of Manpower Statistics, 1972).

17. *Selected Statistics*, *op. cit.*, p. 26.

18. *Manpower Statistics*, *op. cit.*

19. *Ibid.*

20. *Ibid.*

21. Women's Organization (Tehran: 1975).

22. R. Sanghvi, C. German and D. Missen (eds.), *The Revolution of the Shah and the People* (London: Transorient, 1967), p. 7.

23. Ministry of Information (Tehran: 1974), and Women's Organization (Tehran: 1974).

24, Ministry of Information (Tehran: 1975).

Comments and Discussion

The status of women in Iran and their role in furthering development were considered at a plenary session and a special optional
meeting, well attended by participants of both sexes.

In "Dynamics of Women's Condition in Iran," Mamideh Sedghi commented on the changing social status of women in contemporary Iran. Among the factors contributing to change have
been certain provisions of the Iranian Civil Codes dealing with the
age at which women may be married, polygamy and divorce. Ms.
Sedghi also spoke about women's role in production, especially
increasing economic activity by women in urban areas. Significant changes can also be observed in respect to political activity
by women in Iran, although their political participation still lags far
behind that of men. Ms. Sedghi concluded that there has been
increased involvement of women in the development process but
that participation by women in all aspects of Iranian society
should be accelerated considerably.

An Iranian made the following comments on "Dynamics of
Women's Condition in Iran":

1. There is too much emphasis on the erotic and sexual role of
women as something unique to Iranian or Moslem society,

whereas history shows that this has been the lot of women in general in Western society, as well as Eastern society, and in both societies there have been exceptional women who have risen despite cultural limitations and, from behind the scenes, have proved themselves powerful political or literary figures.

2. *Mahrieh* is discussed as though it were "bride price," which is not a sociologically correct analysis of the phenomena. It was, in fact, designed to protect women against, or after, arbitrary divorce so they could be self-supporting.

3. Athough it is stated, *en passant*, that within Islamic laws women were allowed to own property, it was not emphasized that, on marriage, a woman's property did not become that of the husband; that, under Islamic laws of inheritance, daughters inherited one-half of what the sons inherited; and that for a century, while Iranian women were enjoying these property rights, women in Europe had no property rights and on marriage their property became that of the husband.

4. The Education Act of 1290 Solar Year under which education became compulsory for children from seven to 13, regardless of sex, was not mentioned. Under this act, for the first time, government became responsible for education, and women were allowed to go to school. Seven years later the first group of girls graduated from high school. Also not mentioned is the creation of the Voluntary Corps within the White Revolution for young women and men. This fulfilled a double function, on the one hand enabling young women to serve their country side by side with young men while, on the other hand, providing an effective weapon with which to reach and educate rural women. There are at the moment 20,000 members of the female Voluntary Corps active in the field, and it is predicted that, during the course of the Five Year Plan, 150,000 members of the Voluntary Corps will go into the field, of whom 30 percent will be female.

In the discussion that followed, an Iranian noted that the contribution of women to productivity has not been measured accurately, owing partly to the application of Western statistical concepts.

An American warned that as the public sphere expands, the status of women may worsen; the role of the wife/mother may be lessened if the family ceases to be a center of action. Another added that, although the increasing economic activity of urban women was noted, Ms. Sedghi did not really deal with problems that these women, especially lower-class women, are experiencing, including poor wages, employment as children and other special problems.

Special Meeting on the Role of Women

The secretary-general of the Women's Organization of Iran (WOI), an umbrella group for 54 organizations with 260 branches throughout the country, commented on the history of women's organizations in Iran and on some current programs, including educational activities for women, vocational training, family planning programs, day care centers for children and counseling on legal and other matters. Other topics discussed at the meeting included (1) the extent to which the status of women in Iran is really changing, with some optimism expressed despite the strong hold of traditional attitudes, continuing discrimination in some laws and lesser educational opportunities for women; (2) the links between the evolution of women's status in society and economic development, with Iranian women having shown that they are united with men in working for national development; (3) the need for women to enjoy equal educational and employment opportunities in order to contribute to development; (4) the extent of government information programs in the area of family planning and laws governing abortion; and (5) women's movements in other countries, including the United States, where some women liberationists have alienated many women, it was suggested, owing to their view of men as the enemy. The concluding speaker on this subject, an Asian, observed that men and women in Asia have been distressed by processes leading to the breakup of the family unit. There is need to develop family life, he observed, and not only in Iran.

An Iranian commentator provided some figures on the status of women in Iran, pointing out that there are, at the moment, 1,803 female university professors and assistant professors and 86,000 female civil servants (50 percent of all teachers are women). Added to this, women hold positions of responsibility and importance in local and national government.

4. Political and Social Implications of Growth in Iran

Changing Leadership in Iran

Modernization and Changing Leadership in Iran

Amin Alimard and Cyrus Elahi

In this exploratory essay we will briefly discuss political leadership and sociopolitical change in Iran in a context of historical perspective. Before we begin our analysis, it is worthwhile to point out that there are some general differences between elites in Iran and elites in Western industrial societies. In the industrial societies, the concept of elites is quite differentiated: there are political leaders, high government administrators, business and economic leaders, leaders of the masses (*e.g.,* trade union leaders) and military elites.[1]

In Iran, some of these groups do not have the same relative importance. For example, the business elite in Iran does not have nearly the kind of influence that it exercises in the United States or Western European societies. Due to the size of the rural sector and the slow development of labor unions, union leaders do not yet wield the political influence that they exercise in the West. And since the main direction and policies of the military in Iran are largely the decisions of the Shah, it may be thought that the political role of the military is relatively unimportant. However, with the increasing attention paid to the armed forces in Iran, and in the Middle East in general, the role of the military elite may need to be reassessed. On the other hand, the role of religious elites, which has been influential among traditional groups, and the role of intellectuals, which has been no less influential among the educated groups, have not been systematically studied.

Since modernization in Iran is an induced rather than an organic process (as was the case with European societies), the two elites that are obviously important are the political leaders and the high government officials. These groups have been largely responsible for Iran's socioeconomic development and constitute our particular interests in this essay.

In order for an analysis of the modernization process in any particular society to be meaningful, one must pay serious attention to the context and the milieu in which socioeconomic action takes place. That is, in our analysis of socioeconomic change we ought to take into account that cultures, including political cultures, evolve as specialized adaptations to the environments. As a great American anthropologist, Edward Hall, has noted, cultures adapt to their own internal structures, "requiring" their members through their specialized institutions to perform their tasks. Therefore, all cultures are necessarily vulnerable to those institutions that were not significantly featured in their evolution. In this age of increasing international, and therefore crosscultural, communication, we are witnesses to the pressures felt in different cultures precisely because they are vulnerable to each other.

Nevertheless, there are still writers and opinion makers in the West who often forget the fact that the more than 150 states of this world have behind them divergent pasts and are governed by different types of political systems. Critics continue to point out and deplore that "societies" are unequal relative to their degree of "development." Their preconceived notion of modernization and the good society causing an obsession with the inequalities of development at least partly explains the conviction or the illusion that modernization and the main institutional features of industrial societies are transferable at will and in a relatively short time.

What is opposed here is the fanaticism of the ideologists of the 20th century, the great simplifiers and perfectionists who believe that they are in the possession of an infallible formula for economic abundance, freedom and social justice. To doubt these prescriptions for "progress" is far from vulgar skepticism. Rather, it is the voice of knowledge as well as wisdom that confirms the imperfection of all social orders and accepts the difficulties of knowing the future. It is our knowledge that points out the limits of our power and suggests that we gradually improve what exists, instead of suggesting that one can destroy the experience of centuries and start over again.

The major fact about today's Iran is that it is both remarkably like and spectacularly unlike "traditional" Iran, when nearly no one was seriously concerned about "modernization." On the one hand, Iran aspires and exhibits a working commitment to an urban, technological way of life. Yet, as most non-Iranians who have visited Iran know, this society is incomprehensible without elaborate explanations. The outsider readily observes modern technology being used all over Iran to transform the physical aspects of the environment. The difficulty of the intelligent visitor, however, lies in trying to recognize the meaning and purpose of social relations, culture, everything mediated through gesture, sound, image and words. What is important is that those who interpret the amalgam of "old" and "new" in Iran should not purge social reality of its own unique aspects.

One of Marx's most valuable insights is that ideology grows out of practice. Traditionally, one of the most noticeable aspects of political authority in Iran has been its personal character. As one reads Iranian history, it becomes clear that most often the whole society was ruled as if it were the personal possession of the king. Thus, throughout the history of this land, from the time when the Achaemenian kings had made Iran a worldwide empire down to the present day, it had been widely accepted that the king has had the legitimate right to intervene in almost any social and political affair in order to correct improper conduct as the final arbiter. Thus, we might say that Iranian political theory gives the king virtually unlimited power. Now the actual practice of this power can go as far as temperament, personal ambition and capability may take him—which has not been very far for many of Iran's past kings.

To discover the impact of the past on life and society, old prejudices, fears and superstitions must be set aside until the heritage of the past appears for what it really is. For Iran and for many other Asian societies, a significant part of that heritage has been a relatively centralized, authoritarian monarchy that used agricultural surpluses to maintain its army and bureaucracy, leaving the majority of the people powerless, illiterate and poor.

For centuries, the system operated without serious internal problems. A traditional agricultural society composed of peasants and landlords could be managed with relative ease by the political structure. The rural population that comprised the majority had always been defenseless, helpless and thus incapable of causing serious problems. The landlord, although socially and economically superior to the peasants, nevertheless had to depend on the grace of the political authority that he sought through association with political leaders. Often, officials used their position to acquire land, thereby combining two roles into one. As for the peasant, he recognized his helplessness and inability to control the social conditions of his life. Thus, for centuries he endured brutal injustice in a system that offered him no hope whatsoever. Whenever the political authority desired it, the peasant had to furnish the available surplus to finance its operation and pay for its buildings, monuments and lavish tastes.

The contrast between the days when the problems of Tehran politics centered around "meat and bread" and today, faced with the pressures of an ever more demanding society, is alarming. In a sense, today's conditions deviate from what has always seemed "normal" in Iran. The pressing problem for the contemporary political system centers around the question of whether it can continue to increase its productive capacity to satisfy the many basic human needs and wants, such as food, shelter, health, education and a rising living standard.

Obviously, the Shah is the most important elite in Iran. The monarchy has always been the most important political institution in this society. Through centuries of trial and error, the monarchy has evolved as the symbol of Iran's historical continuity; today it is the most important mechanism ensuring continuity amid the social and political changes yet to come.

During World War II, Iran was occupied by the Russians in the north and the British in the south. After the war, she experienced intense foreign subversion whose manifestations were the domestic political turmoil and the disorders of that period. But ever since the consolidation of the political system in the early 1950s, the Shah has effectively controlled the basic patterns of the political process because he felt any other approach to government would be unworkable. In other words, given the fractioned nature of the domestic political scene, such control could not be effective unless it was designed to be managed from a single center of power encompassing the administrative, the executive and the military institutions of Iran. In short, it was felt that a more moderate approach might have resulted in the kind of disorganization the political system could not withstand.

How can we provide meaning for this pattern of leadership? In order to avoid oversimplifying the analysis of political action in Iran, it is necessary to take into account the historical experiences of this land, and her political culture, briefly noted earlier. Furthermore, the early political experiences of the Iranian sovereign should not be overlooked. While he regards those bitter political experiences as a matter of the past, he has drawn from them some hard-learned lessons, calling for structural reforms making possible the implementation of a social revolution. The casual observers who take events out of their historical context and criticize the political systems and policies of other countries on the basis of criteria applicable to European or American societies do not realize that the sudden application of the "liberal formula" in many of these countries could easily give free reign to the centrifugal forces. For the same reason, these observers often tend to take what has already been accomplished in these countries for granted. As for Iran, it is important to dissipate the illusion that even minimal political stability in Iran could have been achieved without difficulty and without danger and that, once established, it could endure by itself.

There are two fundamental points about leadership in Iran's political system: (1) the central role of the Shah in the political process; and (2) his intense determination to transform Iran into a modern industrial society. The drastic reforms that characterized developments in the past decade are mainly the Shah's conscious reaction to the systemic challenges facing Iran. Measures such as land reform; widespread anti-illiteracy campaigns, including the use of young army conscripts as teachers in the rural areas; universal free education, including increasing attention to industrial development; workers' insurance schemes and profit-sharing measures; emancipation of women; and most recently, a serious drive toward political participation and governmental decentralization cannot be fully understood unless the role of the Shah in the political process and his vision of Iran's future are taken into account.

Ever since his achievement of a firm grip over the political process, the Shah has successfully turned toward the recruitment of younger men (often Western-educated)* with modern technical expertise. This practice has seriously decreased the traditional importance of wealth and social status as the prerequisites for political power. One important consequence of this change in Mohammad Reza Shah's recruitment policy is that he is no longer dependent on what has been known in Iran's past as the oligarchy of "the thousand families." Traditionally, the sons of these aristocratic families have been the only source for elite recruitment. As more and more Iranians become experts in various technical fields, the number of men and women eligible to serve the country has increased.

We believe that one of the most important changes in Iranian politics, at all levels of the political system, is this powerful trend toward elite recruitment based on individual achievement rather than social inheritance. Even though some individuals, due to their social (*i.e.*, class) background, wealth or personal relations, may still occupy a few important positions of influence, we argue that despite their possible negative effects, they represent the fringes of the political dynamics. For, despite this hold of the past, *in the mainstream of Iranian politics, property, birth and social class can no longer effectively compete with achievement as the major criterion for elite recruitment*. Furthermore, in view of the availability of free education at all levels, in the future achievement will no longer be determined largely by the social and economic position of individuals.

However, soon after taking their positions in the political system, the young, newly recruited elites discover that the proper use of their field of specialization is at times next to impossible due to the stronghold of some of the irrational, traditional practices of the Iranian bureaucracy. Despite the often-repeated statement concerning the need for a determined movement toward a modern, rational frame of operation, the newly recruited elites learn that to stand up against such practices may lead to a confrontation with other members of the elite who often seek to further their own vested interests.

A meaningful solution to this problem is difficult because it is a part of the process of changing the structural aspects of the political system. The problem is also delicate because many of the individuals whose interests lie in the preservation of the traditional aspects of the society are rather powerful. Some of these elites occupy strategic positions in the political process, providing them access to the flow of messages

---

*Nearly 95 percent of Iranian students studying abroad are to be found in American or Western European universities. This situation has prevailed for over 50 years. Presently, there are over 35,000 Iranian students studying abroad.

throughout the system. An important part of the dynamics of the Iranian political modernization lies in the current efforts to increase the number of the modern-minded elites in strategic political positions.*

At this point, it is important to emphasize that the modernization process in Iran has created a dynamic of its own that has in turn resulted in certain systemic pressures. In its first decade, The Shah and People's Revolution has had two major results. On the one hand, more economic infrastructure has been developed than Iran has ever known. On the other hand, most groups in Iran have developed comparatively high expectations. We are particularly concerned with this high level of expectation because its implications are crucial to the future direction of the Iranian political process. It is the process of social communication, mainly induced by the political system itself, that has brought relatively vast numbers of Iranians with high school and university educations psychologically in touch with life styles and values (e.g., equality) that prevail in Western industrial societies. If the essence of traditional authority was the acceptance of an unchanging and unchangeable set of rules that stood above human affairs, the modernization process, by opening men's perceptions to the possibility of change and the manipulation of the political environment, has caused a shift of one set of attachments to another. In other words, the modernization process has created expectations that did not previously exist. The main results of the shift in attachments and expectations constitutes the key contradiction in most of the modernizing societies: people are learning to expect more of authority than any public authority can bear. This state of affairs carries at least two important political consequences: (1) the legitimacy of governing elites is becoming increasingly dependent upon fulfillment of promised goods; and (2) the elites, increasingly lacking traditional support for their legitimacy, are obviously vulnerable to popular disaffection. In Iran, this situation has been perceived as an opportunity by the new elites for, by being responsive to these new demands and expectations, they are reducing alienation on the one hand, while increasing their own legitimacy on the other.

In order for the political system to bear the large volume and wide range of political and administrative decisions with reasonable effectiveness, the incapacitating factors at work in the machinery of government must be minimized through the rationalization of the political system. Among these incapacitating factors are the inefficiency of the personnel responsible for the implementation of authoritative decisions, the

---

*This new recruitment policy is evident at both ministerial and subministerial levels in many ministries and government organizations. The composition of the Iranians participating in the Aspen Institute/Persepolis Symposium is also an example of the new elite.

inadequacy of the political communication network and, finally, the excessive centralization that exists in Iran as in many developing societies. To overcome these impediments, the Iranian political system is in the beginning stage of implementing necessary changes as well as an administrative revolution.

Although Iran's administrative revolution will be fully implemented, it will not be sufficient. For in order to increase the level of performance with respect to rising expectations, the Iranian political system requires increasingly greater supportive capacity. Polity capacity does not only mean greater bureaucratic and technological efficiency. Rather, we are referring to a special capacity of the socioeconomic and political infrastructure to respond, innovate and adapt to a wide range of demands. In short, society must develop the machinery to manage continuous change. Perhaps the key point about the special capacity required here is the advantage of a political culture of participation. Through the institutionalization of political participation, the new elite is in a position to significantly increase its legitimacy and thereby increase polity capacity. In fact, it is the new elite in various ministries, government organizations and the *Rastakhiz-E-Mellat-E-Iran* that are trying to implement the plans for participation and decentralization.

In order for any government to engage in meaningful activities, two elements are necessary: information and coercion. Information means that type of knowledge that reduces uncertainty.[2] In general, the greater the amount of information available to the political authority, the less coercive is the role of the elites. At any rate, by eliminating or reducing random factors, and thereby uncertainty, information and coercion make possible degrees of predictability as to the results of decisions affecting society. Thus, members of the new elite from different ministries and government organizations frequently make two-day visits to the various *Ostans* in order to gather information on the state of various projects. The meetings held with governors and other *Ostan* officials during these trips have proven to be very effective, since they have enabled Tehran to pinpoint the actual bottlenecks around the country.

During the first decade of the Shah and People's Revolution, the political authority was able to plan and implement decisions without significant open political participation. But in the second decade, as modernization increases, so does complexity, so does uncertainty and so does the need for information. *Rastakhiz-E-Mellat-E-Iran* and the plans for the decentralization of the government came about in view of the political system's need for information and for greater public participation. For the new elites believe that participation is essential to establish responsive government, and that in order to legitimize authority at various levels of decision making there must be responsiveness. Finally, by increasing the capacity of the political infrastructure for the production of power itself, the polity will be able to postpone or reduce the heavy decisional load currently bearing upon the formal machinery of government.

The Iran of today is a self-governing political system. But self-government is more than independence from outside domination. It is important to understand that political systems are partly controlled by the weight of all that has happened to them earlier. This momentum derived from past actions can constrain human organizations in the same sense that an automobile moving at a fast speed cannot stop the moment pressure is applied to the brakes, for the momentum of the past is too great. By the same token, outdated traditional social and political practices cannot be suddenly stopped. It is in the light of this situation that, as we argued earlier, traditional elites, however important as particular individuals, are at the fringes, not the mainstream, of the political process today. It is undeniable that the vast majority of the individuals driving Iran toward greater development and modernization are the new elites.

Today we know that the task of governing any society is crippled without self-correction. As Deutsch puts it, "To the extent that we are able to correct our behavior by presenting increasingly complex responses to our environment, we can say that we have the capacity to learn."[3] As we have noted, traditionally, though not always, Iranian politics have sought to defend illusions, cherished beliefs and to preserve existing practices such as a feudal system of land ownership. What is really new in Iranian politics is that it is in the midst of a learning process. While most leaders and high officials in Iranian history felt they knew all they needed to know, the new elites know that neither they nor other elites anywhere can do without new information and new knowledge. In recent speeches (at the Ramsar Conference, during the first week of September 1975), the new elites discussed the political process as a means of obtaining new knowledge about people's attitudes and values. The critical factor is not the attitude toward the status quo, but toward learning. That is to say, when new problems confront a country, and old answers cannot cope with them, then the society has to learn a set of new habits compatible with the basic patterns of its culture and identity. This is the key idea behind the plans for political participation through *Rastakhiz-E-Mellat-E-Iran*. The driving force in this movement toward new answers is the new elites.

The successful implementation of economic and social programs in Iran was partly intended to build a stable noncommunist society. In other words, Iran's economic growth was—as it is everywhere—infused with certain political values. In the case of this society, the most important value was the preservation of the constitutional monarchy. In fact, the success of "modernization" in Iran has been dependent on maintaining its link with the past through the preservation of the institution of the monarchy. In other words, the strength of Iran's new elites lies in their determination to make use of both traditional roles and values and the creation of new ones.

Conversely, the evolution of "modernization" has created contradictions and is transforming the system. For the changes in a society both influence and are influenced by political leadership, because social development affects any current distribution of power.

What is happening is that the Iranian political system is in the midst of reorganizing its power structure into a mobilization system. Iran can no longer afford incompetence in her administrative system. Thus, traditional criteria for elite recruitment have given way to the standards of achievement and competence that characterize the new Iranian elites of today. These elites are generally impatient and frustrated with the ways of traditional elites.

Despite their country's long and difficult history, Iranians have managed to preserve the feeling of continuity in their national identity. The resilience and astuteness that helped Iranians survive as a nation have also sharpened their national pride. Iranians feel a sense of trust and confidence in their culture, identity and ability. In order to transform the attitudes and actions of citizens in a manner consistent with the requirements of the Great Civilization, it would be necessary for elites to enjoy the active support and confidence of the various groups. It is under such circumstances that political participation becomes increasingly the means to mobilize citizen support for the implementation of economic and social development plans. We firmly believe that given the success of the past with the enlightened leadership that she enjoys at the helm of the political system, Iran will go on modernizing in her own distinctive way, accepting some of the rational aspects of the West but preserving the positive elements of her own values.

Footnotes

1. For background information on elites, see: Raymond Aron, "Social Structure and the Ruling Class," *British Journal of Sociology*, I (March 1950); C. Wright Mills, *The Power Elite* (London: Oxford University Press, 1956); T.B. Bottomore, *Elites and Society* (London, 1964).

2. For an analysis of the role of information in political systems, see: Karl W. Deutsch, *The Nerves of Government* (New York: The Free Press, 1966).

3. *Politics and Government: How People Decide Their Fate* (New York: Houghton-Mifflin Co., 1970), pp. 142–162.

Social Mobilization and Participation in Iran

Gholamreza Afkhami and Cyrus Elahi

Many otherwise futile controversies about development and its problems could become productive if the people discussing it would seek to give meaning to the content of political action by paying serious attention to the context and milieu in which it takes place. The objective of this study is to analyze the nature and necessity of political participation in Iran with proper attention to the historically defined context in which it occurs. We shall, therefore, try to set forth the underlying meaning of the relationship between the political system and its socioeconomic and cultural environment, depicting significant variables that bear upon this relationship.

In Iran, as in many other developing countries, the pattern of the relationship between the political system and its environment has evolved mainly as a result of the simultaneous operations of two types of forces: the traditional culture based on a particular type of economic and social order, and the kind of new consciousness resulting from the experience of colonialism. Ordinarily, the clash of the two types of consciousness creates a multicultural environment where various clusters of value compete for the attention of significant sectors of the society. The elemental notion of consensus must be sought by effective action on the part of the political system.

The pattern of response to the colonial experience moves through various stages. The first expression of nationalism is the ambivalence of xenophobia coupled with great enthusiasm for the institutions of the oppressive country. Internationally it seeks independence defined primarily in legal terms. Soon it is recognized that the essence of colonialism lies in the reality of uneven economic and cultural relationships. The second stage of nationalism is determined by the awareness of this reality. John Kautsky observes:

> Unless they are virtually inaccessible, underdeveloped countries almost by necessity stand economically in a colonial relationship to industrial countries, in which the former serve as the supplier of raw materials (often made available by cheap native labor) and sometimes as the market for the industries of the latter. Anti-colonialism, then, must here be understood as opposition not merely to colonialism narrowly defined but also to a colonial economic structure.[1]

No nationalist movement can feed on negative values forever. The drive for economic emancipation has its logical corollary in economic development. Once the expectation of economic and social development assumes an objective reality, the end of economic growth becomes a moral imperative on the basis of which new patterns of political legitimacy begin to take shape.

The communal consciousness of development revolutionizes the political process by placing the main responsibility for development on the political system. But political development cannot be judged in terms of the value of economic and social decisions made by the political system. What must be the focus of attention is the capability of the political system to make and implement the necessary decisions. The difference between political power and economic foresight is crucial and constitutes a basic principle of this discussion.

The point emerging from the above discussion is that there is a fundamental difference between the pattern of development of the Western societies and that of the so-called developing world. In the first category, change has been organic, that is to say, it has occurred in different parts of the society, creating new expectations and powers. Governments have then responded to such new demands as they have taken shape in their socioeconomic environment. Thus, the total system has maintained its inner cohesion by giving way in time to the new demands, and forming the necessary structures and channels for their articulation and communication. Political development and socioeconomic development have been more or less parallel, though not identical. Thus, ideology becomes a theoretical explanation of the status quo at each point in time. Visions of a radically different future are dismissed as soft-minded expressions of utopia except insofar as they may have referents in the existing social power structure. In spite of the inherent dynamism of the society, its political expression remains static.

In the second category, the process is reversed. The consciousness of development precedes the fact of development and is thereby translated into utopian political ideology. This ideology must of necessity find expression through the political system, regardless of the form of government and the structure of the regime. Its aim is to challenge and change the existing socioeconomic structure in order to achieve the dream of the future. The political system becomes, in essence, a mobilization system.

The capabilities of such a political system are functions of the relationship between the mobilization process and the system goals. The nature of this relationship determines the nature and extent of systemic power, the central concept in the analysis of political development. Systemic power, therefore, may be defined as the capacity of the system to mobilize its resources for the specification and implementation of its goals. This definition of systemic power points to certain concepts that bear significantly on the understanding of the main variables affecting the nature of political development.

The dialectic of change revolves around the manner of posing the problem of identification and the process of mobilization of resources on the one hand, and the capacity to specify and implement goals on the other. It is within this context that we shall try to analyze the condition of social mobilization and political participation in Iran, and the role and the meaning of the *Rastakhiz* for the future development of the country.

Comparing progressive Europe with the then backward America, John Locke observed:

> There cannot be a clearer demonstration of anything than several nations of the Americans are of this, who are rich in land and poor in all the comforts of life; when nature having furnished as liberally as any other people with the materials of plenty, *i.e.,* a fruitful soil, apt to produce in abundance what might serve for food, raiment, and delight—yet, for want of improving it by labour, have not one hundredth part of the conveniences we enjoy. And a king of a large and fruitful territory there, feeds, lodges, and is clad worse than a day labourer in England. . . .

> Thus, in the beginning, all the world was America.[2]

We have learned the lesson that the wealth of material contained within the physical environment is of little value until such time as we develop both the will and the skill to appropriate and use it to our own ends. The lesson is being learned with a vengeance: not only are we opting for material comfort, but we intend to achieve it within a relatively short span of time. The problems and obstacles that must be overcome are only secondarily related to the scarcity of physical resources. The primary obstacles relate to the achievement of the kinds of social organizations, psychological transformations and ideational reorientations necessary to the development of the will and skill to exploit the wealth that remains untapped, in Locke's words, "for want of labour."

Viewed in this perspective, systemic resources assume different degrees of significance. Broadly, a distinction may be made between physical and societal resources. Within the framework of analysis adopted here, physical resources recede to a secondary position. The societal resources include all the qualitative and quantitative factors affecting significantly the society's will and skill to proceed toward the goal of economic and social development. Specifically, these factors appear to be innumerable. Generically, they tend to fall into one of the following broad categories: sociopsychological, organizational and technological. The three are interrelated and together they interact with a fourth category we may call "material." These categories are intended to be suggestive, not exhaustive. They suggest the necessity for cognitive reorientation of the observer. They are not meant to depreciate the significance of other conceivable factors.

The linkage between modernization and sociopsychological transformation has been noted by almost all of the modern writers in the field of comparative politics. The sociopsychological category is perhaps the most important of the determinants of the mobilization process in the transitional systems. It directs our attention to a whole spectrum of differentially mobilized public. For our purposes, four general categories of power resources may be distinguished. The immediately available power resources include that stratum of society that is not only socially mobilized but also tends to share the general ideological posture adopted by the ruling elite. This category, of course, may still be further broken down for purposes of analysis in terms of such factors as articulative capabilities, access to independent sources of power, degrees of integration and the like.

Power resources requiring activation before they become available include the body of disaffected individuals who, although ideationally reoriented, are nevertheless apathetic, primarily as a result of the limited capacity of the political system to coopt them into the ruling process. The major characteristic of this group appears to be what Durkheim has called *anomie,* a condition of normlessness, in this case resulting from the breakdown of old traditional values while the new values are not fully internalized. This stratum presents a major problem for the political system because of its potential availability and its propensity to support any modern movement that can conceivably allow it to participate in the governmental process. In terms of social behavior, the more affluent members of this group tend toward conspicuous consumption while the less affluent resort to such escape from reality devices as narcotics and the like.

The power resources requiring conversion refer to the strata that are mobilized and articulate but remain essentially antiestablishment. This category is normally composed of a variety of heterogeneous elite, each having its own program of action and each contending for power. The ruling elites compete with this category for the mobilization and assimilation of the masses, combining persuasion and force in changing ratios as the circumstances permit.

In Iran, the size of the antiestablishment elites is relatively small. The possibility of action for it is limited. Nevertheless, their existence requires conscious action on the part of the government, and the process of conversion must assume high priority in order to mobilize that part of this society that could assume a leading position in achieving the ends of the revolution. It is for this reason that in most cases avenues seem to be left open for possible rapprochement while animosities continue to exist. At times, complete reconciliation proves difficult, because often the differences pertain to questions of legitimacy and therefore tend to remain noncontrovertible.

The non-mobilized traditional masses constitute the power resources requiring development in the sociopsychological category. To this group belong the rural masses and a substantial portion of the urban elements. To accomplish the ends of development, the political system must find a way to mobilize this resource, the power of which, while potentially enormous, remains dormant. The populist orientation of the Iranian political system points to the fact that it appreciates the potential significance of this category. The emphasis on political education, therefore, is natural and inevitable. Its success depends largely on the efficiency of the system in its drive to control and manage the channels of communication. We shall have occasion to comment on this point later on, though two conclusions seem immediately to follow: (1) parties inevitably play a significant role in the mobilization of the masses, and (2) an immediate advantage accrues to the ruling elite in a one-party political system.

The interaction among these elements occurs within the context of rapid social change. The political system strives to remain one step ahead of the events by spearheading development. However, it does not, and cannot, completely dominate or control either the pattern or rate of social mobilization. Once set in motion, the wheels of social change assume a momentum of their own. Karl Deutsch explains the process:

> Social mobilization is a name given to an overall process of change which happens to substantial parts of the population in countries which are moving from traditional to modern ways of life. It denotes a concept which brackets together a number of more specific processes of change such as changes of residence, of occupation, of social setting, of face-to-face associations, of institutions, roles, and ways of acting, of experiences and expectations, and finally, of personal memories, habits, and needs including the need for new patterns of group affiliations, and new images of personal identity. Singly, and even more in their cumulative impact, these changes tend to influence and sometimes to transform political behavior.[3]

These processes occur simultaneously; they are cumulative in their impact. They are accompanied by a profound psychological transformation, referred to sometimes as "the revolution of rising expectations." But, if not correctly managed, in Daniel Lerner's apt phrase, the disparity between achievement and aspiration leads to a new "revolution of rising frustration." Dissatisfaction spreads because (1) the mass media bring new aspirations to the people, and then since the empathic individual imagination quickly, logarithmically it appears, outruns societal achievement, it brings dissatisfaction conceived as frustration of aspiration; and (2) despite the new evident risks of frustration, the mass media continue to spread around the country inexorably and unilaterally. The seemingly obvious answer to the dilemma is either to increase achievement capabilities of the people or decrease their level of aspiration. Neither solution is easily attainable.

Efforts to increase the achievement capability of the people and, indeed, of the system, must necessarily be exerted as part of the central task of the political system. Presumably, no substantial development can take place without the kind of ideational reorientation we have already alluded to. Somehow, the system must propagate the type of motivational drive that characterizes the emergence of the so-called entrepreneurial man. It appears, however, that achievement capability is intimately bound with the aspirational drives of the individuals. A man with no aspiration is not likely to be found in a position where his capabilities could be discovered or tested. A man with high aspirations is rarely satisfied with his own achievement. Translated into systemic terms, this relationship suggests that the system always tends to have aspirations beyond the boundaries of its achievement capability. Dissatisfaction, therefore, becomes an endemic property of development.

It is always possible to rearrange specific goals and reformulate specific policies. It is not possible to abandon ultimate goals of development. Once begun, development is no longer viewed as a simple matter of change. It becomes a moral problem, a matter of emancipation. As Horowitz suggests:

> Bluntly put, no known society has ever consciously accepted a lower standard of living as a permanent feature of its existence. Indeed, a primary cause of social revolution is the incapacity or inability of an established set of rulers to maintain or accelerate the growth rates of a society. The movement from ruralism to urbanism may appear as simply a matter of change to social scientists, but for a mass of people it is a matter of emancipation. Women are emancipated from domestic obligation. Children are emancipated from the work force. Laborers are emancipated from the vagaries and tyrannies of the land. And human relations as such are emancipated from strict economic necessity.[4]

The possibility of emancipation is accepted as a matter of subjective faith. Objectively, the prospects must be looked at self-consciously because the rate of emancipation or growth, however one chooses to put it, is not measured against the system's previous condition. Rather, it is judged in terms of the existing gaps that separate the country from the developed world. This is, of course, as it ought to be, for it allows the political system to maintain its role as the mobilizing agent in the society and the leading element in the process of change. It is against this background that we shall now try to examine the necessity and the nature of political participation in this country.

True revolutions are always evolutionary. The abrupt change may happen at the end of an evolutionary process that has transformed the basic patterns of power relations in a society. The best example of such a revolution having come to an end of an evolutionary process is the French Revolution. This has been the case in the societies in which development and change have followed an organic pattern. In other cases, revolutions have started after an effective coup d'état. An example of such a revolution is the October Revolution. In effect, a group of people seized power and then set upon a program to change the society after the pattern given by their ideology. The point is that no meaningful revolution ever occurs overnight. Revolutions may be conscious in the sense that certain people form an opinion with respect to the past, present and future and use political power to change their socioeconomic environment.

In Iran we are now at the beginning of the second decade of the Shah and People's Revolution. During the first decade, the socioeconomic infrastructure was changed through the implementation of the 12 principles of the revolution. Among its most important accomplishments have been the change in the landlord-peasant relationship, which affected the majority of the rural population; national control over basic industries; nationalization of a significant part of the country's natural resources; the establishment of a profit-sharing system to extend returns from capital to labor; and perhaps above all, the change in the electoral law allowing for the participation of women in the political process. It has been accomplished with a degree of smoothness not ordinarily seen in other revolutionary experiences.

The people's participation in the first decade was mainly manifested through the original referendum of the Sixth of Bahman. For the most part, the government acted unilaterally to achieve the required socioeconomic transformation with a minimal generation of tension. Nevertheless, the pattern of capital formation in Iran, the centralized nature of decision making, and the insufficiency of channels of communication, have led to socioeconomic discrepancies that must be analyzed.

To be sure, a short-sighted view of the situation may tend to concentrate on contradictions and anomalies of the case. A broader view will see the possibility of the resolution of such contradictions over time.

As the first decade achieved the necessary basic changes in the infrastructure, the emphasis in the second decade must be on popular participation. This emphasis has become a historical necessity, not only in terms of the logic of any revolutionary process, but also due to the requirements of maintaining social integration.

The nature of formation of developmental capital in Iran, coupled with a hegemonial bureaucratic structure acting independently on behalf of the political system, have helped to move the society toward a dichotomization in which those sectors of the public that have greater access to loci of decision making have arrogated a greater part of what there is to themselves. Still some sectors of a society may exist at a per capita income of $200 to $300 or less, if the general per capita level does not exceed $300 or $400. Once the general per capita level moves beyond $1,000 and more, it is no longer possible for the society to absorb discrepancies of such dimensions. On the other hand, as the socioeconomic relations become more complex, changing the distributive pattern may be accomplished only by meaningful changes in systemic structures in order to allow for new power relations to emerge. In other words, the problem is no longer simply economic; it is systemic and basically political. Therefore, it requires systemic and political solutions.

Earlier, we suggested that the first decade of The Shah and People's Revolution in Iran was meant to prepare the infrastructure for moving toward a progressive society based on principles of social justice, equality, freedom and cooperation. The revolution has now entered its second stage: the era of the emergence of mature citizenship acting within the framework of a national political structure designed to allow for optimal participation in the decisions made concerning "authoritative allocation of values." To achieve this situation requires conscious preparatory work. At this juncture, two distinct but interrelated and complementary paths are indicated. The first pertains to the authentication and strengthening of the democratically established representative organs at the various levels of the governmental hierarchy. The second pertains to the process of political mobilization throughout the society.

Concerning the first case, such elective organs already exist. Within a year's time, the hierarchy of representative organs will consist of approximately 50,000 village councils, 440 city councils, 153 provincial councils, 23 Ostan councils leading to the parliament, at the apex composed of the National Consultative Assembly (Majlis) and the Senate. To these must be added the numerous other elective bodies dealing with problems ranging from education to cooperatives and welfare. Potentially, these organs constitute the major channels for the articulation of the political will of the people. Their authenticity depends on the meaningful participation of the people.

There are many factors that affect the rate and range of political participation. The relevant theory maintains that:

> . . . as nations become more economically developed, three major changes occur: (1) the relative size of the upper and middle classes becomes greater; (2) larger numbers of citizens are concentrated in the urban areas; and (3) the density and complexity of economic and secondary organizations increase. These social changes imply political changes. Greater proportions of a population find themselves in life situations which lead to increased political information, political awareness, sense of personal political efficacy, and other relevant attitudes. These attitude changes, in turn, lead to increases in political participation.[5]

The theory concentrates on the cognitive and attitudinal pathways from individuals' positions in the class structure and their involvement in the society's organizational life to their levels of political participation. Leaving aside his position in the class structure for the moment, the individual's cognitive and attitudinal postures are functions of two main clusters of factors: (1) factors bearing on the efficacy of the mobilizational process, of which we shall speak later; and (2) those affecting the authenticity of political structures so that they yield meaningful and tangible returns on political participation. Insofar as it pertains to elective bodies, the second cluster of factors revolves mainly along two axes: (1) the authenticity of the electoral process so those occupying elective seats in the hierarchy of democratic organs feel responsible to their constituencies; and (2) the legal powers of such bodies in the sense that their decisions have significant bearing on the life of the community. Given the political will to achieve the purpose, either case requires both political education and new legal provisions.

The legal aspects of the electoral process are at present under study by different groups. We are moving toward the establishment of single-member electoral districts, permanent registration systems, necessary changes in balloting in order to achieve maximum efficiency and independence for the voter and necessary legal provisions to help reach optimal levels of honesty in elections.

The question of the nature and extent of involvement of the local and provincial democratic councils in political decisions is more complex and merits serious attention. In a bill now before the parliament, new legal powers of participation in decisions concerning allocation of resources have been stipulated for the provincial and *Ostan* councils. Such stipulations, however, assume substance only if corresponding decisions are made at the center to decentralize the governmental structure by delegating relevant decision-making powers in the areas of allocation and administration of development resources to *Ostan*, provincial and local administrators. The decentralization must occur in the realm of planning as well as in administration. A prototype of this process is already in operation in the form of the Plan and Budget Organization's "Special Area Projects," in which allocative decisions are made and implemented in collaboration with provincial councils. This mode of operation should extend systematically to all projects that are not national in scope and character.

Serious efforts in this direction will probably produce two types of results. Given the fact that the bulk of development resources in this country is oil based and therefore centrally generated, decentralization of resource allocation functions will help turn the elective councils into viable institutions through which meaningful popular participation could take place. Otherwise, the activities of such councils will remain limited to the scope provided by the amount of taxes levied on minimal levels of income—a process itself acting as a disincentive for the institutionalization of the councils. Secondly, it will help achieve a modicum of responsibility in administration: the precondition for any progress toward the ends of administrative revolution in Iran.

The organizational form of the proposed decentralization process will probably tend to be modular, *i.e.,* at each level of government relatively self-sufficient decision-making modules composed of relevant executive and legislative bodies act cooperatively to specify and implement their goals. This means that even though decentralization in government is advocated here, at each level of government, powers of the executive are concentrated so that it may be held responsible and responsive to its corresponding legislative organ.

Admittedly, certain constitutional problems present themselves. We are convinced they can be sucessfully tackled and overcome if the necessary conviction and political will exist at the center.

Two lines of argument are generally advanced against the scheme proposed here. Neither is very convincing. One set of reasoning pertains to the scarcity in particular of trained manpower and technological resources at the periphery. Statistically, the argument stands; however, it loses cogency once the problem is posed against the dynamics of socioeconomic relations. While it is true that at the moment capital and technology in Iran are concentrated at the center and in a few large cities, it is also true that unless systemic changes occur in allocative processes, it will be almost impossible to effect a decentralizing pull on these resources.

The second line of argument points to the centrifugal tendencies exhibited in some moments of Iran's history and is apprehensive of possible disintegrative effects of decentralization on society. This argument is patently false because it does not pay proper attention to the historical changes in this country, nor does it recognize the significance of the communication capabilities of the political system. In fact, arguments to the contrary seem more plausible, *i.e.,* opportunities to engage in meaningful political participation coupled with intelligent national policy will lead to higher levels of national integration. Conversely, as we have argued earlier, lack of operational channels of communication in the periphery tends to prevent an equitable distribution of income and privilege, exacerbating the socioeconomic dichotomization of the society. This condition in turn leads to an intensification of social contradictions and will thereby debilitate the bases of political integration.

A different set of questions pertains to the effect of socioeconomic conditions on political participation. It is maintained that the nature of rural-urban divisions and the relatively small size of the middle class in the country preclude the possibility of meaningful participation for a significant proportion of the people. While enjoying some cogency, this line of reasoning is not as solid as it appears to be. Based on the analysis of data taken from the Almond-Verba Five-Nation Study (The Civic Culture), Nie, Powell and Prewitt were able to demonstrate that individuals' levels of social status and organizational involvement were strongly and consistently related to their levels of political participation. But:

> The survey data from five nations showed, further, that organizational involvement was more strongly related to participation, and more consistently from nation to nation, than was social status. Residence in an urban area, contrary to our initial theory, was shown *not* to be related to individual political participation. . . . More advanced nations had, of course, more citizens residing in urban areas, but these individuals did not participate in politics more frequently than their rural counterparts in the same nation.[6]

The study now in progress[7] of the recent national elections in Iran tends to bear out the conclusions reached by the above-named authors. For our purposes, two points emerging from this study are of great interest: (1) that under similar socioeconomic conditions, the difference between rural and urban political participation is negligible; and (2) that it is possible to achieve extensive participation through organized action.

The study of the recent national elections in Iran, although not yet completed, lends tentative support to these conclusions. This means that in spite of the fact that the majority of people live in rural areas under low socioeconomic conditions, given a favorable national policy, they can be involved in political action through effective organizations. Thus arises the possibility not only of achieving a redistribution of power and privilege, but also of a great leap in systemic capacity and power. For indeed, as Clifford Geertz suggests, this process represents not merely "the shifting or transfer of a fixed quantity of power between groups in such a manner that aggregatively the gains of certain groups or individuals match the losses of others, but rather the creation of a new and more efficient machine for the production of power itself, and thus an increase in the general political capacity of the society. This is much more genuinely 'revolutionary' than a mere redistribution, however radical, of power within a given system."[8]

The Rastekhiz (Resurgence) Party of the Iranian Nation

The standard changes effected through decentralization of bureaucracy and authentication of the elective organs at different levels of government pave the way for political participation but do not necessarily achieve it at the desired level. Channels for political communication must be established and utilized in order to mobilize the different sectors of the society for the purpose of participating in the affairs of their community. There is need for qualitative and quantitative development of a communications network capable of enhancing the people's consciousness to the level required for mature, free and equal participation in the political process.

The components of such a communications network include at least two types of channels: the mass media and organizations. The mass media (radio, television, cinema, printed matter, etc.) have a definite and significant part to play in the process of sociopolitical mobilization of the people. Nevertheless, there are certain structural and functional limitations here that must be taken into account. Thus, the use of newspapers, magazines or books is limited by the minimal requirement of literacy. Widespread illiteracy prevents large sectors of the society from meaningful political participation in at least two ways: (1) it inhibits the development of the individual's critical and reflective faculties; and (2) it prevents him from utilizing a very important channel to communicate his needs and observations to the political system. The campaign for meaningful political mobilization must include at its core the campaign for political and social education of which literacy constitutes an inescapable moment. Conversely, success in the eradication of illiteracy can be achieved only if the system generates the kind of political will necessary to mobilize all its ideological and organizational resources in a sustained effort to raise the level of the reflective consciousness of the people.

Radio and television, by overcoming the problem of illiteracy, have a much wider use. Radio in particular, spread around the nation, presents a facile channel for communicating the system's messages to the people. It is, however, a one-way channel; it does not by itself give the listener the opportunity of a dialogue. Moreover, in many cases its messages are not directly assimilated by the recipient; rather, they are mediated through an opinion leader who may or may not interpret the message correctly or favorably. To achieve maximum efficiency, the use of these channels should be coordinated with others of a more immediate nature. Thus, the organizational resources assume particular significance.

For communication purposes, organizational channels of particular utility need not be structurally a part of the political system. In Iran, organizations like the Revolution Corps, the Women's Organization, labor unions, cooperative associations and others can help raise people's political consciousness in their areas of endeavor. However, to be effective, they must be informed and inspired by the values of the system's ideology transmitted through the leadership of the party. This of course is the province of the *Rastakhiz*, the Resurgence Party of the Iranian nation.

The Rastakhiz Party of the Iranian nation was proclaimed by The Shahanshah on 11 Esfand 1353. During the past 10 years, it had become apparent that due to the characteristics of the country's Constitution and its leadership structure, conventional parties, patterned after the Western models, could not properly respond to the political needs of the country. The imperatives of political mobilization and popular participation required an organizational framework inspired by an ideological outlook capable of relating the act of participation to the real loci of power in the polity's decision-making structure. On the other hand, the democratic and equalitarian impulse of the Iranian Constitution and the principles of The Shah and People's Revolution precluded the choice of a one-party system based on some elitist principle that required the exclusion of a large number of the people. The party, therefore, is an all-encompassing entity that potentially includes every member of the nation above the age of 18 who does not deny his adherence to the party's basic principles emanating from the country's cultural and political history and therefore representing the Iranian nationhood. Belief in the historical mission of monarchy, in the Constitution and in the spirit and principles of The Shah and People's Revolution constitutes the means that bind the Iranian people together within the framework of the Rastakhiz Party.

The royal proclamation launching the party stressed the necessity of free and uninhibited dialogue among the members, encouraged by the consensual base created through the party's philosophy. It is the function of the party's leadership and organization to facilitate this dialogue among the mobilized groups and to elicit participating responses in the yet dormant sectors.

The party's organization includes a broad base composed of primary units (*Kanoons*) of 100 to 400 members, depending on whether they are established in the rural or urban areas. These are the primary structures in which political opinions are formed and expressed. In principle, *Kanoons* are admirably suited for the establishment of horizontal relationships among the people of an area as well as between the people and the local government apparatus. Their effectiveness as mobilizing agents depends to a large extent on the organizational and leadership capabilities of the party on the one hand, and success in effecting the decentralization policies alluded to earlier, on the other.

The party's overall organization is composed mainly of two vertical channels: a hierarchy of councils elected upward reaching the Central Council, Executive Committee and the Political Bureau at the apex, and an administrative hierarchy appointed downward but approved at each level by the corresponding elective body. The secretary-general is elected by the party congress, which convenes every four years.

The vertical structure of the party should provide the necessary leadership to encourage greater participation at the base. It should inspire and inform; it should not dominate. It should provide open channels for reciprocal action and reflection. But most important of all, it is the horizontal relations that enrich the citizen's life in the community, that give him a sense of belonging, that help him overcome the alienating forces in his social, economic and cultural environment. The vertical structure can help only if it maintains its openness, absorbs a constant flow of reciprocal information, remains responsive to the needs of the masses, lends them support in their contacts with the bureaucratic structure and provides them with the necessary instruments for the articulation and aggregation of their needs and demands.

All this hinges also upon a serious effort at the decentralization of the governmental structure and activation of the democratic councils based on the pattern we have suggested before. With it, we shall be moving on solid ground; without it, our efforts will be vacuous, devoid of substance. The political atmosphere in Iran, supported by the successes achieved in the country's economic and social life and based on the stability of her political system, strongly suggests the probability of acting vigorously on both fronts.

Footnotes

1. John H. Kautsky, *Political Change in Underdeveloped Countries: Nationalism and Communism* (New York: John Wiley and Sons, 1962), p. 38.

2. John Locke, *The Second Treatise on Government: An Essay Concerning the True Original Extent and End of Civil Government*, J. W. Gough, ed. (New York: Macmillan, 1956), pp. 22–26.

3. Karl W. Deutsch, "Social Mobilization and Political Development," *American Political Science Review*, LV (September 1961), p. 493.

4. Irving Lewis Horowitz, *Three Worlds of Development: The Theory and Practice of International Stratification* (New York: Oxford University Press, 1966), p. 378.

5. Norman H. Nie, G. Bingham Powell, Jr., and Kenneth Prewitt, "Social Structure and Political Participation: Developmental Relationships, II," *American Political Science Review*, 63:3 (September, 1969), pp. 800–832.

6. *Ibid.*, pp. 800–832.

7. This study is being conducted by the Office for the Study of Political Participation and Social Mobilization at the Ministry of Interior.

8. Clifford Geertz, "The Integrative Revolution," in Clifford Geertz (ed.), *Old Societies and New States* (London: Free Press, 1964), p. 121.

Iranian Approaches to Decentralization

M. Bagher Namazi

During the last decade, Iran has become deeply committed to social change and to progressive societal goals. The political will has been mobilized fully to carry out the radical policies needed to transform the social and economic structure of Iran with the objectives of creating a just basis conducive to participation and to ensuring that people from all walks of life are brought into the mainstream of national development.

Through a package reform program spearheaded by land reform, the radical movement of change has been set in motion. This program of reform, commonly known as The Shah and People's Revolution, has created a chain reaction by making its impact felt in all aspects of public life, necessitating more and more changes and reforms to accelerate the pace of modernization—Iranian style.

These changes have also brought into sharp focus some of the glaring deficiencies in the sociopolitical, economic, administrative and institutional framework of the past.

The interaction caused by the reform programs created organized but unarticulated resistance in critical areas of policy making, where key agents of the old system continued to hold power with their old attitudes of feudalism favorable to nepotism, corruption and centralization of decision-making power.

Feudalism has been destroyed where it was most apparent, *i.e.,* in villages, through an effective land distribution program. This aspect of the reform movement was the more physical aspect and perhaps not the most difficult task to perform.

By breaking the back of Iran's landed aristocracy, a basic obstacle to creation of a more fair and just social order was overcome. But the second phase was far more difficult. Two basic actions were required in the second phase:

1. Defining the new societal goals and setting in motion the social institution-building process;

2. Creating the attitudes and habits and social interaction consistent with the new progressive social system.

In the induced-change process, the onus most obviously fell upon the government, which had to:

1. Fill the vacuum created by removal of the feudal forces; and

2. Organize and condition itself to rise to the task in terms of

exercising the necessary leadership and creating the new attitude in the "lead sector" itself.

Feudalism was not a system merely defining and identifying the land-tenure system. It had pervaded the entire social fabric. Building its political and economic strength with a stranglehold over the overwhelming population in the villages, it also controlled the basic part of the national income generated in the agricultural sector. From this seat of power it was able to establish its predominant influence in the judicial, executive and legislative branches of government.

A few of the unfavorable trends encouraged by feudalism are:

- A highly centralized system of public administration top-heavy in Tehran and bedeviled by nepotism and corruption;
- Prevention of progressive legislation that would undermine the feudal power and might spread decision making and resource distribution;
- Prevention of effective, democratically elected participative bodies;
- Stifling of reform programs in the executive branch that the elite had not been able, for various reasons, to prevent in the parliament (the Universal Education Act was a case in point);
- Prevention of individuals from the middle and lower classes from making any incursion into their ranks at the decision-making level.

The initial land reform movement broke the feudal stranglehold on the Iranian economic and social scene. It also released the vast untapped human resources, especially in villages. The supplementary reforms removed barriers created for participation of women—half the population—in public life.

In recognition of the key role of the education system and public administration in shaping the basis of reforms for today and creating the new citizens of tomorrow with the right skills and attitudes, both education and administrative reforms were introduced as part of the reform package, and on both scores the performance fell far short of expectation.

Obviously, the strength of feudalism and its influence on the administrative system, together with the built-in resistance of the bureaucracy, were underestimated. Thirteen years after the introduction of the reform movement, both programs have fallen far short of the goals laid down.

Thus, rural cooperatives have been set up in large numbers, lacking in depth and failing to meet the needs of the rural population. Quantitatively, the education system has expanded; but qualitatively, progress has been unsatisfactory. The education system has failed to respond to the needs of the economy and has failed in inculcating pupils and students with the necessary innovative spirit and analytical mind.

To overcome the critical bottlenecks to social change and to help create the developmental system of public administration, the effort has shifted from only induced reforms from above to the creation of viable participatory bodies at the local level to support and strengthen the reform movement from below. It is also recognized that the supportive drive from below can have a vital "spread effect" and create the strong social roots necessary to sustain and enrich the more progressive new social order.

In addition to this sociopolitical need, the very size of the planned development effort and the investment level has increased in proportions far outstripping the centers' capacity to promote and to control them. A quick glance at the financial size of Iran's plans will be very revealing: The size of development investment in Iran has increased very rapidly during the last three decades. A few figures are indicative of this trend. The size of Iran's First Seven Year Development Plan, launched in 1948, was less than $300 million. The Second Seven Year Plan, ending in 1962, was about $1 billion. The Third Five Year Plan was about $2.5 billion. The Fourth Plan's public investment target reached $7 billion. The original size for 1978 was $30 billion and was recently revised upward to $60 billion. Early predictions for the Sixth Five Year Plan public investment figure are about $150 billion.

Iran's development effort is committed to the political goals of public participation and fairer distribution of income and opportunities. These principles can be realized far more effectively within the context of the more decentralized system responsive and sensitized to felt needs of the people and to the public will. In addition, the questions of efficiency and effective management cannot be settled in a centralized system within the vast increase in the size of public investment.

Even before improvement in the income situation resulting from the increase in the price of oil, Iranian decision makers had given much attention to the need for decentralization and regional development.

Background to the Regionalization Effort

During the First and Second Seven Year Development Plans, special investments were allocated to regional development. The creation of the Khuzestan Development Authority, the Ital Consult Study on Sistan and Baluchestan and cost-sharing projects with municipalities were instances of types of regional development activities promoted and acted upon during the First and Second Plans.

The Third Plan shifted from the listing of projects to more comprehensive approaches to national planning. The planners adopted a more comprehensive approach to regional development. The Third Plan had a special regional development chapter that aimed at institutionalizing the regional development planning system. Specific recommendations were made for setting up regional planning units in the provinces. The Third Plan law also provided the legal base for having projects identified and executed by provincial authorities. Initial steps were taken to set up regional development organizations in limited areas. These development organizations gradually restricted their work to agriculture and were subsequently released from their affiliations with the Plan Organization and were transferred to the Ministry of Agriculture.

The planning units in the provinces in practice became technical operating units to meet the shortage of technical skills in the provinces. These technical units, too, became the provincial branches of the newly created Ministry of Housing and Development.

With the experience of past plans, the Fourth Plan emphasized the study and survey of regions for their economic potential. A large sum of money was invested in comprehensive in-depth studies by consulting engineers in Khorasan, Bandar Abbas and Kermanshah. The results of these studies were not utilized very effectively in actual practice.

The most significant event during the Fourth Plan with respect to regionalization took place in 1350 (1971), when the country was celebrating the 25th century of the founding of the monarchy system in Iran. The celebrations generated a spur to developmental activities. To commemorate the occasion, the Plan Organization promoted a small complex of provincial development projects mainly made up of small-scale education, urban and community development, rural reconstruction, etc.—projects with important local impact. The major point of departure of these projects was the financial decision-making power transferred to provincial authorities for the first time. The zeal for construction created by the celebrations overrode the opposition of centralist forces, which had until then successfully resisted all measures aimed at promoting the political goal of decentralization.

At the same time, another important decentralization objective was put into practice. The constitution of Iran provides for creation of democratically elected local bodies. The Town and Provincial Councils Law was passed. After more than half a century, the provinces were to be given a more effective voice in decision making through these councils.

The provincial project complexes were linked up more effectively to the local councils for more detailed programs approved especially with respect to distribution of the centrally allocated funds within a province and, more specifically, in respect of approval of location of the projects.

During preparation work on the Fifth Plan, an ambitious approach to regional development planning was adopted. A foreign consulting firm was hired to do a study at the regional level and help prepare a strong regional component for the Fifth Plan.

Outlook to the Fifth Development Plan

As the Fourth Plan drew to an end, spurred by a big boost in oil revenues, the economic growth role became accelerated. The Iranian economy became more complicated and sophisticated. The size of the development investment had increased to proportions far beyond expectations.

The rapid increase in the pace of economic growth tended to intensify regional disparities resulting in the danger of serious imbalances. Such regional disparities could not be tolerated by a government committed to social and welfare goals as indicated in the White Revolution Charter of Iran. Despite partial efforts of the past, decentralization and regional development goals had not made a serious impact. The centralized administrative structure had stultified all measures designed to streamline the bureaucracy and create a more rational decentralized system of decision making and resources allocation. Efforts to regionalize the national budget had not been successful.

The centralized system obviously could not respond to the developmental needs of the country. Administrative structures in the region, where most operations were to take place, remained weak and ineffective. The best talents continued to be concentrated in Tehran.

With such a background, the Fifth Plan was formulated with the following objectives in regional development:

- Contributing to the national goals of a fair distribution of income and employment opportunities, raising levels of living of the masses throughout the country (especially less-privileged groups), improving the quality of life and increasing the scope and extent of social services, and creating favorable grounds for the effective participation of all people in the development process;
- Narrowing regional disparities and developing potential regions;
- Utilizing more effectively existing productive capacities;
- Striving to achieve an optimal population settlement pattern;
- Bringing about more effective coordination in the investment process.

Policy Instruments

In order to realize the objectives set out in the Fifth Plan, a number of policy instruments were foreseen. The legal base was envisaged in the

Fifth Plan Law to formalize the system created for provincial project complexes, which were given the term "special regional projects." The law also made it mandatory for the government to gradually regionalize the budget system during the Fifth Plan period.

In order to boost technical and administrative capacity at the provincial level, the following measures were outlined:

- Setting up of strong regional planning units;
- Creation of Provincial Development Authorities (PDA);
- Boosting of the authority of the governors to give them the leading executive role in the regional development process.

The country was divided into 11 development regions, each with an investment program aimed at achieving a certain growth rate. Eleven percent (about 180 billion rials) of the Fifth Plan sectoral funds were allotted for special regional projects.

As the Fifth Plan was launched, the contradictions of the regional plan with the centralized government system began to show itself. In practice, the $2 million study by the consulting firm was not reconciled with sectoral plans, and the two evolved in isolation. The sectoral programs were adopted, and the regional studies and projects identified were put aside.

The division of the country into 11 regions was also rejected because the regions did not conform to the political and administrative divisions. In practice, the government favored the structural divisions in the provinces and the leading role of the governors.

The Provincial Development Authorities formally were limited to two to three provinces during the first two years. The idea of spreading them to all provinces was rejected. It was felt that it was more feasible to concentrate them in the lesser-developed provinces where development capacity was limited. The innovative features of the new PDAs were the combination of political and development authority. The PDAs were headed by governors with development experience. Each operational ministry delegated its powers to the governor who thus had all the necessary decision-making powers and the financial and technical resources required.

Problems and Shortcomings

The long history of centralization in the system of decision making has created complicated sociocultural and administrative barriers impeding the decentralization effort. Some of the problems are listed below:

1. A strong attitude in the bureaucracy to centralize decisions in Tehran. Even highly placed people sometimes moving from Tehran to

the provinces would soon reconcile themselves to the existing tradition of looking to Tehran for all decisions.

2. Most of the regionalization efforts were partial and ineffective. Manpower, especially the highly trained, was discouraged by regulations and the central-based policy-making structure from serving in the provinces.

3. Special regional projects covered less than 10 percent of investment in the region. Thus, the economic situation in the region was basically determined by national projects decided upon by ministries and the Plan and Budget Organization in Tehran.

4. Administrative structures in the regions were replicas of central ministries with no special orientation to the needs of the area or to the potential of the region.

5. The heavy concentration of infrastructure and investment in Tehran added to the location of Tehran as the seat of power for decision making.

6. The data base and flow of information had little provincial base.

Thus, high-level manpower, the most critical factor for providing regions within the capacity for taking a fairer share of the economic cake and putting it to effective use, has been further drawn to Tehran. In this way, centralization continued to feed itself at the expense of the provinces.

A study carried out a few years back shows that 43 percent of the GNP (excluding oil), 67 percent of value added in nonmetallic industries, 60 percent of value added in the construction industries and 76 percent of automobiles produced and imported were concentrated in Tehran.

A careful analysis will reveal that past efforts have not made the necessary impact on the situation. The system had not become decentralized and regional planning had not become a serious part of the planning system. The traditional systematic effort of comprehensive regional planning based on studies had made no impression.

Administrative reform envisaged as part of the revolutionary charter of Iran was closely interlinked with decentralization. And this was the aspect of the reform program that was least successful.

The Leverage Approach

Past experience in Iran has revealed that despite strong policy pronouncements on regional development and decentralization, the built-in resistance of the bureaucracy to changes implied in the regionalization policy prevented the program from making any significant impact.

It was evident that a real and viable regional planning system could not be reconciled with the deep-rooted, centrally structured system of administration. The established centralized decision-making process is strengthened by the highly sectoralized planning system. Thus, the regional planning system had to cope not only with the outside resistance of ministries, but also with the sectoral departments of the Plan Organization. The latter were often able to negate and undermine regional planning from within even more effectively than the ministries.

In such a situation, staff units whose functions cut across sectors were not given a very serious role and voice in resource allocation. The regional planning unit was faced with the same dilemma.

The comprehensive approach to regional development, based on studies and survey of the regions, would make no impact on the sector-oriented system. The administration lacked the capacity at the regional, or even central, level to absorb such studies—thus, the ineffectiveness of the expensive surveys carried out during the Fourth Plan.

To institute the principles of regional development based on decentralization and participation, major and radical changes are needed in the Iranian system of public administration. This means a complete regionalization of the entire government system in order to limit the work of central development ministries to staff functions supported by small and technically viable units in the center. In this way, large armies of staff can be released for operations in the field.

All over the world bureaucracies have developed a built-in system of resistance to change. Thus, the traditional approach of expert group studies and diagnosis and prognosis has not produced the desired results.

A new approach was needed that was fitted to the Iranian sociopolitical and administrative environment. The main problem was to make an impact. To cope with the need, the leverage approach was devised and adapted by the author to induce change in the desired direction. Let us see in a nutshell what the leverage approach is and examine its impact in the Iranian case.

Regional planning and decentralization bring a vast field under their purview. By seeking to tackle the problems on all fronts with the vast ramifications, it is likely to have the limited resources available for this task so thinly spread that no impact can be made.

To concentrate on studies and surveys will make the problem more complicated and difficult to resolve in view of the feeding process of centralization strengthening its hold on the decision-making process. The slow process of mounting comprehensive studies will give the built-in forces of resistance to change time and opportunity to nullify the effort in view of the strong groups of vested interests in the administration.

The new approach is selective and concentrates on few, but very critical, points of impact with the objective of inducing a chain reaction and setting up a process of change in the desired direction of decentralization.

An analysis of the power potential of this critical impact area is needed to minimize the margin of risk and error. Thus, the action and the instruments supporting the action must be carefully weighed. In some ways, it is like waging a strategic and tactical war on vulnerable defense lines of the enemy to break down its resistance. Some of the critical points of impact identified and applied in the Iranian case are as follows:

1. *Taking over gradual control of the development funds for the regions.* Instead of starting with the comprehensive planning approach, the selective project approach was adopted. The Fifth Plan provided that 11 percent of the development funds would be earmarked as special regional projects.

A concentrated effort was mounted to hand over decision-making authority of these projects to local bodies. Around these projects gradual programming capacity was built. Because of the real decision-making potential of these projects to cope to some extent (but effectively and decisively) with locally felt needs, the work became attractive. Thus, the provincial planning units set up around these projects with all powers of the Plan and Budget Organization delegated to them fell into place quickly and were soon accepted by local authorities. The process of acceptance by planning units in the central ministries initiated under the Third Plan took much longer.

Once acceptability had been created, provincial planning was gradually introduced. At present, 11 of the 23 provinces have their own approved medium-term plans, and the rest will follow soon.

2. *Democratization of the local decision-making process with respect to resource distribution.* From the very start, these special regional projects (SRPs) emphasized public participation. The objective was to create a trend of sensitizing the local administration to felt needs of the people and generating the attitude of responsiveness to the expressions given to these needs through the local democratic councils.

The law passed governing the SRPs provided that final approval of the projects would rest with the local district and provincial councils. The chain reaction induced by this approach was far-reaching. A few instances will be cited.

During the second year of the SRP law's implementation, some local councils became conscious of their potential authority. When the cabinet introduced a 30 percent ($100 million) cut in the budget of those projects, councilmen in at least one province took exception to this one-sided decision, came to Tehran and with the help of parliament restored the cut.

Sharp parliamentary discussions were touched off during the budget debates. More time was spent by the parliament examining the impact of these projects than the rest of the budget. Parliamentary debates fed by local councilmen sharply criticized the ministries and the Plan Organization for not responding adequately to the needs expressed by the councils. Executing bodies and ministries came under heavy fire for inefficiency where projects were lagging behind, thus exercising strong pressure on ministries to improve their performance capacity at the provincial level.

Strong pressure was exercised on the government to liberalize regulations governing these projects and increase the size of investment. Instead of programs approved by the center, regulations were changed, compelling the center to restrict its decision-making intervention to global allocation for each province. Local provincial councils would approve the share of each district on the basis of population, size, need, potential and location.

In the revised version of the Fifth Plan, the share of development funds to be handled by the regions increased from 11 percent to 40 percent. Each province was required to have its own plan in the context of the national plan. The government was urged to study the possibilities of introducing administrative changes in order to gear the administration in each province to local needs and objectives spelled out in provincial plans.

A new form of middle-level "area projects" was identified with implementation powers, especially for ratifying project agreements, hiring consulting firms and contractors, delegated to local officials.

3. *Innovation and experimentation*. The emphasis on **innovation and participation** inherent in the SRPs will demonstrate the economic and social feasibility of regionalization.

As the SRPs begin to make impact, the scope of the projects can be increased. With the resulting increase in local technical know-how, gradually the more ambitious and more comprehensive regional development planning system can be created. Thus, comprehensiveness will be achieved on a step-by-step basis. Alongside this work, strong pressure for capacity building will intensify the effort in the provinces.

In addition to the project approach, some administrative innovations and changes in the management of a few projects are also envisaged at the regional level. To prevent these innovative experiments being undermined by the traditional bureaucracy, they are planned to be located as far away as possible from Tehran, where the bureaucracy has not taken too-deep roots.

The Provincial Development Authorities set up already in Bandar Abbas, Sistan, Baluchestan and Kurdestan and headed by the respective governors provide good opportunities for a de facto reorganization of the local administration to respond to regional needs and regional plans.

The special authority vested by the ministers in the heads of the PDAs give the governor an opportunity to informally reorganize the technical staff in the provinces to work across ministerially defined administrative lines. For instance, in Baluchestan and Sistan, all engineers working in the province will be pooled in the Technical Bureau of the PDA. Once any of these formal administrative changes produce results, one will have a working model to demonstrate the shortcomings of the present administration.

Other experiments include integrated socioeconomic approaches to development of geographical zones and communities.

A special comprehensive tribal community development project in Kerman, based on self-aid and participation of the people themselves, has produced remarkable results. The Kerman model is now being tried in several other provinces. In Kerman, the needs of a tribal community were studied by a group of interdisciplinary experts on the orders of the Empress. Development agents were identified from within the community and a respected local leader was recommended as project manager.*

An evaluation of the project has revealed that the return on the investment channeled through such unconventional people-based methods has produced benefits several times those of normal government projects. It has also served to effectively mobilize the participation of the tribal people in project implementation and later upkeep of the facilities created.

Other zonal plans are being conceived that are not linked to the traditional administration. The socioeconomic study of one of the districts of Lorestan is a case in point. Needs and potentials are being studied. On the basis of the study, a comprehensive socioeconomic plan based on popular participation (and increasing capacity for more effective participants) will be drawn up. A light administrative structure will be formed to implement the comprehensive plan. This structure will be dictated by the regional needs and will not correspond to the central administration.

It is expected that before the work on preparation of the Sixth Plan begins, several successful experimental models of regional and zonal development will have been realized. These operationally tested models can then provide an effective basis for a more comprehensive approach to regionalization of the government. By publicizing the results of such real experiments, the challenge to the traditional administration can be made. We will also have set into motion a process of administrative change supported by local authorities in a few regions.

4. *Attack from above.* While the change from below is being effected to demonstrate the inconsistencies of the traditional administration, the top of the structure must not be left without a dent.

---

*The project provides for training of local manpower as development agents. It also provides social services and economic needs, such as cooperative credits. Physical activities, such as building rural roads, drilling wells and setting up warehouses, are also provided.

The nerve center of the public administration in Iran is the Plan and Budget Organization (PBO) itself. The new law made the planning body responsible for coordination of all development policies and investments. So far, the Plan Organization has been based on sectoral units reflecting the ministerial division of work. Until the Fifth Plan, the staff intersectoral units, such as the Economic and Social Policy Bureau and the Regional Development Division, did not play a major role in decision making. Thus, like other planning set-ups, the staff work needed to bring about "interrelatedness" in policy and the coordination of investment decisions were not very effective.

With the new organization of PBO, staff units have been given a far greater role. A regionalization department at the undersecretarial level has been set up. However, the sectoral ministry-oriented units still prevail. A more radical approach would be to scrap the sectoral units and transfer all work on sectoral planning to the ministries. The PBO would then have units concentrating mainly on interdisciplinary and intersectoral work. In this way, project, program and plan recommendations coming from ministries would be analyzed and examined in a far greater and more meaningful perspective.

Such an outlook by PBO, which controls allocation of the tremendous financial resources of the country, would provide a new outlook to investment and policy issues. It would also reveal gaps and overlaps resulting from present ministry- and sector-oriented structures. By systematic and continuous interdisciplinary staff work the inconsistencies would be revealed more and more and the crucial need to revitalize the present system would become more evident.

5. *Capacity building.* Such efforts from below and from above have to be supported by qualified and trained staff. The need for action-oriented study and research and the capacity for conducting them is evident. Unfortunately, the increasing viability of the private sector and the attraction of high-level administrative posts offered to trained and qualified economists and social scientists in the large number of ministries in the center make it difficult for PBO to mobilize sufficient brainpower in its traditional structure, governed by normal recruitment policies.

Thus, a National Development Institute for Planning Operation Research and Training has been foreseen. This institute, which is gradually being built up with the most capable staff, is designed to attract the best talents to give scientific support to the new effort. At present, the focus of the institute, which has started as a joint Iranian-U. N. project, is on regional development issues.

At the provincial level, planning units have been set up as viable branches of the Plan Organization. With respect to regional plans and projects, they have been vested with the authority and responsibility of PBO. With a few innovations, especially delegation of decision-making authority, some of the able talents of PBO have been attracted to the field. These units, which are very slowly but very definitely developing their staff, have a key role to play in the new process. Starting with the special regional projects, some of them are now moving gradually to comprehensive planning. They thus provide the needed staff support at the local level.

Recommendations

Several effective leverages have been created to strengthen the decentralization and democratization of the decision-making process. Some of these are more important than the others in speeding up the change process and mounting strong pressure upon the decision-making process to respond.

The key leverage of change lies in the vast potential of the participatory bodies such as provincial, district and village councils. By concentrating on increasing the powers of these councils with respect to resource distribution, the councils will become more and more attractive for drawing the best of the local talents to its folds. These better quality local decision makers will do a better job of ensuring that local projects conform to local needs. They will also keep up and intensify pressure for supplementary reforms and changes, especially in sensitization of the local administration to community needs.

Together, these councils, using support of the parliament in the center and working all over the country, will bring such pressure on the central administration to revitalize and rid itself of remnants of feudal attitudes and deadwood that no government will be able to or dare resist.

The bureaucracy in the center must be effectively curtailed, both to prevent red tape and centralization from hampering innovation and effective action at the local level, and to release much-needed manpower from routine work in the center for creative and productive activity in the field.

Thus, the pressure of change and delegation of power to the regions generated by the elected members of the councils will help in inducing the difficult decision of scrapping several ministries and streamlining them into more viable departments, exercising staff function supporting the field work.

Has the leverage approach worked? It is too early to make a definite appraisal. Perhaps this question can be answered to some extent at the end of the Fifth Plan. The power has been delegated to the provinces. Local councils have come to play a leading role in resource allocation. For the next year, 11 development ministries have been required to decentralize their budget; planning consciousness at the provincial level has been created to a large extent. Regional authorities such as Regional Development Banks have been founded.

However, the real test will come in the Sixth Plan, when reorganizing the government system on a decentralized basis, and regionalization of the whole planning system itself, will have to be put into effect.

Comments and Discussion

Discussion at several plenary sessions of the symposium dealt with the changing leadership in Iran.

In introducing "Modernization and Changing Leadership in Iran," Amin Alimard observed, first, that the monarchy has always been the most important political institution in Iran and that the Shah is the most important elite. The central role of the Shah in the political process is a fundamental point. The other essential point to understand in considering Iranian leadership is the determination of the Shah to transform Iran into a modern industrial society. Mr. Alimard commented on the major reforms undertaken by the Shah in reaction to the systematic challenges facing Iran; on his recruitment of younger men with technical expertise, *i.e.*, individuals who have achieved something and not just persons of wealth and social status; on certain economic, political and social results of The Shah and People's Revolution, including rising levels of expectation; and on administrative and political changes undertaken to strengthen government, mobilize the population for development and increase participation in the political process.

The nature of, and need for, political participation in Iran were discussed by Gholamreza Afkhami in introducing "Social Mobilization and Participation in Iran." Mr. Afkhami commented first on Iran's political response to the colonial experience and then on the perceived responsibility of the political process for achieving development. Mr. Afkhami noted that development was very different in the West, where it was organic, from what it has been in Iran, where the process has been reversed, with consciousness of development preceding the fact of development. Mr. Afkhami described Iran's political system and the accomplishments of The Shah and People's Revolution. At the same time, some factors, including the pattern of capital formation, the centralization of decision making and the insufficiency of channels of communication, have led to some socioeconomic discrepancies. Mr. Afkhami stressed the importance of popular participation in the second decade of the revolution and suggested some possible consequences of moves toward decentralization. He commented also on the need for new communications networks and on the role of the Rastakhiz (Resurgence) Party in mobilizing popular participation.

Mr. Elahi suggested that The Shah and People's Revolution has led to several political developments, namely, an increased infrastructure, rising expectations that will affect the political system for years to come, increasing dependency of government's legitimacy on its ability to fulfill material aspirations and increasingly vulnerable elites. These developments obviously present some problems; they may also offer opportunities since the elites can increase their legitimacy by responding to demands and meeting needs. In many countries, regimes have no option but control and repression; in Iran, the government, seeking to change society, needs power to mobilize people for development, to create conditions that permit people to act like citizens and to respond to popular demands. The function of the Resurgence Party is to change the status quo, not preserve it.

In "Iranian Approaches to Decentralization," M. Bagher Namazi described Iran's attempts to share decision making between national and local levels. He cited the regional development goals of the Fifth Plan, including fair income distribution and employment opportunities, lessened disparities among the regions, more effective utilization of producing capacities, optimal population settlement and more effective coordination of investments. Mr. Namazi observed that Iran's political goals are clear; ways are being sought to carry them out. Land reform created the basis for participation by the rural population. The central government is mainly responsible for national development, and the public administration system needed to be revitalized for the land reform task. As a result, administrative changes have been included in the overall social reform program. Since decentralization is not being achieved so rapidly as was hoped, new approaches—including the "leverage approach" to decentralization, involving selective use of development funds for the regions, local decision making about resource use, innovation, a new role for the Plan and Budget Organization and capacity building—are being tried. Mr. Namazi concluded that the subjects of all three essays presented—the development of new elites, social mobilization, popular participation, and decentralization—are entwined.

In the discussion that followed these presentations, participants focused on political structures and their roles, popular participation in the political process, human freedom and decentralization.

Political Power in Iran

Observing that social vocabulary is not always easy to translate into political reality, a European asked what is really involved in "activating" and "converting" "power resources," including "disaffected individuals."* One could infer from this that manipulation of society is perceived as being normal. The speaker asked how the ruling elite is structured, what its attitudes are, how it interprets its goals and how dialogue occurs, including within regional and local units and within the Resurgence Party. Without dialogue, the powerful elite may be isolated.

An Iranian responding to these questions observed that the issue is not personal power but systemic power, how society

---

*Language used by Messrs. Afkhami and Elahi in "Social Mobilization and Participation in Iran"; see page 228 of this book.

mobilizes its resources to achieve its goals; that "activating resources" does not imply power by one group over another but, rather, interaction and mobilization of an otherwise dormant group; that development in Iran is a serious, overriding concern; that the political system must reorient itself so as to involve people in politics and mobilize them for development; and that dialogue is seen as a two-way exchange to bring about changes in political attitudes.

Responding to a European's suggestion that if the government seeks to mobilize acceptance of tenets from on high, this is a method of imposing, not sharing, power, an Iranian affirmed the government's genuine concern for getting more grass-roots participation by Iranians in saying what their needs and priorities are. It seeks dialogue with the people so that it may set national priorities on the basis of knowledge of their views. Until such time as everyone can participate effectively, Iran's elites, who come from all sectors of society, are trying now to make decisions that will shape the future. Another Iranian stressed that the question of mobilization is directly related to such questions as income distribution and development. The situation in Iran is very different from that in the West.

Question of the One-Party State

The nature and role of the Resurgence Party and opportunities for dissent in Iran were discussed at length.

Various non-Iranians commented with respect to one-party states that national parties in one-party states can become mere vehicles for control; that one-party systems often fail to maintain the probity of those in power and/or to renew themselves, sometimes becoming arrogant or concerned only with maintaining themselves; and that Westerners should keep an open mind about political structures: there may be no need for two parties as long as there is room for dissent.

Iranian responses to these and other comments indicated, first, that there is ample place for dissent within the party, which includes two wings—one called "progressive" and the other "constructive." (But there is no obligation to belong to either wing, and many party members, particularly the rank and file, are not identified with either group.) Both wings are represented throughout the country. Discussion goes on in party cells and councils at district, town and village levels, with different views expressed at all levels. If consensus is reached at a lower level, it is transmitted up through the structure of the party. The Central Council and Executive Committee of the party make final decisions on the basis of proposals from lower levels.

The sincerity of the one-party system in Iran was emphasized by one participant, who noted that many Iranians are now participating actively in politics who refused to do so earlier when there were two parties, mainly because they saw no difference between the former parties and no opportunity for playing a real role. On the contrary, today there is very open dialogue within the party, including freedom of dissent over political and social issues. Another speaker stressed that the party is open to all Iranian citizens, with only three obligatory principles: members must adhere to the institution of monarchy, the constitution and the principles of the White Revolution (The Shah and People's Revolution). Differing views on any other subjects are acceptable within the party.

Responding to a question about whether changing conditions might make it appropriate at some future date to modify the present one-party system, a member of the Executive Council of the Resurgence Party indicated that the party's structure would change when circumstances change; at the moment a single structure is needed to reach people outside the political system and engage them in dialogue. As time goes by, in 10, 15 or 20 years, when political participation takes root and illiteracy is completely eliminated, conditions may become right for two political parties to operate. But there is no basis for a two-party system now. Economic, political and social goals—including literacy, better income distribution and the sharing of the fruits of development—must first be achieved. Another speaker recalled that Iran had tried a two-party system and that it failed to solve problems of development or mobilize human resources. Another Iranian concurred that the chaos that followed World War II and the succeeding period of a two-party system, which favored landed aristocracy and feudal lords, did not further economic or social development; the present system is Iran's third attempt and is proving far more successful. The one-party system was seen by another speaker as an effective tool for mobilizing the people to participate in development; if there were a variety of political structures, people might participate for the wrong reasons, in the hope of personal gain. As it is, the party provides an inspirational ideology and a means for allowing people to organize themselves and debate relevant issues.

Responding to questions about renewal of party leadership, several Iranians observed that changing the elite, replacing the old elite by younger members with different backgrounds and bringing in new blood at all times may save the party from the "arrogance" of power, and that new elites are constantly being developed through education, including, especially, young people from lower classes trained in Iran. A question about party membership requirements was answered by an Iranian who explained that there is no obligation to belong to the party. Individuals in the private (business) sector find no problems in not belonging, but politically ambitious persons in the public sector (government) probably should belong, with all the possibilities for dissent described above. No one is punished for deferring membership—just as no one was penalized for not voting in the last election, despite rumors to the contrary that came from outside Iran.

The general question of limits on freedom of expression in Iran was raised in connection with the discussion of a one-party system. Several non-Iranians expressed the view that political structure matters less than freedom to express dissent. Various Iranians indicated that, except for challenges to the institution of monarchy, the constitution and the principles of The Shah and People's Revolution, Iranians are free to speak about any matter; that the question of balance between individual freedoms and the interests of the state is an age-old question; and that there is frequent open criticism of the government on domestic matters, including in the offical party journal. The need for each state to resolve these questions for itself, in light of its stage of development and cultural and historical background, was affirmed by a non-Iranian, who shared the view that social discipline may be needed to devise and implement desirable social programs, *e.g.,* schooling for children. This is acceptable as long as the system is open to criticism from within and capable of change. The final Iranian speaker on this point affirmed that the system tolerates constructive dissent and criticism and suggested that the proceedings of the present symposium are witness to this fact. The government must respect individual rights but, given the fact that over 50 percent of the population is still illiterate, it cannot allow the misuse of individual freedoms by some who aim at the creation of discord and chaos in the interests of bygone feudal lords, foreign powers or ultraconservative and reactionary groups opposing women's emancipation or the like. A non-Iranian concluded that American and other foreign visitors must recognize government as "the art of the possible"; an American added that many questions by non-Iranians stemmed from their high expectations of Iran's capacity for greatness.

Rapidity and Extent of Popular Participation

Responding to an observation that forces at work may lead to greater social tensions and quite different problems from those of the past decade—with the possible result that people may drop out of the political process and/or develop resistance to government—several Iranians suggested that Iran has successfully met challenges so far and that Iranians will probably accept new values; moreover, the creation of a new political infrastructure through new party cells should increase popular participation and, by bringing nonparticipants into the political system, decrease some pressures. Another Iranian concurred that participation is essential but anticipated some future conflicts. Development is fraught with tension. It will be necessary to create a dynamic balance among forces in society, to help them move ahead, to develop an open process and to establish a society based on a meaningful concept of justice. An Iranian added that participation is a complex question but expressed the view that people will participate if they feel it can make a difference in their lives.

(An American warned, however, that successful participation by low-income groups—resulting in material gains—could work to the detriment of economic growth since "payoffs" necessitated by political considerations could slow concentrated efforts to achieve growth.)

Decentralization in Iran

Responding to questions about the extent of decentralization in Iran, various Iranians observed that visits by cabinet members and other government officials to the provinces, where they meet with provincial councils, are achieving results. The councils do challenge some broad development strategies in areas like rural development and rural education, and their views are having an effect on decision making. Some decisions not well related to local needs have been set aside. The councils also play a role in deciding how to spend the 10 percent of development funds allocated by the center to the provinces. Groundwork is being laid for more effective participation. As people feel that they can improve their villages and provinces by electing representatives to their local councils, they will participate more fully.

A non-Iranian wondered if it is wise to decentralize as much as envisaged: if regional bodies are formed, they may seek autonomy. Responding to his question about how to keep provincial bodies from overreaching the authority of the central government, an Iranian explained that there are strong checks to prevent decentralization's leading to antinationalism, including a manpower check (the provinces are dependent on the center for supplies of trained manpower) and a financial check (funds from the center). Moreover, the national planning system has not been changed; regional activities will emerge within the framework of the national planning system. Planners are merely seeking to assure popular participation and responsiveness of national plans to local needs. In addition, people performing administrative functions in the regions are, to a great extent, responsible to the center (although they should ideally be increasingly responsive to needs expressed by local councils).

The possibility that decentralization may work against development by stimulating demands for consumer goods, leading to an enormous burden 20 years from now, was mentioned by one American. But an Iranian questioned this view, observing that provinces cannot be allowed to "die" as the result of population movement to Tehran. (Moreover, Tehran cannot support more than 5½ million people owing to limited water resources.) The government must pursue a policy of balanced growth and bring industry and employment to the regions. In any case, it is desirable to seek participation in policy formulation by all sectors of the population, even if this represents a risk to economic growth. Other Iranians concurred that decentralization is important for other than material reasons; it gives people a chance to shape their lives.

The question of how decentralization will affect different ethnic groups was discussed briefly. An Iranian pointed out that since 1962 the government has made a special effort to study the problems and needs of various tribes in the rural areas; a good bit of research and some action have gone forward. Land reform has benefited the tribes by removing land holdings from tribal chiefs, and tribes are establishing cooperatives in many areas. Although many tribes are nomadic, the government has created mobile tribal schools on a large scale, as well as free tribal boarding schools in cities like Shiraz to provide high school courses for the children of those who cannot afford boarding costs in cities.

The possible transfer of taxing powers to the provinces was mentioned by a non-Iranian as potentially important in the future when industry will have supplanted oil as the basis of the economy. An Iranian noted that the new Local Council Law includes provision for local taxation by councils in limited areas, but this is relatively unimportant now since oil revenues—the major source of development financing—are centralized and being expended in the regions by the center.

Income Distribution in Iran

Income Distribution and Its Major Determinants in Iran

M. H. Pesaran

An equitable distribution of income has long been recognized to be a prerequisite of economic and political stability and is central to the economic welfare of both developed and developing countries. In spite of this general concern about income distribution, until quite recently the accent in the developing countries has been placed largely upon growth and industrialization, and relatively little attention has been paid to problems connected with income distribution. The rationale behind this approach to development planning is the belief that, in the early stages of rapid economic development, inequalities in the distribution of income among households, economic sectors and regions are bound to increase, but as development proceeds and exceeds a certain threshold level, income distribution will "automatically" improve, and the gap between rich and poor will eventually narrow.

Recent experiences of most developing countries as well as a greater theoretical understanding of the issues concerning the relationship between income distribution and the development process have put under suspicion the view that economic growth by itself can solve or even ease the problem of income distribution within any reasonable time period. A joint study by the World Bank's Development Research Center and the Institute of Development Studies at the University of Sussex also reaches similar conclusions and advocates a reexamination of policies of growth and income distribution in developing countries.

It is the purpose of this essay to investigate the interrelationship of growth and distribution in the Iranian economy. In the first section we shall briefly review the past and the present trends of income distribution in Iran. In the second section we shall make a preliminary attempt at identifying the socioeconomic and demographic characteristics of households by expenditure classes. In the third section we shall briefly discuss the theoretical and empirical attempts that have been made for determining the factors influencing the size distribution of income. In this section we shall also consider the cross-section evidence concerning the distribution of household expenditure in the major regions of the country and derive an econometric relationship for explaining variations in the size distribution of expenditure of different regions of the country in terms of several economic, social and demographic variables such as the level of development, the ratio of urban to rural household expenditure, age distribution and the rate of participation of households in economic activities. In this way, we hope to single out the major factors that have been responsible for the inequality of incomes in Iran.

Statistical Evidence on Income Distribution

There are no official statistics on income distribution in Iran. Income tax data, due to their very small coverage, are of little use. In spite of these data problems, it is, nevertheless, possible to employ household expenditure figures from sample surveys to arrive at some reasonable estimates of the distribution of income and its trends, as has already been argued in a previous paper.[1]

The annual household expenditure surveys of Bank Markazi Iran (BMI) give the distribution of household expenditures by expenditure brackets in urban areas, and the surveys carried out by the Statistical Center of Iran (SCI) provide expenditure distributions for both urban and rural areas.

The decile distribution of household expenditure for urban areas has been computed for the years 1959–60 and 1969–70 to 1973–74 on the basis of BMI surveys. The results are given in Table 51 (all tables appear in the appendix following this essay), which shows that in the last year of the survey—namely, 1973–74—the bottom 10 percent of households in urban areas spent 1.37 percent of the total household expenditure, while the top 10 percent spent about 38 percent of the total expenditure.

Over the period 1959–60 to 1973–74, certain changes have occurred in the distribution of income in urban areas. There has been a general trend toward a more unequal distribution of expenditure. This trend is particularly noticeable over the years 1959–60 to 1971–72. There seems to be a tendency for the expenditure distribution to stabilize or even improve slightly over the two years 1972–73 and 1973–74. The expenditure share of the bottom 10 percent of households has decreased uniformly from 1.77 percent in 1959–60 to 1.34 percent in 1971–72, but this trend was reversed in the following two years, and the expenditure share of this decile increased slightly to 1.37 percent. Similarly, the share of the top 10 percent of households increased from 35.4 percent in 1959–60 to the very high level of 39.5 percent in 1971–72, but it declined sharply to 36.95 percent in 1972–73 with a subsequent increase in 1973–74. The decile distribution tabulated in Table 51 also shows the relative stability of the share of households in the upper-middle deciles.

In order to illustrate these trends more clearly, we have computed four well-known measures of inequality for expenditure in urban areas. One of these measures is the coefficient of concentration, or the Gini coefficient, which gives an overall impression of the degree of inequality. The other three measures, which are based on decile distribution, give the expenditure share of the top 20 percent, the middle 40 percent and the bottom 40 percent of households. The estimates of these four measures over the years for which reliable expenditure figures are available are given in Table 52.

Our conclusion that until 1971–72 expenditure distribution was becoming more skewed is in fact verified both by the trend in the Gini coefficient and the estimates of the share of the top 20 percent and the bottom 40 percent of the households. Although the share of the middle 40 percent declined over the period 1959–60 to 1969–70, it has been relatively constant and on the average has amounted to about 26 percent.

The expenditure distribution for households in both urban and rural areas can be obtained from the household expenditure surveys carried out by the Statistical Center of Iran. Using the results of these surveys, we have computed the decile distribution of household expenditure for urban areas, rural areas and for the country as a whole. These distributions are given in Table 53, which, as expected, shows that expenditure is more unequally distributed in the urban areas than in the rural areas. While the share of the bottom 20 percent of households in urban areas in 1971–72 was 5.7 percent, for the rural areas it was higher and amounted to 6.6 percent. Similarly, the share of the top 20 percent of households in urban areas was 48.3 percent, considerably higher than the corresponding share in rural areas (45.7 percent). In fact, measuring the overall degree of inequality by the Gini coefficient, we find that this coefficient for the urban areas was 0.4152, while for the rural areas it stood at the lower level of 0.3899.

Due to the considerable disparity between average household expenditures in urban and rural areas in 1971–72, the expenditure distribution for the economy as a whole was more unequal than either the urban or the rural areas. The share of the bottom 10 percent was 2 percent, as compared with the share of the top 10 percent, which was over 34 percent. The Gini coefficient of expenditure for the whole country was 0.4363. Over the period 1969–70 to 1972–73, the inequality in expenditure distribution underwent important changes. The observed change in the overall inequality from 1969–70 to 1970–71 is very drastic. The Gini coefficient increased from 0.4188 in 1969–70 to 0.4545 in 1970–71. Most of this sudden and sharp increase in inequality can be explained in terms of the widening gap between urban and rural average household expenditures. In fact, the ratio of urban to rural per capita expenditures increased from 1.91 in 1969–70 to 2.3 in 1970–71. From 1970–71 to 1972–73 , however, there has been a general tendency for the inequality in household expenditures to decrease.

Various summary measures of inequality for urban and rural areas of the country over the years 1969–70 to 1972–73 are given in Table 54. There does not seem to be any specific trend in the Gini coefficient in urban areas. There is, nevertheless, a marked and definite upward trend in the share of the middle 40 percent of households, which is a clear indication of the rise of the urban middle class in Iran, especially over the last few years. In spite of this rising share of the middle-expenditure classes, the share of the bottom 40 percent of households in urban areas has not decreased. In fact, it has even increased slightly. In effect, there seems to have been a distribution of expenditure from the very high- to the middle- and lower-expenditure brackets. The household expenditure surveys of BMI and SCI for urban areas differ in a number of respects. First, the inequality of expenditure in urban areas turns out to be significantly greater if estimated from BMI surveys than when SCI surveys are used. Second, as we have already mentioned, unlike the SCI data, the BMI statistics do not support the hypothesis of a rising share of middle-expenditure classes.

In order to infer inequality in the distribution of incomes from the results given above, it will be necessary to specify the shape of the saving function of the cross section of households. Due to data limitations, this function cannot be estimated satisfactorily. But since households with very low incomes normally save less and those with high incomes save proportionately more, then inequality in the distribution of income will be generally greater than the inequality in the distribution of expenditure. Furthermore, given no significant change in the cross-section saving function, the trend in expenditure distribution can be taken to be a very good approximation to the trend in inequality of the distribution of income.

It should be pointed out that there is no necessary connection between the trends in inequality of incomes or consumption expenditures and the poverty or the standard of living of households. It is highly possible in circumstances of rising incomes for poverty, however defined, to decrease while there is an upward trend in the inequality of incomes. As this paper is confined to an analysis of income distribution, no specific discussion of the problems of "poverty" in Iran will be undertaken, in spite of its great importance. It is, nevertheless, possible to infer from national income statistics and consumption expenditure surveys that the number of people below the poverty line in Iran has been declining over the past few years.

Household Characteristics by Expenditure Classes

Before starting an econometric explanation of the observed inequality in the distribution of expenditure in Iran, it is helpful to identify, as far as the available data allow, the socioeconomic characteristics of households in different expenditure brackets. Of the various factors influencing income distribution, such household characteristics as age distribution, sex composition, race, family size, level of education and occupation of the household head, have recently attracted a great deal of attention. The larger the proportion of those below 15 years of age and the larger the sex ratio (the ratio of males to females, *ceteris paribus*), the more unequal income distribution will be. Differences in the educational attainments of household members also result in greater inequalities as long as there is a positive relation between education and income. Similar arguments can also be put forward in terms of other household characteristics.

In the case of Iran, very little effort has so far been made at a cross-tabulation of income (or expenditures) and household characteristics. But the Statistical Center of Iran has recently started such a tabulation on a limited scale. The SCI Household Budget Surveys of 1971–72 include, among other things, information on education, employment and occupation of the household head by expenditure classes. The proportions of households in the survey with no literate member are shown in Table 55 according to expenditure classes. From this table it is first clear that a much larger proportion of urban households than rural households have at least one literate member. Second, a smaller proportion of households in the higher expenditure brackets have no literate members. In fact, there is a definite inverse relationship between the proportion of households with no literate member in a given expenditure bracket and household expenditure in both urban and rural areas. While about 82 percent of households in the lowest expenditure class were without a literate person, only 6 percent of households in the highest expenditure bracket had the same characteristic. It follows that only an educational program with a particular emphasis upon coverage will be successful in reducing the degree of income inequality among households. At present the distribution of educational attainment of households is severely skewed, but with the efforts of the past few years to widen the educational base in both urban and rural areas, one might expect the educational attainment to have a more favorable impact upon income distribution in the future than has hitherto been the case.

Full employment has long been recognized as the single most important objective of economic policy, both for obtaining a high level of domestic production and for improving income distribution. The exact relationship between employment and income distribution does, however, depend on the capital intensity of production techniques. The larger the capital intensity is, the weaker the employment-income distribution relationship will be. In order to make a preliminary investigation of how employment (or unemployment) affects income distribution in Iran, we have computed the proportion of households with no employed member in each household decile. The results are summarized in Table 56, which clearly shows a significantly higher unemployment rate for the bottom 20 percent of households as compared with the rest. A larger proportion of households in urban areas, as compared with rural areas had no employed person. This proportion was 11.8 percent and 6.8 percent for urban and rural areas, respectively. It is interesting to note that, as shown in the previous section, expenditure has been more equally distributed in rural areas where a smaller proportion of households were without an employed person than in urban areas. A further interesting feature of the employment characteristic of households is the slightly larger rate of unemployment for households in the top deciles as compared with those in the middle deciles. This might be because a significant part of the income of rich families comes from property rather than employment.

Other characteristics of households for which data are available are the sector of employment and the occupation of the household head by expenditure classes. While the majority of household heads in the low-expenditure classes are employed in the agricultural and construction sectors, household heads in the high-expenditure classes are generally employed in the service sector. The heads of most households in the low-expenditure classes are wage and salary earners. This is more so in the urban than in the rural areas. About 24 percent of household heads in rural areas and about 33 percent of household heads in urban areas are wage and salary earners. Due to the widespread prevalence of subsistence farming, about 65 percent of household heads in rural areas are own-account workers, and this proportion tends to increase with household expenditure.

As no cross-tabulation of age and sex distribution by expenditure classes is yet available, a direct study of the impact of these demographic variables upon income distribution in Iran is not possible. However, in the next section an attempt will be made to assess the significance of these factors on income distribution in Iran indirectly by means of a spatial model.

Determinants of Income Inequality in Iran—A Cross Section of Evidence

The determination of the laws governing the distribution of income has preoccupied economists and social scientists alike, ever since Ricardo considered it to be the principal problem of political economy. In spite of concerted efforts by both classical and neoclassical economists to formulate meaningful theories of income distribution, because of the emphasis they place upon the functional distribution of income between labor and capital, no satisfactory theoretical framework for the explanation of income inequality among households is yet available. The inadequacy of the existing theories stems from the fact that in most developing countries the poor are generally illiterate and are either unemployed or self-employed, and the rich derive a significant proportion of their incomes from property. It is clear that under these circumstances any theory that focuses upon the division of output between wages and profits will be of only limited value for the purpose of explaining the distribution of income among households. Furthermore, most of the theories that explicitly attempt the determination of the size distribution of income among households or individuals are based on random processes, and income inequality is explained either by pure chance or by the skewed distribution of certain attributes claimed to be inherent in human nature.[2] Clearly, such random models are also of little relevance.[3]

In the light of the failure of theoretical investigations to yield testable hypotheses concerning the variations in the size distribution of income, our analysis of the factors determining income distribution in Iran follows that of other research workers insofar as we have considered those variables that have been related to income distribution in the literature.

Earlier it was shown how employment, educational attainment and the occupation of household members varied with expenditure or income. Apart from these factors, other variables, such as the rate of industrialization, the differential productivity growth in the modern and the traditional sectors, the magnitude and the pattern of government expenditure, the rate of inflation, the sex and age composition of the population, the disparity of rural and urban incomes and the rate of rural-urban migration, can affect the size distribution of income.

In view of the very short span of time series data available on income distribution, we based our analysis upon cross-section data on the distribution of household expenditure in 1971–72 and the results of the 1966 Census of Population. Information on regional variations in expenditure distribution is not only of relevance to a study of factors determining income distribution but is also of great importance when formulating regional economic policy. In Table 57 we have computed the decile distribution of household expenditures by 14 regions of the country in 1971–72.[4] The share of the bottom 10 percent of households in the Central and Fars regions is 1.76 percent and 1.75 percent, respectively, which is lower than the country's average. The shares of the top 10 percent of households in these two regions were 37.11 percent and 38.3 percent, as compared with 34.2 percent in the country as a whole. The share of the bottom 10 percent of households in the other regions ranged between 2 and 3.62 percent.

Regional variations in the upper end of the household expenditure distribution are much greater than in the lower end. The share of the top 10 percent of households in the 14 regions ranges between 26.17 percent and 38.48 percent. The shares of the top 10 percent of households in Sistan and Baluchestan, Fars, West Azarbaijan and Central Province are computed to be 38.48, 38.3, 37.2 and 37.11, respectively, which are considerably higher than the percentage for the country as a whole.

In order to give an overall impression of interregional variations in expenditure inequality, we have computed the Gini coefficient and three other measures of inequality in 1971–72 for each of the 14 regions by urban and rural areas. The results are summarized in Table 58.

In the case of the majority of regions, inequality is greater in urban than in rural areas. For regions with a more developed rural sector, the inequality is greater in rural than in urban areas. The Gini coefficients for rural areas of Gilan and Mazandaran are estimated to be 0.3821 and 0.4160, respectively, while the Gini coefficients for urban areas of these two predominantly agricultural regions are smaller and stand at 0.3634 and 0.3752, respectively. In short, Central Province, which has the highest per capita expenditures, and Kerman, with the lowest per capita expenditure, have the most equally distributed expenditure in the country. It should be noted that the relation between average household expenditure (or per capita income) and inequality in a given region is not a simple one. In fact, Gilan, with an average household expenditure second to that of Central Province, has a Gini coefficient of only 0.3786, which is much less than the similar coefficient for Khorasan or Fars and many other regions. A similar argument can also be made for East Azarbaijan or Khordestan.

The ratio of rural to urban household expenditure seems also to be a significant factor explaining interregional variations in inequality. As is clear from Table 59, of those regions with similar average household expenditures, those with a lower ratio of urban to rural household expenditure have a more equal expenditure distribution. For instance, in spite of the fact that the average household expenditure in West Azarbaijan is slightly larger than in Fars (7,492 rials per month as against 7,326 rials per month), the inequality is greater in Fars than in West Azarbaijan mainly because the ratio of urban to rural household expenditure is higher in Fars (1.96) than in West Azarbaijan (1.12).

In order to formalize the evidence in Tables 58 and 59, we have estimated an equation relating the Gini coefficient (GINI) of each region to the logarithm of household expenditure (y) and the ratio of urban to rural household expenditure (RUR) of that region. For the purpose of testing the nonlinear hypothesis put forward by Kuznets for the relationship between inequality and the "level of development," we have also included the income variable in quadratic form in the regression relation.

274   Iran: Past, Present and Future

This functional form, which has also been used by Ahluwalia in his explanation of the crosscountry evidence on income distribution[5], indicates an inverted U-shaped relationship when the coefficient of y is positive and that of y^2 is negative.

Using the data given in Table 59, the following estimate was obtained[6]:

$$\text{GINI} = -12.19 + 2.80y - 0.1569y^2 + 0.0478\text{RUR} \qquad (A)$$
$$(-1.20) \quad (1.21) \quad (-1.18) \quad (2.27)$$

R^2, unadjusted $= 0.4372$
R^2, adjusted $= 0.2684$

Thus, there is some evidence supporting Kuznets' hypothesis of a nonlinear relationship between inequality and the level of development in the Iranian economy. The evidence is not, however, very significant. The coefficients of y and y^2 have the signs expected *a priori* and indicate that regions with low per capita incomes are likely to have less inequality, unless a certain threshold level of per capita income is reached and above which high per capita incomes will not necessarily be accompanied by greater inequality.

The variable RUR, the ratio of urban to rural household expenditure, is quite significant and indicates a direct relationship between inequality and the disparity between rural and urban living standards. The greater the gap between rural and urban expenditure, the greater the inequality is likely to be.

A similar relation was also estimated for explaining the share of the bottom 40 percent of households, which is of importance especially in policy formulations with respect to poorer households. Denoting this share by SB40 we obtained:

$$\text{SB40} = 670.6 - 145.78y + 8.16y^2 - 2.29\text{RUR} \qquad (B)$$
$$(1.61) \quad (-1.54) \quad (1.50) \quad (-2.67)$$

R^2, unadjusted $= 0.5288$
R^2, adjusted $= 0.3875$,

which is even more significant than the relation we estimated for explaining variations in regional Gini coefficients. Note that, as expected, the signs of the coefficients of y, y^2 and RUR in the above relation are opposite to the signs of the corresponding coefficients in relation (A).

In order to test the effect of other factors likely to have some influence upon the degree of inequality we reestimated relations (A) and (B) with the following variables[7]:

- The ratio of males to females in each region—sex ratio (Z_1);
- The proportion of the population below 20 years of age in each region (Z_2);

- The proportion of the population having at least six years of formal education in each region (Z_3);
- The ratio of agricultural employment to total employment in each region (Z_4);
- The amount of government development expenditure in each region during the Fourth Development Plan in billions of rials (Z_5).

Of the above five variables we found that the variables representing the sex composition and the age distribution in each region were not at all significant. This might be because of the small amount of variation in these variables over the regions. The employment ratio that reflects the degree of industrialization of each region did not prove to be significant either, possibly because of its correlation with household average expenditure.

The relation we found to be the most satisfactory in explaining regional differences in inequality is the following:

$$SB40 = 1145.6 - 256.15y + 14.59y^2 - 2.43RUR + 0.0681Z_5 - 0.2754Z_3$$
$$(2.50) \quad (-2.42) \quad (2.39) \quad (-2.46) \quad (2.04) \quad (-1.50)$$

R^2, unadjusted $= 0.7037$
R^2, adjusted $= 0.5185$,

in which both government development expenditure and, to a lesser extent, the formal education variable have shown to be statistically significant in explaining inequality. It is interesting to note that the inclusion of these two variables in relation (B) have not only increased the overall explanatory power of the relation but have also increased the level of significance of y, the average household expenditure. Since the coefficient of Z_5 is positive, it follows that larger government development expenditure, *ceteris paribus*, is likely to raise the share of the bottom 40 percent of households. The negative coefficient for Z_3 is indicative of the unfavorable impact that education might have upon the distribution of expenditure. This result is in line with the observation we made when we discussed household characteristics by expenditure classes. Note, however, that Z_3 is only marginally significant and this result should be treated with caution. Furthermore, the negative coefficient of Z_3 should not be taken to mean that an education program with the widest possible coverage will be unfavorable to the cause of equality. The negative coefficient is the result of the existing skewed distribution of formal education (or human capital) and its undesirable consequences on income distribution. Clearly, a more equal distribution of human capital is likely to favor a better income distribution than otherwise.

Summary

On the basis of the results obtained in the previous sections, several conclusions may be drawn.

1.   It appears that until 1971–72, the inequality in income distribution in Iran was increasing. But over the period 1971–72 to 1973–74, there seems to have been a general tendency for inequality in household expenditure to stabilize or even decline slightly.

2.   The distribution of income in rural areas is less equal than in urban areas.

3.   According to Statistical Center of Iran surveys, there is some evidence that in urban areas the share of middle-income classes has been rising, but Bank Markazi Iran surveys do not support this conclusion.

4.   Households in the bottom deciles usually have no literate member and have a high rate of unemployment. Furthermore, their heads are either own-account workers (in rural areas) or wage and salary earners (in urban areas).

5.   There are considerable variations in regional expenditure inequality. Rich regions, such as Fars and Central Province, show a high degree of inequality, while inequality in poor regions, such as Kerman, is relatively low. The relationship between the "level of development" and inequality also depends on the urban-rural expenditure disparity.

6.   We found some evidence to support Kuznets' hypothesis that income inequality in the early phases of development is likely to decline in the later stages of development.

7.   The ratio of urban to rural expenditure, government development expenditure and the overall educational attainment of households and its distribution have a large and significant influence upon income distribution in Iran. A policy that emphasizes reducing the gap between urban and rural areas, between rich and poor regions by a balanced regional government development expenditure is very likely to succeed in reducing income inequalities in Iran. Furthermore, an educational program with a wide regional coverage, which in the long run reduces regional income disparities, will also be instrumental in achieving an improved income distribution. Finally, the creation of relatively well-paid jobs for unskilled and semiskilled laborers in small urban centers is also likely to reduce income inequality in urban areas.

Table 51
Decile Distribution of Household Expenditure — Urban Areas
(percent)

Deciles (lowest to highest)	1959-1960	1969-1970	1970-1971	1971-1972	1972-1973	1973-1974
1st	1.77	1.59	1.48	1.34	1.37	1.37
2nd	2.96	2.86	2.62	2.39	2.51	2.40
3rd	4.09	3.96	4.07	3.60	3.36	3.42
4th	5.08	4.58	4.54	4.32	4.64	4.77
5th	6.17	5.94	5.60	5.66	5.16	5.08
6th	7.37	7.96	7.68	6.94	6.98	6.85
7th	8.92	8.48	8.23	8.57	9.51	9.36
8th	11.85	11.72	11.48	11.70	11.14	11.19
9th	16.42	16.05	16.18	16.00	18.38	17.57
10th	35.37	36.86	38.12	39.48	36.95	37.99

Source: Bank Markazi Iran survey.

Table 52
Four Measures of Inequality of Consumption Expenditure in Urban Areas

Years	Gini Coefficient	Share of Top 20 Percent (percent)	Share of Middle 20 Percent (percent)	Share of Bottom 20 Percent (percent)
1959-60	0.4552	51.79	27.54	13.90
1969-70	0.4710	52.91	26.96	12.99
1970-71	0.4849	54.30	26.05	12.71
1971-72	0.5051	55.48	25.49	11.65
1972-73	0.4916	55.33	26.29	11.88
1973-74	0.4946	55.56	26.06	11.96

Source: Bank Markazi Iran survey.

Table 53
Decile Distribution of Household Expenditures in 1971-72

Deciles (lowest to highest)	Urban Areas (percent)	Rural Areas (percent)	Total (percent)
1st	2.17	2.79	1.96
2nd	3.56	3.82	3.51
3rd	4.56	5.04	4.37
4th	5.96	5.90	5.14
5th	6.66	6.98	6.24
6th	7.67	8.14	8.39
7th	9.35	9.56	8.51
8th	11.74	12.10	11.88
9th	16.21	14.48	15.80
10th	32.12	31.19	34.20

Source: Statistical Center of Iran Survey (Plan and Budget Organization).

Table 54
Four Measures of Inequality of Consumption Expenditure

	1969-70	1970-71	1971-72	1972-73
Rural				
Gini Coefficient	0.3559	0.3685	0.3899	0.3659
Share of Top 20 Percent	44.88	45.85	45.67	43.59
Share of Middle 40 Percent	32.08	31.62	30.58	31.73
Share of Bottom 40 Percent	18.03	18.17	17.55	18.40
Urban				
Gini Coefficient	0.4161	0.4227	0.4152	0.4032
Share of Top 20 Percent	49.24	47.83	48.33	47.11
Share of Middle 40 Percent	27.99	28.43	29.64	30.21
Share of Bottom 40 Percent	16.06	15.36	16.25	16.69
Total				
Gini Coefficient	0.4188	0.4545	0.4363	0.4228
Share of Top 20 Percent	49.66	52.48	50.00	48.83
Share of Middle 40 Percent	28.91	26.25	28.28	28.89
Share of Bottom 40 Percent	16.77	14.41	14.98	15.40

Source: Statistical Center of Iran Survey (Plan and Budget Organization).

Table 55
Proportion of Households Without a Literate Member
by Expenditure Classes in 1971-72

Expenditure Classes (per month; in rials)	Urban Areas	Rural Areas	Total
Under 2,000	76.3	83.2	81.5
2,000-2,999	55.2	67.0	63.6
3,000-3,999	38.5	53.9	48.2
4,000-4,999	25.4	44.9	35.9
5,000-7,499	15.0	39.0	25.1
7,500-9,999	7.8	30.9	15.0
10,000-12,499	3.3	23.3	8.2
12,500-14,999	2.5	20.5	6.3
15,000-19,999	2.5	20.2	5.5
20,000-29,999	1.2	17.1	3.5
30,000 and Over	1.3	18.6	4.1
All Classes	19.8	53.1	36.0

Source: Statistical Center of Iran (Plan and Budget Organization).

Table 56
The Percentage of Households Within a Given Decile
Without an Employed Member

Household Deciles (lowest to highest)	Urban Areas	Rural Areas	Total
1st	26.9	22.0	25.9
2nd	12.7	14.8	9.1
3rd	10.1	5.9	7.8
4th	9.6	5.3	6.9
5th	9.5	4.5	6.3
6th	9.4	3.9	6.7
7th	9.2	3.4	6.7
8th	10.3	3.5	7.2
9th	10.2	2.2	8.4
10th	9.9	2.2	8.7
All	11.8	6.8	9.4

Source: Statistical Center of Iran (Plan and Budget Organization).

Table 57
Decile Distribution of Household Expenditure by Regions in 1971-72

(From Lowest to Highest)	Central	Gilan	Mazandaran	East Azarbaijan	West Azarbaijan	Kermanshah and Lorestan	Khuzestan and Bakhtiari	Fars	Kerman	Khorasan	Estahan and Yazd	Sistan and Baluchestan	Kordestan	Oman Sea Ports and Persian Gulf Ports
1st	1.76	2.48	2.00	2.49	2.19	2.39	2.26	1.75	3.62	2.62	2.37	2.65	2.51	2.44
2nd	2.83	3.71	3.71	3.82	3.33	3.94	3.53	3.10	3.63	3.20	3.68	2.66	3.90	4.04
3rd	3.63	5.01	4.89	4.68	4.45	4.78	4.49	3.76	6.24	4.77	4.27	2.83	4.94	4.51
4th	4.72	6.42	5.77	5.69	4.81	5.52	5.58	4.77	6.56	5.50	5.86	4.93	5.73	5.35
5th	6.02	7.41	6.90	7.07	5.94	6.97	7.05	5.93	7.29	6.69	6.37	5.20	7.12	6.91
6th	6.97	7.73	8.86	7.07	7.51	9.00	8.60	7.57	8.99	7.77	7.57	6.93	8.63	8.46
7th	8.66	10.33	8.86	9.60	8.15	9.48	9.29	8.31	9.58	9.28	10.18	8.67	8.62	9.76
8th	11.75	12.34	12.28	11.34	11.28	12.08	12.11	10.85	12.17	11.47	10.61	11.90	11.88	12.46
9th	16.55	15.66	15.39	16.00	15.14	15.15	16.38	15.66	15.75	15.14	15.61	15.75	15.50	16.13
10th	37.11	28.91	31.34	32.24	37.20	30.69	30.71	38.30	26.17	33.56	33.48	38.48	31.17	29.94

Source: Statistical Center of Iran (Plan and Budget Organization).

Table 58a

Four Measures of Inequality of Consumption Expenditure by Regions in 1971-72

(Part One)

	Central	Gilan	Mazan-daran	East Azar-baijan	West Azar-baijan	Kerman-shah and Lores-tan	Khuzes-tan and Bakh-tiari
Rural							
Gini Coefficient	0.3471	0.3821	0.4160	0.3356	0.4795	0.3767	0.3622
Share of Top 20 Percent	42.33	44.48	47.89	41.89	54.22	44.90	43.05
Share of Middle 40 Percent	32.44	32.46	30.17	33.56	25.96	32.15	31.86
Share of Bottom 40 Percent	19.95	16.66	15.84	20.17	14.60	17.68	18.60
Urban							
Gini Coefficient	0.4257	0.3634	0.3752	0.4112	0.4287	0.3935	0.3727
Share of Top 20 Percent	49.30	44.06	45.42	47.78	49.72	45.99	44.43
Share of Middle 40 Percent	28.48	31.56	31.54	29.62	28.41	30.89	31.98
Share of Bottom 40 Percent	15.57	18.83	18.31	16.24	15.46	16.65	18.22
Total							
Gini Coefficient	0.4781	0.3786	0.4031	0.4089	0.4572	0.3935	0.4060
Share of Top 20 Percent	53.65	44.57	46.73	48.24	52.34	45.84	47.09
Share of Middle 40 Percent	26.37	31.89	30.39	29.43	26.41	30.97	30.52
Share of Bottom 40 Percent	12.93	17.62	16.37	16.68	14.78	16.63	15.89

Source: Statistical Center of Iran survey.

Table 58b

Four Measures of Inequality of Consumption Expenditure by Regions in 1971-72

(Part Two)

	Fars	Kerman	Khor-asan	Esfahan and Yazd	Sistan and Bluches-tan	Kordes-tan	Oman and Persian Gulf Ports
Rural							
Gini Coefficient	0.4480	0.2712	0.3433	0.3024	0.4034	0.3659	0.3229
Share of Top 20 Percent	50.29	37.06	42.34	38.66	48.16	44.03	40.89
Share of Middle 40 Percent	27.94	36.47	32.79	34.27	28.47	31.59	32.37
Share of Bottom 40 Percent	15.39	23.43	19.66	21.64	16.07	19.42	20.72
Urban							
Gini Coefficient	0.4356	0.3331	0.4186	0.3857	0.4430	0.3572	0.3604
Share of Top 20 Percent	50.02	40.97	48.49	46.05	50.28	43.62	42.62
Share of Middle 40 Percent	28.44	34.39	29.10	30.93	29.40	31.18	32.98
Share of Bottom 40 Percent	15.18	19.60	15.89	18.05	14.31	19.77	18.37
Total							
Gini Coefficient	0.4778	0.3342	0.4193	0.4201	0.4849	0.3943	0.3959
Share of Top 20 Percent	53.96	41.92	48.70	49.09	54.23	46.67	46.07
Share of Middle 40 Percent	26.58	32.42	29.24	29.98	25.73	30.10	30.48
Share of Bottom 40 Percent	13.38	20.05	16.09	16.18	13.07	17.08	16.34

Source: Statistical Center of Iran survey.

Table 59
Relation Between Gini Coefficient, Household Expenditure and
the Ratio of Urban to Rural Expenditure, 1971-72

Regions	Gini Coeffi-cient	Average Monthly Household Expen-diture (rials)	Ratio of Urban to Rural Household Expenditure
Central	0.4781	10,204	2.96
Gilan	0.3786	8,329	1.36
Mazandaran	0.4031	6,886	1.28
East Azarbaijan	0.4089	8,711	1.74
West Azarbaijan	0.4572	7,492	1.12
Kermanshah and Lorestan	0.3935	6,431	1.30
Khuzestan and Bakhtiari	0.4060	7,139	1.93
Fars	0.4778	7,326	1.96
Kerman	0.3342	3,845	1.71
Khorasan	0.4193	5,235	1.91
Esfahan and Yazd	0.4201	5,956	2.40
Sistan and Baluchestan	0.4849	5,012	2.49
Kordestan	0.3943	7,090	1.77
Oman and Persian Gulf Ports	0.3959	6,206	2.04

Source: Computed on the basis of Urban and Rural Household Budget Surveys 1971-72—
Statistical Center of Iran, Plan and Budget Organization.

Footnotes

1. M.H. Pesaran, *Income Distribution Trends in Rural and Urban Iran*, presented to the International Conference on the Social Sciences and Problems of Development—Persepolis, Iran, 1974.

2. See D.G. Champerowne, "A Model of Income Distribution," *Economic Journal* (June 1953); and B. Mandelbrot, "Stable Paretian Random Functions and the Multiplicative Variations of Income," *Econometrics* (October 1961).

3. There have recently been a number of attempts at integrating the stochastic model relating to inherent distribution of skills among individuals with the economic models explaining factor shares. See, for example, J.E. Stiglitz, "Distribution of Income and Wealth among Individuals," *Econometrics* (July 1969).

4. The data published by the Statistical Center of Iran gives the distribution of expenditure for 14 provinces and eight Farmandariekols (independent general government rates). We have included the eight *Farmandariekols* in the neighboring provinces so that a more reasonable area distribution is made in the analysis.

5. See the Appendix to M.S. Ahluwalia, "Income Inequality: Some Dimensions of the Problem," in *Redistribution with Growth*, World Bank and the Institute of Development Studies at the University of Sussex.

6. The figures in parentheses are t-ratios and R^2 is the multiple correlation coefficient.

7. The values of variable Z_1 to Z_4 are computed from the 1966 National Census of Population.

Comments and Discussion

In "Income Distribution and Its Major Determinants in Iran," M.H. Pesaran stressed the importance of equitable income distribution to economic and political stability. Although most planners have taken for granted that income distribution will automatically start improving when development reaches a certain level, this view is now being questioned as a result of the recent experiences of most developing countries. It is important to know more about the interrelationship of growth and income distribution in the Iranian economy. Mr. Pesaran offered some statistical evidence on income distribution in Iran, described the characteristics of households in different expenditure brackets and suggested some factors that may be responsible for income inequality in Iran. He concluded by observing that inequality in income distribution was increasing until 1971–72 but may have stabilized in the past two years; that income distribution is less equal in rural areas than urban areas; that there are variations in income distribution patterns among the regions; and that income inequalities in Iran will probably be reduced as a result of development and special government measures benefiting rural areas.

In the discussion that followed, the question of income distribution was considered mainly in relation to social mobility, popular participation and decentralization. Iranian participants differed somewhat in their predictions. Several specialists re-affirmed the view that the income gap between rich and poor will continue to widen, at least for a while. But oil revenues are being used to provide social services and subsidies for the rural population that directly benefit people in the rural areas even if their incomes are not raised. Moreover, the government is committed in the long run to achieve a better income distribution pattern and has undertaken its policy of decentralization toward this end. An Iranian observed that government cannot rely on income distribution alone or mobilization alone to bring about desired changes: they go hand in hand. Although social mobilization was stressed in the information presented at the symposium, definite measures are also needed to achieve more equitable income distribution, especially in the rural areas. Processes already initiated under decentralization must be supplemented.

Another Iranian questioned the view that the income gap will continue to widen and cited a number of government measures and economic developments that are benefiting the rural sector and should lead to more equitable income distribution, including the meat price rise, guaranteed minimum prices for five commodities, investments in rural areas, the establishment of cooperative stores providing goods at low prices, the sale of company shares to workers and farmers, etc. Growth of the manufacturing sector, the spread of industry to rural areas and the rise of industrial salaries can be expected also to contribute to more equitable income distribution.

5. Iran in World Affairs

The Economics of Oil

Economics of Oil

R. Fallah

Historical Background

It appears to me that before talking about the highly controversial subject of the economics of oil today, which forms the center of attention of all international discussions, it would be proper to make a reference to its historical background.

At the outset it is fair to say that the oil-producing countries should express praise and appreciation of the oil companies, which acted as pioneers more than half a century ago, utilizing their technology, risking their capital and laboring under adverse conditions to search for, discover and produce petroleum in the various areas of the world.

The criticism that could, however, be leveled at these companies is that from those early days onward, and up to recent years, they have acted as self-appointed masters of the reserves they discovered. In many instances they showed little consideration for the rightful interests of the real owners of this valuable commodity, not only insofar as it concerned the return of an adequate income to the countries concerned, but also in the somewhat indifferent methods of producing the oil fields, which were not always in keeping with the best oil industry practice.

The modest and vitally important industrial and agricultural programs that had begun in some of the producing countries, notably in my country, gained momentum and brought into sharp focus the ever-increasing imbalance between our meager petroleum revenues and the soaring costs of machinery and equipment imported from the West. The oil companies did not, or perhaps under the prevailing circumstances could not, adjust crude oil prices to a more realistic level, and the producers had no alternative but to take matters into their own hands and make the proper adjustment themselves.

The companies could have argued that the antitrust laws, the rules of supply and demand and other considerations in an allegedly competitive—free market would have prevented them from following a reasonable course of action, but the bitter truth is that the laws of some countries cannot be tolerated once they prove to be detrimental to the vital interests of other sovereign nations. The Western industrialization has been based on the supply of cheap energy at the expense of developing nations, and this had to be corrected one day. Had this process taken place gradually over the past decade, the energy crisis and the abrupt dislocation in the Western economy could have been avoided.

In fact, what actually did happen was a gradual decline in crude oil prices, while costs of goods and services provided by the industrialized nations to the developing countries against this precious but vanishing commodity were continually on the increase, due not only to inflation but also to the fact that even at constant money values, bigger profits had to be realized by the Western nations in order to provide for higher and better standards of living for their people. Under such conditions, the transfer to the producing countries of the oil companies' power to determine prices was inevitable.

There is one more general consideration. Reluctantly or not, the realistic observer must admit that most primary energy is a finite treasure that human society could decide to consume in a fast gulp or treat with care and foresight. Giving it away at a price way below the cost of developing other sources of energy cannot serve a justifiable purpose. Doing that means just catering to the momentary wishes of an industrial society that was built on the error of giveaway energy, and it means compounding this error at the expense of future generations.

The Industrialized Nations

Energy is, and will remain, an essential item in everybody's life. It is estimated that more than 70 percent of all energy consumed throughout the world is utilized for productive and business purposes, making its abundant availability a condition of the function of world industry.

Jolted out of their complacency, the industrial countries have embarked upon a program, meant to be rapid, of creating new sources of energy. It so happens that there is no chance either in America or in the prolific oil fields of the North Sea or of Alaska to develop new production of oil at a price much lower than the OPEC price. His Imperial Majesty has been telling the world for a long time that the only measure of the economic fairness of the new world price of oil was the West's ability to create alternative sources of energy at a lower cost. In the short and medium term, there is just no chance to accomplish this aim.

As to the progress that is being made in the fields of producing fuel from coal, shale and tar sands, and in developing solar, nuclear, geothermal and tidal power and other similar systems, it is generally believed that it will not affect the growing reliance of the world on petroleum over the next decade. The "Projects Independence and Interdependence," sponsored by the U.S., met with little success, and the enthusiastic launching of ERDA by the administration and the Congress, supported by large appropriations for energy research, resulted in the conclusion that there is no scientific shortcut that will make the West independent of OPEC oil for many years to come. It is anticipated that oil consumption in 1985 will be almost double that of 1970, and that the petroleum industry's global financial needs up to 1985, taking into account an average 10 percent inflation rate, will be in excess of $2 trillion—a formidable sum by any standard. The future, in other words, shows increasing development of the oil industry.

In the immediate past much has happened. The effect of the revaluation of oil on the world scene was profound. It was also confused and highly emotional. Unfortunately for all concerned, the great economic issue of a fair price for energy and of its consequences for the future welfare of the developing countries become deeply enmeshed in the passions aroused by the embargo on oil exports following the outbreak of the Arab-Israeli War. Clearly this was only a coincidence, and any analysis of the world oil problem must proceed free from the resentment awakened by this foreign and totally unrelated matter.

Even without the embargo complication, the reaction of the consuming countries was deeply partisan. There was an outcry against the increase in the cost of Western living, and there were dire predictions of impending catastrophe. Almost two years after the event it seems certain that the prophets of gloom have been wrong. To recognize that does not mean to belittle the problems caused by the revaluation. It is only a warning against hasty and biased judgment. In the forum of this seminar, objectivity should be our prime target.

First let us review the economic events. The OPEC price as set in October 1973 became immediately the world market price. The transition, despite the gigantic shift in value, was smooth. Even the serious issue of the boycott did not bring havoc to the affected countries, mostly because of the resourcefulness of the international oil companies, which displayed a masterly ability to use their vast distributing and transportation facilities to their best advantage. The OPEC price would today be the universal price had it not been for two notable exceptions: the United States and Canada. These two countries are both importers of OPEC oil and producers of oil in their own territories. Having to pay the OPEC price for their imports, they chose to impose an artificial price on their own production. The latter is close to the old price, approximately 40 percent of the accepted world market price of today. The Canadian system is simplicity in the extreme, the U.S. system more complicated and confusing.

It is a modern paradox that two countries proclaiming their unshakable commitment to a free market economy have established drastic bureaucratic controls of the industry, while it is anticipated that the two other potential oil producers of the Western world headed by socialistic governments, the U.K. and Norway, would let their people pay the market price. The fact that these two present producers act not only in conflict with the intention of the two future producers of oil but also with the idea of economic freedom and nonintervention in business is ample evidence that the economics of oil cannot be dealt with in a summary fashion solely with the rules of 19th-century liberalism. Nor is it correct to say that the departure from market freedom in America is caused only by the intervention of the Mideastern governments in the price mechanism of oil. There is no way of maintaining an efficient oil industry without having some policies of production and pricing formulated and applied. This has always been the case. The only difference is that in the past the prevailing dictate was that of the oil companies. Among their aims, the most urgent was to lift our oil resources at the fastest possible rate. Maximizing production obviously meant minimizing the price of oil.

In the case of any commodity produced under conditions such as those of oil in the Middle East, where production can be substantially augmented at a relatively modest cost, as compared to the value of the increment in production, the choices open to the producers are whether a finite stock of a natural resource should be exhausted slowly, moderately or quickly, and there is just no way of avoiding the central regulation of production and marketing. The West should stop chastising us for interference and rather join us in working out a system of developing oil that is both fair and rational from the consumers' and producers' points of view.

Let us compare briefly the political and social reasonings behind the American price ceiling and the OPEC price floor. The Western action was designed to protect the consumer. It was in fact directed against the domestic producer who was being prevented from reaping the windfall benefits of the sharp advance in world prices. The action of the governments of the producing countries was designed to achieve a modest change in the distribution of the industrial product of the world by moving a very small fraction of industrial countries' gross national product into the hands of the poor masses of the developing world. We understand, even if we do not always approve, the political actions of our friends in the West. It is self-evident that the interest of our people also required governmental action, and what government action can be more important than the defense of the terms of trade of the most valuable physical resource we possess?

If I say that I do not agree with the price ceilings on the North American continent, it is because they contain the worst contradiction in Western oil policies. Generally speaking, the policies pursued in both Canada and the United States tend to prevent the generation of sufficient funds for an energetic search for petroleum. They follow three objectives that have been proclaimed again and again: (1) protection of the consumer; (2) reduction of imports; and (3) encouragement of domestic oil production. Objectives two and three go together: the higher the domestic production, the lower the imports; the higher the price, the greater the imports. But two and three together do not go with one. There is no political magic, however tortuous, that can square the circle of prices kept low and of hopes for increased production kept high.

Coming back to OPEC action, we do deny that the revaluation of oil was a burden to the consumer. The price increase of 1973 meant for most highly industrialized countries an increase in the cost of energy equal to 2 or 3 percent of their gross national product. Thus the average citizen of the Western world was less rich by that percentage. I would like to speak for a moment strictly as an Iranian, as a citizen of a nation of 33 million intelligent, hardworking and ambitious people. A 2 or 3 percent reduction in the gross national product of the West meant a more than 40 percent increase in our gross national product. If you want to compare the social value of the loss in the West against that of the gain in our country the answer, I believe, is clear.

Regretfully, I must quickly add that the consequences for the West went beyond the measure of the quantitative burden of the price increase. The producers' action happened at a time of inflation, and the factors behind inflation are known to feed on themselves. A general massive cost increase such as the one launched by the revaluation of oil loosens the resistance against other price increases not directly related to oil. The wave of higher prices due to oil was followed by other markets exploiting what appeared to be a weak resistance against inflationary pressures. In that sense, the burden for the West may have been greater than the direct cost of higher-priced oil. If there was weakness, it was inherent in the economic system of the West. The oil producers cannot be accused of causing this accelerated effect, especially since they paid their share of it in the price of their imports.

Price of Crude Oil

A correct and adequate price for crude oil would be that which would compare with the cost of producing an alternative commodity that would serve similar purposes, including the production of evergy. Crude oil, which has been termed by our sovereign a "noble product," cannot be compared to, let us say, nuclear or solar power, as they do not perform identical functions. What may be produced from coal, shale oil or tar sands may be considered to fall into the same category. Not exacting any penalty for the fact that the West had done little to produce such alternative sources of evergy mainly because of the overproduction of crude oil, resulting in ridiculously cheap prices, the present values placed on crude oil are very reasonable.

Since low-cost petroleum resources available to the OPEC nations will definitely vanish within the foreseeable future, it would be grossly unjust to expect them to dispose of their wealth at prices lower than what they would have to pay the West for its equivalent when their own reserves have been exhausted.

Some American and European government and financial authorities are totally wrong in maintaining that the laws of supply and demand, at some point in time, will depress crude oil prices. In arriving at this assumption they ignore the fact that the conventional market forces that usually bring about fluctuations in prices of some commodities are no longer applicable to the producing countries of OPEC. The reason is obviously due to the fact that the total income of the OPEC nations from sales of petroleum is very much in excess of what they need.

In the days of cheap energy, OPEC never succeeded in drafting an acceptable resolution outlining pro-rationing because every country was pressing for higher sales. Today, thanks to a large surplus on the balance of payments of certain OPEC nations, the position is not the same, and I anticipate that even a decrease in production in some of these countries would be welcome. As far as Iranian policy within OPEC is concerned, supplies at all times should equate with demand and therefore there should be no surpluses due to overproduction and no shortages due to political embargoes.

So long as there is no sound policy based on determination to return to the discipline of stable money it is imperative that, for adjusting crude oil prices, a certain system of indexing be adopted to maintain the purchasing power of the oil income and safeguard it against inflation. Periodic revision of crude oil prices has been announced and explained in detail by His Imperial Majesty in the course of several audiences granted to the press and American and European television networks.

Coping with the Crisis

I would be the last person to deny that there has been and still remains a crisis of energy facing the world that, together with other events, has to some extent dislocated the Western economy and has caused hardship among the nations of the Third World.

I do not bring any instant miracles to alleviate the problems facing the industrialized nations as well as the Third World. These problems have many deep-rooted causes including, of course, the higher costs of energy of recent years. However, the combined effects of the following suggestions, which are by no means offered as a final blueprint, may help the world's finances to settle down again to a new equilibrium.

First, some of the members of the Western world should apply themselves more diligently to production and export, expect a smaller growth in their standard of living than they had come to anticipate and tolerate a certain transfer of wealth to the developing countries, thereby narrowing the wide gap between the rich and the poor and contributing to the creation of a more stable and more homogeneous world community.

Fortunately, all the industrialized nations are now taking effective measures to contain inflation within tolerable limits, and, even in democracies, such as the U.K., where interference by the government in such matters as the workers' right of free collective bargaining or price control tends to be regarded as outrageous, consideration is now being given to the introduction of rigid statutory controls.

I am glad to say that in this connection and at the moment of compiling these notes, the world economy is already beginning to improve and it may be effectively disinflated if there are further rises in employment. More and more economic indicators are heralding a business recovery in spite of high energy costs, and the rate of price inflation appears to have been curbed, and is on the decline. There are cheerful Washington predictions of economic recovery in the United States, perhaps in the near future. Most experts also agree that Europe generally will continue to remain in recession but that the economy will turn around soon after the United States' recovery begins.

Second, the surplus oil funds could be used partly for investment abroad in the purchase of equity shares in foreign companies or real estate. There are obvious limitations to this course of action since no country would wish to see control by way of foreign ownership established on its soil on a large scale, as the OPEC nations themselves have good cause to remember.

Investment in gold, on a massive scale, is hazardous for surplus-fund nations, for while stockpiling it they would be at the mercy of speculators, and whenever the time came to dispose of it, since gold has very few industrial uses, the customers might not exist.

Third, the oil companies may be relieved of a part of the tremendous financial burden of providing the world with its energy requirements. Those oil companies operating within the OPEC areas, subject, wherever possible, to the concurrence of the governments of the producing countries, could be relieved of the local burden of capital investments by their host countries against suitable and commensurate considerations. The capital required by all the companies operating in OPEC regions for the development of the petroleum industry could thus be furnished by the producing countries and, considering the large sums involved, this should be of help to the balance of payments of the industrialized nations.

Fourth, an approach I suggested not long ago, applicable to countries that accumulate a large surplus of oil funds in the form of paper money and cannot utilize them in more profitable ways, would be to trade at least part of the oil against a special convertible energy bond. This does not apply to those countries that recycle their oil incomes for internal development, as such countries have no adverse effect on the balance of trade of the West. At the end of May, Saudi Arabia, the world's leading exporter of oil, had become the second largest holder of international monetary reserves, with $20.5 billion, pushing the United States into third place. This is only a beginning, and concerns only one country; considerably higher overall figures can be foreseen for the years to come.

Periodic corrective measures in the pricing of oil would, of course, safeguard its purchasing power at any given time. But what about the staggering sums of paper money earned in previous years and placed in reserves that are fast losing their value?

The above suggestion, which might put an end to the present crisis, would be to deposit some or all of the remaining surplus oil funds in a special energy bank, which could be an entirely new and independent organization or function under the auspices of the World Bank.

Against the funds deposited, the new bank would issue interest-bearing long-term convertible energy bonds, the nominal value of which would be expressed in units of both energy and currency that would correspond with the cash value of the energy on the date of issue. At maturity the bank would, at the discretion of the depositors, either arrange for the return of an equivalent amount of energy of a similar type, or its prevailing market value, or just the nominal value of the bond. Such repayments could of course be extended over a period of time to be agreed on.

Needless to say, it would be necessary to draw up a suitable banking and legal instrument guaranteeing the bonds and providing safeguards satisfactory to all parties involved. Such an arrangement would remove the petroleum-exporting countries' fear of inflation and would encourage them to produce sufficient oil for the world's energy needs during the transitional period in which we must, all of us, switch over from our present wasteful consumption of our irreplaceable hydrocarbon reserves. Otherwise a further threat to world stability may be that oil producers, caught between galloping inflation on the one hand and diminishing petroleum reserves on the other, may be more and more tempted to let the value of their oil appreciate in the ground, rather than produce it to exchange for paper money.

The adoption of such a scheme would prove beneficial to both sides, as it would provide a good safeguard for the producers by maintaining the value of their surplus funds while giving the consumers a moratorium—which is needed—during which to produce similar alternative sources of energy.

This suggestion has been treated with mixed feelings in certain international circles but has met with a favorable reaction from some

Iran: Past, Present and Future

economic and banking authorities, who agree that under this scheme a substantial part of the surplus oil funds would be taken out of the ordinary financial system, with their reemergence, in a different form, postponed for a number of years.

The Third and Fourth Worlds

This essay would not be complete without mentioning the nations of the Third World that have, by comparison, suffered more than the industrialized nations from the crisis of energy and that have also had to pay higher costs for goods and services received from the West.

Following the lead given by OPEC, the Third World is developing an accelerated drive for economic self-determination and the assurance of fair prices for its products, which the Western world has had the benefit of using far too cheaply for far too long.

The Paris Conference, composed of the representatives of the industrialized nations, the oil-producing countries and the Third World, which was convened early this year, was intended to be a first step toward examining and coordinating the various views and seeking a compromise solution for a satisfactory pricing mechanism acceptable to all parties concerned. Unfortunately, this conference did not achieve its purpose, but it is hoped that at a future date it will be reconvened, perhaps under a somewhat different agenda, enabling the producers of commodities and raw materials to play a more dominant role than hitherto. The new era must of necessity bring about changes in the international economic structure.

The vital importance of such changes becomes apparent when we consider the problems facing what has been called the Fourth World— that section of the Third World, comprising between one-third and one-half of the whole, that lacks even primary agricultural products in quantities sufficient to generate the minimum requirements of foreign exchange needed for the import of the goods and services necessary for development. These countries need special treatment, and with the utmost urgency.

In 1972, the world's population was estimated at 3.7 billion, divided between 1.2 billion in the richer countries and 2.5 billion in the remainder. At present the rich countries are growing relatively richer and their population is increasing by about 1 percent annually, while the poorer countries are getting relatively poorer and their population is growing at a rate of 2.5 percent a year. It is generally agreed that if the world continues along these lines, it faces an ominous future, for the tensions now building up must one day find violent release. Shall we avoid this through international cooperation, planning and agreement, or must we learn the hard way, through world disaster?

The one-third or less of mankind in the richer countries accounted for some 83 percent of total world energy consumption in 1972, while the two-thirds or more in all the other countries consumed only 17 percent. Moreover, the high consumption of the first group was increasing faster than the low consumption of the second.

The very close correlation between energy use and national income indicates that the Third World in general and the Fourth World in particular will have to raise their energy consumption considerably if they are to make significant economic progress. But as we have noted, some countries are not generating sufficient income to pay for their energy imports.

It has been suggested by Professor F. Kohler of Vienna University that the solution might be a graduated energy tax in the industrial countries, the proceeds of which would be used to help the needier countries to pay for the energy, goods and services necessary for their development. Whether the industrial countries would ever agree to such an arrangement is problematical, but there is a possibility that the growing menace of a rich-poor confrontation may induce them to accept.

In any case, proposals such as this will no doubt come up for discussion at the reconvened dialogue between the petroleum-exporting and -importing countries and the Third World, where it is to be hoped that the question of aid to the Fourth World will receive particular attention. It matters little what form that aid takes, so long as it is provided on a massive—shall I say a Marshall Plan?—scale. I need hardly add that cooperation between the industrial countries and the OPEC states is a prerequisite for success.

Until such time as the nations of the Third and Fourth Worlds can stand on their own feet, achieve some measure of economic independence and provide a minimum acceptable standard of living for their people, it is up to both OPEC and the industrialized nations to provide them with the necessary financial and technological assistance. Iran, away from the limelight and political considerations, has been doing and will continue to do her fair share in this rescue operation.

Iran's Petrodollars: Surplus or Deficit?—An Examination of Alternative Iranian Policies

Fereidun Fesharaki

The aims of this essay are threefold: to show how (1) Iran has dealt with her petrodollar receipts in 1974–75; (2) how Iran could change her expenditure policy in the face of declining oil revenues; and (3) the extent by which Iran's investment strategy can produce returns to supplement the country's foreign exchange requirements in the future. Thus, the options open to the Government of Iran and its priorities will be examined. While we look at the general investment policy of Iran, attention is focused particularly on petroleum-related activities at home and abroad. The specific impact of such investments on the dynamics of the Iranian economy is left to other participants.

The Problem

The quantum increase in oil prices in the last quarter of 1975 and the subsequent price rises resulting from increasing participation of the Persian Gulf Arab Oil Producers in equity shares of the oil companies (which benefited Iran through the "balancing margin principle" of the 1973 Sales and Purchase Agreement), called for an increase in the price of benchmark light Arabian crude from $3.01 per barrel on October 1, 1973, to $10.46 per barrel on January 1, 1975. The government per-barrel take during the same period rose from $1.76 to $10.12. The largest ever transfer of capital from one group of nations to others took place in 1974–75. The total OPEC receipts rose from $23 billion in 1973 to around $90 billion in 1974. As it can be seen in Table 60 (all tables appear in the appendix to this essay), the five small Arab producers, with only 4 percent of the total population, received 45 percent of the revenues. These are the countries with the lowest level of absorptive capacity and the highest magnitude of surplus petrodollars. The non-oil exports, which can be a rough indicator of the stage of economic development in these countries, show that the five richest countries' (see Table 60) non-oil exports were in total 21 percent less than Iran's non-oil exports in 1974. As a result of the differing levels of development among the oil producers, a total surplus of around $55 billion, amounting to 10 percent of the world trade, could not be internally utilized.[1]

Iran's petrodollar position is particularly important, not only because of the way it will affect the future development of the Iranian economy, but also in the way it will dictate Iran's investment strategy and foreign policy abroad. In 1974, Iran was the second largest oil exporter in the world; at the same time, Iran has the most sophisticated economy among the oil producers and a well-organized planning machinery capable of absorbing these funds.

Iran's Fifth Development Plan (March 21, 1973, to March 21, 1978) was revised in late 1974 to take into account the new developments in the oil industry. The anticipated foreign exchange receipts during the plan period are to total $114 billion, but the oil sector alone was expected to provide $102 billion, or 90 percent of the total receipts (see Table 61). These figures are based on a production capacity and international demand that is not likely to be realized. As a result, a considerable shortfall of revenues may occur that requires a modification and reappraisal of the government objectives. But before we go on any further, let us elaborate on the causes of such a possible shortfall.

Future Exporting Prospects

The 1973 Sales and Purchase Agreement, which replaced the former Consortium Agreement, laid down specific guidelines for Iran's exports from the southern oil fields for the duration of contract 1973–93. These guidelines were based on the size of Iranian proven and recoverable reserves. The agreement itself marked the recognition of two important factors: (1) Iranian production is near its peak capacity and cannot be substantially expanded; and (2) the prospect of discovering new oil-bearing fields is small. Thus, the largest group of oil fields responsible for 90 percent of Iranian production in the past two decades will cease to export in 1993. The total Khuzestan (formerly Consortium) production was expected to reach its peak of 7.6 million barrels a day (mb/d) by 1978 and remain relatively steady for six years. Thereafter, the production will fall until 1993, when the total production will be capable of supplying only the domestic demand. During this 20-year period, the Khuzestan area will produce 42.5 billion barrels of oil, 29.3 billion barrels of which are to be sold to the former Consortium participants; 7.2 billion barrels will be directly exported by the National Iranian Oil Company (NIOC); and 6 billion barrels will be internally utilized. Together with two dozen or so foreign operators producing in Iran, the total installed capacity was estimated to reach around 8.5 mb/d by the late 1970s.

Unofficial estimates of Iranian proven reserves range from 45 billion barrels to 100 billion barrels[2], though the most recently quoted figure is 60 to 70 billion barrels. But how flexible are the proven reserves of any country? Such reserves are governed by two factors: (1) the finite quantity of oil-in-place and the recovery rate—this means that one day this finite quantity will be entirely exhausted, but secondary recovery methods can increase the recoverable volume; and (2) reserves are a function of market price, thus, if the price of oil rises, many oil fields that had previously been shut down as noncommercial (for being high-cost or small-producer) will become economically viable. Also, a great deal of offshore exploration will become economically acceptable. Thus, the rise in Iranian oil prices from $1.50 per barrel in 1970 to, say, $10.50 in 1975 will obviously mean a substantial increase in the reserves, but by how much no one knows. In terms of relative volume of reserves, however, the Iranian position will not substantially change, since the other producers' reserves will also rise. Gas reinjection is expected to boost the recovery factor for oil in place from 20 to 30 percent attainable by primary depletion up to 40 percent—with a corresponding increase in reserves. Initially, seven of the larger oil fields—Agha Jari, Ahwaz-Asmari, Marum, Gachsaran, Haftgell, Bibi-Hakimeh and Paris—will carry out the program. Haftgell will receive the first injection of 300 million cubic feet daily (cfd) from the gas cap of Naft-e-Sefid in 1975; other fields will follow by 1977. By the end of the decade, smaller fields producing as little as 30,000 b/d may well be included in the program. Thus, valuable quantities of gas, which are flared in large volumes today and soon will be exportable, must be used to sustain the productivity of the oil fields. This we will consider in greater detail when we look at the future of gas exports later on.

Decline in Demand

The economic recession in the industrial countries, coupled with higher oil prices, has substantially reduced the demand for Iranian oil. From January to May 1975, the Iranian production averaged 5.5 mb/d, down 10.5 percent from the same period in 1974. April production was 5.1 mb/d, down 17.6 percent from April 1974.[3] As a result, Iran's exports in 1975 are likely to range between 4.7 to 5.0 mb/d, compared to around 5.7 mb/d in 1974. Whether the decline in the demand for oil is the result of higher prices and the structural changes in energy saving in the West, or the decline in demand is due to a temporary recession in the West, is outside the scope of this study. However, the fall in demand has given the authorities in Iran a longer time to plan the increase in oil productivity of the fields and adjust their overall expenditure policy.

Estimated Foreign Exchange Receipts

Given the above two factors on the productivity of the Iranian oil fields and the decline in demand, we may proceed to make a simple forecast of the revenues from the petroleum sector in Table 62. The underlying assumption is that by 1976 the Western demand has recovered and Iran can produce at peak capacity.

It can be seen that the forecasted revenues fall 13 to 19 percent short of the $102 billion anticipated in the Fifth Plan. Even with the price of over $11.50 per barrel, which may well be prevailing from September 1975 (after the OPEC meeting), still the plan target will not be reached. At first sight, one may conclude that there will be no problems, because Iran's balance of payments shows a surplus of $17.5 billion (see Table 61), approximately equal to the size of the deficit. The problem is, of course, not so simple. Iran has already made such aid and investment commitments that she may not deem appropriate to discontinue. Furthermore, the gap may continue to widen during the Sixth Plan (1977-78–1982-83) and adjustments need to be made as soon as possible. In the budget year 1974–75, the government faced a shortfall of $2 billion in its petroleum receipts. In the current year, the shortfall may even be larger.

In the Fifth Plan, importation of goods is expected to total $79.1 billion. Based on the 1972 import figure of $2.57 billion, this would imply a growth rate in imports of just under 100 percent. Despite the possible shortfalls in the foreign exchange receipts of Iran in the Fifth Plan, such a high level of imports may be maintained by cutting down on other foreign exchange expenditures, but if the imports are allowed to grow at these rates in the Sixth Plan, the most optimistic production forecasts may not provide the necessary foreign exchange.

Options Open to Iran

In the following we will discuss all kinds of expenditures Iran has undertaken or planned in the current plan period. We will also examine the future trends and the possibility of return on foreign investment.

Domestic Investment

The Fifth Plan is to undertake expenditures of $69.6 billion in the five-year period. The public sector investment amounts to $46.2 billion, or 66 percent of the total, at an annual growth rate of 38.1 percent, compared to 14.1 percent in the Fourth Development Plan. These include investments in capital goods, oil and gas, infrastructure and social welfare, etc. With the present level of government commitment at home, it is highly unlikely that public spending will be cut down drastically. Thus, it is reasonable to assume that the government will attempt to fulfill its domestic commitments at their planned levels.

Domestic Hydrocarbon Investments

As a means of increasing its future export potential, the government has in the past few years concentrated its efforts on three major hydrocarbon fields: domestic export refineries, petrochemicals and gas.

Domestic Export Refineries. These types of refinery have for long been an attractive proposition to the producing countries, particularly Iran, which has carefully been watching the export potentials of the Consortium-operated Abadan export refinery. Export refineries provide two main advantages for the oil producers. It would provide them with the value added involved in the refining process and a stronger political control on the supply. Because the refineries have since the late 1940s concentrated in the consuming areas, the consumers could switch the source of crude in cases of difficulty (embargo or higher prices), but with the refineries in the producing areas, the consumers will not have such a flexibility.

Iran's drive to substitute product exports for crude started with the takeover of the Abadan Refinery in 1973. Since then a number of preliminary agreements have been signed with Japanese, European and American concerns. So far, none of the agreements has been finalized, because of lack of cooperation from consumers and Iran's insistence in some cases to link the refinery construction to the construction of an adjoining petrochemical complex that can use naphtha produced from the refinery as its feedstock.

Though Iran has not succeeded in bringing refineries home so far, the future trend is unmistakable. NIOC will seek partners that have an extensive marketing network abroad, and most probably will provide incentives such as discounts, lower fuel costs (cheap natural gas), long-term guarantees, as well as accessibility to capital. One can expect a general movement in the direction of home refineries for Iran as well as other producers, but such a movement may be slower than has been anticipated, particularly in view of the present excess capacity of refineries around the world. Iran's export of refined products is unlikely to exceed its crude exports, given the lifespan of Iran's reserves of oil and the state of refining operations around the world. Thus, Iran cannot look to export refineries as a major potential earner of foreign exchange in the foreseeable future.

Table 63 shows the government's investment plans for oil. Investment in the oil industry in the Fifth Plan is projected at $9.3 billion: $5 billion from general revenues, $3 billion through NIOC and the remainder from the private sector. Refining absorbs the lion's share of investment: 44 percent of the total. Domestic refineries at Isfahan, Tabriz (proposed), and Shiraz and Tehran II refineries, constructed in the plan period, will not absorb more than half of the allocations. This shows the government's hopes for heavy investment in export refineries, which may not be fully realized. Apart from refineries, other investment commitments are expected to be realized in full.

Petrochemicals. Another important future source of income for Iran will be petrochemical exports. National Petrochemical Company (NPC), an NIOC subsidiary, was established in 1965 and has built up an industry with an investment value of $400 million, comprising two wholly owned subsidiaries (Shahpour Chemical Company and Iran Chemical Fertilizer Company) and two joint ventures with U.S. companies. The joint ventures are Abadan Petrochemical Company (B.F. Goodrich—26 percent, NPC—74 percent) and Kharg Chemical Company (Indiana Standard—50 percent, NPC—50 percent). Table 64 shows the production of these ventures in the first quarter of 1974. Plans are underway to increase the capacity of these plants by 100 percent in three years. Three other petrochemical projects are now being implemented, and a wide range of other projects is under discussion.[4]

The basic idea behind investment in petrochemicals is similar to that for export refineries: to capture the value added. But the difference is that the value added in petrochemicals is substantially above that of refining. At the same time, export refineries are complementary to petrochemicals plants as the former's output is an important feedstock for the latter.

Iran offers an attractive opportunity for petrochemical investments to foreign partners: cheap gas, security of feedstock and a possible geographical advantage due to its location between Europe and Asia. Iran plans to spend $8 billion in a 10-year investment program that may be the first step toward shifting the petrochemical world's center of gravity to the Persian Gulf. By 1983 Iran aims to be producing 5 to 10 percent of the world's basic petrochemical needs and thereafter to supply 10 percent of the annual growth in the world demand.[5]

Whether the investment figures quoted above can be realized or not, it is clear that Iran is moving fast in the direction of petrochemical exports as the most economic way of utilizing oil.

Iran: Past, Present and Future

Gas. At a time when Iran's oil production is leveling off, Iran's gas industry is geared to assume a major role in the expansion of the Iranian economy. Iran has ambitious plans to utilize its associated and nonassociated natural gas for domestic consumption, refinery and petrochemical feedstock, gas reinjection to maintain pressure at the oilfields and exports.

All of the gas produced in Iran is associated gas (produced with oil and a free good in that sense), 58 percent of which was flared in 1973. A total of 4.8 billion cubic feet daily was produced in 1973, of which 2 billion cfd were utilized. Gas consumption in the same year for domestic commercial, industrial and petrochemical uses amounted to 229 million cfd, oil field consumption was 816 million cfd, and exports, to the Soviet Union through IGAT (Iranian Gas Trunkline) amounted to 840 million cfd. Exports to the Soviet Union were expected to reach 1 billion cfd by the end of 1974 and then level off (see Table 67).

The future export potential of gas and oil in Iran is dominated by the key issue of reservoir reinjection for secondary recovery in the Khuzestan oil fields (discussed earlier). A look at the figures will explain why. Estimates of the amount required for gas reinjection vary between 8 and 13 billion cfd, compared to the available flare-associated gas of 2 billion cfd by 1980. To fill this gap, NIOC is planning to use gas caps in suitable oil reservoirs, known gas fields and new gas discoveries, which it is confident of making.

Two important points have to be made at this point concerning reservoir reinjection. First, reinjection is a costly venture involving collection of the gas, drilling reinjection wells and reinjection. Second, gas reinjection does not mean a **loss** of gas, but rather a delay in its utilization. One may expect around 85 percent of the reinjected gas to be recovered in 20 years or so, depending on the characteristics of the reservoirs.

Iran's gas exports are one of the government's hopes for the future. Although quite a few letters of intent have been signed, only two contracts have been finalized. One is the exports to the Soviet Union, which started a few years ago, and a major trilateral deal that was finalized in April 1975. The trilateral deal involves Iran, the Soviet Union and West Germany. The U.S.S.R. will receive 1.3 billion cfd of gas from Iran and will deliver 1 billion cfd annually to Germany over 25 years on account of Iran. The gas will be delivered in 1981 through a 900-mile pipeline that joins the southern gas fields to the Soviet border at Astara. At present prices, this would mean an annual income of $250 million for Iran and $60 million for the U.S.S.R. According to West German sources, part of Iranian gas may be sold to Italy or Austria.[6]

Another serious contender for Iranian gas is El Paso Natural Gas of the U.S., and two Belgian companies, Sopex and Distrigaz, have signed a letter of intent with the National Iranian Gas Company (NIGC), a NIOC subsidiary. The project involves LNG (liquid natural gas) exports to

Europe and the U.S. of 2 billion initially, rising to 3 billion cfd from the early 1980s.[7]

Iran's gas reserves are the largest in the Middle East and possibly the second largest in the world next to the Soviet Union. Earlier estimates put Iran's reserves at 270 trillion cubic feet or 65 percent of the Middle East reserves. After the discovery of large gas deposits by Egoco of reportedly 175 trillion cubic feet, the estimates were revised upward. The Egoco discovery is said to be probably the largest gas field in the world.[8] Present estimates put Iran's reserves at 250 trillion to 600 trillion cubic feet, half of which is located offshore. It is believed that the true magnitude is closer to the upper range (Soviet gas reserves are estimated at 550 trillion cubic feet).

As was mentioned before, the key to Iran's gas export potential is the amount required for secondary recovery through reinjection. Domestic consumption, gas export projects and gas required for reinjection would demand gas production of around 15 billion to 20 billion cfd by 1980, in comparison with the projected associated gas production of around 5 billion cfd in 1980. Thus, the natural gas fields have to be tapped to supplement the associated gas produced as a by-product of oil. According to the Fifth Plan guidelines, $2.5 billion will be invested in the gas industry: $0.77 billion from the government, $1 billion from NIGC and the remainder from foreign investment. However, 57 percent of the total investment will be directed toward exports and 34 percent to refining and transport. No allocation is made for exploration, which indicates that sufficient resources are already known or that future exploration will be carried out by foreign companies. The total investment may well be sufficient to increase production to the desired levels. Thus, to ensure the availability of financing for gas, the plan states that, "Investment in the development of the gas industry will not be subject to financial limitations and, if necessary, changes will be made in the projected credits."

Export refineries, petrochemicals and gas offer attractive opportunities for Iran's future. The government is committed to large expenditures in these fields and the likelihood of a sizable cut in these investments is remote. At the same time, these ventures have little export potential in the short term, though their long-term future will no doubt be bright.

External Expenditures

In the following we shall consider Iran's foreign investments, as well as aid and loan policy, and try to evaluate the importance and the future trend of such policies.

Financial and Physical Assets

Unlike many other OPEC surplus countries, Iran's investment in physical assets (real estate, etc.) is nonexistent. There is also no indication of a movement of funds to buy government securities, unit trusts or holding large sums of money in bank deposits for investment purposes. Insofar as equities are concerned, there has been no rush for indiscriminate purchase, although in July 1974, Iran bought 25.02 percent of the shares in the steelworks of Krupp Industries of Germany for $100 million. Another deal was approved in April 1975, giving Iran 25.02 percent of shares in Deutsche Babcock & Wilcox AG, at a cost of $75 million. The firm is a leading manufacturer of power-generating equipment, produces nuclear power plant components and is active in a number of other industrial and engineering fields.

Iran's purchase of equity shares abroad is governed by three major criteria: effect on domestic economy (through technology, training, etc.), enhancing economic and political cooperation between Iran and industrial countries and the financial viability of the project. The Krupp and Babcock purchases are directly related to the future industrial needs of Iran in steel production and technology as well as nuclear power generation.

In general, such equity purchases have been relatively small in relation to Iran's petrodollar receipts. At the same time, it is likely that such purchases in the future will be few, selective and based on the above criteria.

Hydrocarbon Investment Abroad

Iran's investment in oil and oil-related activities abroad have been relatively limited in the past. In the following we will consider exploration, transportation, refining and marketing.

Exploration. NIOC went into partnership with British Petroleum a few years ago for exploration in the British sector of the North Sea, through its subsidiary Iranian Oil Company (UK). Very little information is available on the operation of this joint venture, though it is reported that no successful find has been made. In April 1975, NIOC won a concession to explore and exploit for oil in the continental shelf of western Greenland. NIOC's fully owned subsidiary in Denmark has a 25 percent share in a consortium comprising British Petroleum, Standard Oil of

California and SAGA. The agreement covers an area of 10 offshore blocks. The soundness of investment in such "upstream operations" cannot be factually determined without more information, but for a national entity such as NIOC this may not be the most important factor. If NIOC wishes to gain experience through partnership with foreign partners, these joint ventures will provide such opportunity.

Transportation. Iran's entry into international oil transportation started with the establishment of the National Iranian Tanker Company (NITC), a NIOC subsidiary, in 1955 (Iran has no pipeline ownership abroad). By 1974, the fleet included four ocean-going tankers, two with a capacity of 55,000 dead weight tons (dwt) each and another two, each with a capacity of 35,000 dwt. In 1973, two supertankers with a capacity of 230,000 dwt each were ordered from Japan, the first of which was delivered in April 1975. Iran has also agreed to buy a number of tankers from BP Tanker Company and pool them with the British Company under a unified (British) management late in 1975. Iran's ownership of tankers is very small in relation to Iran's export requirements, and the bulk of Iranian crude will no doubt be exported in the future through the traditional mediums. Furthermore, Iran has no immediate use for the tankers bought recently. The Japanese-made supertanker has been leased to a Japanese company, while the BP Tanker Company will manage the Iranian Tanker Company in a joint venture. In the future, Iran may use its own tankers, particularly in view of NIOC's increasing direct sales. In general, Iran's purchase of tankers is a small, limited operation, and there is no indication of a surge into tanker business in the future.

Refining and Marketing. NIOC participates in two joint venture refineries abroad but has no foreign distribution facilities. The two foreign refineries are Madras refinery in India (operational in 1969) and Sassolburg refinery in South Africa (operational in 1971). In both cases, NIOC provided expertise, part of the capital expenditure and crude throughput on a long-term basis. In July 1971, NIOC acquired 24.5 percent of the shares of the Madras Fertilizer Plant, the largest and most modern fertilizer complex in India.

After the February 1971 Tehran agreement, when oil prices started to rise for the first time after 11 years, NIOC undertook a series of studies for expanding its refining and marketing operations in Europe and the U.S. A number of letters of intent were signed with Greek, German, U.S. and Belgian concerns. The Greek deal involved participation in ownership of Asperoprygos refinery and marketing of its products. The German agreement entailed participation of NIOC in a number of refineries in Germany as well as equity participation in 1,300 service stations.[9] The

U.S. deal provided for participation of NIOC in 50 percent equity owner-ship of Ashland Oil Company. Ashland has a 60,000 b/d refinery and a petrochemical complex in Buffalo, as well as 180 service stations in New York State.[10] Another U.S. deal between Shell and other U.S. companies for construction of a 500,000 b/d refinery in Iran and a joint marketing venture in service stations on the U.S. east coast was signed in 1974, but was postponed indefinitely in 1975.[11]

Aid to Developing Countries

Iran's aid prior to 1975 was very small indeed. As we can see from Table 68, this aid amounted to $3.8 million in 1973. As of 1974, the petrodollar surplus allowed Iran to enter the big aid league within the span of one year. The total committed Iranian aid in 1974 amounted to $3,280 million, of which $953 million was disbursed.

Iran's aid may be divided into two broad categories: bilateral and multilateral aid (see Tables 69 and 70). The recipients of the bilateral aid are a heterogeneous lot. Aid has been awarded to these countries on three major criteria: (1) to strengthen Iran's links with these countries; (2) to help these countries establish industries and export their finished or intermediate product to Iran; and (3) aid for humanitarian purposes. Needless to say, as is to be expected, the countries in the first two categories have received the lion's share of the allocations. The Iranian aid, though it may be project-tied, is not source-tied, and thus it is much more advantageous to the recipient countries than traditional western aid. This is to say, the recipients are not required to spend their aid money on Iranian-produced goods. The value of aid (which includes loans) to recipient countries can be measured in terms of grant element (grant equivalent), which shows what aid is worth to the recipient as an outright grant. Every loan has three major features: interest rate, grace period and repayment period. The Iranian loans carry low interest rates and long repayment and grace periods and thus have a large grant-element component. Unfortunately, the lack of detailed information on the terms of loans makes it impossible to arrive at a total grant-element figure for Iranian aid, though in some specific cases it is known that the grant element ranges from 40 percent in the case of India to 100 percent in the case of Ethiopia. Furthermore, Iranian aid, unlike the OECD aid, has no imperialistic inclinations. This aid is used neither to keep a par-ticular regime in power nor to help sustain a country under Iran's political influence.

Iran's aid in 1974 amounted to 6.9 percent of her GNP in terms of committed aid and 2.1 percent of her GNP in terms of disbursed aid. In all, Iran was the second largest donor in OPEC after Saudi Arabia.

Economic Cooperation with Industrial Countries

In a bid to obtain technological cooperation and show her goodwill to industrial nations, Iran has engaged in a number of loan and trade deals with these countries. The major deals involve the United Kingdom, France, Italy and the United States:

1. United Kingdom—A loan of $1.2 billion carrying commercial interest rates and guaranteed by the British Government. The loan will open lines of credit to public sector industries, will be given over three years and is repayable after five years from the entry into effect of each part of the loan. Four hundred million dollars has been disbursed.

2. Italy—A series of preliminary agreements has been signed with Italy, aiming at $3 billion of trade and cooperation between the two countries. The agreements include a steel mill based on the direct reduction method with a capacity of three million tons a year at Bandar Abbas, a satellite town with 80,000 inhabitants; shipbuilding facilities with a capacity of 750,000 tons per annum; another tire factory by Pirelli with a capacity of 400,000 tons a year; and a NIOC-ENI joint venture for refining and distribution of oil products in Europe and Africa. Other agreements include petrochemicals, aluminum, textiles, construction, agriculture and capital goods manufacture. No actual disbursements have taken place.

3. France—A series of preliminary and final agreements worth $7.8 billion, including $1.8 billion for the two French atomic power plants. Other projects are a 41-mile underground subway for Tehran; production of 100,000 Renault cars in Iran as a joint venture; construction of 200,000 housing units; a color TV system for Iran based on the French "Secam" system; 26 turbo trains as well as electrification and modernization of the Iranian rail network; a fleet of methane tankers; and a $270-million steel plant. Other projects include cooperation in agriculture, petrochemicals and energy. One billion dollars has actually been disbursed.

4. United States—The largest-ever single agreement between two countries was signed by Iran and the U.S. in March 1975, involving $15 billion over five years. Five billion dollars will be in normal trade items, representing an increase of some 20 percent per year in non-oil trade; another $5 billion is for the sale of U.S. military equipment to Iran; and another $5 billion in actual U.S. involvement in the Iranian economy. The latter includes eight nuclear plants of 1,000 megawatts each; associated desalination plants; 20 prefabricated factories, 100,000 apartments, five hospitals with a total of 3,000 beds; the establishment of an integrated electronics industry; the building of a major port; joint ventures to produce fertilizers, pesticides, farm machinery and processed food; and superhighways and vocational training centers. No actual disbursements have taken place.

It is important to note that, based on the information available, these agreements have not included a direct oil-for-technology exchange, though the oil component may indeed be hidden among various clauses. Except for U.K. and U.S. deals, no time limits have been set, and indeed, so far, only $1.4 billion of the total committed $27 billion has been disbursed. Disbursement of the remainder will, no doubt, depend on Iran's foreign exchange position in the next few years.

Defense Expenditure

Iran's defense expenditures have been the largest single foreign exchange receiver. Traditionally, defense expenditures have accounted for between 25 and 50 percent of the total government disbursements. In 1962, defense and security expenditures amounted to $210 million; in 1966, $360 million; in 1970, $820 million; and in 1972, $1.4 billion. After the increase in oil prices in 1973, the government's general budget increased from $4.8 billion in 1972 to $23.7 billion in 1974–75 and to $26.5 billion in the proposed 1975–76 budget. However, the share of defense and security expenditures remained surprisingly stable at $5.3 billion and $7.8 billion for the last two budgets. The Fifth Plan anticipates total government receipts of $122.8 billion, of which $29.1 billion, or 24 percent, will be spent on defense. Available data do not show the foreign exchange component of such expenditures (imports), but it is reported that between 50 and 80 percent of such expenditures are imports. (Table 69 shows the expenditures in the Middle East on defense.)

Iran's defense expenditures, like those of most other countries, place a heavy burden on its resources. The ever-increasing importance of oil and the increase in oil revenues and prices have made the Persian Gulf region politically more sensitive as well as an increasingly important lifeline for the west. Iran's intentions are, in cooperation with neighboring countries, to ensure the safety of this lifeline and to keep the area free from the Big Power rivalries.

Summary

In the course of this essay we discussed the future foreign exchange position of Iran. Although the simplistic calculation shows that Iran is likely to face a foreign exchange shortfall in the Fifth Plan, the present foreign exchange reserves of around $7 billion ensure that Iran is in no immediate danger. However, adjustment must be made soon if Iran is to avoid becoming a deficit country in a few years' time.

Future export earning hopes on gas, petrochemicals and export refineries are misplaced. To be sure, these industries may have a bright long-term future, but in the short term Iran cannot expect substantial earnings from these sources.

Iran has correctly curtailed its downstream activities abroad. There is no great financial advantage to be gained from these ventures, except possibly as a matter of corporate strategy on a very small scale. Iran's proposed investment in foreign oil ventures in the Fifth Plan amounts to $460 million, indicating 5 percent of the total investments in the five-year period.

Iran's aid to developing countries has been generous, although the direction of aid has been clearly tied to future Iranian political links in the region. A great deal of humanitarian aid has also been granted to African nations. Egypt, as an Arab country, is the largest recipient of aid from Iran; India, the giant nation with nuclear capabilities, is in the second place; and Pakistan—Iran's old CENTO ally—is in the third place. Committed aid to these three countries accounts for most of the aid promised by Iran in 1974. Despite the tensions between India, Pakistan and Afghanistan, Iran has managed to maintain a delicate balance in between. Trade and loans to the industrial countries have also been on a substantial scale, including the particularly worst hit countries, such as Italy and the U.K., as well as the U.S. and France. The total proposed deals with the industrial countries amount to $27 billion—5 percent of which has already been disbursed.

Defense expenditures by Iran have continued at a high rate from $1.4 billion in 1972 to $7.8 billion in 1975–76. But The Shahanshah has made it clear that Iran has no intention of territorial expansion or political domination in the Gulf; rather he wishes that the local governments in the region would conclude an alliance to replace the U.S. and Soviet presence in the Persian Gulf and Indian Ocean, as well as reduce the risk of subversion by Marxist elements.

One thing is certain: Iran will not be able to keep up expenditures at home, or aid and loan and defense expenditures at present high levels of 1974 and 1975. Iran's Fifth Plan shows that the country expects to invest $11 billion abroad and receive a return of $2 billion in the five-year period. Both these figures may prove to be overly optimistic. In any case, the expected return will not be sufficient to maintain the present level of expenditures. From the three components referred to above, aid and foreign investment will be the first to go. Defense may also be cut before any large-scale reductions in domestic expenditures are undertaken.

Whether domestic expenditure should be reduced or the government should go back to the capital markets to borrow funds is a matter beyond the scope of this study. However, a few general observations may be made: the inflow of imports in 1974 was around $10 billion, compared to $3.6 billion in 1973. The imports included a large component of consumer goods and food items that can be reduced to ease the foreign exchange shortfall. This can be done by raising tariff barriers back to the previous levels in 1974 (in 1975 tariffs were substantially reduced). Only food import subsidies in 1974 amounted to over $1 billion. The infrastructure is already showing signs of strain. The Fifth Plan forecasts a shortage of over 720,000 workers. Only 10,000 of the shortage is in the unskilled category: the bulk is highly skilled and semi-skilled labor, which Iran lacks. In 1974 alone, Iran had to pay $100 million in fines to shipowners for delays in unloading cargo in Iranian ports. Customs posts are jammed, and the government did not, at the time, have enough warehouses to store the imported wheat.

The Government of Iran is clearly interested in distributing its newly found affluence to the bulk of the populace. It hopes to maintain this affluence through a dynamic free enterprise economy, with the help of foreign technology and labor. But maybe the injection of capital and imported goods into the economy is too fast for the infrastructure and the economy as a whole. If Iran is to experience a shortfall in foreign exchange requirements, with a direct impact on the standard of living of the people (*e.g.,* cutting food import subsidies), the nation will find it more difficult to adjust itself to a lower standard of living after a few years of affluence. Perhaps the government should consider maintaining its development goals, but implement them at a slower pace, keeping in mind the future position of Iran's foreign exchange.

Table 60
Estimated OPEC Oil Revenues and GNP

Country	Population (millions) 1973*	Oil Revenues (millions of U.S. dollars) 1973	1974	Non-oil Exports 1973	GNP Per Capita** (U.S. dollars) 1973	1974
Rich Oil Countries	11.2	10,600	40,300	683		
Saudi Arabia	7.8	5,100	20,000		980	2,900
Kuwait	1.0	1,900	7,000	577	4,100	8,500
Qatar	0.2	400	1,600		3,300	>10,000
Abu Dhabi†	0.1	900	4,100		9,000	>10,000
Libya	2.1	2,300	7,600	106	3,000	5,800
Middle-income Oil Countries	75.2	9,500	39,700	2,388		
Iran	31.2	4,100	17,400	864	520	940
Venezuela	11.2	2,800	10,600	1,232	1,150	1,850
Iraq	10.4	1,500	6,800	22	430	930
Algeria	15.4	900	3,700	270	350	530
Ecuador	6.5	100	800	n.a.	320	420
Gabon	0.5	100	400	n.a.	900	1,540
Low-income Oil Countries	183.4	2,900	10,000	2,210		
Indonesia	124.0	900	3,000	1,923	80	100
Nigeria	59.4	2,000	7,000	287	150	230
Grand Total	269.8	23,000	90,000	5,281		

Source: IMF Survey, February 3, 1975, p. 38.

*Population figures extrapolated from 1971 data as shown in World Bank Atlas.
**GNP figures were estimated on the basis of both oil revenues and non-oil productive activities.
†Member of the United Arab Emirates.

Table 61
Summary of Iran's Balance of Payments During the Fifth Plan
(billions of dollars)

Current Receipts		114.0
Receipts from oil sector	102.2	
Foreign exchange earnings from export of goods	4.9	
Foreign exchange earnings from export of services	4.9	
Foreign exchange earnings from investments abroad	2.0	
Current Payments		94.7
Sale of foreign exchange for import of goods	79.1	
Sale of foreign exchange for import of services	14.3	
Servicing of foreign loans	1.3	
Current Balance		19.3
Receipts on Capital Account		4.7
Foreign loans and credits received by the government	2.2	
Other loans and foreign private investment	2.5	
Payments on Capital Account		6.5
Repayment of principal of government loans and credits	6.0	
Repayment of private loans and transfer abroad of private capital	0.5	
Capital Balance		-1.8
Net Balance on Current and Capital Account		17.5

Source: The Fifth Development Plan of Iran, *op. cit.,* p. 62.

Table 62
Iran's Receipts from the Oil Sector
(thousands of barrels per day and current billions of dollars)

	1973	1974	1975	1976	1977	1978	1979	1980
Planned Output*	5314	5676	6322	6958	7596	7603	7606	7610
Likely Output**	5860	6030	5500	6000	6200	6500	6500	6500
Internal Demands[†]	266	297	365	447	514	584	660	752
Stock Change and Loss	24	63	—	—	—	—	—	—
Exports	5570	5670	5135	5553	5686	5916	5840	5748
Revenue I[††]	3.8	18.0	18.9	20.5	21.0	21.8	21.5	21.2
Revenue II[†††]	3.8	18.0	19.5	22.5	25.4	29.1	31.5	34.2

Source: Derived by the author.

Note: 1973 and 1974 data are actual.

*Relates to Khuzestan production only. Other production was anticipated to be around one million barrels per day by the end of the decade.

**Based on technical and engineering capacities from 1976 onwards.

[†]Based on 1974 projections by the Distribution Department of NIOC (unpublished).

[††]Based on a government take of $10.12 per barrel from January 1975.

[†††]Based on a 10 percent annual increase in government take from October 1975.

Table 63

Fixed Capital Formation for Oil During the Fifth Plan

(billions of rials)

Program	Public Sector	Private Sector	Total
Exploration and Production	187.4	—	187.4
Refining	212.4	64.0	276.4
Transport and Distribution	73.6	—	73.6
Non-basic Affairs	8.0	—	8.0
Operations Outside Iran	30.7	—	30.7
Investment in Affili- ated Companies	23.8	23.8	47.6
Total	535.9	87.8	623.7

Source: Iran's Fifth Development Plan (Revised), January 1975, p. 274.

Note: Investments in oil are not subject to credit limitations and may increase.

Table 64

Production of Iran's Petrochemicals—First Quarter of 1974

Name of Company and Products	Production (metric tons)	Sales
Shahpour Chemical Company		
Ammonia	39,950	25,664
Urea	29,728	28,161
Sulphur	69,639	44,381
Sulphuric Acid	74,811	972
Phosphoric Acid	23,532	—
Ammonium Phosphate	53,496	55,319
Kharg Chemical Company		
Sulphur	68,845	80,900
Propane (barrels)	350,507	378,348
Butane (barrels)	280,620	210,123
Light Naphtha (barrels)	208,191	207,259
Abadan Petrochemical Company		
Caustic Soda	5,259	4,468
D. D. B.	3,195	3,454
P. V. C.	4,801	4,506
Polyca Products	673	716
Iran Chemical Fertilizer Company		
Ammonium Nitrate	8,243	8,258
Urea	13,558	11,794
Light Sodium Carbonate	1,173	160
Heavy Sodium Carbonate	6,691	2,263
Sodium Bicarbonate	525	66

Source: *Iran Oil Journal,* August 1974.

Iran: Past, Present and Future

Table 65
Associated Gas Production 1973
(thousand cubic feet)

Company	Gas Produced	Gas Utilized	Gas Flared	Gas Utilized (percent)
NIOC/OSCO	1,615,683,300	724,292,941	891,390,356	44.6
IPAC	58,837,200	14,479,300	44,357,900	24.6
IMINOGO	27,057,000	1,000,000	26,057,000	3.7
LAPCO	26,692,774	1,457,000	25,235,274	5.5
SIRIP	10,991,900	1,157,500	9,934,400	10.5
NIOC (Naft-e-Shah)	4,316,900	463,100	3.	
Total	1,743,579,074	742,850,341	1,000,728,733	42.6

Note: This table overstates the amount of gas utilized, since some recipients (including IGAT and Kharg Chemical) flare a portion of the gas received.

Associated Gas Production and Utilization (million cubic feet daily)

	1970	1973	1975	1980
Production	2,772.0	4,784.0	4,249.0	5,793.0
Consumption				
Domestic, Commercial Industrial and Petrochemical	67.5	228.6	796.0	1,401.0
Oil Fields Consumption	924.0	816.4	1,164.0	1,307.0
Export	83.5	840.0	1,016.0	1,016.0
Total	1,085.0	1,885.0	2,976.0	3,784.0
Balance	1,687.0	2,899.0	1,973.0	2,000.0

Note: Export figures are for IGAT only. Balance indicated will be used for secondary recovery and other projects.

Table 65 (cont'd)
Domestic Gas Consumption (Associated and Nonassociated)
(million cubic feet daily)

	1970	1973	1975	1980
Oil Field Consumption	924.0	816.0	1,184.0	1,367.0
Domestic and Commercial	0.3	1.2	4.0	42.8
Electricity Generating	2.0	58.8	156.4	724.6
Industries	15.1	63.0	180.5	1,085.0
Total	841.4	844.0	1,504.9	3,170.4

Note: Does not include gas to be used for reinjection purposes. Industries heading includes direct reduction steel mill and petrochemicals.

Source: The National Iranian Gas Company, in Supplement to the *Middle East Economic Survey,* February 7, 1975.

Iran: Past, Present and Future

Table 66

Components of Committed and Disbursed Iranian Aid

(millions of dollars)

	1970		1971		1972		1973		1974		1975	
	C	D	C	D	C	D	C	D	C	D	C	D
ODA:*												
Bilateral	—	3.0	—	2.6	2.1	3.7	10.2	0.8	1745.1	358.1	121.0	126.0
Multilateral	—		32.0	0.3	1.8	—	1.6	—	171.0	—	—	—
Total		3.0	32.0	2.9	3.9	3.7	11.8	0.8	1916.1	358.1	121.0	126.0
Other:												
Bilateral	—	—	—	—	—	—	—	—	524.2	—	304.8	—
Multilateral	4.0	4.0	1.0	1.0	8.5	8.5	3.0	3.0	839.8	595.6	1013.8	34.0
Total	4.0	4.0	1.0	1.0	8.5	8.5	3.0	3.0	1364.0	595.6	1318.6	34.0
Total	4.0	7.0	33.0	3.9	12.4	12.2	14.8	3.8	3280.1	953.7	1439.6	160.0
Total as a Percent of GNP	0.04	0.06	0.25	0.03	0.08	0.07	0.7	0.02	6.9	2.1	—	—

Source: Based on data collected from the World Bank.

Note: 1975 data are for the first quarter only.

*Official Development Aid. Includes flows for which terms are unknown, but the type of project would probably attract ODA.

Table 67
Bilateral Committed and Disbursed Iranian Aid
(millions of dollars)

Recipient	1974		1975	
	C	D	C	D
Afghanistan	10.0	—	—	—
Bangladesh	15.0	—	—	—
Egypt	860.0	50.0	120.0	—
Ethiopia	0.1	0.1	—	—
India*	133.0	133.0	—	—
Indonesia	—	—	200.0	—
Jordan	11.0	—	4.8	—
Lebanon	345.5	—	—	—
Lesotho	1.0	—	—	—
Morocco	30.0	—	—	—
Pakistan	647.0	125.0	1.0	126.0
Peru	—	—	100.0	—
Senegal	15.7	—	—	—
Sri Lanka	67.0	—	—	—
Sudan	130.0	50.0	—	—
Tunisia	4.0	—	—	—
Total	2,296.3	358.1	425.8	126.0

Source: Based on data collected from the World Bank.

Note: 1975 figures are for the first quarter only.

*Aid to India as reported by the World Bank is substantially lower than the figure of $900 million reported by IMF and the Iranian press.

Table 68
Multilateral Committed and Disbursed Iranian Aid
(millions of dollars)

Recipient	1974		1975	
	C	D	C	D
IMF Oil Facility*	476.0	306.8	1,000.0	20.2
UNDP**	1.0	—	—	—
UN Emergency Special Fund	150.0	—	—	—
UN Emergency Special Account	20.0	—	—	—
World Bank	363.8	288.8	13.8	13.8
Total	1,010.8	595.6	1,013.8	34.0

Source: Based on data collected from the World Bank.

Note: The above table excludes Iran's $150 million commitment to the OPEC Fund.

*Includes only the portion for the 1975 Oil Facility committed to developing countries.

**United Nations Development Programme.

Table 69
Defense Expenditures in Middle East

Country	Expenditure (billions of dollars)	Per Capita (dollars)	Percent of GNP
Algeria	0.404	25	3.3
Bahrain	0.008	35	2.2
Egypt	3.117	85	35.8
Iraq	0.803	76	7.0
Jordan	0.142	54	10.9
Kuwait	0.162	154	1.5
Lebanon	0.133	42	4.3
Libya	0.402	178	3.5
Morocco	0.190	11	3.0
Oman	0.169	228	15.4
Qatar	0.023	130	1.1
Saudi Arabia	1.808	228	5.7
Sudan	0.118	7	5.9
Syria	0.460	65	16.4
Tunisia	0.043	8	1.5
UAE	0.140	821	2.8
North Yemen	0.058	9	3.6
South Yemen	0.029	18	4.8
Total 18 Arab States	8.209	60	7.1
Israel	3.688	1,131	42.4
Iran	5.328	165	13.3
U.S.	85.500	400	6.2

Source: *Middle East Economic Survey,* February 21, 1975.

Iran: Past, Present and Future

Footnotes

1. For details of the OPEC recycling policies and their implications, see F. Fesharaki, "The Development of Iranian Oil Industry—International and Domestic Aspects," to be published by Praeger Publishers, Inc., in Fall 1975. Also, see J. Amuzegar, "Reassessing the Effects of Oil Price Hikes," in *Kayhan International,* February 22, 1975.

2. Iran Almanac and the Book of Facts, Tehran, 1969; Speech by Dr. R. Fallah in *Kayhan International,* July 21, 1973. Iranian proven reserves are not as a matter of policy published in NIOC.

3. *Petroleum Intelligence Weekly,* June 23, 1975, p. 7.

4. *Middle East Economic Survey* (Supplement), "Iran: Gas on the Move," February 7, 1975.

5. *European Chemical News,* June 7, 1974.

6. *Kayhan International,* April 12, 1975.

7. *Middle East Economic Survey,* January 3, 1975.

8. Economist Intelligence Unit, "Oil Production, Revenues and Economic Development," QER Special No. 13, 1975, p. 9.

9. *Kayhan International,* December 8, 1973 (Farsi Edition).

10. Petroleum Press Service, September 1973.

11. *Petroleum Intelligence Weekly,* April 28, 1975.

Comments and Discussion

The broad question of Iran's role in world affairs was considered in several parts, with participants focusing on such elements as the economics of oil, Iran's role in the world economic setting and Iran's foreign policy.

Discussion of the economics of oil was begun with the presentations of "Economics of Oil" and "Iran's Petrodollars: Surplus or Deficit?". R. Fallah observed, first, that the oil industry still has pricing and marketing policies, but that these are now controlled from Tehran, not London. When the oil companies failed to adjust crude oil prices to realistic levels—levels required by the producing countries to support modest industrial and agricultural development programs—the producers had no alternative but to take matters into their own hands and themselves make proper price adjustments. The industrial countries are now seeking new sources of energy, but there is no possibility that new production of oil will be developed in the short- or medium-term future at a price lower than the OPEC price. What has happened in the United States and Canada is paradoxical: the OPEC price would be the universal price today if the United States and Canada—two countries proclaiming commitment to a free-market economy—

had not imposed artificial prices on their own production. Although the oil price rise of 1973 resulted in a burden to consumers, the two or three percent reduction in the GNP of the West was more than offset, in terms of social gain, by the 40 percent increase in Iran's GNP. Mr. Fallah observed that the correct price of crude oil, in Iran's view, is a price that compares with the cost of producing an alternative commodity serving similar purposes. (Nuclear or solar power cannot be compared, but oil produced from coal, shale or tar sands is comparable.) Mr. Fallah then offered some suggestions for coping with the world energy crisis, among them (1) steps by the Western world to narrow the gap between rich and poor nations, including increased production and expenditure, slowed growth rate and acceptance of a transfer of wealth to developing countries; (2) foreign investments by producing states of surplus petrodollars; (3) transfers of responsibility for local capital investments from the oil companies to the host governments in some OPEC states; and (4) trading oil that generates surplus funds in some countries, e.g., Saudi Arabia, for convertible energy bonds. Mr. Fallah concluded by endorsing renewed dialogue among the oil-exporting and -importing countries and Third World countries concerning aid to the Fourth World.

Mr. Fesharaki focused first on the petrodollar position of Iran; although Iran in 1974 was the second largest exporter of oil in the world, it has the most sophisticated economy among the oil producers and well-organized machinery for utilizing oil revenues. Noting that Iran's Fifth Plan anticipated oil revenues of $102 billion in the plan period (March 1973—March 1978), Mr. Fesharaki indicated that these revenues will probably not be realized owing to Iran's production capacity and reduced international demand. In his view, revenues will fall 16 to 19 percent short of the projected $102 billion, even if an oil price rise is effected following the September 1975 OPEC meeting. Although this appears not to present a problem, owing to Iran's balance-of-payments surplus—about equal to the shortfall—the situation is more complex, partly because of Iran's aid and investment commitments. Furthermore, the gap may continue to widen during the Sixth Plan. Mr. Fesharaki then outlined expenditures anticipated by Iran in the current plan period that are dependent on foreign exchange, including domestic investments (hydrocarbons; export refineries;

petrochemicals for export; and gas to be used for domestic consumption, refinery and petrochemical feedstock, reinjection to maintain pressure at oil fields and export) and external expenditures (foreign equity purchases; hydrocarbon investments; oil explorations in joint ventures with foreign partners; oil transport, refining and marketing; aid to developing countries; loan and trade agreements with industrial countries; and defense expenditures—the largest single foreign exchange receiver). Mr. Fesharaki concluded that if expenditures must be reduced owing to a shortfall in foreign exchange, foreign investments should be cut first. Other measures, such as cutting food imports, would significantly affect Iran's standard of living. Perhaps development goals should be maintained but implemented at a somewhat slower pace.

Oil Supply Policies

An Iranian indicated that Iran's policy within OPEC has been that oil supply should equal demand; it has opposed surpluses that push prices down and shortages, owing to embargoes or other factors, that drive prices up. Members of OPEC have held different views on this matter, owing partly to huge surpluses of petrodollars in some OPEC countries. Some countries favor holding oil for the future rather than accepting "paper money" now.

An American argued that Iran should not exhaust its oil reserves in 20 or 30 years if this would enable the government to achieve its development goals; a preservation policy would force industrial countries to consume less oil. A new world attitude is needed toward energy consumption.

Oil Pricing Policies

Several Iranians reiterated Iran's view that the correct price for oil is the price the West would have to pay for alternative sources of energy. The West has suggested that Iran reduce its price because it cannot absorb $20 billion in oil revenues, but this is a self-interested argument. There is no "fair" price for oil, it was suggested—only "a" price, the market price, determined by the interaction of supply and demand. An American concurred that arguments about what constitutes a fair price are not useful; the view that a nonrenewable resource should be priced at the cost of possible alternative resources is sensible since it wil yield revenues Iran must have to import needed commodities.

Another way of looking at price, an Iranian observed, is to estimate the cost Iran will have to pay 20 or 30 years from now to obtain equivalent resources. This is the *true* "opportunity cost." But it is difficult to calculate since inflation and other factors must be taken into account. Another consideration affecting price is the cost to Iran (and other developing countries) of importing manufactured goods from the West; there should be some link between what Iran receives for its oil exports and what it must pay for industrial goods, a participant suggested.

An American specialist warned, however, that new increases in the price of crude oil will lead to increases in the price of gasoline and all other products deriving from crude oil—a merry-go-round of price increases. As for the view that crude oil prices should be set at the cost of producing fuel from coal, once oil prices are raised, coal prices will go up since coal has the same utility value as oil; this means that the cost of producing fuel from coal will rise, justifying, in turn, another rise in the price of oil and so forth. Crude oil prices could easily reach $50 a barrel by these means. The speaker argued strongly that oil prices cannot be determined on this basis. A reasonable compromise is needed so that Iran may proceed with deliberate speed toward its development goals without destroying the world economy. At a subsequent point in the symposium, this participant added that OPEC exports in 1980 will not be significantly larger in volume than they were in 1973–74. If Iran is to increase its revenues from oil in order to sustain its rate of development, it will have to increase oil prices. But it cannot raise prices sharply without impairing world economic stability. Iran has never followed the policy of increasing its revenues by simply increasing the price of oil. As it has shown in the past, Iran can adjust its development programs to accord with the revenues available.

Convertible Energy Bond Proposal

Mr. Fallah's proposal that oil in countries with surplus petrodollars be traded for convertible energy bonds was discussed briefly. An American specialist suggested that investors might welcome such bonds initially but would soon become skeptical, especially if the producers of other commodities adopted this practice and the world became full of unpaid bonds. The fact that OPEC would determine the price of oil and the creditor would determine the conversion price is another handicap.

Another American acknowledged some disadvantages but saw value in the fact that such bonds would take surplus money out of circulation and preserve its value against inflation or devaluation. Iranians added that, unlike oil, an indispensable commodity, other commodities are not qualified to issue such bonds. It was also suggested that OPEC would not determine future fuel prices. America's supply of coal and shale is enough to meet world energy requirements for centuries, and coal—not oil—will set future energy prices.

"Cash Flow" Problem

In a brief exchange, an American observed that Iran is experiencing a cash flow problem: it is delaying payments on contracts, borrowing abroad at high interest rates and receiving 16 percent less revenue from oil exports than last year. An Iranian replied that borrowing abroad is not a sign of weakness; Western countries borrow, too. In his view, the shortfall in oil revenues is temporary and attributable to the mild recession in Western Europe. Iran will make it up.

Relationship Between Oil Revenues and Development Goals

A number of points were made with respect to the importance of oil revenues to Iran's economy, problems that may be encountered in pursuing development goals at the rapid rate envisaged and the need for a "fall-back" position if oil revenues are less than anticipated.

An American shared the views expressed by several Iranians that the demand for oil will remain high, that there are no immediate prospects of alternative sources of fuel, that Iran will continue to discover oil and that it has approximately 20 years in which to use oil revenues for the development of agriculture and competitive industry. But he warned against pursuing rapid economic growth at the expense of viability. Several Americans added that other countries have tried to develop too rapidly and have fallen back, causing great waste.

Iran's growth has not been balanced, an Iranian observed, owing to oil revenues. The government must try to deal with the side effects of oil-produced growth and to achieve greater equality in income distribution and more balanced growth. A European also observed that there has been a close correlation between oil price rises and inflation in Iran, that the rapid growth of GNP has benefited only half the people since half are outside the market and monetary systems and that food imports are rising. She warned that oil revenues may be contributing to a dangerously split society. An American specialist concurred that if Iran achieves its GNP growth rate goals, this may produce stresses that will seriously harm society. In his view Iran should consider a slower growth rate. GNP is not everything. The happiness of the individual and the stability of society are also important.

An Iranian acknowledged that the need for substantial agricultural imports, resulting from population increase and a very rapid rise in per capita consumption of all food items, represents a danger to the economy. But he expressed optimism about the development of industrial exports and the outcome of mineral explorations; even without oil Iran was developing rapidly. Another Iranian indicated that inflation and higher prices have led to a larger import bill; it is hoped that revenues spent in Iran will produce goods and services to meet local demands and reduce the need for imports. Everything possible is being done to increase food production, but limited water supply and other factors make this difficult. Another speaker stressed that Iran does not want "to become Italy"; it wants only to achieve the same standard of living. GNP may not be a perfect measurement, but some index is needed to assess social and economic progress. ("Gross National Happiness" would be even harder to measure!) The government is seeking the betterment of the people of Iran and to maintain their dignity as human beings. They cannot have dignity when they lack food, health care and schooling. The government seeks only to improve the basic quality of their lives.

An American specialist warned that oil revenues cannot be considered "real" income over the long term; they will have to be replaced by savings resulting from people's efforts and hard work. Meanwhile, if Iran hopes to achieve a European standard of living in 10 years, the contribution of the non-oil sector to GNP must rise dramatically—from $15 billion in 1974 to $90 billion annually (or half the GNP of the United Kingdom). This would be an incredible leap, especially since Iran is entering a period of foreign currency account deficits owing to its significant increases in foreign currency expenditures, now about $20 billion to $22 billion. But, an Iranian observed, increasing the contribution of the industrial sector from $15 billion to $90 billion means an annual growth rate, compounded, of only 20 percent. This has been achieved and can be sustained. The difficulties involved in transforming public sector responsibility, in the form of oil revenues, to private sector savings are real, but this can be achieved over time. The speaker also anticipated that Iran will have a balance in its overall currency account and that its exchange reserves will be maintained at $8.5 billion. An Iranian added that Iran has always set its development goals beyond what it expected to achieve—yet all were **understated.** Iranians have reason for optimism about future growth.

Responding to an American's question about whether Iran has a "fall-back" plan if economic and political problems severely affect world stability and cause a decline in oil revenues, several Iranians replied that Iran would return to a lower economic growth rate—lower, that is, than what it has experienced in the last two years but several times higher than the rate accepted by the United Nations. Iran's economy would adjust as the world's economy adjusted. It would borrow less and settle for a slower rate of growth.

Proposed Investments Relating to Oil

The question of whether Iran can successfully develop petrochemicals for export was discussed. An American asked whether other

OPEC countries have similar plans and if world demand for pet-rochemicals has been analyzed. Another American strongly doubted that Iran will succeed in exporting oil and gas deriva-tives. An American specialist concurred that every Persian Gulf country will try to develop oil-related industries; the market situa-tion is not clear. Moreover, petrochemical industries are not labor-intensive and will not provide employment opportunities. (An Iranian observed on this point that Iran favors capital-intensive industries partly because it lacks skilled workers; capital-intensive production suits Iran.) Another participant agreed that other oil-producing countries will move to establish refineries, produce petrochemicals and build tankers; this is a natural de-velopment. Although Iran at the moment has more technical know-how, Saudi Arabia has more money and can catch up. The possibility of competition among the oil-producing states in pet-rochemical production was noted by one speaker, who suggested that such competition could be harmful to OPEC.

The need to import modern technology from the West in order to become competitive in areas like petrochemicals was noted by an Iranian speaker.

Alternate Energy Sources

Responding to an American's question about whether Iran is in-vesting oil revenues in searches for alternative sources of energy, an Iranian noted that Iran is undertaking some foreign investments and is in the midst of building several nuclear plants. It expects also to save some gas. There is, however, little near-term prospect of running short of fuel.

Defense Spending and Control of the Military

Several Americans commented on Iran's high rate of expenditures for defense, the fact that military expenditures always escalate rapidly and the difficulty of controlling military expenses. One asked whether highly sophisticated, expensive weaponry—which outdates rapidly—is really needed by Iran.

Various Iranians replied that Iran needs an adequate defense system to guard the lifeline to the Persian Gulf and maintain its national integrity in order to develop. (See the following section.) Officials responsible for developing the Fifth Plan considered military expenditures carefully. Like other elements of the national budget, military expenditures are controlled by the Plan and Budget Organization, with final decisions being taken by His Imperial Majesty The Shah. As for the sophistication and expense of weapons purchased by Iran, the West should make them simpler and cheaper!

Aid to the Fourth World

A number of participants commented on the severe effects of oil price rises on the Third and Fourth Worlds. (In 1973–74, Ghana, for example, had to spend $150 million more to import oil, at a time when cocoa prices were declining.) The deficits of all developing countries have risen sharply, partly because of the higher cost of oil imports and partly because the industrial countries have passed on their own higher cost of oil in the form of higher prices for manufactured exports. Various speakers appealed for programs to aid the Third and Fourth Worlds, including projects such as the drawing fund to cover budget deficits proposed by the Shah to OPEC. One Iranian said that it is unfair to relate the deficit problems of Third and Fourth World countries, like Ghana, to the price of oil. In 1960 Ghana could purchase a tractor from an industrial country for the export price of one ton of cocoa. In 1972, before the oil price increase, Ghana had to export five tons of cocoa to pay for the importation of a single tractor. Today it must export even more.

With respect to the proposed establishment of a two-tier system of oil prices, with lower prices for the Third World, an Iranian commented that studies have shown this would not be feasible. He and others expressed the view that OPEC, and Iranian, aid to the Third World has been generous. OPEC countries have given substantially more soft-term loans than the OECD countries, with aid amounting to 2.3 percent of their GNP, as compared with less than .5 percent in the advanced countries. Iran would like OPEC aid to be mixed institutionally with OECD aid so that OPEC could not be charged with exercising political influence. Iran had hoped that the Paris Conference convened earlier this year would consider how to help the developing countries increase their commodity exports, but this was not included on the agenda of the conference. New steps will be needed to help the Third and Fourth Worlds offset the harmful effects of international inflation and new oil price rises. An American said, however, that developing countries should not be encouraged to form producer associations for their commodities: substitutes exist that limit their ability to raise prices; moreover, 50 percent of all commodities are produced outside developing countries. In his view, the General Agreement on Tariffs and Trade (GATT) or a new trade organization should, rather, seek the elimination of all advanced country tariff barriers on imports from developing countries. This will not be easy to achieve in the United States, but it can be done. The final speaker on this point affirmed that neither OPEC nor OECD is doing enough for the Fourth World. Its basic, imperative needs are not being met. New measures must be taken.

Iran in the World Economic Setting

Iran in the World Economic Setting

Hassan Ali Mehran

The present century, which has witnessed accomplishments beyond man's wildest dreams, has entered its last quarter at a time when the world at large is beset by a variety of economic problems. An alarming inflation, a creeping and widespread recession, a serious preoccupation with a possible breakdown of the international monetary system, and chaos in international economic order have confronted the world community with one of its most difficult periods. The basic causes of these problems must be sought not in the context of one particular development but in the complexities of the fundamental issues facing the world today.

Indeed, the present problems of the international economic community are caused by the imbalances and inequities that were primarily responsible for the accelerated economic growth of a handful of industrial countries through the transfer of real resources from the rest of the world to these countries in the form of cheap raw materials. For years the world economy functioned under a system that allowed a few economically advanced countries to prosper while the masses of the people in a great many developing countries remained in want of the minimum amenities of life. Whereas declining prices of raw materials caused a continuous drain on the natural wealth of the developing countries, the industrialized countries indulged in wasteful consumption. Furthermore, the rising prices of their manufactured products frustrated the efforts of the nonindustrial world for economic development.

The most significant attempt at introducing a degree of rationality and justice into the system of international economic relations was made by the Organization of Petroleum Exporting Countries, OPEC, in which Iran has been an active member since its inception. In what may be considered a landmark in the field of primary commodities, the OPEC countries in their negotiations with major international oil companies, held in February 1971 in Tehran, succeeded not only in raising crude oil prices, which had actually fallen since 1948, but also in establishing a foundation that gave them a voice in the future determination of prices. The success of OPEC was duly hailed as the first major breakthrough in the struggle of the developing countries to seek an equitable solution to the difficult problem of exporting their raw materials at fair prices to the world markets.

However, the role of Iran in the international economic scene has gone beyond its activities as an OPEC member in the field of primary commodities. In line with the noble aims set by my august sovereign, His Imperial Majesty Shahanshah Aryamehr, Iran has pursued at home, in the context of The Shah and People's Revolution, such objectives as accelerated economic growth, social welfare and justice and a sustained increase in the living standards of all the strata of society. Abroad, both at the bilateral and multilateral levels, Iran has employed her newly acquired financial capabilities to promote international economic cooperation on the basis of equity, sovereign equality, interdependence, common interest and cooperation among all states.

In this context Iran has embarked on an all-embracing program of aid to the developing countries. On a bilateral basis, Iran's program includes extensive measures aimed at easing the problems of the less-developed countries. In the continents of Asia and Africa, this has taken the form, in highly concessionary terms, of assistance to a dozen countries. It ranges from aid in the development of natural resources to the implementation of manufacturing projects, reconstruction and rehabilitation schemes, utilization of idle industrial capacities, as well as help in development and educational programs, balance-of-payments assistance, emergency aids and, in some cases, outright grants.

In the developed countries, Iran's initiatives have been aimed at easing balance-of-payments difficulties. They have also taken the form of joint ventures in, and outside of, Iran as well as the prepayment of Iran's loans to creditor countries.

In the multilateral context, Iran was the first to announce its support of the IMF's oil facility and has financed a substantial part of this facility's resources. It has also made significant contributions to the World Bank in the form of loans and purchase of the bank's bonds.

Total commitments by Iran in bilateral and multinational forms thus far exceed $10 billion. To appreciate the magnitude of Iran's foreign assistance, it will help to recall that during the entire period of the Marshall Plan, total U.S. aid amounted to $11.4 billion. This constituted 0.77 percent of her gross national product for that period. In 1973, the total aid outflow of the DAC countries was no more than two-thirds of 1 percent of their GNP. Against this background, Iran's total assistance program is expected to reach nearly 6 percent of her GNP in the next four years.

In addition to her role as a donor country, Iran has extensive economic and trade relations with the rest of the world. The policies that govern these relations and the mechanism through which they are implemented are the subject for review in this paper. The important fact to recognize at the outset is that economic cooperation has served Iran in accelerating the pace of her economic development. Without access to advanced technology, machinery and equipment, skilled manpower and a share in international markets, sustained economic development could not have been achieved. The government policy has therefore been to devise a mechanism that would ensure that these elements are readily available and fully utilized in an orderly manner for the promotion of economic development in the country. In this context the question may be raised as to the part governments can play in furthering economic and trade relations between nations. With all the information available to them and the various instruments of economic policy at their disposal, the governments are in an ideal position to actively encourage the expansion of economic cooperation in mutually beneficial areas. To do this, a continuous dialogue between the governments has to be established and maintained. Iran has been one of the first countries in the world to use the system of joint commissions. Over the years this mechanism has come to be widely used by a great number of countries for promotion of bilateral trade, economic, technical and scientific cooperation with other countries. Through the establishment of this body with an increasing number of countries, Iran has been able to expand and diversify her external economic relations, increase her exports, gain access to new production techniques and processes, diversify her industrial base and, in short, accelerate her pace of economic development.

Iran's International Economic Relations Prior To 1962

Prior to the year 1962, Iran's economic relations with other countries were limited to the field of trade. The major objectives of her foreign trade policy during the period before World War II were to achieve a balance between export and import trade, and to raise revenue for the government.

To meet these objectives, a number of barter trade agreements were signed between Iran and some of her trading partners. By the year 1940, for instance, Iran had barter trade agreements with the Soviet Union and Germany. After World War II, Iran had extended such agreements to France, Italy, Czechoslovakia, Poland and Hungary. The main purpose of these agreements was to establish a balance in bilateral trade, a condition that had become necessary because of the foreign exchange shortage prevalent in that period. Throughout the 1940s and early 1950s, the foreign exchange constraint continued to dominate Iran's foreign trade policy and the objectives remained as before.

The increase in foreign exchange revenue and an accelerated pace in industrial development starting in the late 1950s gradually led to a wider concept of foreign trade policy. The instruments of this policy, such as export-import regulations, began to be used less for the purpose of raising revenue and restricting imports to save foreign exchange, and more to support other objectives of economic policy, namely, to assist the industrial development of the country.

The Years 1962–68

Since 1962 the expansion of Iran's foreign trade and economic relations has kept a rapid pace. The development of these relations since that year falls into two distinct periods: (1) the period 1962–68, during which Iran began establishing joint ministerial commissions or committees for trade, economic and technical cooperation with the Socialist countries of Eastern Europe and concluding trade, payments and economic cooperation agreements with them, and (2) the period 1969–75, during which the number of these joint commissions multiplied and important trade and economic cooperation agreements were signed with Western European and North American countries, as well as certain countries in Asia and Africa.

The main purpose for establishment of joint commisions,which normally met at the ministerial level, was to review trade and economic relations between the two countries, to discuss ways and means for the development of these relations, and to adopt measures to facilitate and expand bilateral economic cooperation.

During the period 1962–68, Iran established joint ministerial commissions and concluded trade and payments as well as economic and technical cooperation agreements with practically all the countries of Eastern Europe. The trade and payments agreements allowed for expansion of the volume of trade through setting indicative quotas for commodities to be exchanged between the two countries. The first of these agreements was signed in 1964 with the Soviet Union. Under economic cooperation agreements concluded separately, lines of credit were made available to Iran by the respective countries for the purchase of plants and equipments. Repayment of principals and payments of interest was to take the form of export of Iranian goods. The first of these agreements was signed with Czechoslovakia, followed by Hungary in 1965.

Within the context of the joint ministerial commissions and the agreements signed during the above period, Iran succeeded in promoting bilateral trade relations and expanding economic cooperation. Iran's export to the Socialist countries, which was $30 million in 1962, had, by the end of 1973, reached the figure of $153 million, thereby establishing a firm footing in the markets of these countries with regard to Iran's industrial products.

By 1973, about 83 percent of Iran's export of shoes, 58 percent of her export of detergent, and 66 percent of her exported textiles went to the countries of Eastern Europe. The import from these countries also steadily increased, rising from $25 million in 1962 to $330 million in 1973, thereby increasing the share of the Socialist countries in Iran's total imports from 4.5 percent to 8.8 percent.

Along with increased trade, closer economic cooperation with Eastern European countries contributed significantly to the industrial development of Iran. The Aryamehr Steel Mill, the Aras Dam, the machine tool plant, the tractor factory, and the machine building plant are some of the major projects that were initiated and completed in the context of joint commissions with Eastern European countries.

The Years 1969–75

After 1970 there was a very sharp rise in the number of joint commissions with different countries, with the number increasing from seven in 1969 to 34 in 1975.

In 1971 the establishment of the joint commission with Belgium was the first important measure taken for the expansion of Iran's relations through this mechanism with Western European and other industrial countries. After this, joint commissions were formed with Austria, the United Kingdom, and in 1973 with the Federal Republic of Germany. By 1974, Iran had formed joint commissions with other countries such as France, Italy, the United States, Canada, Sweden and Denmark.

In 1974, the countries having joint commissions with Iran accounted for nearly three-quarters of her foreign trade. Furthermore, as a result of the agreements reached with these countries in the framework of the newly established joint commissions, large-scale industrial projects with far-reaching effects on the country's economic development were initiated in Iran. Among these projects, mention may be made of the nuclear power stations, direct reduction iron ore plants, the special steel plant and a great number of industrial units in the area of mechanical and electrical engineering, chemical and petrochemical fields, electronics, automotive industry, agricultural machinery and agribusiness.

Under these agreements, Iran also actively pursued her policy of promoting exports of manufactured goods to the markets of the industrialized countries and removing obstacles in the way of their expansion so that the composition of Iran's foreign trade could fully reflect the many changes taking place in the industrial structure of her economy.

These agreements further included provisions for Iran's investment in those countries as well as the setting up of joint venture projects in third-party countries. Protocols signed within the context of the joint commissions that once included provisions for extension of credit to, and direct investments in, Iran now reflected Iran's new role in world affairs and her commitment to cooperate in the development efforts of other countries, developing and developed alike.

It is, however, important to note that, while some of these developments would have taken place regardless of the work of the commissions, the commissions have been instrumental for the orderly manner in which these occurred, and have served as a mechanism through which obstacles have been removed in time for the projects to be completed.

Iran's Relations with International Financial Organizations

Iran has continued to maintain excellent relations with the international financial organizations. She has been a founding member of the International Monetary Fund and the International Bank for Reconstruction and Development.

Though Iran is not a party to the General Agreement on Tariff and Trade (GATT), she has been working toward the essential goals of GATT and actively participates in the multilateral trade negotiations that aim at devising measures for the solution of such basic problems of the international economy as the reduction of tariff and nontariff barriers, monetary reform and improvement of the international framework for the conduct of world trade.

With a totally nondiscriminatory import regime, Iran has in the past few years gone a long way in liberalizing imports, lowering or removing import charges, and reducing or eliminating protection for her fast-growing domestic industries. She has made these major efforts unilaterally and without expectation of reciprocity, ensuring at the same time that the benefits of these measures are shared without discrimination by all of Iran's trading partners.

At this juncture, it is relevant to make a brief reference to Iran's relations with the European Economic Community (EEC). Iran was the first country in the world to sign, in 1962, a nonpreferential trade agreement with the EEC, Iran's largest trading partner. However, with the general reduction of tariff brought about by the Kennedy round of trade negotiations, and the rapid economic development of Iran, the significance of the agreement gradually declined and in 1973 it was not renewed. In the last few years, during which the EEC entered into a network of preferential arrangements with selected countries, Iran has consistently voiced her criticism of the discriminatory effects of such arrangements and announced her readiness to negotiate with the EEC for the conclusion of a new agreement that would remove all discriminations against Iranian exports in the EEC markets. To this end, negotiations have been held at different levels between Iranian and EEC authorities.

In other important economic organizations such as the United Nations Conference on Trade and Development (UNCTAD) and the Industrial Development Organization (UNIDO), Iran has been an active member ever since their inception.

Summary

This survey was an attempt to show the course Iran has followed in her international economic relations. Her emergence as a creditor nation in the world economic scene has placed her in a position to participate actively in efforts aimed at creating a new international economic order in which the just aspirations of all nations are realized. Indeed, the new position of Iran in the world economic setting has provided an opportunity for this country to endeavor to effect the same reforms on an international scale that she has successfully carried out at home. Fully conscious of her international responsibilities and of the fact that no nation can take pride in affluence in a world plagued with hunger, misery and disease and that international development is a shared and common responsibility of all countries, Iran will continue to pursue its present course in international affairs, cooperating with all nations—developing, centrally planned and industrial alike—on a bilateral basis as well as in a multilateral setting, to establish a new international economic order under which the sovereign equality of all states and equal participation of all countries in the solving of world economic problems could be secured in the common interest of all mankind.

Iran's International Economic Outlook

Mohsen A. Fardi

The objectives of this essay are twofold: (1) to evaluate briefly the past performance of Iran's foreign trade sector, and (2) to outline the future outlook for Iran's foreign trade.

Early Development of Foreign Trade

One of the oldest countries in the world and at the crossroads of Eastern and Western civilizations, Iran has been exposed to, and in turn has left its own mark on, other cultures and economies. However, in the modern era, *i.e.,* since the Industrial Revolution took place in England, the development of Iran's international trade did not keep pace with the rising volume of world trade. This situation was somewhat changed when oil was discovered in Iran and when Iran, through a concession with the Anglo-Iranian Oil Company, began to export oil in significant amounts in the early 1920s. However, up to the nationalization of the oil industry in 1951, the contributions of the oil exports were rather insignificant to the national economy.

From 1954, though, Iran's revenues from exports of oil and the rise in the volume of oil exported increased steadily, yet due to the falling price of crude oil, both in nominal and in real terms, up to the late 1960s Iran was only able to maintain her relative share in the world's total trade. As shown in Table 70 (all tables appear in the appendix to this essay), Iran's share in the value of world exports fluctuated around 0.7 of 1 percent from 1959 to 1966, briefly rising to 1 percent in 1967 and falling back to 0.86 of 1 percent in 1969. From 1970 on, due to a significant improvement in Iran's terms of trade, her share in the value of world exports began to rise, reaching the level of 1.33 percent in 1973.

Compared to the performance of the exports by developing countries, the rise in Iran's exports has been very remarkable, this share rising from 3.3 percent in 1966 to 6.4 percent in 1973. In comparison to the exports from the Middle East region, Iran's exports increased from 16.8 percent in 1966 to 23.8 percent in 1973. Since oil exports by other countries in the Middle East have increased as rapidly as in Iran, part of the rise in Iran's share is due to the relatively rapid development of non-oil exports in Iran.

Growth in the Volume of Exports and Imports and the Changing Orientation of the Economy from 1960 to 1973

Iran's economy in the last decade, as outlined in other papers presented to this symposium, has experienced a very rapid growth. Iran's GNP increased from $4.6 billion in 1960 to $44.0 billion in 1974. Obviously, a great deal of this very rapid growth, especially since 1970, has been due to oil exports and to the public sector's programs for using oil exports to finance current and development expenditures. Oil exports have also assisted the rapid development of the economy by providing an ample supply of foreign exchange to draw on for financing the increasing amounts of imports.

As Iran's economy has developed, its orientation toward foreign trade and her interdependence with the world economy have been enhanced. As shown in Table 71, the share of exports in Iran's GNP increased from about 20 percent in 1969 to 57 percent in 1974. The rise in non-oil exports and services, at least up to 1973, was about equal to the growth in GNP. Almost all of the change in the rising share of exports in the GNP has been due to the rising volume and value of oil exports. Iran's total exchange receipts from exports including oil,* traditional goods, industrial goods and services, increased from $528 million in 1960 to $6.2 billion in 1973, and further to $21.1 in 1974. Though exports of goods grew in this period by at least sixfold and the export of services by at most 28-fold, due to a very rapid increase in the exchange receipts from the oil sector, the share of non-oil exports in total exchange revenues has decreased from 32.0 percent in 1960 to 11.7 percent in 1974.

Iran's payments for imports of goods and services have increased from $600 million in 1960 to $12,600 million in 1974, an increase of 21 times, with the share of goods relatively constant at about 84 percent. Though in the 1960s Iran experienced a consistent deficit in her current accounts, which was financed by borrowing from abroad, in the last two years the rise in oil prices has improved the current balance position to the tune of $8.5 billion. This development has enabled Iran to launch a vigorous policy for the development of the domestic economy and to use the surplus for assisting countries faced with a deficit in their balance-of-payments through international financial institutions and bilateral agreements.

---

*Less factor payments abroad.

Changing Composition of Iran's Foreign Trade: Exports

Aside from the export of oil, which has contributed increasingly to Iran's foreign trade, earning, as noted above, between 68 percent and 88 percent of total exchange receipts during the 1960–74 period, Iran's major exports consist of traditional goods such as carpets, cotton, animal hides and skins, minerals and manufactured products such as textiles, soaps, detergents, shoes, clothing and transportation equipment. The value of these exports increased from $112 million in 1960 to $610 in 1974, or a 5.5-fold increase. As shown in Table 73, about one-fifth of Iran's normal exports of goods consists of carpets and another one-fifth of cotton. Dried and fresh fruits make up about 15 percent and animal by-products about 6 percent. The most significant development in Iran's non-oil exports has been the emergence of industrial goods as a significant share of Iran's exports, increasing from less than 1 percent in 1960 to 23 percent in 1974.

Imports

For sustaining the tempo of her economic growth, Iran has relied on the international market to provide her with industrial raw and intermediate materials, machinery and equipment and food. Between 1960 and 1974, total imports of goods increased about 10 times from $688 million to $6,615 million. In Iran, imports have been used effectively in the past for meeting domestic shortages and thus controlling the rate of inflation, unavoidable in the face of rapid growth and structural change. The main concern has been to regulate imports in such a manner as to provide enough incentives and protection for the emerging domestic industries. Yet whenever domestic supply has fallen short of the domestic demand, imports have been encouraged by lowering tariff rates and by providing government subsidies.

Iran's major import categories are machinery and equipment, food and industrial raw and intermediate products such as iron, steel and chemical products. Import of machinery including transport, though still significant, has fallen from 40 percent of the total in 1970 to 32 percent in 1974, due to increasingly more domestic production and import substitution. Meanwhile, the share of food has increased from 7 percent in 1970 to 17 percent in 1974, in spite of the emphasis placed on the growth of the agricultural sector in Iran's economic plans. The rise in food imports has been unavoidable in the face of high income elasticity of demand for food, rising income and population, and unprecedented rising prices.

Yet in the long run, Iran must rely more on her domestic resources if the economy and its balance of payments are not to be overburdened by rising food imports. Among other major imports are iron and steel and petrochemicals, together taking up 27.3 percent of total imports in 1974. Given Iran's potential comparative advantage in raw material and energy-intensive industries, it should be expected that Iran provide for her domestic iron and steel chemical requirements in addition to exporting significant amounts in the future.

The Pattern and Direction of Iran's Foreign Trade Exports

Since Iran's economy began growing rapidly in the late 1950s, the direction of Iran's total exports, including oil, has shifted more toward the nonsocialist developed countries. Data collected by the International Monetary Fund and published in the form of computer tapes in the Direction of Trade (DOT) series show that whereas in 1960 about 77 percent of the value of total exports went to the developed countries, and in 1965, 71 percent, by 1973 this ratio had increased to 90 percent. This, of course, indicates that as oil exports have increased, trade with the developed countries—particularly Japan and the Common Market countries—has become increasingly more important. In contrast, the share of other regions, covering the rest of the world, had declined to a mere 10 percent by 1973. Among the developed countries, the share of Japan increased from 3 percent in 1960 to 38 percent in 1970, then fell to 29 percent by 1973. It is noteworthy that the share of the United States, not so dependent on oil imports from Iran, declined from 6 percent in 1960 to 2.5 percent in 1970, but increased again to 5.7 percent by 1973. The Federal Republic of Germany and England also experienced a relative decline in their respective shares in Iran's exports.

Table 76 shows more clearly the changing geographic distribution of Iran's exports. Between 1960 and 1973, total exports increased by seven times. Meanwhile, exports to Japan increased by 77 times, followed by The Netherlands (20 times), Italy (15 times), the United States (seven times) and England (four times). In contrast to the above, exports to Africa and to Asia, other than Japan, increased by only three times, and exports to the Middle Eastern countries declined to about 84 percent of the 1960 level.

This means that, as Iran's economy has developed, its rate of growth has become more dependent on the rate of economic growth in a few select countries. Thus, Iran cannot be indifferent to a slow-down in the economies of the industrialized countries. Iran's foreign trade and international policymakers in the last two years have repeatedly emphasized this point and have drawn up Iran's foreign economic policies accordingly.

Imports

Unlike exports, which are few in kind, as just noted, Iran imports a diverse number of goods. With the exception of trade with the Soviet bloc, Iran's trade with the rest of the world is generally, up to now, on a multilateral basis. Yet similar to the pattern of exports, over 85 percent of Iran's imports in 1973 originated from the developed countries. Only 6 percent of it originated from the Soviet bloc and 9 percent from the rest of the world. As shown in Table 77, the geographic pattern of Iran's imports, with the exception of trade with Japan, the U.S. and the U.K., has been relatively stable since 1960. During this period, Japan succeeded in increasing her share in Iran's import market from 6.4 percent in 1960 to 14.3 percent in 1973. Meanwhile, the shares of the U.K. and the U.S. decreased by four and six percentage points, respectively. (Preliminary figures for 1974 show that the U.S. share of Iran's import market increased again to about 20 percent).*

From 1960 to 1973, Iran's import market increased by about six times; Japan, France and the Soviet bloc, by pursuing a more aggressive drive to capture Iran's market, were able to increase their respective exports to Iran at a faster rate than what was achieved by other major countries (see Table 78).

The Future Outlook

Given Iran's rapid economic development in the last decade, her new international strength, particularly in the world petroleum market and the plans envisaged for the coming decade, Iran's international outlook appears brighter than ever. The goal established by His Imperial Majesty for Iran is to reach the prevailing level of economic development in Western Europe in 10 years' time.** The implications of this goal are varied and worth many careful examinations. Though such considera-

----

*Bank Markazi Iran Annual Report for 1974.

**HIM interview with Johannes Engel as quoted by Bahman Abadian, *A Review of Iran's Development Prospects,* Tehran, 1974, p. 13.

tions are beyond the scope of this study, nevertheless, to put the magnitudes of Iran's foreign trade by the year 1984 into perspective, it is necessary to look at the size of some European countries' GNP and their share of foreign trade in order to define the required rate of growth of Iran's exports that would be compatible with such an objective.

Table 79 shows the GNP level on a total and a per capita basis for some European countries and Japan, ranging from the Federal Republic of Germany, one of the most developed, to Spain, one of the least developed.

Iran's GNP in 1974 reached the level of $44 billion, or $1,344 on a per capita basis.* For Iran's per capita GNP to reach that of 1973 Germany in 1984, the former has to increase to $5,600 per capita, and to $240 billion on the gross basis. This corresponds to an annual rate of growth of 18.5 percent. In contrast, for Iran's GNP to reach that of Italy, its required rate of growth is only 8.5 percent. Comparable required rates of growth for other countries are shown in Table 10.

Whereas maintaining an annual rate of growth of 18.5 percent for 10 years is difficult to foresee, the rates lying in the range of 8 to 12 percent are quite feasible, and the rate of 16 percent probable. For the sake of outlining in more detail the foreign trade implications of Iran's overall growth targets, two alternative GNP growth rates of 8.5 percent and 16.3 percent are selected for a more detailed examination.

The foreign trade structure of the countries under discussion shows a great degree of similarity. As Table 80 shows, high rates of economic growth since 1967 have been associated with a larger share of foreign trade in the respective national economies. For example, the share of imports in England's GNP increased from 19 percent to 26 percent and for Italy from 16 percent to 23 percent during the 1967–73 period.

Iran's orientation toward foreign trade is already very strong, even at a relatively low level of GNP. With oil and gas remaining important export products during the next decade, and Iran's plans for building infrastructure and industrial production capacities, it is not too unlikely for the average share of imports to remain at about 30 percent of Iran's GNP. This implies import requirements ranging between $32 billion and $60 billion, corresponding to the above two alternative growth rates. This in turn implies import growth rates ranging between 10 and 17 percent per year, respectively.

The question that should be raised is whether the growth in Iran's exports will be adequate to finance such levels of imports. To answer this question, we must examine Iran's future export prospects. (See Table 81.)

---

*Bank Markazi Iran preliminary figures.

During the next 10 years, oil should remain Iran's major export and foreign exchange supplier. The rate of growth of oil exports will be dependent on the strength of world demand for petroleum. It is true that the growth in demand for imported oil, following its price adjustment in 1973–74 and due to a general economic slow-down in the industrial countries and the efforts of oil-importing countries to conserve energy, has slowed down. However, with economic recovery overdue, it should be expected that the demand for oil will soon begin to rise again. In the longer-term context, in the absence of major technological breakthroughs replacing oil as a primary source of energy, the demand for oil should continue to grow fast enough for Iran to maintain at least the current level of exports.

On the supply side, Iranian reserves of crude oil are estimated to be between 60 billion and 70 billion barrels, which would last at least 30 years at production levels ranging between 5.5 million and 6.5 million barrels per day. Given this and the assumption that oil prices remain constant in real terms, Iran may continue receiving an inflow of over $20 billion annually from crude oil exports during the next decade.

But Iran is not content with production and export of crude oil. As Iran's economic plans materialize, she would be drawing on her crude oil reserve for expanding the domestic economy and for providing the raw materials needed in petrochemical, oil products and industrial manufacturing.

It is very likely that in the future Iran shall be an exporter of a host of industrial products derived from petroleum. Since the net value added* for these products is positive to the extent the plans for processing crude oil in Iran into some of its 70,000 by-products are materialized, proceeds from oil-related exports should exceed the existing levels of $16 billion to $20 billion per year. Consequently, it is conceivable that without any major efforts, $25 billion to $30 billion of Iran's import requirements could be financed by drawing on exports of crude oil and oil-related products. This means a real rate of growth for the oil-related exports ranging between 3 and 5 percent annually.

For financing the remainder, the Iranian policymakers and planners must look hard at her other resources, both actual and potential.

Iran's traditional exports reached the level of $530 million in 1973 but fell to $470 million in 1974, a year in which domestic demand was very strong. Iran's future prospects for exporting these products are not high, due to two important factors: (1) as Iran's economy develops, much of the raw and agricultural products making up the traditional exports would be taken up by the domestic industries and consumers; and (2)

---

*Value added less import requirements.

raw material and labor-factor prices should be expected to rise rapidly in the face of strong domestic demand and shortage of supply, making production of labor-intensive exports, such as carpets, extremely expensive. Thus, exports of traditional raw materials and agricultural goods cannot grow much beyond 5 to 7 percent annually in real terms.

The new industrial products, yet to be developed, hold a more promising prospect. Iran's new industrial exports have increased from less than $1 million in 1960 to $141 million in 1974, or about 3 percent of the $4.7 billion value added by industries and mines during the later year. For Iran to export significant amounts of industrial products in the next decade, at least three things must take place:

- The cost of production and the quality of output must change to make export of a variety of industrial goods possible;
- Secure markets must be developed by introducing Iranian manufactured goods in foreign markets and by signing bilateral and multilateral agreements for lowering trade barriers and duties;
- Domestic output must grow fast enough to satisfy a major share of the rapidly growing domestic demand and have some excess capacity for supplying the export markets. Thus to export, say $2 billion to $4 billion worth of industrial goods, and assuming that 15 percent of domestic production can be exported, value added by industries must rise to $13 billion to $27 billion, an annual rate of growth ranging between 11 and 19 percent. Whether Iran's physical and human resources permit such a sustaining rate of growth in industrial output depends on factors beyond the scope of this study; nevertheless, in the author's judgment, it is feasible. Given these considerations, it is assumed that the rate of growth of industrial goods exports would lie between 25 and 40 percent per year.

Another export potential that remains to be developed is Iran's rich natural gas endowment. Iran's gas reserves are tentatively estimated at about 600 trillion cubic feet, perhaps the largest reserve in the world. Yet Iran exported only $130 million worth of gas in 1974. Conceivably, Iran could, with minor efforts, increase her gas exports to $2 billion to $5 billion by 1984. This implies an annual rate of growth in gas exports ranging between 30 and 45 percent.

Export of services and open market transactions of exporters brought Iran an additional $1.7 billion in 1974. Income from Iran's investments abroad, interest on short-term assets of the Central Bank and increasing inflow of tourists from abroad may provide Iran with at least $4 billion to $5 billion foreign exchange by 1984, or an annual rate of growth between 9 and 11 percent.

Given the above considerations, the value of total exports could increase to amounts ranging from $33 billion to $46 billion during the next decade. This implies that Iran, with no major difficulties, may finance the import requirements of an economy comparable on a per capita GNP basis to those of Japan, the United Kingdom and Italy in 1973.

For Iran's economy to grow faster than 13 percent, one requirement is that imports should grow by rates ranging between 17 and 19 percent. This means imports reaching $60 billion to $70 billion by 1984. Whether Iran's total exports could possibly grow to this level requires further consideration. Obviously, the rate of growth in exports as just projected would not be sufficient to finance this level of imports.

In order to avoid a serious deficit in the balance-of-payments serving as a constraint to the growth of the economy, exports must grow faster, and imports at slower rates than just projected. Given the low base of non-oil exports prevailing up to now and the optimistic rates assumed for their growth, revenues from exports of oil and related products must increase beyond $30 billion per year.

To end with an optimistic note, the discovery of additional oil reserves, a higher-than-projected growth in demand for energy and the forging of Iran's plans for oil conservation and its export in processed forms may give rise to revenues from oil exports to exceed $30 billion by 1984. In the meantime, the challenge facing Iran's economy is to expand the industrial base of the economy in order to become relatively less dependent on imports and more competitive in non-oil exports.

The Necessity to Expand Non-oil Exports

Iran's economy, due to its relatively small size and its historical orientation toward foreign trade, cannot become in the foreseeable future independent of foreign trade. The future prospects for exports of oil, gas and their related products are good, and Iran may count on her rich natural resources for at least one to two more decades. Meantime, oil-induced growth, because of the inherent characteristics of the raw material export industry, i.e., weak backward and forward linkages, relatively large share of rent and depletion allowance in the value added and the fact that income generated by production and export of oil and gas do not accrue to all strata of the society equitably, has been a mixed blessing to the economy.

On the one hand, large inflows of foreign exchange from the export of crude oil has permitted the public sector to launch massive economic and social development plans and programs for subsidizing basic consumptions and services. It has also afforded the citizens a standard of living much above what the productivity and efficiency of the non-oil economy warrant. On the other hand, an abundant supply of foreign exchange and the public sector's concern in turning the exchange earned into the domestic currency has given rise to a market rate of exchange for trial above the rate that efficiency and the international competitiveness of the non-oil sectors warrant. These factors have given rise to a rate of exchange too high for the domestic economy to be able to compete effectively under relatively free trade conditions with foreign producers, both inside and outside the borders. It is true that the domestic industries have been protected from undue foreign competition by tariffs and commercial profit taxes. However, this situation has left no incentive for the domestic producers to lower their costs of production, to become technological innovators and to expand their exports.

Iran's balanced growth in the long run cannot be dependent on oil exports alone. Other sectors of the economy, particularly agriculture, industry and human resources, must develop in harmony with the growth of oil exports. The balanced growth of the above sectors cannot be completely dependent on the national economy. In order to benefit from the advantages of economies of scale and the improvement of quality, the industries in which Iran has actual or potential comparative advantage must be able to compete with others in the international markets.

In the longer term, Iran needs to replace her oil exports with exports of energy and raw-material-intensive products. Iran's oil resources, rich as they may be, are bound to be exhausted. The economy must be prepared for this eventually. Even if resources are not exhausted, the growth of domestic demand for oil as a basic source of raw materials will not permit its export in crude form.

Iran's economy, no matter how fast it grows, cannot become independent of imports. Indeed, many of the consumer and capital goods that were imported 10 years ago are now being produced domestically. This trend will continue. However, economic growth, technological change and the consumer's taste for variety would lead to increasing imports. To finance the costs of these imports, and in order to prevent the deficit in balance-of-payments from serving as a constraint to growth, Iran must develop her non-oil exports.

Appendix

Table 70
The Share of Iran's Exports and Imports in World and Regional Trade
(percent)

	1960	1965	1970	1972	1973
Exports					
World	0.75	0.79	0.94	1.27	1.33
Developing Countries	3.16	3.64	4.83	6.44	6.37
Middle East	17.14	18.22	22.82	23.73	23.84
Imports					
World	0.48	0.49	0.56	0.63	0.64
Developing Countries	1.93	2.29	2.93	3.36	3.50
Middle East	13.65	14.95	18.78	20.55	20.46

Source: IMF, International Financial Statistics, 1972 Supplement and January 1975 issues.

Table 71
Shares of Exports and Imports in Iran's GNP
(percent in current prices)

	1960	1965	1970	1973	1974
Exports	19.6	22.2	25.4	47.8	56.6
Oil	16.3	18.7	22.2	44.2	54.4
Non-oil Goods	2.9	3.0	2.7	2.8	1.7
Services	0.4	0.5	0.5	0.8	0.5
Imports	16.1	15.3	19.9	20.9	23.0
Goods	15.1	14.2	18.4	19.9	22.2
Services*	1.0	1.1	1.5	1.0	0.8

*Excludes factor payment to the foreign oil companies.

Table 72
Iran's Foreign Exchange Receipts and Payments
(millions of dollars)

	1960		1965		1970		1973		1974*	
	Value	Percent	Value	Percent	Value	Percent	Value	Percent	Value	Percent
Current Receipts	528	100.0	817	100.0	1,690	100.0	6,284	100.0	21,145	100.0
Oil Sector	359	68.0	608	74.4	1,268	75.1	5,067	80.6	18,671	88.3
Exports of Goods**	106	20.0	132	16.1	259	15.3	635	10.1	694	3.3
Exports of Services	64	12.0	78	9.5	163	9.6	582	9.3	1,780	8.4
Current Payments	598	100.0	933	100.0	2,365	100.0	5,900	100.0	12,647	100.0
Import of Goods†	505	84.5	792	85.0	1,986	84.0	4,955	84.0	10,386	82.0
Import of Services	93	15.5	141	15.0	379	16.0	945	16.0	2,261	18.0
Net Current Account	-70	—	-116	—	-675	—	384	—	8,498	—

Source: Bank Markazi Iran Annual Report and Balance Sheet 1970-1974.

*Provisional
**Including gas
†Including non-monetary gold

Table 73
Composition of Non-Oil Exports from Iran
(percent)

	1960	1965	1970	1973	1974
Carpets	19.8	25.1	19.8	17.0	19.5
Cotton	23.6	27.7	20.8	23.6	13.5
Dried and Fresh Fruits	17.2	12.7	12.7	14.9	16.9
Animal Hides and Skins	8.7	6.4	6.8	5.8	5.9
Mineral Ores	3.7	5.9	7.2	3.8	5.4
Industrial Goods	0.6	1.5	16.8	16.7	23.1
All Other Goods	26.4	20.7	15.9	18.2	15.7
Value of Non-Oil Exports (millions of dollars)	111.5	180.8	272.6	634.7	610.0

Source: Iran Foreign Trade statistics.

Table 74
Composition of Iran's Imports of Goods
(percent)

	1960	1965	1970	1973	1974
Food and Live Animals	14.1	12.5	6.6	10.5	16.7
Non-edible Raw Materials	3.9	6.5	5.3	5.4	5.4
Chemical Products	8.1	8.5	9.2	9.5	9.8
Iron and Steel	14.0	14.6	15.1	15.6	17.5
Machinery Including Transport	36.3	31.3	40.5	37.5	31.9
All Other Goods	23.6	26.6	23.3	21.5	18.7
Value of Imports of Goods (millions of dollars)	688	899	1677	3737	6616

Source: Bank Markazi Iran, Annual Report 1974, and Foreign Trade Statistics of Iran.

Table 75
Direction of Iran's Exports*

	1960	1965	1970	1972	1973
Developed Countries	77.3	71.4	81.2	87.1	89.7
Japan	(2.9)	(15.8)	(38.3)	(33.3)	(29.0)
Federal Republic of Germany	(15.1)	(3.5)	(8.5)	(8.5)	(9.6)
U.K.	(14.4)	(12.3)	(6.3)	(7.0)	(8.8)
Netherlands	(2.9)	(8.3)	(6.5)	(7.4)	(8.2)
Italy	(3.2)	(4.0)	(4.2)	(8.5)	(6.8)
U.S.	(6.0)	(5.3)	(2.5)	(5.0)	(5.7)
France	(3.8)	(5.8)	(3.3)	(4.3)	(4.7)
Middle East	3.8	7.2	2.1	0.5	0.5
Other Asia	13.7	12.7	11.1	7.1	6.1
Africa	5.1	4.4	3.6	2.3	2.5
Soviet Bloc	—	3.0	1.1	0.9	—
Other Areas	0.1	1.3	0.9	2.0	1.2

Source: IMF, Direction of Trade. Tape File.

*Includes oil exports.

Iran: Past, Present and Future

Table 76

Index Value of Iran's Exports to Major Trading Regions and Countries

	1960	1965	1970	1972	1973
Developed Countries	100	140	290	524	816
Japan	100	907	3,986	5,892	7,703
Germany	100	36	155	263	450
U.K.	100	129	120	227	430
Netherlands	100	440	621	1,204	2,013
Italy	100	190	355	1,228	1,485
U.S.	100	135	117	390	669
France	100	231	241	535	874
Middle East	100	290	155	65	84
Other Asia	100	141	224	242	315
Africa	100	130	195	208	332
Total	100	152	276	467	703

Source: IMF, Direction of Trade, Tape File.

Note: 1960=100

Table 77
Direction of Iran's Imports

	1960	1965	1970	1972	1973
Developed Countries	81.2	84.9	81.3	88.3	85.8
Germany	(21.0)	(19.8)	(21.1)	(17.2)	(19.4)
Japan	(6.4)	(7.8)	(11.9)	(12.4)	(14.3)
U.S.	(19.6)	(18.0)*	(13.0)*	(16.7)*	(14.0)*
U.K.	(14.3)	(13.0)	(10.5)	(11.9)	(10.0)
France	(3.7)	(5.7)	(4.5)	(5.1)	(4.8)
Italy	(4.0)	(4.5)	(5.5)	(5.9)	(3.6)
Netherlands	(3.5)	(2.8)	(2.7)	(3.2)	(2.4)
Middle East	4.5	3.9	1.5	2.3	2.2
Other Asia	8.4	6.0	4.2	2.6	3.1
Africa	0.4	0.1	0.3	0.2	0.4
Soviet Bloc	5.4	4.5	12.4*	6.0*	6.3*
Other Countries	0.1	0.6	0.3	0.6	2.2

Source: IMF, Direction of Trade, Tape File.

*Adjusted by data given in Bank Markazi Iran Annual Reports for 1970, 1974.

Table 78
Index Value of Iran's Imports from Major Trading Regions and Countries

	1960	1965	1970	1972	1973
Developed Countries	100	161	334	549	620
Germany	100	145	299	392	560
Japan	100	190	554	1008	1363
U.S.	100	127*	162*	319*	363*
U.K.	100	140	217	399	426
France	100	284	361	660	774
Italy	100	173	410	715	550
Netherlands	100	124	234	443	423
Middle East	100	132	96	243	245
Other Asia	100	112	185	149	228
Africa	100	23	245	295	573
Soviet Bloc	100	128	621*	460*	985*
Total	100	154	247	479	606

Source: IMF, Direction of Trade, Tape File.

Note: 1960=100

*Adjusted by Bank Markazi Iran figures.

Table 79

Comparative GNP's of Some European Countries and Japan in 1973 and the Required Level of Iran's GNP to Reach Them by 1984

	GNP (billions of dollars)	1973 Population (millions)	Per Capita GNP (dollars)	GNP Requirement		Import Requirement	
				Value (billions of dollars)	Annual Growth Rate	Value (billions of dollars)	Annual Growth Rate
Germany	348	62.0	5600	241	18.5	72	19.0
France*	240	52.1	4600	198	16.3	60	17.0
Japan*	366	108.4	3380	145	12.7	44	13.3
U.K.	176	55.9	3150	135	10.7	41	12.5
Italy	138	54.9	2500	108	8.5	32	9.7
Spain	60	34.0	1720	74	4.9	22	5.7
Iran**	44	32.8	1344	—	—	—	—

Source: All countries except Iran, IMF, International Financial Statistics, Country Pages, February 1975.

*For France and Japan, 1973 rate of growth in GNP was used to bring 1972 figures up to date.

**Iran data from Bank Markazi Iran, 1974 Annual Report (Provisional). Iran's population for 1984 assumed to reach 43 million.

Table 80
The Share of Exports and Imports in the GNP for
Selected Countries Based on National Currencies
(percent)

	1967		1970		1973	
	Exports	Imports	Exports	Imports	Exports	Imports
Germany	21.4	18.0	22.0	20.3	23.1	20.3
U.K.	18.1	19.1	22.1	21.3	23.0	25.5
Italy	17.0	15.8	19.1	19.0	21.0	23.3
France	13.7	13.6	13.1	12.8	17.3*	16.4*
Spain	11.0	14.1	15.1	16.3	16.9	18.6
Japan	9.7	9.7	11.2	10.0	10.8*	8.5*
Iran	22.9	18.2	25.4	19.9	47.8	20.9

Source: All countries except Iran from IMF, International Financial Statistics, February 1975; Iran data from Bank Markazi Iran National Income Statistics.
*1972 data.

Table 81
Actual and Prospective Balance of Trade
(1974 constant millions of dollars)

	Actual 1974	1984 Prospects		Hypothetical Rates of Growth	
		Variety 1	Variety 2	Variety 1	Variety 2
Oil Industry Products	18,670	25,090	30,410	3.0	5.0
Traditional Goods	470	800	1,010	5.5	8.0
Industrial Goods	140	1,300	4,050	25.0	40.0
Gas Exports	130	1,800	5,340	30.0	45.0
Services	1,780	4,020	5,050	8.5	11.0
Total Exports	21,190	33,010	45,860	4.5	8.1
Import Requirements	12,650	32,000	60,000	9.7	17.0
Surplus or Deficit	+8,540	+1,010	−14,140	—	—

Source: 1974 data from Bank Markazi Iran, 1353 (1974) Annual Report (Provisional); other data are hypothetical.

Comments and Discussion

In "Iran in the World Economic Setting," Hassan Ali Mehran observed that Iran exists in a world with basic problems, including inflation, recession and chaotic monetary and economic systems, and with tremendous disparities among nations. The rich countries continue to get richer and the poor poorer, with the accelerated growth of the rich countries owing partly to the fact that they have benefited from the resources of the developing countries at artificially low prices. The first major breakthrough in achieving a new world order was OPEC's action to fix oil prices. It is hoped that the producers of other commodities will follow suit. Mr. Mehran observed that Iran's international role is not limited to OPEC members. It has undertaken assistance programs for several countries in the Third and Fourth Worlds. Iran also has extensive economic and trade relations with the rest of the world. The establishment of a joint commission with Belgium in 1971 was the first important step through such a mechanism toward trade relations with Western Europe; by 1974 countries with joint commissions with Iran accounted for three-quarters of Iran's foreign trade. Mr. Mehran concluded that Iran will continue to work for the elimination of tariff and nontariff barriers to free trade.

In "Iran's International Economic Outlook," Mohsen A. Fardi called participants' attention to four tables showing the significant increase in Iran's share of exports and imports in world and regional trade; the contribution of exports, mainly oil, to Iran's rising GNP; the rise in foreign exchange receipts; and the composition of non-oil exports. In his view, the prospects for Iran attaining "a European standard of living" in 10 years are very good. Oil exports are likely to remain high, but Iran hopes to change their nature, from crude oil to refined products. As for non-oil exports, Iran hopes to produce manufactured goods of sufficiently high quality and low cost to capture markets abroad. Looking ahead, Mr. Fardi suggested that Iran must either significantly increase its non-oil exports, modify the rate of exchange or effect economies in the non-oil sector.

Export Prospects

In the discussion, various speakers stressed the need for Iran to build up its industrial exports as a long-term substitute for oil and as a means of providing employment for the populace presently located in rural sectors in order to achieve more equitable income distribution. But a number of Iranian and non-Iranian participants expressed some pessimism about the feasibility of a large export buildup, emphasizing that Iranian products will have to be competitive in terms of quality and price. An American urged that Iran prepare a careful list of desired exports and warned that such items as cars and trucks would face very stiff competition from Japan.

Trade Relations with Other Areas

Responding to questions about trade with the Middle East, the European Economic Community and the Soviet Union, Iranians observed that Middle East trade is relatively small since Iran does not export oil to the Middle East (with the exception of Israel—a courageous act, in the view of some Americans) and since the kinds of things Iran used to export to the Middle East, *e.g.,* food products, are now consumed at home; that Iran has had many difficulties trading with the EEC and hopes for future modification of the EEC's extensive trade networks with former colonies; and that the Soviet Union is an old trading partner. Iran is also supplying gas to the German Democratic Republic through the Soviet Union under one agreement and is planning another agreement covering the shipment of gas to Western Europe through an Iranian/Soviet pipeline.

Worldwide Inflation

Responding to a question about what Iran can do to help combat worldwide inflation, an Iranian noted that His Imperial Majesty has expressed concern about this point and wants Iran to cooperate in efforts to check inflation. In the speaker's view, the advanced nations must not scramble for commodities; this leads to continuing inflation.

Interdependence

Predicting that the world will become far more interdependent in future, an American questioned whether any country or group of countries should exercise unilateral control over any matter that vitally affects the welfare of other states. He wondered what restraints nations should accept on their own sovereignty in order not to impair the sovereignty of others. Responding to this point an Iranian observed that the notion of interdependence is not new; that Iran considers Western prosperity to be important; and that relations among nations involve faith in each other and not just economics. Another noted that the colonial powers exploited the developing world for centuries without acknowledging the interdependence of mankind. When a barber in New York City earns eight to ten times as much as the worker in a developing country who produces the coffee that the barber drinks, he does not realize that this situation is leading developing countries to redefine "interdependence."

Iran's Foreign Policy

Iran's International Position: An Interpretation

Ahmad Ghoreyshi and Cyrus Elahi

Any study of an international political situation must be cognizant of the connections between historical and political analyses and psychological, sociological or anthropological studies of international conflict. It is important to note that the final outcome of such inquiries will not be fully informative until the examples cited and the situations interpreted are seen "against the background of a real political complex."[1] In other words, psychosocial studies that attempt to clarify the determinants of foreign policy in the modern international system are complementary to a political study of a problem; they do not take its place.[2]

Beyond making reference to the psychosociology of the actor, any explanation of the international behavior of a given state must take into account the relation of forces in a given historical area. Whether decisions are made by one man, by a few individuals or as a result of a variety of forces, we must clarify the actor's goals, his conception of the world and the mode of action he tends to adopt. In order to explain a decision, we must clarify the actor's image of the circumstances, an image that may not necessarily be "objective."[3] Moreover, for each actor, the circumstances are not formed by the calculable relations of power components alone, but rather by the probabilistic behavior of its foes, allies and other neutral actors. Thus, like gambling, international political behavior is based on probabilities.

To begin with, we clearly acknowledge the passing of the bipolar world that characterized the Cold War period—a world rigidly divided into two rival blocs, wherein each superpower was a master of its respective "camp." Today's world is tending toward five major units—the U.S., the Soviet Union, China, Japan and Western Europe. This world is infinitely more complex; the breakdown of former empires has resulted in many independent states, and the superpowers find much of their power unusable or unrewarding. Nevertheless, to a very significant extent Iran's future in the international system is affected by the behavior of the Soviet Union and the United States.

For Iran, as for other states, the notion of "state independence" is partly illusory and requires a bit of semantic clarification.[4] Whether we are speaking of industrial or non-industrial states, "The national society is now so penetrated by the external world that it is no longer the only source of legitimacy."[5] Given the awareness of new relationships, it is completely unrealistic to persist in old habits, ideological tendencies or conceptual frameworks based on outmoded national-international distinctions. Instead, it should be recognized that what happens in Iran, or any other state, is no longer intelligible in terms of parochial events and forces. Rather, such developments must be seen as part of a world transformation in which Iran is working out her role.[6]

As a non-Arab oil-producing state in the Middle East, Iran's position is closely interrelated with developments both within and among her neighbors. Yet despite the importance of her regional ties, a global perspective seems the most relevant approach for the analysis of the foreign policy of Iran.

The first factor accounting for this position is the strategic location of Iran with respect to key transportation and communication routes. A geographical position is bound to impose upon the diplomatic behavior of a political unit certain orientations that tend to be quite enduring. And, "the more this position is designed in physical terms, the more durable the orientation. The more stable the diplomatic system, the less a change of regime will modify these orientations."[7]

The second factor in favor of a global systemic perspective is Iran's status as a major oil-producing state in the world. Side by side with her strategic importance, the problems associated with the production, marketing and pricing of oil constitute a central issue area in Iranian politics, both domestic and international.

As stated earlier, in the analysis of international political behavior, reference to the relation of forces is essential. An analysis of power relations may start by indicating that continuous involvement with the Soviet Union is a persistent feature. In the course of her relations, Iran has been subjected to various forms and degrees of pressure from her northern neighbor. Large portions of the bordering lands and areas (e.g., Caucasian provinces), now well within Soviet boundaries, were under Iranian jurisdiction until the early part of the 19th century. In the 20th century, the Russians have invaded and occupied Iranian territory three times, from 1909 to 1911, 1914 to 1918 and 1941 to 1948. Since the 1917 Revolution, the Russians have tried to establish two separate Soviet Republics, one in Mahabad and the other in Azerbaijan. Iranians vividly recall the Soviet occupation of northern Iran in both wars and their refusal to evacuate after World War II.

Today, even though Russian engineers and technicians are involved in the operation of a steel mill in Esfahan, it is occasionally reported that Communist authorities somewhere in the Soviet bloc still permit Iranian exiles to make anti-Iranian broadcasts.[8] Clearly, Russian influence on the course of modern Iranian history has been tremendous. Furthermore, the Soviets turn their pressure on and off in accordance with the existing degree of rapprochement between the two states.

Modern Iranian history has been largely shaped by the Great Powers pursuing their interests in the Middle East.[9] Long before American professors began conceptualizing about "intervention" and "penetration," Iran had become a thoroughly "penetrated" political unit. Even though it is often pointed out that Iran has not been subjugated to direct colonial rule and has always preserved her status as a sovereign state, the contemporary Iranian perception of her role in world politics, her preoccupation with security, and her image of the superpowers, has its roots in nearly a century and a half of Russian-British rivalry for the domination and exploitation of Iran.

Iran's geographic importance to England had a high priority, for as long as India constituted an integral portion of British interests. But with the discovery of oil in Iran, and with the conversion of the British navy from coal to oil use, British interests increased. As the control of Iranian oil fields became a matter of practical importance to Britain's self-interest, British policy became increasingly important to the course of Iranian politics. Although American efforts to force the withdrawal of Soviet troops from Azarbaijan had been instrumental, it was not until the fall of Dr. Mossadegh that the role of Britain seriously declined and the United States became deeply involved with Iran.

With the reaffirmation of the monarchy, the immediate problem facing the Iranian Government was its precarious security vis-à-vis its northern neighbor. In search of support, Iran joined the Baghdad Pact

(1955) to seek aid in the United States. Accordingly, the Shah sought more arms, and a commitment to Iran's defense in the United States. Toward that end, on March 13, 1959, the United States-Iran Bilateral Treaty was signed. But despite the achievement of a formal alliance with the United States, the Shah remained dissatisfied: America had agreed neither to join the Baghdad Pact, nor to supply Iran with the missiles she had requested. In view of these dissatisfactions and the limitations of the treaty (it did not guarantee Iran's security), Iran sought new alternatives.

When Iran joined the Baghdad Pact in 1955, the Soviet Union applied pressure on her to leave the pact, or at least to guarantee that her territory would not be used against the U.S.S.R. With the signing of the United States-Iran Bilateral Treaty, Soviet resentment intensified and was expressed with aggressive propaganda.[10] Nevertheless, hoping to convince Iran to disengage herself from a pro-Western position, Soviet behavior fluctuated in a dialectic of persuasion and subversion. By 1962, Iran had adopted an attitude of friendship toward the Soviet Union, followed by increased Soviet-Iranian trade and a barter transaction to build a steel mill here, while in return Iran would sell natural gas to the Russians. Finally, in February 1966, a Soviet-Iranian arms deal took place.

Today, Iran is pursuing an independent foreign policy and makes no effort to express a commitment in favor of policies that would identify closely with either of the "Big Two." This policy is centered around Iranian national interests and reflects the proud and confident character of today's Iran. But the really significant point is that, under present circumstances, both superpowers have learned to accept Iran's foreign policy.

As a result of the normalization of relations with the Soviet Union and a remarkable degree of political stability, Iranian oil continuously flows to Western markets and to Japan. In return, Iran receives steadily increasing revenues that are essential for the continuation of current sociopolitical and economic trends. Finally, in view of these trends, Western and Japanese corporate interests as well as those of East European countries can and do take advantage of investment opportunities in Iran.[11]

Clearly, the active international role currently pursued by Iran could not have materialized without the supremacy of the Shah over the political process. Yet, while this domestic condition is necessary, it is not sufficient as the determinant of Iran's current international position. For, in addition to the Shah's effective leadership, the emergence of Iran's "independent" foreign policy necessitated the development of policies known as détente.

As long as the essential features of the international political system remain as they are, Iran's international position will remain potentially dangerous. There are no assurances that under different circumstances (e.g., a breakdown of the present détente) Soviet pressures would not be renewed. Nor can we rule out reactions from the United States, should she perceive the changing circumstances as contrary to her interests. The numerous prejudiced articles critical of Iran that appeared in the American press in the past two years (the period of the "energy crisis") are examples of such a reaction. Finally, we cannot rule out violence in the form of intervention, subversion and a "show of force."

In view of the nature of Soviet-American interests in Iran, her relative independence can remain meaningful only if the rules of diplomatic-strategic behavior are manipulated with subtlety and imagination. Here everything depends almost exclusively on the decision of the head of the state—that is, the Shah, whose diplomatic achievements speak for themselves.

Beyond the critical importance of Soviet-American relations in the larger international system, as pointed out earlier, Iran's current diplomatic situation is partly related to her position relative to the power structure in the Middle East subsystem. Iran has shifted her attention to a more active role in western Asia and the Persian Gulf. In general, Turkey, Pakistan and Afghanistan are not perceived to represent a threat. The situation in the Persian Gulf region is fluid. But Iran's relations with the Arab states can be characterized as very friendly. Preliminary discussions are underway concerning an Iran-Arab defense pact to keep the control of the Persian Gulf in the hands of riparian states. In other words, it has become an accepted principle among regional powers that in order to preserve order in the Persian Gulf area and minimize Big Power interference, it is necessary for Iran and all other riparian states to cooperate.[12]

The Union of Arab Emirates, formed of Abu Dhabi, Dubai, Sharja, Ajman, Fujaira, and Umm al-Quaiwain, has emerged as the newest Arab state.[13] Ras al-Khaima later joined the union, and Bahrain and Qatar have both become independent states. Iranian troops have reasserted the islands of Abu Musa, Greater Tunb and Lesser Tunb at the entrance of the Gulf.[14] At the invitation of Sultan Qabus, Iranian troops and U.S. Government military assistance are helping the ruler of Oman in a guerrilla war waged by Dhofari rebels (of the Popular Front for the Liberation of Oman and the Arab Gulf [PFLOAG]). The United States has established naval stations on Bahrain and the Diego Garcia.[15] The Soviet Union has been the principal supplier of arms and technical assistance to Iraq. The Soviets are reported to be helping to build the new Iraqi deep-water port at Umm al-Qasr. Moscow has also been providing weapons to the Dhofari rebels (PFLOAG). Finally, the Russians either have constructed or are in the midst of constructing a naval base on the Somali Coast.

We cannot yet tell the consequences of these developments. It is only certain that the tangle of relations in the area will not be the same again. In general, the Persian Gulf area remains vulnerable to change. There is too little experience of effective government in the emirates to ensure the viability of the vulnerable new states. There is oil, there are weak governments, traditional political structures and opportunities for subversion and insurgency. If the union shows signs of ineffectiveness, or if there is a leftist coup d'état in any of the member sheikdoms, either Saudi Arabia, Iraq, or both, could take action (e.g., make territorial claims) that would bring reaction from Iran. Much will depend on two factors: the future relations of Saudi Arabia, Iraq, Iran and mutual cooperation with Kuwait on the one hand, and the attitude and understanding of the United States, Soviet Union and, to some extent, China, on the other.[16]

A word of caution may be in order with respect to the Soviet Union's interests: the usual clichés about "the need for an outlet to the open seas" as the main determinant of the Soviet policy toward Iran are generally mistaken. General statements concerning the determinants of foreign policy, like the rules of caution based on experience, may be dangerous if they are formulated without a clear definition of the conditions in which they are applicable. For Soviet leaders at any given period, the importance of free access to the sea depends on strategic considerations that change as the methods of warfare change, and on the importance attributed to the maintenance of peace. This is not to deny that the Soviet Union hopes to increase its thorough penetration and control over the Red Sea-Persian Gulf-Indian Ocean complex. But more important for political and ideological considerations, Iran is an integral portion of a general territorial area along her southern borders over which the Soviet Union hopes to establish political and perhaps economic hegemony.

The uncertainties for the future of the Persian Gulf area are in turn related to the unknown future of the most important regional problem: the Arab-Israeli conflict. Before June 1967, Egyptian soldiers were engaged in combat in Yemen, and Egypt was involved in fermenting a nationalist revolutionary movement in South Arabia, Kuwait and the Trucial Sheikdoms. Radio Cairo's propaganda supported Syrian and Iraqi claims that the Iranian province of Khuzestan is part of the "Arab homeland."

Long before Britain's withdrawal from the Persian Gulf area at the end of 1971, Iran and Saudi Arabia agreed to cooperate to prevent the growth of revolutionary forces in that region.[17] Iraqi threats to Kuwait during Qassem's rule, and the Egyptian military activities in Yemen were sufficient cause for the Governments of Kuwait and Saudi Arabia to share a common interest with Iran against the growth of revolutionary Arab movements. The Shah has repeatedly expressed Iran's determination to play an active role in the preservation of a regional balance of power in order to maintain and control navigation routes in the Persian Gulf.

At any given time, the nature and outcome of Arab reaction to Iran's policies will largely depend upon the relative capabilities and the particular circumstances in which Egypt and Iraq may find themselves.

Iran's relations with Egypt have been improving steadily and are symbolized by the very warm reception President Sadat received in his recent visit to Tehran (April 29, 1975). As a concrete example of Iran's friendly relations with Egypt, we can cite the loan provided by Iran and her position that the territories occupied by Israel (since 1967) should be returned to the Arabs.

Hostility between Iran and Iraq continued after the demise of Qassem, and conflict, mutual antagonism and profound mistrust characterized relations between them until very recently. The major points in the conflict concerned hegemony over the Persian Gulf, navigation in Shatt al-Arab, the status of the minority community of Persians residing in Iraq and Iranian support of the Kurdish revolt. But ever since March 6, 1975 (during the OPEC conference in Algeria), when it was announced that Iran and Iraq would cooperate to resolve their differences, relations have sharply improved. Iran has discontinued her support for Kurdish rebels and, after a series of meetings, all the other problems mentioned above were resolved.

In part due to her membership in the Moslem community, and partly to improve relations with Saudi Arabia and throughout the Persian Gulf area, the Shah has expressed Iran's sympathies for Palestinian refugees and supported the Arab demand for the return of territories occupied in June 1967. Yet Iran's de facto recognition of Israel continues, and she remains a staunch supporter of the guaranteed independence of all states in the area, including Israel.

When Prime Minister Harold Wilson announced in 1968 that London could no longer afford to maintain a military presence "east of Suez," Washington was not the only capital that experienced considerable alarm. Tehran, Riyadh and Kuwait City recognized that Mr. Wilson's statement meant a major turning point in their international positions. In January 1968, a few months after Mr. Wilson's statement, President Nixon took office and the Persian Gulf was perceived as a major security concern of the new administration.

Preoccupied with Iran's national security, the Iranian monarch embarked on the expansion of military power on land, in the air and on sea in order to play an active role in the area. Between 1971 and 1973, Iran and Saudi Arabia jointly spent $3.6 billion on American weapons, which is a threefold increase of what they spent during the preceding 20 years. Iran is now the principal importer of American military aircraft, and Saudi-Kuwaiti purchases are in the billions of dollars and steadily increasing.[18]

While a detailed analysis of Iran's military capability is not intended here,[19] it is worth pointing out that the expansion of her forces has been the subject of a variety of comments and speculations. These comments range from a perception of Iran as a country located in a volatile area of the world trying to protect herself, to those who are simply puzzled by the

Iranian military buildup, and finally to those who suggest that Iran may be pursuing an expansionist policy. The diplo-military behavior of Iran, as is the case with other states, is a function of multiple factors: their local situations, the technology of weaponry, their broad ideological preferences and their fears and expectations.

In a world of autonomous political units, security or the aspiration to survive is a primary objective of each state. As pointed out earlier, it was the insecurity of the region and the need for economic and military assistance that motivated Iran to join the U.S.-sponsored Baghdad Pact. Today, as then, the Shah is trying as much as possible to ensure Iran's stability against internal or external threats. Mohammad Reza Shah Pahlavi has long experience in political life, and much of this experience throughout the 1940s and early 1950s has been bitter. He is determined not to allow Iran to continue to suffer the humiliations she has had to endure for so long.

In addition to having witnessed the forced exit of his father, Reza Shah the Great, the Anglo-Soviet occupation of Iran, the Tudeh Party's subversive activities until the early 1950s, the Shah has "seen" the Anglo-French-Israeli attack on Egypt, the Iraqi Revolution in 1958, the dismemberment of Pakistan and the violent death of young King Faisal. These events have left their imprints in Tehran.

If the 1958 Iraqi Revolution indicated that the Baghdad Pact cannot adequately ensure the survival of Middle Eastern governments involved, the second Kashmir War and the Indo-Pakistani War of 1972 demonstrated the ineffectiveness of bilateral agreements with the U.S. as a measure to ensure national security.

Prime Minister Hoveyda's comments with respect to the Indo-Pakistani War illustrate Iran's conception of national security: "Pakistan, an ally of the United States through two multinational and one bilateral treaty, has been attacked and dismembered without as much as a ripple of serious protest. There is no reason why Pakistan's plight should be treated as an isolated case that could not be repeated elsewhere in the region."[20]

Although Tehran favors a just and peaceful resolution of the Arab-Israeli conflict, the specific outcome of this problem will have a significant effect on Iran's national security. For if there is an overwhelming victory by the Israelis, "radical" Arab leaders like Libya's Colonel Qaddafi may indeed increase in number throughout the Arab world. Should such a situation arise, political instability would probably increase in the Arab states. Iran would certainly view such a circumstance as potentially dangerous. On the other hand, if the turn of events causes the destruction of Israel, Arab-Iranian relations may be perceived and defined in new, dangerous ways.

All the talk about disarmament, stability and regional security agreements are meaningless if nations believe that at the 11th hour everyone is on his own. We can go further and say that the Shah's attitude toward defense involves an ideological aspect; like General de Gaulle, the Shah believes that a state that cannot protect itself cannot be independent and therefore will not be a full-fledged state.

The problem of peace is difficult because it has to do with man's humanity. The mouse, having recognized the superior power of the adversary, yields. Man on the other hand, is capable of preferring revolt to humiliation and his own subjective truth to life itself. States, like individuals, desire not only life but honor, not only security but dignity. For example, even though in terms of military capability Iran is hardly comparable with either of the "Big Two," in the event of an attack, say, by either of the two—very improbable as things stand today—the Iranians would like to put up a fight even for a few days, long enough to attract world public opinion in order to avoid the fate of Czechoslovakia and the Dominican Republic.

The stakes in the Persian Gulf area are very high. Saudi Arabia, which occupies most of the Arabian peninsula, including a 250-mile strip along the gulf, holds nearly one-fourth of the world's known oil reserves (approximately 130 billion barrels). Kuwait, with a population of 800,000, situated at the extreme western end of the gulf, holds another one-fifth of world petroleum reserves (75 billion barrels). Iran, which occupies the entire northern boundary of the Persian Gulf (including the strategic Strait of Hormoz at the Persian Gulf's eastern entrance into the Indian Ocean), has estimated reserves of 65 billion barrels and large deposits of natural gas. Iraq also claims large petroleum reserves (estimated at 30 billion barrels). These oil reserves, together with the holdings of Abu Dhabi and other small sheikdoms of the lower Persian Gulf, constitute two-thirds of the world's proven reserves. Almost all the Persian Gulf oil is transported by tankers to Western markets and Japan. It would take the sinking of a few ships to block or at least highly limit the capacity of the gulf's navigation routes. For Iran, one could say that it is a matter of life and death for these routes to be kept open. As the most populated state in the area, the Shah is determined that Iran develop a strong, flexible military capability to cope with possible disruptions perceived as a threat to Iran's security.

Despite what may be regarded as "high" oil prices, in the absence of a cheaper alternative source of energy, the United States believes that whoever controls the Persian Gulf controls the key to industrial life in the West. The importance of the Persian Gulf in the eyes of the United States can be seen by this quote from a 1969 study by the Georgetown University Center for Strategic Studies, an institution that generally shares the conception of national security held by the defense establishment in Washington: "The strategic interests of the non-Communist world would be in grave jeopardy if freedom of movement in and out of the gulf were curtailed or denied."[21]

These strategic concerns on the part of the United States are complemented by important economic considerations. In view of recent oil price increases, it is argued that the United States (and some other arms-producing Western nations) can regain some of the petrodollars that otherwise could act as an independent variable to threaten the American economy. From the perspective of the Pentagon, the rationale for an increased export of arms to Middle Eastern states links economic considerations to national security. Thus, Deputy Secretary of Defense William P. Clemens told Congress in 1973 that any restriction in the sale of arms "decreases the potential contribution of sales . . . to strengthening both free world security and the U.S. economy and balance-of-payments positions."[22] This is not to argue, however, that Iran is obliged to buy arms from the United States. If another country offered a technologically more sophisticated weapon, or a better price for comparable weapons, Iran would immediately pursue the offer.

As stated earlier, oil revenues are essential for the government and the socioeconomic development of Iran. Iranians argue that the impact of higher oil prices upon other prices, output, employment and the balance-of-payments problems all over the world are partial and relatively insignificant. The major burden for these problems, Iranians argue, should rest on the imbalances inherent in the international economic system that led to the plunder of the natural resources in the Third World countries and created excessive levels of consumption and waste in the industrialized countries.

At any rate, they do not feel guilty for the economic dislocations of today's world. They argue that had the oil prices increased at the mere rate of 5.5 percent per annum since the end of World War II, today's government "take" prices would have been over $12 per barrel (today's government "take" prices for light and heavy oil combined is around $10.40 per barrel). On the basis of this calculation only, between 1960 and 1972 Iran would have received over $100 billion more than she has indeed received.

In conclusion, in view of the arms race in the Middle East and throughout the world, Iran is likely to continue to increase her military capability in order to be able to conduct her affairs from a position of strength. With respect to foreign trade in general and the sale of oil in particular, she will demand better terms of trade. Finally, in the pursuit of her national interests, the core operational features of Iran's actions will be negotiations, persuasion and accommodation.

Table 82
Number of Foreign Investors in Iran According to Year of Decree
and Country of Investors

Year of Decree	U.S.	Federal Republic of Germany	Japan	England	Switzerland	France	Mixed Company	Other*	Total
1956	—	—	—	—	—	1	—	—	1
1957	1	—	—	—	—	1	—	—	2
1958	1	—	—	—	—	—	—	1	2
1959	2	—	—	1	—	—	—	—	3
1960	—	1	—	2	—	—	1	2	6
1961	1	—	—	—	—	—	—	2	3
1962	1	1	—	—	—	—	1	1	4
1963	1	—	—	—	1	—	—	1	3
1964	3	—	—	—	—	—	—	5	8
1965	2	2	—	1	1	—	1	2	9
1966	4	2	1	1	—	2	—	—	10
1967	2	4	1	—	—	1	1	4	13
1968	1	1	1	—	2	—	1	1	7
1969	5	1	1	2	1	1	2	2	15
1970	3	6	3	3	—	1	1	3	20
1971	—	1	2	—	1	1	3	1	9
1972	1	1	2	2	5	1	2	2	16
1973	6	1	6	2	—	2	1	2	20
1974	9	2	6	6	2	1	3	3	32
Total	43	23	23	20	13	12	17	32	183

Source: Mostafa Moini, *A Study of Private Foreign Investment in Iran* (Tehran: The Institute for International Political and Economic Studies, July 1975), p. 118.

*This category includes the following: Italy and Denmark, 5 each, Sweden and Netherlands, 4 each, Belgium and Luxembourg, 3 each, Israel 2, and the following countries 1 each: Australia, Austria, Greece, India, Kenya, Panama.

Table 83
Imported Capital in Iran as of Bahman 30, 1974, According to Year of Decree and Country of Investor
(millions of rials)

Year of Decree	U.S.	Federal Republic of Germany	Japan	England	Switzer-land	France	Mixed Company	Other*	Total
1956	—	—	—	—	—	118	—	—	118
1957	16	—	—	—	—	188	—	—	204
1958	495	—	—	—	—	—	—	20	515
1959	202	—	—	116	—	—	—	—	318
1960	—	61	—	21	—	—	13	98	193
1961	136	—	—	—	—	—	—	215	351
1962	11	47	—	—	—	—	16	64	138
1963	88	—	—	—	64	—	—	12	164
1964	265	—	—	—	—	—	—	104	369
1965	1,698	127	—	5	965	—	59	23	2,877
1966	717	73	26	63	—	117	—	—	996
1967	459	325	4	—	—	14	213	230	1,245
1968	21	24	60	—	80	—	29	45	259
1969	160	300	87	24	19	53	209	207	1,059
1970	157	561	169	25	—	9	123	150	1,194
1971	—	6	13	—	22	14	401	83	539
1972	686	23	95	38	210	23	273	15	1,363
1973	255	122	2,252	32	—	11	16	15	2,703
1974	345	—	31	23	—	—	83	142	624
TOTAL	5,711	1,669	2,737	347	1,360	547	1,435	1,423	15,227

Source: Mostafa Moini, *A Study of Private Foreign Investment in Iran* (Tehran: The Institute for International Political and Economic Studies, July 1975), p. 119.

*Same as in Table 82.

Iran: Past, Present and Future

Table 84
U.S. Exports to Iran
(dollars)

	1971	1972	1973	1974 (January-May)
Food and Live Animals	31,825,747	58,265,191	90,462,920	51,040,959
Beverages and Tobacco	2,027,807	1,339,295	3,637,346	1,620,960
Crude Materials, Inedible, Except Fuel	4,481,758	5,753,001	7,263,910	10,019,290
Minerals, Fuels, Lubes	1,452,440	1,528,778	2,746,567	2,568,525
Oil and Fats, Animal and Vegetable	26,988,868	16,606,831	17,861,131	40,915,017
Chemicals	20,893,908	23,442,742	38,435,434	22,456,379
Manufactured Goods by Chief Material	23,290,205	46,917,243	51,494,277	32,511,912
Machinery and Transportation Equipment	202,703,150	240,691,624	327,605,192	150,816,070
Miscellaneous Manufactured Articles, n.e.c.	11,566,420	10,101,558	12,373,652	7,363,222
Items Not Classified by Kind	2,366,653	4,404,473	4,392,157	2,657,445
Special Category*	153,553,170	148,812,088	213,147,092	122,526,976
Total	481,140,126	557,862,806	769,419,678	444,510,755

*Consists of arms, ammunition and other military items generally under the export control jurisdiction of the Department of State.

Table 85
Import of Goods from the Socialist Countries
(millions of dollars)

Country	1959	1960	1961	1962	1963	1964	1965	1966	1967	1968	1969	1970	1971	1972	1973
U.S.S.R.	17.9	19.3	18.1	14.1	22.2	22.6	16.6	28.7	33.3	44.9	115.8	130.5	141.4	72.0	213.9
Czecho-slovakia	9.0	7.4	5.1	4.5	5.0	7.3	7.0	7.6	13.5	13.8	16.6	20.8	28.1	24.6	22.7
Poland	1.4	2.5	2.1	3.0	2.9	4.6	5.6	7.3	4.9	12.2	5.7	5.1	5.1	5.6	15.0
Hungary	3.5	3.4	4.3	2.5	6.1	8.3	4.8	4.1	7.1	8.3	9.1	14.3	14.5	13.3	20.9
Romania	—	0.2	0.4	0.4	0.4	0.5	0.7	7.0	13.7	15.1	27.4	31.2	39.8	34.2	47.4
Bulgaria	0.3	0.6	0.4	0.3	0.2	1.1	1.5	5.1	2.7	2.6	4.0	5.4	4.0	4.0	9.1
Total	32.1	33.4	30.4	24.8	38.8	44.4	36.2	59.8	75.2	96.9	178.6	207.3	232.9	153.7	329.0

Source: Foreign Trade Statistics of Iran.

Iran: Past, Present and Future

Table 86
United States Soviet Navy Port Calls in the Indian Ocean

	1968 U.S.	1968 U.S.S.R.	1969 U.S.	1969 U.S.S.R.	1970 U.S.	1970 U.S.S.R.	1971 U.S.	1971 U.S.S.R.	1972 U.S.	1972 U.S.S.R.	1973 U.S.	1973 U.S.S.R.
Ethiopia	14	0	13	1	10	1	10	1	8	1	12	1
India	9	8	9	2	8	6	11	1	0	4	0	7
Iran	1	3	2	7	10	0	6	2	8	2	8	0
Iraq	0	3	0	8	0	2	0	11	0	14	0	16
Kenya	7	5	9	0	8	3	9	0	12	2	22	4
Kuwait	0	0	2	1	1	0	3	0	1	0	2	0
Malagasy Republic	6	0	5	1	7	0	13	0	11	0	19	0
Maldives	0	1	0	1	1	0	1	1	1	0	0	1
Mauritius	18	2	10	4	7	17	16	5	7	20	19	11
Pakistan	6	2	9	2	7	2	11	0	10	0	11	0
Seychelles Islands	6	0	6	0	3	0	9	0	6	3	10	0
Somalia*	1	3	0	13	0	18	2	11	0	38	0	97
South Yemen	0	4	0	13	0	7	0	13	0	12	0	7
Sri Lanka	3	4	6	8	3	2	4	2	10	14	10	9
Sudan	0	0	0	2	0	2	0	0	0	0	1	0
Tanzapia	0	4	0	2	0	2	2	0	0	0	1	0
UAR (Port Suez)	0	3	0	1	0	0	0	0	0	0	0	0
Yemen	0	0	0	2	0	3	0	0	0	0	0	0
Total Port Calls per Year	71	42	71	68	65	65	97	47	74	110	115	153

Source: U.S. Congress, House of Representatives, Committee on Foreign Affairs, *Proposed Expansion of U.S. Military Facilities in the Indian Ocean,* 93rd Congress, 2nd Session, 1974, p. 159.

Note: "Port calls" reflect every entry of each Soviet naval ship into a foreign port but do not reflect the duration of the visits, which varied from one day to 18 months. Port calls by oceanographic research and space event support ships are included in the totals because the data available for 1968 through 1971 are not categorized by ship. Singapore is not included in the table because it is a Pacific Ocean port. However, Soviet ships from the Indian Ocean occasionally call there and Soviet naval auxiliaries are overhauled in Singapore's shipyards. In addition, ships engaged in long-term harbor clearing operations in Bangladesh are not considered to be conducting routine port calls, and therefore are not included.

*The large increase in visits to Somalia since 1971 reflects the U.S.S.R.'s development and use of the port of Berbera for naval support. Most of the remaining port visits in the Indian Ocean—particularly those by combatants—were undertaken for diplomatic purposes.

Table 87
General Purpose Forces Deployments of Out-of-Home Area Into Indian Ocean
(ship days)

	1968	1969	1970	1971	1972	1973
Surface Combatants (including amphibious and auxiliary ships):						
Soviet	1,760	3,668	3,579	3,804	8,007	8,543
United States	1,688	1,315	1,246	1,337	1,435	2,154

Source: U.S. Congress, House of Representatives, Committee on Foreign Affairs, *Proposed Expansion of U.S. Military Facilities in the Indian Ocean,* 93rd Congress, 2nd Session, 1974, p. 138.

Table 88

Exports of Significant Defense Articles from the Persian Gulf Area on the U.S. Munitions List

(dollars)

Country	FISCAL YEAR					
	1963 (second half)	1969	1970	1971	1972	1973
Bahrain						
Iran:						
Commercial	25,749,000	11,875,000	4,474,000	33,198,000	35,308,724	10,757,006
FMS	8,612,000	44,246,000	66,046,000	(1) 78,880,000	198,461,000	143,521,000
MAP		28,097,000	7,839,000	346,000		
Total	34,361,000	84,218,000	78,359,000	112,424,000	233,769,724	154,278,006
Iraq						
Kuwait						
Oman: Commercial					173,934	
Qajar						
Saudi Arabia:						
Commercial	6,295,000	16,389,000		3,536,000	229,448	522,467
FMS	12,581,000	1,454,000	1,670,000	4,318,000	2,455,000	66,127,000
Total	18,876,000	17,843,000	1,670,000	7,854,000	2,684,448	66,619,467
United Arab Emirates:						
Commercial					437,062	56,357
Persian Gulf Area Total	53,237,000	102,061,000	80,029,000	120,278,000	237,065,168	220,983,830

Source: U.S. Congress, House of Representatives, Committee on Foreign Affairs, *The Persian Gulf, 1974: Money, Politics, Arms, and Power*, 93rd Congress, 2nd Session, 1974, p. 48.

Iran: Past, Present and Future

Footnotes

1. Raymond Aron, "Conflict and War from the Viewpoint of Historical Sociology," *The Nature of Conflict, Studies on the Sociological Aspects of International Relations*, the International Sociological Association in collaboration with Jesse Bernard *et al.* (Paris: UNESCO, 1957), p. 185.

2. Raymond Aron, *Peace and War* (New York: Doubleday, 1966), pp. 279–366. Also see Stanley Hoffmann, *The State of War* (New York: Praeger, 1965), p. 15.

3. Kenneth E. Boulding, "National Images and International Systems," *International Politics and Foreign Policy* (rev. ed.), ed. James N. Rosenau (New York: The Free Press, 1969), pp. 422–431.

4. See Richard W. Cottam, *Competitive Interference and Twentieth Century Diplomacy* (Pittsburgh: University of Pittsburgh Press, 1967), and Miles Copeland, *The Game of Nations* (New York: Simon and Schuster, 1969).

5. James N. Rosenau, "Pre-theories and Theories of Foreign Policy," *Approaches to Comparative and International Politics*, ed. R. Barry Farrell (Evanston, Il.: Northwestern University Press, 1966), p. 63.

6. For information and analysis on the politics and foreign policy of Iran see H.I.M. Mohammad Reza Shah Pahlavi, *Mission for My Country* (London: Hutchinson and Co., 1961); James A. Bill, *The Politics of Iran: Groups, Classes, and Modernization* (Columbus, Ohio: Charles E. Merrill, 1972); Leonard Binder, *Iran: Political Development in a Changing Society* (Berkeley: University of California Press, 1971); Marvin Zonis, *The Political Elite of Iran* (Princeton, N.J.: Princeton University Press, 1971); Rouhollah K. Ramazani, *The Foreign Policy of Iran* (Charlottesville, Va.: University of Virginia Press, 1966); Shahram Chubin and Sepehr Zabih, *The Foreign Relations of Iran* (Berkeley: University of California Press, 1974); and Leonard Binder, *Factors Influencing Iran's International Situation* (Santa Monica: The Rand Corporation, RM-5968 FF, October, 1969).

7. Raymond Aron, *Peace and War, op. cit.*, p. 287.

8. *The New York Times*, June 8, 1969.

9. See Firuz Kazemzadeh, *Russia and Britain in Persia 1694–1914* (New Haven: Yale University Press, 1968); see also Tareq Y. Ismael, *The Middle East in World Politics* (Syracuse, N.Y.: Syracuse University Press, 1974).

10. For a good summary of these events and their larger context, see Firuz Kazemzadeh, "Soviet-Iranian Relations: A Quarter-Century of Freeze and Thaw," *The Soviet Union and the Middle East: The Post-World War II Era*, ed. Ivo J. Lederer and Wayne S. Vucinich (Stanford, Calif.: Hoover Institute Press, 1974), pp. 55–77.

11. See Tables 1, 2, 3 and 4.

12. For background information on the Persian Gulf, see Sharam Chubin and Sepehr Zabih, *op. cit.*, pp. 193–271; J.C. Hurewitz, *The Persian Gulf: Prospects for Stability* (N.Y.: Foreign Policy Association, Inc., April, 1974); U.S. Congress, House of Representatives, Committee on Foreign Affairs, *The Persian Gulf, 1974: Money, Politics, Arms, and Power*, 93rd Congress, 2nd Session, 1974; U.S. Congress, House of Representatives, Committee on Foreign Affairs, *Proposed Expansion of U.S. Military Facilities in the Indian Ocean*, 93rd Congress, 2nd Session, 1974.

13. *The New York Times*, December 3, 1971.

14. For an informative interview on Iran's position on the Persian Gulf, see "Shah of Iran Warns Outsiders Against Gulf Military Position," *The New York Times*, January 17, 1972.

15. See *Proposed Expansion of U.S. Military Facilities in the Indian Ocean, op. cit.*

16. See Tables 5 and 6.

17. *The New York Times*, November 17, 1968.

18. See Table 7.

19. See *The Military Balance, 1973–1974* (London: The International Institute for Strategic Studies, 1974).

20. Quoted by C.L. Sulzberger, "It's Everyone for Himself," *The New York Times*, February 9, 1972.

21. Quoted by Michael T. Klare, "The Political Economy of Arms Sales, The American Empire at Bay," *The Persian Gulf, 1974: Money, Politics, Arms, and Power, op. cit.*, p. 221.

22. *Ibid.*, p. 220.

The Instruments of Iranian Foreign Policy

Rouhollah K. Ramazani

Iran's resurgence in international politics is generally acknowledged, but scholars and statesmen differ in their interpretation of its causes and effects. While some might attribute it principally to political stability or economic development within Iran, others might consider it the by-product of a more favorable international system. There is little doubt, for example, that the consolidation of political authority within Iran contributes considerably to the country's greater capability to play a more active role in world affairs today as Reza Shah's establishment of internal security and political control performed a somewhat similar function in the past. Or, to be sure, the tempo of socioeconomic change, accelerated by a vigorous land-reform program, increasing oil revenues and the cumulative impact of spectacular rates of economic growth over the years, significantly undergirds the expansion, complexity and diversity of Iran's relations with an ever-widening circle of nations in the world arena.

Also, to be sure, changes in the international system tend to maximize Iran's relative freedom of action in world politics. The process of transition from rigid bipolarity to a more flexible and complicated multipolarity has a profound impact on Iran's relations with superpowers as well as other states. By the same token, the more abrupt subsystemic changes resulting from the British withdrawal from the vast areas "east of Suez" tend to expand the margin of Iran's freedom of action in regional affairs. But neither systemic nor subsystemic changes, nor the efficacy of domestic political control and rapid economic growth can separately or jointly, I submit, provide a satisfactory explanation of Iran's resurgence in world politics. The convergence of these changes that I have called domestic-international transitions lies at the heart of Iran's new opportunity to play a more dynamic role in world politics, but the opportunity to play that role is not the same as the ability to do it. In other words, granted a more favorable domestic and international environment during the last decade, how has Iran tried to play its new role in world politics? Obviously, there is no single way of approaching this question, but a fruitful way, I suggest, might be to identify the principal instruments of Iranian foreign policy. I shall try to do so in this essay in the hope of stimulating discussions toward a more balanced assessment of the problems and prospects of Iran's contemporary foreign policy.

The Military

No discussion of the instruments of Iranian foreign policy can escape the role of military force. Iran is the chief military power in the Persian Gulf today. Although the tradition of acquisition of military equipment from the United States can be traced back to 1947, the fact remains that the rapid military buildup of Iran began in earnest in the wake of the 1968 announcement of the British decision to withdraw from the Persian Gulf. President Johnson agreed to help build up the Iranian defense system with more sophisticated weapons, as evidenced by the delivery of the long-sought Phantom II, through the U.S. Navy. There is no need to reiterate here the well-publicized news of Iran's actual or planned purchase of military hardware, including the F-4 Phantom fighter-bombers, the F-14 and the F-15 fighter planes and, more recently, the F-17 lightweight fighter planes. What is of interest to me here is the overall place of military force in Iranian foreign policy. This will require an analysis of the actual practice in the conduct of Iranian foreign policy rather than an inventory of military hardware or an examination of the share of military expenditure in the Iranian budget or of the ratio of military cost to the GNP.

Only a few instances of actual practice exist. One instance in which Iran demonstrated its military capability was the landing of forces on the three islands of Abu Musa and the two Tunbs (1971). Iran believed in 1971, as it believes today, that it possessed "vital interests" in the security of the Persian Gulf and the Straits of Hormuz, and its presence on these islands was necessary for the protection of those interests. The circumstances surrounding its decision are instructive. First, the politico-military situation at the time did not seem to provide a viable alternative to the use of force. On the one hand, Iran could not rely upon collective action to maintain local security by local powers; CENTO seemed irrelevant and included outside powers. On the other hand, the future security and stability of the lower Persian Gulf was uncertain despite the planned Arab Federation. Second, the landing of forces on the two Tunbs took place only after many months of protracted and unsuccessful negotiations. And third, as a result of the use of diplomacy through negotiations, Iran succeeded in concluding an agreement with the Sheikh of Sharjah **prior** to the landing of its forces on the island of Abu Musa.

Another instance of actual military action is the case of Oman. Given the strategic location of Oman, the foreign-supported rebellion in Dhofar and the avowed determination of the Dhofari rebels to overthrow the regimes of such gulf states as Iran, the Iranian Government committed forces there in support of the Sultan's fight against insurgency. Given the Arab-Israeli disengagement agreement; Egypt's rapprochement with

Iran; the settlement of the Iraqi-Iranian dispute; and, most important of all, defections among the rebels, the success of Iranian forces in clearing the road from Thamarit to Salalah, and the possibility of South Yemen's reconciliation with Oman, the chances for Arab military participation in the Sultan's fight against the rebels and for Iranian withdrawal may be improving. But the principal point of this discussion is that Iranian intervention took place at the invitation of the Sultan of Oman and in the face of the failure of Arab states to fulfill promises of assistance.

The third instance that might shed some light on the place of the use of force in Iranian foreign policy is the conflict with Iraq. There is no need to describe here the festering nature of the conflict or the escalation of border clashes between the two countries over the years. The important point here is that neither side seemed prepared under the circumstances to commit its forces beyond the point they actually had by March 1975. In the case of Iran, it would seem clear from a statement of the Shah that Iran was reluctant to get sucked into a full-fledged armed conflict with Iraq. In connection with the Kurds, the Shah said, according to Joseph Kraft, that they were making no progress in the war and that they were running. The Shah then added, "We Iranians would have had to do the fighting. I decided I didn't want to have a war with Iraq at a time when the Near East was a powder keg, and the Russians supported Iraq and the United States suffered from a Watergate complex."

Speculations about nuclear weapons and Iran's foreign policy are rampant. Obviously, it is absurd to talk about nuclear arms as an instrument of Iranian foreign policy at this time, when Iran does not even possess such weapons. But Iran's determination to acquire numerous nuclear plants with the assistance of the United States, the Federal Republic of Germany and France on the one hand, and its interest in Australian and Canadian uranium on the other, cause speculations about the technical possibility of diversion of nuclear energy to nuclear weapons, as evidenced by the example of India. Iran is a party to the NPT, took the initiative to acquire United Nations' support for declaring the Middle East a "nuclear-free zone" and has repeatedly proclaimed that it is "a cardinal point," to borrow the Shah's words, of Iranian policy, not to produce nuclear weapons. However, the Shah also has reportedly stated if every little country obtained a few atomic bombs, Iran would be forced to reconsider its position.

Diplomacy

Diplomacy seldom makes as much sensational news as war, but this truism does not excuse scholars' failure to give it adequate treatment. The resurgence of Iran in world politics during the past decade has paralleled the emergence of unprecedented diplomatic ties between Iran and numerous states. It has also involved an unprecedented degree of the use of multilateral diplomacy through regional and universal organizations regarding a great variety of economic, social and political issues of concern to Iran. But the details of such diplomatic activities are beyond the scope of this study. I am concerned here with diplomacy as an instrument of Iranian foreign policy. More specifically, I am concerned with the use of diplomacy as a method of settling disputes.

Almost all the cases of major dispute settlement of the recent past have involved Iran's relations with various regional powers. The greatest number of these disputes fall under one category: these involve Iran's claim to the continental shelf in the Persian Gulf. Within the span of a few years, most of these disputes have been settled by diplomatic means, although the dispute with Saudi Arabia involved sovereign claim and counterclaim regarding the islands of Farsi and Arabi in addition to the sea bed. The shelf agreement with Saudi Arabia was heralded as the first of its kind. It was signed in 1968 and went into force a year later. The precedent-setting agreement was the result of years of quiet negotiations between the two major gulf states. It was followed by Iran's agreement with Qatar. This agreement was signed in 1969 and went into force in 1970. In the following year, Iran signed still another agreement with Bahrain that went into effect in 1972. In 1971, an agreement was also initialed with Abu Dhabi, and a memorandum of understanding was signed with Sharjah as well. Finally, an agreement was reached between Iran and Oman in 1974. The continental shelf delimitation problems between Iran and Iraq and Kuwait have yet to be settled. The triangular nature of the problems and the long-standing Irano-Iraqi conflict, on the one hand, and the Iraqi-Kuwaiti conflict on the other, complicated the settlement of the relevant shelf disputes until recently. With the settlement of the larger Irano-Iraqi conflict over the river boundary in the Shatt al-Arab, it would seem reasonable to hope that the continental shelf disputes with Iraq and Kuwait will also be settled, before long, through diplomacy.

Diplomacy has been utilized for the settlement of three other major disputes within the Middle East region. Until recently, the most spectacular example of pacific settlement of a dispute by Iran was the case of Bahrain. There is little doubt that the age-old dispute between Iran and Britain over Bahrain was settled in 1970 primarily because by then the parties found it compatible with their mutual interest to do so. In anticipation of the British departure from the Persian Gulf by the end of 1971, the parties realized that political accommodation in regard to Bahrain would ultimately serve their larger strategic and political interests in the Persian Gulf in the future.

But the choice of the kind of diplomatic means by which Iran decided to settle the dispute was also significant. Iran's initiative to involve the office of the Secretary-General of the United Nations was indicative of its concern not only with power but also with legitimacy. The settlement of the Bahrain dispute involved the principle of self-determination on the one hand, and that of peaceful settlement of disputes on the other. These two principles of the U.N. Charter were included in the Shah's initial policy statement on Bahrain in New Delhi; in the relevant British and Iranian correspondence with the U.N. Secretary-General; in the latter's instructions to his personal representative; in the report of the head of the U.N. mission to Bahrain and in the endorsing resolution of the Security Council. The general assessment of the United Nations by Inis Claude seems applicable to the case of the Bahrain settlement by Iran. He states that the function of "collective legitimization is one of the most significant elements in the pattern of political activity that the United Nations has evolved in response to the set of limitations and possibilities posed by the political realities of our time." I would add that for over a century Iran had pleaded historical legitimacy for its claim of "incontestable sovereign right" to Bahrain, but it relinquished that claim in 1970 by utilizing the machinery of collective legitimization of the United Nations for both internal and external reasons.

Iran's most spectacular use of diplomacy as a means of settling disputes is the Shatt al-Arab case. As already mentioned, the age-old conflict between the two neighboring countries involved escalation of armed clashes across the border over the years with no prospects of settlement in sight. Neither the concern of the United Nations nor the prolonged negotiations between the parties seemed to prove successful. Iran's preparedness to resort to third-party adjudication as a means of settling the dispute peacefully proved equally ineffective. But the Shah and Saddam Husain suddenly agreed to settle the dispute as the result of mediation by President Boumédienne of Algeria. No basic change had occurred in March 1975, in either the patterns of power rivalry between the two neighboring states or in the complexion of their political systems to obviate underlying differences between them, but by then a variety of considerations seemed to converge in favor of a rapid settlement of the dispute. Iran's post-October War annoyance with the Israeli position in peace negotiations was finding increasing favor in Iraq. Iraq's greater desire to break out of its self-imposed isolation was watched with increasing interest in Tehran. And the emerging Iraqi disappointment with the Soviets fitted Iran's campaign to neutralize the rise of Great Power influence in the Persian Gulf. Furthermore, the pressure for a unified front within OPEC was probably also influential in the settlement of the conflict because the organization was preparing at the time for a unified front for negotiations in a preliminary meeting in Paris with the representatives of the oil-consuming countries.

Whatever domestic and external considerations might have indeed influenced the decision to reach the Algiers accord, the real point of this discussion is that the settlement represented another major instance of the use of diplomacy in Iranian foreign policy at a time of the greatest military buildup during the past decade. The larger significance of the agreement transcends, I submit, the specific and quid pro quo of the Iraqi acceptance of the principle of *thalweg* in settling the river boundary in the Shatt al-Arab for the Iranian relinquishment of support for the Kurds. The settlement has spurred unprecedented interest in the principle of regional security by regional powers that Iran has advocated ever since 1968, when the British first announced the decision to withdraw their forces from the Persian Gulf.

Finally, diplomacy as an instrument of foreign policy was used once again toward the settlement of another ancient dispute between Iran and a regional power in recent years. As early as 1959, the Shah appointed General Jahanbani to search for a solution to the Irano-Afghan dispute over the Helmand River. The search was pursued further in the 1960s without definitive results. But after some seven months of strenuous negotiations in 1973, it seemed that Iran and Afghanistan were on the verge of a historic breakthrough. Iran signed a treaty to settle the dispute in March, and the Majlis approved it on July 17. On the same day, however, the Afghan army toppled vacationing King Muhammad Zahir Shah in a bloodless coup d'état. Nevertheless, the Iranian Senate approved the treaty in August. It remains uncertain, however, whether Afghanistan will ratify the treaty in spite of continuing improvement in the relations of the two neighboring countries after the formation of the new republic under President Daud Khan. Even if no ratification is forthcoming, the fact still remains that Iran, in this case as in other cases mentioned before, resorted to the instrument of diplomacy in an attempt to settle another major dispute with a regional power.

Economics

No discussion of the instruments of Iranian foreign policy today can escape its economic instruments. Iran's resurgence in world politics has paralleled unprecedented expansion and diversification of its foreign economic activities. These activities embrace a wide variety of fields ranging from trade, energy and investment to aid. Granted the interplay between economic, diplomatic and military instruments of any state's foreign policy, I shall attempt here to identify the principal economic instruments of Iranian foreign policy.

Oil

Oil is not merely Iran's greatest natural resource and source of revenues. It is also a major instrument of its foreign policy. Iran's age-old national goal of controlling the oil was achieved finally in 1973 when, according to Prime Minister Hoveyda, the Nationalization Act was implemented "in its fullest sense after a lapse of 23 years." During most of those 23 years, Iran pursued two separate but interrelated oil policies. First, the Shah set the goal of transforming the NIOC into an "integrated international oil company." Toward this goal, the NIOC was enabled by the Petroleum Law of 1957 to enter into a wide variety of relations with foreign private and public corporations regarding the exploration and exploitation of Iranian oil outside the agreement area, operated primarily by the Consortium. Second, Iran sought through extensive negotiations with the Consortium during the 1960s and early 1970s to increase its oil production and revenues. In spite of all the adjustments in Iran-Consortium relations over the years, the decision-making power rested in the hands of the Consortium. The 1973 agreement satisfied Iran's historic quest for the control of the oil industry as an instrument of its own policy without prejudice to the established interests of the Consortium as a buyer of Iranian oil.

Instrumentality of oil and gas takes many forms in Iran's relations with numerous foreign private and public corporations, and directly with a variety of states. Oil and gas have been used to serve Iran's foreign policy goals in maintaining not only its basic economic ties with the West, but also in forging new ties with the Soviet Union and East European states. Oil has also served Iran in creating new, or expanding old, ties with Third World countries.

Iran possesses a cosmopolitan network of ties with the Americans, British, Dutch, French, Germans, Italians, Indians, Spanish and others. These ties take the form of partnership such as with Agip Mineraria and Pan American Petroleum Company, or contracts such as with the ERAP group, or investment in refining and marketing. This latter type of transaction was attempted without success with Ashland Oil Company. More recently, Iran has been negotiating with the Shell Oil Company for investment in a gasoline-marketing network in the United States. Barter agreements for oil sale with Bulgaria, Czechoslovakia, Romania, and gas sale to, and through, the Soviet Union, are examples of deals with the Socialist states. Assistance to Libya and Algeria in petroleum technology and the interest in exchanging oil technology with Mexico are examples of transactions with Third World countries. Iran's cooperation with the OPEC countries of the Persian Gulf in reaching the Tehran agreement with the international oil companies in 1971 and in negotiating with the oil-consuming countries in 1975, are further examples of the instrumentality of oil in Iranian policy toward Third World states.

Trade

Trade is another major instrument of Iranian foreign policy. It has served, for example, the objective of Iran's "normalization" of its relations with the Soviet Union. Given the unsatisfactory nature of traditional Irano-Soviet Union trade relations, stabilization of trade and transit relations between Iran and the Soviet Union in recent years has been a major achievement. The earliest breach in the pattern of Iran's traditionally unstable trade with the Soviet Union was made in 1964, followed by major trade agreements in 1967 and 1970. The 1970 agreement is to last for a period of five years, during which time the value of trade between the two countries is to increase over $1 billion. As viewed from Tehran at the time of the signing of the agreement, Soviet markets would constitute the largest single market for Iranian manufactured goods. The creation of a mixed Irano-Soviet company in the same year was for the purpose of facilitating transit trade. The prospects for transit trade improved in 1971 with the establishment of a regular shipping line between the two neighboring countries.

Cooperation

Economic cooperation is another major instrument of Iranian foreign policy. It has also served, for example, Iran's objective of closer relations with the Soviet Union ever since 1966. In that year, Iran signed an agreement with the Soviet Union for the construction of a steel mill, a gas pipeline and a mechanical engineering plant, which were completed in 1973, 1970 and 1972, respectively. In 1971 also, the construction of hydraulic engineering installations on the Aras River was completed. This year (1975), Iran signed the largest economic cooperation agreement with the Soviet Union. It includes a joint venture to build a large paper complex in Russia with Iranian credit.

Economic cooperation has also constituted a major instrument of Iranian policy toward the United States. For example, this year (1975), Iran and the United States signed a mammoth economic agreement that calls for $15 billion of non-oil trade, including, among other items, the purchase of nuclear plants, military equipment, prefabricated factories, apartments and hospitals. Other examples may be cited from Iran's purchase of nuclear plants from France and Germany as well as the economic cooperation agreement signed this year (1975) between Iran and Britain.

Finally, economic aid is the most recent instrument of Iranian foreign policy. To be sure, this new instrument has been strengthened by the spectacular rise of oil prices after the October War, but the Iranian foreign-aid program was established before that war. Iran's own rate of economic growth made its foreign aid program possible. This same growth made it possible as early as 1967 for the United States to terminate its long-standing direct economic aid to Iran. As President Johnson stated at the time, the termination of the aid was celebrated as an achievement, not as an ending. He declared it "a milestone in Iran's continuing progress." Iran's direct economic aid to, and cooperation with, an increasing number of Third World states such as Egypt, Senegal, India and Afghanistan, to mention a few, are matched by its various proposals to aid the poor nations. For example, it proposed in 1974 the creation of a development fund in cooperation with the International Bank for Reconstruction and Development and the International Monetary Fund.

Summary

In conclusion, let us see what propositions I can reasonably make on the basis of this broad and brief discussion of the major instruments of Iranian foreign policy.

1. The instruments of Iranian foreign policy have been expanded and diversified in the last decade. Contrary to prevalent opinion, this expansion and diversification is not confined to military instruments. Diplomatic and economic instruments have undergone even more dramatic changes. In the economic field, trade, economic cooperation and aid serve Iran's objectives at the international and regional levels as evidenced by its unprecedented economic ties with not only an ever-increasing number of states but also with a wide variety of private and public foreign corporations. Diplomatically, Iran has established new ties not only with a variety of states of different ideological persuasions and political systems, but, more important, has resorted boldly to various techniques of diplomacy for the pacific settlement of age-old, as well as new, disputes.

2. No valid proposition can be offered at the present time regarding the relative use of military as contrasted with diplomatic instruments of Iranian foreign policy. A couple of observers have suggested recently that in regional and local relations Iran "emphasizes might in derogation of diplomacy." My fundamental objection to this hypothesis is that it is not supported by evidence. As I discussed before, Iran has resorted to the use of force only in two instances during the last decade. In the case of landing forces on the three Persian Gulf islands two fundamental points must be recalled. First, the politico-military situation at the time did not seem to provide a viable alternative for the protection of Iran's vital interests in the area. Second, the recourse to force was a matter of last resort in view of the fact that it followed many months of protracted and eventually unsuccessful negotiations regarding the two Tunbs. Furthermore, the landing on the island of Abu Musa was in compliance with an agreement made with the Sheikh of Sharjeh. In the case of Oman,

Iran's military involvement began at the invitation of Sultan Oabus. No question of resort to diplomatic means could arise and hence no derogation of diplomacy could make sense. Neither of these two cases, nor the decision of Iran to avoid a war with Iraq, provides a sufficient basis for generalization about the relationship of military to diplomatic instruments in Iranian foreign policy. Just as I do not believe that the actual practice of Iran *as yet* supports the proposition that Iran emphasizes might in derogation of diplomacy, I do not find it possible to suggest the opposite, either. There is simply not enough evidence at the present time. Prudence suggests greater caution in making generalizations until actual practice over a longer span of time can produce, in the future, observable patterns of behavior as a basis for reliable propositions.

3. As I look ahead, there is little doubt that the instruments of Iranian foreign policy will continue to mulitply and diversify in the near future as they have in the last decade. And as this growth and diversifying of the instruments of foreign policy proceed apace with Iran's increasing power and activities in world affairs, they will have to face new challenges. In concluding a project of nearly 20 years of research and writing on Iranian foreign policy, I have recently suggested elsewhere that the most profound future challenge of Iranian foreign policy will be philosophical. During the last decade, Iran has insisted, quite successfully, on the protection of its national interests, but is there any scheme of higher values that Iran's emerging power will try to serve? This is a normative question that, I submit, should concern Iranian thinkers far more in the future. The founders of ancient Iran were concerned with normative problems. According to Adda B. Bozeman, the Iranians posed "for the first time in historically known terms" the problem of moral principles and national interest in foreign policy. I suggest that the Iranian heritage contains the germ of the notion that Santayana calls "the harmony of the whole which does not destroy the vitality of the parts." The incessant quest for national autonomy within the international system inclines Iran, like all modernizing nations in this age of nationalism, to emphasize today the vitality of the parts. But the real question for now and tomorrow may be whether Iran can develop out of its own rich and cosmopolitan heritage and the realities of an increasingly interdependent world a concept of order that would simultaneously contribute to greater harmony of the international community as well as the Iranian goal of a Great Civilization. I conclude this essay, therefore, with a call for the study of philosophy of Iranian foreign policy.

Comments and Discussion

In "Iran's International Position: An Interpretation," Ahmad Ghoreyshi observed that security is a fundamental concern of Iran's foreign policy, especially in light of its strategic location and its status as a major oil-producing state. Iran's long involvement with the Soviet Union is a persistent feature of Iran's foreign relations; Iran has often been subjected in the past to pressure from her northern neighbor and has been invaded and occupied by Russia three times within this century. Although relations with the Soviet Union have been stable since 1962, when Iran agreed to prohibit stationing of U.S. missiles, the existence of a giant neighbor can make one nervous. Mr. Ghoreyshi then commented on Iran's place in the Middle Eastern power system. Iran has a great stake in the Persian Gulf. When Britain announced its withdrawal from positions east of the Suez, Iran's first concern was the stability and security of the Persian Gulf area. If a hostile force were to take power in the Persian Gulf, Iran's very existence would be endangered. This cannot be allowed to happen. A tenet of Iranian foreign policy is military dominance in the Persian Gulf area. Mr. Ghoreyshi observed in this regard that Iran cannot count on the United States to protect its interests. (The Indo-Pakistani War of 1972 demonstrated the ineffectiveness of bilateral agreements with the United States, which allowed Pakistan to be attacked and dismantled without the slightest reaction.) Moreover, no one knows who is in charge of U.S. foreign policy. As for questions about whether Iran really needs highly sophisticated weapons, as long as these are made and sold to others in the region Iran must buy them. Iran seeks deterrent strength, Mr. Ghoreyshi emphasized—it does not plan aggression. In concluding, he observed that the outcome of the Middle East Arab-Israeli conflict will have implications for Iran: if the Israelis win overwhelmingly, the number of radical leaders in the Arab world could grow, and political instability could increase. If Israel is destroyed, relations with the Arab world may be perceived in new, dangerous ways.

In "The Instruments of Iranian Foreign Policy," Rouhollah K. Ramazani observed that Westerners and Iranians have different perceptions of the Persian Gulf situation. Westerners, he feels, incline either to the "pawn perspective" (that small states are manipulated by large states), the "powder keg perspective" (that conflict in the area may draw in the superpowers) or the "petrodollar perspective" (that whatever OPEC gains the West loses). Iranians tend to feel that the Persian Gulf countries, including Iran, are mainly interested in controlling their own destinies. Iran's determination to preserve its independence has been *the* salient feature of Iranian foreign policy for 450 years, Mr. Ramazani affirmed. Mr. Ramazani defined Iran's instruments of foreign policy as including military force, diplomacy and economic instruments, especially oil. Of these, military force, designed to preserve the security of the Persian Gulf area, is a key element. Americans will never convince Iran to reduce its military strength by using economic arguments. Iran will never consider slowing its arms purchases until there is an effective arms agreement between the United States and the Soviet Union. In Mr. Ramazani's view, Iran does not emphasize military strength to the detriment of development. Mr. Ramazani concluded by citing diplomatic initiatives taken by Iran to resolve disputes in the Persian Gulf area.

Factors Affecting Iranian Foreign Policy

An Iranian commented on the major factors identified by the opening speakers as affecting Iranian foreign policy. In his view, foreign policy is an extension of internal policies. For a long time Iran responded to initiatives taken by others, but today it is an "actor" on the world stage; it has, accordingly, adopted an active foreign policy, including initiating proposals that the Middle East be a non-nuclear zone and that the Indian Ocean be free from Big Power rivalries. Factors affecting Iranian foreign policy, in addition to those already mentioned, include détente, although Iran's own détente with the Soviet Union preceded the relaxation of tensions between the U.S.S.R. and the United States; international events, e.g., the Arab-Israeli conflict and British withdrawal from the Persian Gulf; the accomplishments of The Shah and People's Revolution, and oil revenues, which have permitted Iran both to develop internally and to fashion economic tools for use in international politics; and the increase in Iran's military strength, which is intended to deter aggression.

On the question of how détente between the United States and the Soviet Union affects Iranian foreign policy, an Iranian expressed the hope that it would be extended to the Persian Gulf area; détente is incompatible with wars of liberation and support for subversion in the Persian Gulf area. Détente is seen by Iranians as potentially beneficial, whereas conflict between the U.S.S.R. and the United States is regarded as harmful.

On the question of security in the Persian Gulf area and regional cooperation, an Iranian doubted that anyone is actively working for instability, but there are some potentially dangerous elements, including the Arab-Israeli conflict and some rebellious elements (of which the foreign-supported rebellion in Dhofar was an example), although these rebellious elements are now largely under control. Within Iran, the overthrow of the Shah and his government is inconceivable; there is only a very small force of terrorists and they are not effective. Another Iranian expressed some reservations about a pact in the Persian Gulf area that might limit Iran's freedom to act and/or involve Iran in rescue operations.

Other Iranians called for a regional economic policy and economic cooperation, as well as political and military cooperation, although there are questions to be resolved, including how to define the region and whether military cooperation should precede or follow economic cooperation.

Responding to a question about Iran's policy regarding the conflict between Russia and China, several Iranians indicated that China has not as yet openly fostered dissidence in Iran although it has supported some rebellious elements in the Persian Gulf area, e.g., the Dhofar rebels. Officially, Iran is on good terms with the U.S.S.R., with which it has some 1,500 kilometers of common frontier, but it does not perceive China as a threat, at least for the near future.

Iran's Role in World Affairs

An American asked what will happen if Iran attains all its goals and becomes strong; beyond achieving economic development and security in the Persian Gulf area, does Iran have a role in the world? In the speaker's view, new international institutions are needed "in which the strong must row the hardest"—institutions concerned with the economy and security of the whole world. Oil, like food, is in some sense a world resource. Questions relating to the use of nonrenewable resources, production policies and markets for non-oil exports should be worked out on a world basis. What Iran does about the Persian Gulf and proliferation of nuclear weapons will also be subjects for the development of new international arrangements. Iran will, and should, exercise international influence.

Iran's Growing Military Strength

A number of non-Iranian participants commented on Iran's defense program and expenditures. In an early intervention, one American, who concurred that Iran needs some level of military capability, suggested that the problem is to determine how much and what kind. The United States has not solved this problem well.

By not effectively perceiving its own security requirements, America has stimulated arms competition, including huge shipments of arms to the Middle East; America has also provoked strategic weapons competition because it sought superiority rather than a modest deterrent level of strength. Even the strongest military power will not survive unless it addresses itself to other concerns, including domestic concerns. In the speaker's view, Iran's policies have implications for its relations with the Soviet Union, where there is great apprehension that the next world crisis—five years hence—will occur in the Persian Gulf area. The Soviets see Iran as a focal point, owing largely to the quantity and types of weapons Iran is buying. Enlarged military capabilities can have bad effects, create apprehensions. The speaker observed that Americans are currently more realistic in their attitudes toward the Soviet Union than they were during either the Cold War or détente periods. They have two perspectives on the Soviet Union: the sense that nuclear war is the world's greatest danger and the feeling that domestic developments within the U.S.S.R., especially economic developments, may lead to some constraints on détente aims. There are also new factors in the world that could lead to new tensions, suggesting the need for new forms of organization. The speaker concluded that, if we are fully to appreciate security requirements, we must understand that military might alone is not the sole consideration. We must be able to understand changing factors, harmonize our economic and political structures and move toward a new international system for resolving problems. Tensions larger than balance-of-power considerations may tear the world apart.

Another American observed that the United States has been infatuated with GNP and military imperatives. In his view, Iran cannot continue its economic development programs and simultaneously expand its military power; it will have to choose between building badly needed civilian ports and naval bases.

A European acknowledged Iran's stake in the Persian Gulf area and commented on the odd fact that Americans appear to be both selling arms to Iran and decrying the arms race in the Persian Gulf. He wondered, however, (1) what Iran sees as a specific threat to which it must tailor its military force, *e.g.*, an attack by the Soviet Union or the United States, confrontation with Arab states, or terrorism and upheaval; (2) what relative strength Iran feels it must have, *e.g.*, twice as much strength as the next strongest or stronger than all together; and (3) what Iran would consider the lowest satisfactory percentage of GNP to be spent on military force. Another European joined in asking whether Iran's deterrent force was supposed to preserve it for a few days—too short a period for U.S. intervention—and whether Iran's force should be equal to the total of all Arab forces. With respect to the latter, he noted that Iran has been successful diplomatically in the region, that Saudi Arabia cannot increase its armed forces rapidly and that Iraq is very backward.

Various Iranians responded, in general, that Iran does not want to waste money on military power but it has seen events in Czechoslovakia, Pakistan and the Dominican Republic and must keep these in mind; that the stakes are too high to take chances; that Iran has no aggressive intentions, only defensive ones, but that it does not want to be threatened by other states in the region; that it is difficult to say how much military capability is needed (although it is worth noting that the October War in 1973 was fought with very modern weapons); that, generally speaking, Iran is spending less of its GNP on defense than Israel, Egypt and several other Middle Eastern countries; and that Iran's military strength has preserved peace in the Persian Gulf area.

On the question of whether Iran could hope to hold out against a Soviet invasion without nuclear arms, an Iranian indicated that Iran could not resist a Great Power aggression but, by being strong, it might deter one. Iran does not plan to develop nuclear weapons, but if other states in the Middle East, *e.g.*, Israel or Egypt, develop nuclear weapons, Iran will have to follow suit.

Relations with Other World Areas

Several speakers asked about Iran's policies toward Southeast Asia, including possible development aid programs, and Iran's expectations regarding regional economic, political, military and/or cultural relations with Western Europe. A European asked also about Iran's ties with such similar countries as Algeria and with the nonaligned world generally.

Relations with the United States

An American suggested that there is some possibility of Iran and the United States being on a collision course. If Iran increases oil prices in order to sustain its economic and military drives, this could contribute to American feelings of "strangulation" and lead to economic and political conflicts that would impair the basic relationship. If Iran could lower its sights now, a future generation of leaders—U.S.-trained—might adopt moderate positions in matters affecting the industrial nations, and Iran could play the role of a true partner in an interdependent world. (This observation prompted an Iranian to recall Porfirio Diaz' comment, "Poor Mexico, so far from God and so near to the United States!", for which he substituted a contemporary version: "Happy Iran, so near to God and so far from the United States!")

Another American doubted that relations between Iran and the United States would become strained, pointing out that Secretary of State Henry Kissinger's mention of "strangulation" referred to the oil embargo and not to oil price rises. In recent months, Iran has contributed less to America's problems than some other countries, partly because it has been investing its petrodollars outside Iran.

Two concluding Iranian speakers suggested that Iran cannot wait to see what happens in the world before it formulates a foreign policy; that it cannot be complacent about security; that it has been moderate in world affairs; that there is no evidence of a "collision course" with America (although there may be some chance of lessened friendship owing to Secretary Kissinger's remarks about "securing the sources of oil" and his subsequent explanations of these remarks); that there are more parallel interests between the United States and Iran than otherwise, especially given America's position of non-involvement in the Persian Gulf area, which it relies on Iran to secure; and that the oil price question can, and will, be discussed, with Iran always being willing to enter into a dialogue with friends.

6.   Cultural Development in Iran

Cultural Development in Iran

Ehsan Yarshater

The beginnings of Iranian culture are inevitably to be sought in Iranian myths and legends. Myths not only reflect the earliest conception of a people about the universe around them, but also their earliest responses to the challenges of their environment. Such responses could develop into a higher and more sophisticated mode of living, called culture. The cultures that developed on the plains of Mesopotamia, the valley of the Nile, in China, India, Persia and Greece in ancient times are cases in point.

The Iranian cultural development began in the Eurasian Steppes around the Caspian Sea, most probably in western central Asia, when tribal life with an agro-pastural economy prevailed. In the rich collection of myths and legends preserved for us in the Avesta, as well as in Persian epic literature, the early struggles of the Iranian people against physical hazards and hostile neighbors are clearly reflected. We read in the *Avesta* of the monstrous demon of drought, Azidahaka (which later appears in Persian and Arabic sources in the form of the tyrant Zahhak) trying to destroy the good world of Ahura Mazda. We read in the *Vendidād* of the various evils and calamities, such as extreme hot and cold winds, venomous insects, locusts and other pests, all created by Ahriman, the adversary of good creation. We read in the second chapter of the *Vendidād* about the earth extending itself three times in order to be able to house an increasing number of men, animals, plants and hearth fires. We read in Ferdowsi's *Shāhnāma* of the struggle of the earliest kings from Hushang to Jamshid against the *divs*, incarnations of hostile forces, and the success of these kings in harnessing them and utilizing them for human purposes. Tahmurath is said to have saddled Ahriman in the form of a horse and ridden on him from one end of the earth to the other, and Jamshid is reported to have subdued all manner of *divs* and employed them in building houses for men.

The events and exploits, which appear in the *Avesta* on a mythical plane and in the *Shāhnāma* in a legendary form, represent a dramatized expression of the earliest fears, hopes, struggles, reverses and triumphs of the early Iranian tribes in their effort to meet the challenges of their environment and in developing a distinct form of culture.

A more conscious account of the development of this culture is found in the early parts of the *Shāhnāma*, where the Pishdadi kings are credited with having initiated the various acts or stages of civilization.

For instance, we read that Hushang was the first to extract iron from ore, to draw water from rivers for irrigation, and to instruct people how to sow seeds and harvest crops, whereas before him people lived on fruits alone. His successor, Tahmurath, released the secret of writing from demons, and Jamshid succeeded in making metal weapons and in spinning cotton, wool, slik and floss, and in weaving cloth. He divided the people into four classes, according to their professions, and with the help of the *divs* erected houses with stone.

Such accounts, although obviously late in origin, present a measure of rationalization about the development of culture. The *divs* may represent in this context alien peoples whom the Iranians defeated, subdued and employed in the course of their progress from a localized and primitive society towards the military and political leadership of the ancient Middle East.

It is to be noted that from the earliest times the Iranian people had a clear concept of themselves as a distinct nation and took pride in their identity. This is clear from the *Avesta* where Iran-vēj, the homeland of the Iranians, is depicted as the favorite land of the gods. It is even clearer in Darius' inscriptions, where he takes pride not only in his tribal affiliation as a Persian, but also in being an Aryan, literally, "noble." In the national legends, Iranshahr, the kingdom of Iran, constitutes the heart of *Khunirath*, the central clime of the world, which was given to Iraj, the favorite son of Fereydun, when he divided the world among his three sons. The Sasanians had a very clear notion of their identity as the kings of a well-defined nation, that of Iran, and they clearly distinguished between Iran and other countries and regions under their rule. The latter they called *Anērān, i.e.,* "non-Iran."

It is often said that nationalism, as we know it today, is an importation of the West during the 19th century. There is some justification for this, since Islam tended to blur the older national boundaries, but in pre-Islamic Iran a very strong sense of nationalism, nurtured by common aspirations and ideals, a common tradition and common ethnic and linguistic background, prevailed. This nationalism did not entirely fade out in the Islamic commonwealth. During long centuries it continued its simmering existence, until finally the Safavids, almost inadvertently, gave it a more dramatic expression in the 16th century through the formation of a national state. The Persian language and the *Shāhnāma*, which embodies the myths, legends and historical memories of a proud past, stood during all these centuries as pillars of an unmistakable identity.

I have particularly emphasized Iranian nationalism and its reflection in legend, history and literature because Iranian culture in the course of its development has been exposed to a number of strong influences from neighboring traditions, as it has been itself an agent of widespread impact outside of its boundaries. It is this conscious notion of a distinct identity that lends definition to the cultural endeavors of the people in the midst of a multitude of adoptions and adaptations.

It is not given to every culture to achieve the same degree of strength in all branches of artistic and intellectual expression. In India and Greece, for instance, whereas calligraphy had little import, sculpture reached an extraordinary level of expression, and in China music and dance did not rival the art of the brush or that of the potter, and it is a well-known fact that French music cannot compete with the fame of French architecture or painting.

In Persia, secular philosophy never achieved prominence and remained mostly subordinated to theology, and in pre-Islamic Persia, painting does not show an inspiring record. Even in Islamic times Persian painting, despite its extraordinary beauty and distinction, displays limited scope.

In discussing the cultural development in Iran during historical times it would be useful at the outset to distinguish the salient features of the culture and point out areas where national effort has been more successful. In order to facilitate discussion, we may consider responses to spiritual, material and aesthetic needs separately.

The Spiritual Culture

In a general survey of Persian cultural history, our attention is unfailingly drawn to the development of religious thought. Persia has been not only the birthplace of one of the earliest higher religions, namely Zoroastrianism, but also a continuing source of religious thinking and contribution. A religion hardly ever arises in a vacuum. It is generally a radical reform of previous religious thought and practices and a remodeling of spiritual concepts that we call a new religion. Moses, Zoroaster, Buddha, Jesus and Mohammed all fashioned a new religion on existing foundations. What social, economic and political conditions anticipate the rise of a new set of spiritual principles is outside the scope of this paper. But in the case of the all-embracing religions, such as Zoroastrianism and Islam, and unlike Confucianism and Buddhism, we are dealing with not only an expression of faith but also a system of beliefs, precepts and laws that purport to regulate all aspects of human conduct. Zoroastrianism, accordingly, is to be regarded as the embodiment of a set of coordinated religious, social, ethical and legal precepts sanctioned by metaphysical beliefs. For more than a millennium this religion held the Iranian society together, providing it with ethical underpinnings, social stability, an ideal for the present and hope for the future.

Here we might consider some of the characteristics of Iranian religious thought and try to follow their implications in the course of Iranian history.

I have already referred to the concept of the *divs* in the Iranian myths. The opposition between good and evil seems to characterize

Iranian thinking from pre-Zoroastrian times. Whether this dualism, which manifests itself clearly in the *Yashts* of the *Avesta* on a mythical level, has its roots in the raids of opposing neighboring tribes, or in the hostility between a nascent agricultural society and the adjacent nomadic marauders, whether it derives from the conflicts between the desired and the permissible in the mind of the people, or whether it reflects hostility between the believers of two opposing religions, need not detain us here. The fact remains that Iranian religious thought is strongly colored by a dualistic concept of the universe. In explaining the nature and origin of evil—a question that has preoccupied theologians everywhere— Zoroastrianism adopted a highly original stand. The existence and independence of evil, whether moral, physical or social, is clearly recognized and attributed to Ahriman, the Evil Spirit, who, unlike Satan, is not a creation of Good *(Ahura Mazda)*, but his adversary. He is out to destroy the peaceful world of Hormozd and manages to pollute it with death, diseases, poisonous creatures and other assorted pestilences. The Zoroastrian theologians are spared the well-nigh-impossible task of explaining evil as a creation of God, a task imposed by the strict monotheism of higher Semitic religions. Our world is pictured instead as an admixture of good and evil and as a battlefield of the forces of Hormozd and Ahriman in a continuing flight for the ultimate victory, which is projected to belong to Hormozd.

This basic, dualistic concept is also the core of Mani's religious system, which was strongly influenced by Zoroastrianism. Although widely different in outlook from Zoroaster, Mani, too, embraced the view of the dichotomy of the two principles, that of light and darkness. The aim of his precepts, like those of Zoroaster, was to eliminate evil and purify the world of its contamination. However, his strong ascetic tendency and his pessimistic view of the world as reflected in his cosmology is a far cry from the positive view of life in Zoroaster's preaching.

The little we know of the doctrine of Mazdak, a religious reformer of the late 5th century and early 6th century, shows the same dualistic notion of the world with a strong ethical bias against social inequities.

Islam, however, preached a different outlook and its adamant monotheism made the association of any other gods with Allah *(shirk)* the gravest of all sins. The most drastic change of concept, after the advent of Islam, was for a Zoroastrian now to believe that all creatures were created by one and the same God, a notion that had been held unthinkable for so long. Persian theologians endeavored valiantly, along with others in the Moslem world, to prove the necessity of evil and to explain away its apparent contradiction to the will of God.

When Islam conquered Persia, it looked for a time as if creative thought in the spiritual field had lost its vigor, but soon this proved to be a mistaken view. In the wake of the downfall of the Persian Empire we notice the emergence of a series of religio-political movements, some with reformist Zoroastrian tendencies, some displaying Islamic influence, and yet others showing a Mazdakite spirit. But the same latent causes that brought about the collapse of the Sasanian state and its allied church most probably also prevented any of these movements from taking root. In the end Islam emerged triumphant and the Persians, in the spirit of good faith, channeled their contributions toward the enrichment of a new mode of thinking. The simple precepts of Islam, which for a while had gone forth by the inspired strength of a rising religion, now needed amplification and philosophical justification in order to meet the challenge of more sophisticated minds. In this task, which gave birth to Islamic theology, Persians made vital contributions. They were prominent among the Mutazilite and Shicite theologians, as well as among the groups like the *Ikhwān al-Safā* (Brethren of Purity), who aimed at spreading knowledge and enlightenment. But perhaps their major contribution is revealed in the development of Islamic mystical thought.

Historically, Islamic mysticism rose from among the circles of men of outstanding piety, who, in seeking the true spirit of Islam, shunned the pleasures of the world and focused on purifying their souls as a way of attaining truth and approaching God. Their broader interpretation of Islamic precepts enabled them to be more tolerant and more humble, while devoting themselves to the love of God and the service of men. In Persia the inspiration of divine love moved the poets and writers among them to produce works of great beauty, which have enriched Persian literature to a great extent.

In the course of its development, this mysticism embraced a mode of thinking which had a long tradition in Persia, namely the gnostic way of thought *(Irfān)*. Briefly stated, gnostic creeds are based on the belief that man's soul, being of heavenly or divine substance and a stranger in this world, has been entrapped within our bodies and chained by our earthly needs. Like any living being that is cut off from its native home, it seeks to return to its origin but only too often is its vision darkened by the temptations of the senses and its true path lost by neglect. In order for the soul to rise from the abyss of its worldly existence and soar to the heights of freedom and salvation, it is in need of a savior, a savior who will awaken it from its slumber, reveal to it its divine origin, and show it the way to redemption. Generally, gnostic religions, of which Manichaeism is a highly developed one, postulate the captivity of the soul in the world of matter, the necessity of a redeemer and the enlightening knowledge by which salvation could be achieved. This illuminating "knowledge" *(gnosis, cirfān)*, is not scholastic learning but an inspired recognition of the nature of one's soul and its origin that can be imparted by an inspired leader or mentor. Once this illumination is gained, a spiritual journey may be undertaken, which guides the soul through various stages, until it is completely divested of material attachments and becomes impervious to the temptations of the world, and finally achieves divine character. These are, in fact, also the underlying principles of Islamic *cirfān*. In a sense, *cirfān* is a unifying element in the religious thinking of the pre-Islamic Middle East and the Islamic world. It can be easily seen that the basic concept in this mode of thinking is a belief in the duality of two divergent principles: matter and spirit, body and soul, light and darkness or good and evil, a belief, which, as I pointed out earlier, is a characteristic feature of Persian religious thought. A Sufi is engaged in a continual struggle against his evil self (*nafs* or *nafs-i ammāra*). He is constantly being tempted and ambushed by the villain within him, his id, to borrow a Freudian term, which seeks to plunge him deeper and deeper into the pit of worldly attachments and away from the loftiness and serenity of his original existence. To harness, emaciate and efface the self successfully is the principal task of a Sufi.

A second feature of Iranian spiritual life concerns the place of man in the universe. Here, however, historical changes seem to have affected the original thinking of the Iranians more drastically. In the Zoroastrian system man was created by Ahura Mazda and was conceived as his helper in the struggle against evil. He was subject to the temptations of Ahriman and was harassed and troubled by him, but he was free to choose the path of righteousness in order to defeat Ahriman's designs. This choice required him to be morally upright and to enhance the prosperity of the world by irrigating the land, planting trees, sowing grain and bringing forth children. This optimistic view of the world and the license to enjoy life stand in contrast to the original tenets of most religions, if not all. But the vicissitudes of Iranian history have not made for rigid attitudes. The basic optimism met in Zoroastrian religion developed at a time of great vitality and drive. In the third century A.D., on the other hand, the Manichaean view gave vent to an entirely different picture of man. He was conceived by Mani as having been devised by the demons in order to contain and confine the divine light stolen by them in a prison of lust and greed. The best way to regain one's soul and set it free, thought Mani, was to ignore, weaken and destroy the body. The normal acts of living such as marriage, the breeding of children and the making of food and earning a livelihood, were only reluctantly tolerated.

Much of this attitude was later mirrored, as we have seen, in the thinking of Persian mystics. The attention of the theologians, however, was focused mostly on the question of whether man was endowed with a free will or whether his actions were predestined and, if so, as most of the Muslims came eventually to believe by their understanding of the Koran, how was one to account for the punishment and reward attached to man's deeds. The attitude of the Persian thinkers has remained mostly ambiguous in this respect. Here the thinking of individuals like Saadi, a preacher by profession, and Jalal al-Din Rumi, a teacher and educator, are perhaps of greater significance than those of systematic philosophers and theologians, since they reflect more clearly the natural views of the people with all their insights and contradictions. Although the prevalence of the will of God and the inability of man to change the dictates of fate were generally recognized, the necessity of endeavor was also emphasized.

A consideration of Iranian philosophy need not keep us long. Iranian response to spiritual needs has been expressed within the context of religious thought. Therefore philosophy, as divorced from religious beliefs, made little headway. This doesn't mean that philosophy was neglected. In fact *hekmat* continued to be one of the most respected intellectual exercises in Islamic Persia. It is sufficient to recall the names of Farabi, Avicenna and Mulla Sadra to realize that some of the greatest names in Islamic philosophy belong to the annals of Persian achievements. Only it is to be noted that Islamic philosophy generally borrowed the Greek method of argumentation and logic in order to prove the principles inspired by Islam.

The Material Culture

Not being an economic historian or an anthropologist, I would leave it to others to trace the development of material culture in Iran. I would only venture that in the sciences, which have to do mostly with the mastery of nature and the improvement of the material life, the Iranian contribution ranks high. Again, this can be demonstrated by recalling the names of the celebrated scientists who were born or nurtured in Iran and contributed to the scientific achievement of the Islamic world. Among these may be mentioned the encyclopaedic scientist Biruni, the mathematicians and astronomers Abu Macshar Balkhi, Musa Khwarazmi, Omar-i Khayyami and Ghiath al-Din Jamshid Kashani, and the physicians Avicenna and Razi, all of whom are internationally recognized and have a place in the history of science. The fact that Persian science has an eclectic basis and has benefited from Babylonian, Greek and Indian sciences does not detract from its significance since, here, as in a number of other areas, the Persian contribution has been not only one of innovation but most importantly one of synthesis and systemization, one of shaping a comprehensive whole out of diverse elements.

The Aesthetic Culture

I should like now to focus on the response given in Iran to the aesthetic needs.

Our attention is drawn first to the attractive painted figures and geometrical designs on ancient pottery found, among other sites, in Sialk, Susa, and Tepe Gian. These represent a high degree of artistic perception and a sophisticated sense of rhythm and stylization. Although this art belongs to people who inhabited Persia prior to the coming of the Aryans, it provided an artistic base for the Aryan conquerors, once they settled down to a sedentary life and absorbed the native traditions.

The artistic accomplishments of the Aryans arrest us suddenly with the rising columns and graceful remains of the Achaemenid monuments in Pasargedae, Persepolis and Susa. They represent the culminating point of ancient Middle Eastern art and also its last brilliant phase. The splendid columns, polished sculpture and spacious halls of Persepolis palaces stand as a visual monument to the power of the Achaemenid kings of kings and the glory of a vast empire. Here again, the artistic merit lies less in innovative elements or processes, but true to the Achaemenid spirit of universality and peace, in creating a harmonious whole out of diverse traditions. In Achaemenid architecture the Mesopotamian, Egyptian, Elamite, Anatolian, Urartan and Greek contributions are combined and harmonized in an unprecedented manner. It is the artistic conception and the successful synthesis in these monuments that constitute their claim to greatness.

The Greek rule in Persia and numerous Greek colonies and city-states after the fall of the Achaemenids naturally could not leave Persian life and art unaffected, and the impact of Hellenism can be seen in Parthian coins, in the Greek alphabet of Kushan inscriptions, in the Buddhist art of Gandhara and in such monuments as the temple of Anahita near Kangavar. Xenophobia is not a feature of Persian culture and the ease with which Persia has adopted without prejudice what had seemed useful or appealing has been a source of enrichment to all Persian art. But this eagerness and ease of adoption has been always balanced by a conscious control and an unerring artistic taste that time and again have succeeded in turning a borrowed feature into an element of national art. Otherwise Persian art could not have claimed that distinction it possesses. The most salient examples are the adaptation of Chinese features in painting and pottery and of Arabic prosody in poetry, areas in which Persian art is justly renowned.

An awakening of the national consciousness is the hallmark of Sasanian attitude. The Greek features of the Parthian period, a period the Sasanians liked to picture as one of the Dark Ages, were gradually shed and a national policy inspired the unison of church and state. And yet, even in this period Persia did not remain insensitive to Greek science and philosophy, to Indian mathematics and to Byzantine art and military and administrative processes. True to her artistic and scientific spirit, she resisted prejudice against the achievements of other nations, while strongly defending a vigorous national policy.

By the end of the Sasanian period, some 14 centuries had elapsed from the days when the Iranians fashioned their first empire under the Medes. During these centuries they created four powerful empires, with many military and administrative feats to their credit. For about 200 years, under the Achaemenids, they ruled practically over the whole of the ancient Middle East and, sometimes, over much more. Towards the 7th century A.D., however, the country had exhausted its energy. Its institutions had become rigid and the dedication of its leaders to public purposes had weakened. Had not the Muslim armies struck from without, the empire would probably have crumbled from within. As it was, the Muslim forces rid the Persians of a collection of burdensome institutions and hackneyed procedures, while presenting them with a simple code of religious, ethical and social principles, the attraction of which could not be lost, in the long run, on the majority of the Persians.

It took about 200 years, however, before the Persians could recover from the impact of the astounding events and the profound changes attendant on the acceptance of Islam, and collect themselves in the context of a new mode of life. From the 9th century A.D., local dynasties began to be established on Persian soil and to provide generous support for the arts.

Under the Samanids (903–99) eastern Persia pioneered in a renaissance of Persian art and literature, giving Greater Khorasan a lead over the rest of the country. With the injunction of Islam against the making of images, sculpture was not allowed to develop, and wall painting, which had had a remarkable tradition in central Asia and pre-Islamic Persia, suffered somewhat. Painted pottery in all forms and colors, as well as architecture, were among the earlier arts that flourished. Book arts, that is, calligraphy, binding, illumination and illustrative painting, commonly called miniature, were naturally slower to develop, since they had to wait for the currency of Arabic script. One should bear in mind, however, that from the time of the Omayyads and throughout the Abbasid period, the artistic accomplishments of the Persians should be viewed not only through what was done in Persia, or in Persian, but also through major contributions made by the Iranian peoples to the development of Islamic art in general. The Abbasid court drew heavily on Persian precedence, not only in administrative procedures, but also in the arts and in refinements of court life. Much of the artistic work achieved in Baghdad, Basra, Kufa and Samarra derived directly or indirectly from a Persian milieu.

Rather than tracing the development of various arts, I would comment on some of their general features.

Although Persian pictorial art is grounded in figurative painting, it does not, generally, aim at a strictly realistic rendering of nature. Accordingly, the rules of perspective and the use of shadow and light are not attempted in traditional Persian painting, nor is the expression of emotions in the facial features and the movements of the characters a preoccupation of the artist. On the other hand, the artist takes great pains to decorate his painting with details of architectural design, clothes, carpets and flowers in order to heighten our aesthetic pleasure. Again, the artist shows an extraordinary gift for the use of bright and pure colors with a sense of harmony unsurpassed in the arts of the Islamic world. A decorative tendency and a strong sense of color harmony, in fact, characterize the visual arts of Persia. Since Persian painting is by and large illustrative, it does not leave much room for abstraction, but in textile design, pottery, tile work and illumination, ingenious and extensive use of stylization and abstraction is made with best decorative effect.

Ornamentation is also an obvious attribute of Persian music and poetry, as I have tried to demonstrate elsewhere.* Ornament should not be considered an accident of Persian art but an integral part of its essence. If Persian poetry, music or painting is robbed of its ornamental aspect, it often loses not only its attraction but also its character. Decoration, in fact, may be considered the most emphatic tendency of Persian art in general.

A third characteristic of Persian art may be called lyricism. Applied to different media, of course, this characteristic assumes different aspects. In poetry, it denotes the passionate but controlled and measured expression of intimate emotions with appropriate imagery and effective orchestration of sounds. In painting, it is seen mostly not in the subject matter, but in the indulgence of the artist in the flow of the dancing lines and meandering curves. The rapturous flow of the line finds its most exquisite expression in the cursive style of calligraphy (shikasta), which marks the delicate and dextrous movement of the artist's pen. The arabesques seen on the domes of Persian mosques or on Persian metal work or carpets are other instances of lyricism of line and design.

We must now turn our attention to the Persian literary arts, which have a special place in the history of Persian culture. Of these, poetry holds a unique position, not only among the Persian arts, but also among the literatures of the Islamic world. The earliest Avestan hymns, those of Zoroaster himself, as well as the hymns to various Iranian deities in the Yashts of the Avesta, are metrical, and not uncommonly endowed with beautiful imagery. There is also appealing poetry to be found among the Manichaean hymns. But it is in the Islamic period that poetry rises to unprecedented heights and gives the world one of its richest literatures. What gives Persian poetry its unique status is that, apart from its poetic

---

*"Affinities Between Persian Poetry and Music," Studies in Art and Literature of the Middle East, ed. by P. Chelkowski (Salt Lake City: The Middle East Center, University of Utah) and (New York: New York University Press, 1974, pp. 59–78).

quality, it encompasses a wealth of ideas, often in succinct form. Nowhere is the Persian experience of life and Persian wisdom better expressed than in its poetry. In other words, Persian poetry not only responds to our aesthetic needs, but also engages, to a large measure, our intellect, although it must be emphasized that its merit depends primarily on its quality as art, rather than as thought.

The salient genres of Persian poetry may be briefly discussed here. One is epic poetry. Epic poetry developed early in Islamic Persia on the models of the epic literature of Sasanian times. Such a model is still preserved in the *Ayādegār-i Zarērān*, a short poem about a battle between the Iranians and the Turanians during the reign of Gushtasp, in which Zarēr, the warrior brother of the king, is struck down by the enemy and then duly avenged by his young son. The epic art soon reached its highest moment in the latter part of the 10th century with Ferdowsi's *Shāhnāma*. The poem, which has been a pillar of the Persian language and a living monument of Persian nationalism, is counted among the few great world epics. The creation of a great epic requires not only heroic content and a masterful poet, but also a particular taste and temperament, which seems to have been confined to few nations. Despite the fact that Persian literature has had a wide influence in countries from India to Turkey, with the model of the *Shāhnāma* and other epics there for everyone to read and appreciate, no other nation of the Islamic world has produced an epic remotely comparable to the work of Ferdowsi or even to the romances of Nizami.

From the point of view of content, the *Shāhnāma* is a comprehensive history of Iran, from the beginning of kingship to the fall of the Sasanian Empire. No distinction is made between myth, legend and factual history, since to Iranians history was not a mere collection of facts, but an enlightening record of significant events, whether factual or legendary. The theme of the *Shāhnāma* is the preservation and the integrity of the Iranian sovereignty and the defense of its boundaries against its enemies. As pictured in the *Shāhnāma*, this is done through the efforts of a succession of Iranian monarchs, who symbolize the unity of the nation and the national virtues. To the Persians, history has always been an instrument of social cohesion and moral instruction. The *Shāhnāma* and its predecessor, the Sasanian *Khwadaynāmag*, aimed not at a lifeless record of details but at a rhetorical, entertaining and edifying record of the Persian experience. It aimed at maintaining the national ideals by the example of the deeds and the conduct of its kings and heroes. In a sense, the *Shāhnāma* is a long hymn to honor valor, widsom and patriotism, virtues that were conceived in the springtime of the nation's career and sustained during its heroic age.

Lyric poetry, another important genre of Persian literature, had its beginning also under the Samanids and reached its zenith with Hafiz in the 14th century. Persian poets have never tired of singing the praises of love and describing the beauty of the beloved in passionate terms. But lyric poetry of Persia would not have enriched our experience so remarkably were it not for the fact that it is also a storehouse of mystical thinking, subtle social satire and ethical comments. It is these aspects of lyrical poetry that make it the most revealing expression of Persian thought and sentiment.

A few words about the court poetry, another major genre of Persian literature, may be in order. It has been fashionable of late to decry the works of the court poets on moral grounds. Although we may not cherish their flattering attitude toward unjust and tyrannical patrons, the literary value of such poetry cannot be made dependent on the moral and social assumptions of a differing age. The court poets of Persia were, like most medieval artisans, in need of patrons to support their art. It is to the credit of the Persian courts and their courtiers that they did provide this patronage throughout the Islamic period, thereby affording added impetus for the development of literary arts and their refinement. If we don't approve of the content of court panegyrics, we cannot fault the poets on the quality of their art and craftsmanship. Persia, having had a tradition of monarchy from the beginning of its history, has relied, until the turn of the century, chiefly on the patronage of the courts for the maintenance and advancement of its arts and sciences. So strong has the tradition of court patronage been that the foreign invaders from central Asia who so often conquered Iran and ruled the country, ended up by becoming mostly not only generous patrons of poets and writers but also frequently the practitioners of Persian art and poetry.

The Decline of Persian Arts

As is the case with political power, artistic energy and creative vitality cannot be maintained forever. There comes a time, at last, when exhaustion sets in, creative energy dries up and derivative art becomes the order of the day. Persian culture has proved no exception to this general rule. After rising to the height of its excellence with Hafiz, Persian poetry embarked almost immediately on a course of decline, even though good poetry was still produced and, in some respects, the Isfahani school represented a conscious effort to breathe new life into a weary and debilitated poetry. The visual arts still continued strong in the earlier parts of the Safavid period, but after Shah Abbas the Great, whose period presented a *tour de force* of political, economic and artistic effort, they, too, began to show an all-too-obvious downhill trend. Even the religious zeal and enthusiasm that had bestowed a new gleam to the spiritual life of the country, when Shiism was made the official faith of the land, could not be maintained at its high pitch after Shah Abbas and

Iran: Past, Present and Future

religious writing settled mostly in lifeless commentaries and annotations of the works of earlier jurists and theologians. The collapse of the Safavid power symbolized the exhaustion of a brilliant cultural effort that had sustained itself for nearly 1,000 years after Islam.

The Qajars inherited a weakened tradition and a declining culture that war further threatened by internal strife, foreign interventions and an increasing absence of dedication and public responsibility. The decline, which was noticeable in all spheres of cultural, social and political life, was not lost on some of the intelligent and public-spirited figures of the Qajar period. The solution to the social ills was sought variously by attempts at removing the Qajars from the throne, at effecting a union among the Islamic countries, at adhering to inspiring religious movements or at initiating educational and administrative reforms on the model of the West. In the literary world, a turning away from the jaded style of the Safavid poets led to the revival of the style of some of the old masters. In the arts, the Western examples were allowed an ever-widening influence. But in the end, nothing short of a revolution that led eventually to the elimination of the Qajars from the throne and prepared the way for a new start could stop the downhill trend.

Iran's Cultural Identity and the Present Day World

Ehsan Naraghi

For years and years my heart demanded
the cup of Jamshid*; but my heart
itself was what it demanded from another.

(Hafiz)

The Essential Elements of Iranian Culture

Born at the crossroads of different civilizations, Iranian culture, whose quintessence reaches us through the intermingling of many different beliefs and traditions, appears as a distinct entity. To speak about it in a few words, and to discover its characteristics and essential spirit, we have to look closely at three of its most significant elements—religion, language and the pre-Islamic past.

Religion

The religion of the country is Shiite Islam which, though true to the basic principles of Islam, advocates the belief that the 12 Imams, descendants of the Prophet, were the sole repositories of the true faith and the only ones able to lead Moslem communities. The Iranians have always shown profound veneration for the Prophet's family, especially for his son-in-law, Ali, and the latter's offspring, Imam Hossein, who had attacked the legitimacy of the temporal and spiritual reign of the Omayyad caliphs. The martyrdom of Hossein kindled the wrath of the Shiites against the political and religious domination of the caliphs. Comparable to the

---

*According to Persian legend, the entire universe was reflected in the cup of Jamshid, making it as yearned for as was the Holy Grail in Western civilization.

separation between Rome and Byzantium, the Shiah faith introduced an original spiritual element with Islam. The 12th Imam (Mhadi) is at present in hiding, and his reappearance will herald the end of the Shiites' sufferings and the reign of justice and equity throughout the world. The disappearance and the reappearance of the Imam signify an undying hope among the faithful. The notion of the Imam in hiding points to a virtual, underlying presence that, from a social point of view, makes up for the imperfections in the community today and, where belief is concerned, implies a more personal dimension to a faith in which mysticism occupies an important place.

The Iranian Literary Renaissance and the Cultural Influence of the Persian Language

Modern Persian, or Farsi, is derived from Pahlavi, which was the language of the Iranians in the 7th century, that is, before the Arab invasion. After the conquest, Arabic became the language of religion and administration, which influenced the Persian language all the more because the latter was in any event transcribed in Arabic characters.

During the 9th century, Persian made its official appearance in the courts of the Iranian dynasties of Khorasan, thus preparing official circles for the emergence of the great Ferdowsi. In the 10th century, Ferdowsi wrote the national epic in 60,000 lines, in a form of Persian that was still close to Pahlavi. Ferdowsi's great work *Shāhnāma* ("The Book of Kings") is an important landmark, not only in the renaissance of a language and a literature that had remained practically unchanged for 1,000 years, but also in its expression of a national identity. Having undergone Arab domination for more than three centuries, and having assimilated the Moslem faith to make a new culture out of it, the Iranians saw themselves described in "The Book of Kings" as a people possessed of ancient traditions yet imbued with fresh vitality and aspirations. Ferdowsi is one of the rare authors who manages to depict vividly the whole soul of a people. His heroes and their struggle for justice stem from the most ancient popular traditions and from all the legends of Iranian mythology in which any Iranian can recognize himself. But the most remarkable thing about "The Book of Kings" is that, throughout this pageant of splendid ages and illustrious dynasties that have vanished on distant horizons, there is no trace of resentment or bitterness. The melancholy that these tales inspire in us comes rather from the destiny of man and the passing nature of his greatness. Ferdowsi spoke of the Arab conquerors without hatred or desire for vengeance, insofar as the main social and philosophical values of Islam (and especially its feeling for justice) re-echoed the central ideas that had long since flourished in Iran itself. If today the storytellers in the villages and the singers in the physical training cultural centers still recite Ferdowsi's poems, this is because "The Book of Kings" reflects the Iranian taste for dreams and wonders, proudly reminding them of their glories and defeats, the joys and sufferings, of their past.

For 1,000 years the Persian philosophers and scholars had joined forces with the Arab philosophers, scholars and lawyers, in a form of cililization that Islam was able to create, through an extraordinary blend of people and cultures, and in which the Arabic language had become the everyday language. Thus, they obtained an enrichment of religious faith and of a subtly contrived jurisprudence, and fostered every form of learning by assimilating the Graeco-Roman and Indian inheritances. With their abundant intellectual vitality, the Persians even left their own imprint upon the Arab language and grammar. Yet the presence of a pre-Islamic past is no less living in the souls of these same men who devoted themselves entirely to the flowering of Moslem civilization.

The Pre-Islamic Past

All through Moslem history, the Persians maintained their own personality. In the realm of the mind and intellectual research, they acted in accordance with the standards common to the whole Moslem community, whereas in their personal, emotional and aesthetic lives they lived in a different world. Avicenna, who was to remain for centuries the unrivaled master of a type of medicine of unprecedented philosophical and psychological dimensions, and who produced outstanding treatises on philosophy and medicine in the Arab tongue, also composed poems in Persian, in which, for instance, we find him modestly declaring "a thousand suns have shone in my mind, but I have never succeeded in plumbing the mystery of a single part of the universe."

This feeling of dissatisfaction with oneself, and this confession of man's inability to explain the mysteries of life, reach philosophical skepticism in the work of Omar Khayyam, whose *Robayyats* (quatrains) express it with deep melancholy and sadness. In order to assuage his anguish, this mathematician and astronomer sought in the wisdom of nations an explanation that he never found. To escape the vanity of philosophers and theologians, he took refuge in a kind of epicureanism. And at a time when the Crusades had exalted men's religious faith, he protested daringly, yet unassumingly, against religious and philosophical dogmas. The toleration that emerges from Omar Khayyam's thought, his refusal to submit to occult forces and the philosophy of doubt that he preached, are characteristic of Iranian culture and literature and are to be found at all times in Persian poetry and thought. One of the spiritual guides in this school of thought, Djelal el-Din Rumi, declares in one of his poems, "I am neither Muslim nor Christian, Jew nor Zoroastrian, I am neither of the earth nor of the heavens, I am neither body nor soul; yet, I am all of these, at one and the same time."

Poetry as a Privileged Form of Expression

Saadi, Hafiz and all the Persian poets have exalted love above religion and race, and have sung of wine as the symbol of self-forgetfulness and the antidote to the vanities of life. "It is in the flowing bowl that we have found the reason for our unending drunkenness." Rarely has poetry played such an important part in the life of a people. It is the most widespread form of artistic and literary expression. Even in philosophical treatises and historical tales it has remained the privileged language, and it is certainly also the heaven of cultural unity. In daily conversation, it is considered as a reference system and the mirror of values to which a whole nation feels bound. Thus, poetry has become the symbol of language itself. For a people that has suffered so many invasions and destructions, and so much violence, was not poetry also the only way of keeping alive the secrets of the message and the memories of its ancestors? Among innumerable definitions of culture, there is one I like best: culture is the collective memory that links a people's past to its present and reminds it of its differences from other peoples; a memory that enables it to bridge the gaps created by history. If culture is memory, then memory in Iran is chiefly poetry. But this poetry, which is the repository of history and language, is not the work of a few aesthetes or subtle minds given over to fancy and tricks of style. It has a deep-seated emotive force, without which it would never have attained its characteristic diversity and universality.

Whether we are dealing with the divine love of Djelal el-Din Rumi, the sublime kingdom of Hafiz, the cult of beauty in Saadi, the free thinking and skepticism of Omar Khayyam, or the rhyming tales of Nizami, there is one common source that nourished the work of all these men; this is mysticism in its most varied forms.

Originality and Universality of Iranian Thought

Apart from the legal and utilitarian aspect of Islam, the mystics were attracted by another side of the Prophet's message, which appeals particularly to the conscience of men. Official Islam (*Shariat*), with its ritual and strict legal teaching, became one with a coercive and dominating power, whereas the mystics were in quest of a warmer and more spontaneous atmosphere. They found it among the members of a brotherhood (*Tariqat*) where an esoteric practice based on personal experience offered them greater satisfaction. This practice provided oneness of heart and thought between the faithful and involved them in an inexhaustible search for spiritual enrichment. Such an effort was only possible with the help of a spiritual guide (a pole of "pir," as the Persians say) who, by a kind of inner élan and an extensive knowledge of the world without (*Zaher*) and within (*Baten*), was above the doctrine of established rules. In his whole existence, and his knowledge of men and things and his way of life, this guide was to be an example and a leader for the faithful.

Henry Corbin, the French philosopher who has just completed a monumental work in four volumes entitled, *In Iranian Islam—Spiritual and Philosophical Aspects*, published by Gallimard (Paris), has managed to provide us with a clear and exhaustive picture of 1,000 years' development in philosophical and religious thought, in which the mystical side of this thought stands out. The originality of Mr. Corbin's work lies especially in its hermeneutic approach. He himself defines his method as "a phenomenology, studying the 'religious object' as 'a first phenomenon,' which cannot be explained in any other way, *i.e.*, by political, social, ethnic, economic or geographical circumstances." He says that he became the spiritual guest of Islam in order to understand it. "You cannot describe a building which you have never entered."

Mr. Corbin's work will certainly prove a landmark, not only in the understanding of the psychological depths of Iranian civilization, but also in the questions it raises with regard to the philosophical prospects of the West itself.

Referring to this question in his recent work*, Gilbert Durand refers to Corbin's theories and says, "This work marks the end of a misunderstanding dating from the time of the Crusades. One might say to summarize Henry Corbin's masterly thesis that all the West has done is to repeat the erroneous assumption made by the peripatetic scholastics of the Middle Ages, namely: that the philosophy of Islam could be reduced to the Arab thought of the caliphs, and 'had vanished lost in the sands in Andalousia with the Averoes (*Ibn Roshd*),' who died in 1198." Speaking of the realm of the imaginary, and recent theories in psychology and psychoanalysis (Freud, Jung, Piaget), Durand says how revealing Corbin's work has been for him and declares that the Persian philosophers, from Solrawardi (12th century) to the contemporary Skeikhi school, "base the specific working of the human psyche, not on reason and the logical springs of judgment, or even on perceptions—as the whole psychologi-

---

Human Science and Tradition—The New Spirit in Anthropology.

cal philosophy of the West has endeavoured to—but on 'knowledge through the heart' (*ma' rifat qalbiya*), inner vision (*basirat al-batin*), which is to normal vision with its long chains of determinisms and reasons what feeling (*batin*)—or the linear nature of time (*zaman anfosi*) is in relation to the letter (*zahir*)."

Corbin, while demonstrating the originality of the intuitive method, says: "Western anthropology, sidetracked by the fables of the positivist ideology of objectivity, has quite recently discovered the notion of understanding (*Verstehen*) whereas the Muslim gnostic from the very beginning, and especially since the 17th century with Molla Sadra, had placed this existential internationalization in the forefront of the sociological or historical event."

Already in the 14th century a Shiite theosophist, Jaafar Kashi, had established the supremacy of "understanding" (*Tafhim*) over other ways of knowledge (*Tafshir*, for example). It would take us too long to show here how Corbin managed to pick out from a mass of works (manuscripts, for the most part) philosophical reflections almost uninterrupted in Iran over 1,000 years. Moreover, Corbin expresses his surprise that so many European travelers and scholars (Orientalists included) who visited Iran from the 15th century on were unaware of the existence of such living and varied schools of thought. In our opinion, this ignorance may be explained in three ways: (1) the esoteric character of the Shiite gnosis; (2) the humility of mystic thinkers; and (3) Ketman (keeping silence when insecurity and violence are rife). But it would be wrong to believe that this absence of impact was the result of a hermetic side of the philosophical and religious thought, or that it signified a refusal to appear openly.

Unity of the Culture and its Integration Within the Community

The dazzling proof of the socially positive nature of Sufiism is the notion of chivalry (*Javanmard*), an ethical category that confers a spiritual character on any group of men, which for centuries lay behind the organization of the corporations of arts and crafts and became the unwritten law in Moslem cities. This notion of chivalry may be compared with the notion of knights of the Holy Grail in the West. Its equivalent in Arabic is *Fotowwat*, which (as Corbin says) "designates a form of life which declared itself in vast areas of Muslim civilization, but plainly bears the Shiite imprint wherever it is found." Indeed, Corbin, in the above-mentioned work and in his research on the work of Sohrawardi, takes the theme of spiritual chivalry as an example of Iran's vocation in forming links between the Abrahamic tradition and the Zoroastrian. "With Sohrawardi, the resurrector in Iranian Islam and Islamic Iran of the ancient Persians, we have witnessed the transformation of the heroic epic of ancient Iranian chivalry into the mystical epic of the pilgrims of God, within Iranian Sufiism." Thus, Persian Sufiism, thanks to an extraordinary metamorphosis, manages to transform what is epic into what is ethical. Besides, this blending (of which Hafiz provides a telling example) is one of the features of Persian humanism.

In the realm of art, music, painting or architecture, mytho-poetic thought is ever present. Here everything and, indeed, the whole of nature becomes the symbolized appearance of the Being. Music, for instance, which cannot be imagined without poetry, expresses the same movement between the lover and the loved one, between the joy of union and that of being loved (vassal) as well as the despair of parting (Hejran). This is why we can see in Persian music a perpetual to-and-fro movement between dazzling enchantment and heartrending laments.

In a remarkable essay dealing with Iranian art and commissioned by UNESCO from Darius Shayegan, we read these words: "And the image of what poetry and music are seeking distractedly in this absence which is also a presence is reflected by art in the enchanting welcome of the blue domes waiting at the edge of the oasis, in the vaulted space of the rooms which radiate waiting, in the paradisiac dream of the carpets which gather up the steps, and in the gardens with reflecting pools where dreams eternity." Elsewhere we read:

> There is correspondence between the realities and the forms which they symbolise; this is why the forms of miniatures look like images 'in suspense' located, as Sohrawardi says, in the country of nowhere (Na Koja abad)—a sort of Utopia, a place which is not contained in a topos, but a nowhere which is the where of everything. That also is why everything is so marvelous, so strangely impregnated with the freshness appropriate to the vision of children, and so absorbed in that metallic light which formerly crowned the magi and sovereigns of ancient Persia with a halo, like a light of glory, and therefore of the soul.

> The carpets, where the richness of composition, the exuberance of forms and the harmony of the colours attain the zenith of decorative art, reveal the same archetype so dear to Iran— the garden of Paradise.

Here, briefly called up, is the philosophical/religious and poetic/aesthetic universe of what might be called the Iranian world, or Iranian culture. Despite the apparently blurred contours, its inner cohesion remains perfect. Foreign Orientalists and scholars, despite praiseworthy efforts, have rarely managed to grasp the spirit behind such works.

In a philological study of the poetry, or in an aesthetic analysis of the miniatures, for example, if we do not take account of this world as a whole, with its laws and its system of measurement, we may easily reach incomplete or erroneous conclusions.

Henry Corbin's work shows us that if we enter this mansion on tiptoe, making of ourselves "a dwelling place for its spirituality," we are received, as he says, as spiritual guests; and we gradually become able to hear and see everything, as long as we leave at the door of the house all our prejudices and preconceived ideas, just as we take off our shoes in Iran before entering a holy place.

Culture and the Two Major Temptations: Westernization and "Developmentism"

In the West, since the last war, the social scientists have had much to say on the subject of "resistance to change." They have claimed that the culture, traditions and beliefs in non-Western societies are a barrier to progress. Such an allegation reflects two attitudes, sometimes found separately, and sometimes complementing one another. The first is consciously or unconsciously dominating and seeks to establish a Western hegemony over the whole world, considering as negative anything that may appear to obstruct this hegemony; the second is an ethnocentric Western attitude founded on a Judaeo-Christian vision of history, linear and professist, seeking to mold the world according to a Western model. The Western achievements in technology serve as an argument, and often as an alibi, to justify such an attempt at uniformity.

During the last two decades, universities and research centers in the West have more or less fallen in line with these two attitudes. They have based all their studies on development upon a linear, Westernizing conception of progress, exalting the merits of the quantitativist school. They have adopted Western society as their system of reference, rejecting all phenomena that were not part and parcel of this system, considering them retrograde or at least superfluous. Thus, they have been to all intents and purposes led to disregard the cultural dimension, and this attitude in many cases resulted in the enforcement of an exogenous abstract model of development, to the neglect of anything that was specifically or creatively endogenous.

The elite of the Third World who attended Western universities have not been free from such mishaps. The institutions of the United Nations have embarked more or less on the same course, and, in the belief that they were acting beneficially, have committed grave mistakes. The events of these last years in the Third World, and the slow and painful road that certain dominated peoples have had to travel to obtain their independence and assert their national and cultural identity in the face of so-called progress, are a proof of this. All the more so because disappointments and unlooked-for events of a sociocultural or even economic kind, at the level of technocratic reasoning, have demonstrated, if not the arrogance, at least the limits of a "developmentism" of a Western type; have led to the appearance of a deep-seated malaise in the West; and have further aroused doubts as to the unconditional validity of such a model. As far as Iranian culture and the Iranian mentality are concerned, it should be remarked that for the last 150 years, the components representing, or expressing, Iranian culture, were never opposed to a technological or institutional modernization of the country.

Many of the political writings and travel impressions of Iranian thinkers in the second half of the last century deal with the agonizing problem of the technical and economic backwardness of Iran. All the social and religious movements in the country were animated by the quest for a new solution to this problem.

Evidence of this lies in the fact that the most conservative elements in political and religious life at the end of the 19th century and at the beginning of the 20th—namely, the religious authorities—were in the forefront of a movement for national recovery and of advocating the Belgian constitution to the geopolitical conditions and to the traditions of the country; they also played a reforming role in modifying the legal apparatus of the country of which, by tradition, they were the sole repositories.

At the beginning of the century, there was a great enthusiasm for the adoption of the Western model. Taqizadeh, one of the most respected representatives of this elite, had openly declared, "We must Westernize ourselves, body and soul." Fifty years afterward, in the 1960s, he repented and admitted the importance of a cultural identity. Today, among the new generation of poets, writers and artists hailing from the most diverse schools of thought, not one wishes to become Western "in body and soul." How has this change of attitude come about?

First, since the display of optimism at the beginning of the century over unconditional Westernization, disappointment has been widespread. The process of modernization, as interpreted or encouraged by the West, contained many erroneous elements and much veiled domination. The values of freedom, democracy and justice that the West appeared willing to establish everywhere have often become a mere means of barter, used in the West's interests with a resultant gradual separation between the notion of modernization and the notion of Westernization.

On the other hand, the cosmopolitanism, advocated in the guise of various doctrines by the West in the 19th century, never really became a living reality even among Western nations. In the economic-political sphere, as well as at the ethnic-cultural level, every time an occasion arose, their nationalism was fully asserted. Thus, the Iranian elite, suffering for several decades from the aftermath of two world wars and the ups and downs of the appropriation of one of their resources—oil—realized that a strong national identity is vital for the salvation and unity of a country. They realized also that in the modern world the loss of such identity leads inevitably to subordination.

The demands of rationality and objectivity constitute the very foundations of the Western outlook. If such an outlook has resulted in great achievements where machinery and the physical world are concerned, we must admit that it has been much less successful in dealing with the human condition. Human sciences, founded on rational objectivity, are today suffering setbacks and defeats. Is it not important that, having exalted rationality to ensure human happiness, we should now be induced to invent a special discipline—psychoanalysis—to cure the ills arising from an overrationally organized life that is deprived of its basic relationship with the nonrational? It is hardly necessary to emphasize that since psychoanalysis itself is the outcome of a rational and objective approach, it has been unable to fulfill the task it set itself. Why should cultures like ours, in which man is considered in all his aspects, be deprived of their substance by following a so-called rational course at the end of which lies the vast expanse of the nonrational and the impossibility of receiving an answer to our questions? Why should this wealth of feeling and emotion that has reached us after centuries of tradition and mystical-poetic experience, and which is one of the outstanding features of the Iranian personality in history, have to be considered as something shameful and subjective that we must rid ourselves of? Like the river that flows naturally toward the sea, this emotional wealth bears man toward communion with other people and so with the community at large. The whole tradition of love, brotherhood and comradeship, which is a living element in our culture, must be considered as an antidote to the risk of isolation and emotional indifference today threatening Western society. Anguish, depression, neurosis and schizophrenia are Western maladies, new varieties of which the "specialists" are explaining to us with every passing day.

As for administration and industry, they have to appeal to an increasing number of sociologists and psychologists so as to lessen the evils of a dehumanizing bureaucracy. Why should we follow the same road? Do we have to assess our degree of civilization by reference to the ills of Western civilization? We can certainly adapt the techniques and methods of industrial and administrative organization to the demands of our social and cultural life, as long as we do not forget the value that our tradition attaches to man and to human relationships. This being so, culture ceases to be a mere aid to economic development, or a legacy of the past, preserved in the museums and restored according to the taste of a few aesthetes and art lovers. Our culture is a deep and daily reality for the great mass of the Iranian people. Classical poetry, popular poetry and songs, tales, proverbs and ancestral wisdom express a deep-seated humanism that guides men and women in their daily lives. It would be hard to find in Iran a single urban or rural community without its own holy places, where the memory of a descendant of the Prophet or of a spiritual guide (*pir*) or a knight (*Javanmard*) is honored: historical or legendary figures, they all symbolize some virtue sùch as the sense of devotion, moral courage or justice, to which the whole community is attached.

Thus, we see that every village and every district has its own historical or spiritual personality, with the result that it cannot be viewed merely in terms of an economic function. The people have needs and aspirations that are not purely material.

The same phenomenon is to be found in craftsmanship and the popular arts enshrining a whole symbolism and a whole philosophy of life, as well as a close knowledge of nature (plants, for instance), and these have to be taken into consideration when, in aid of some probably questionable economic advantage, an attempt is made to replace craftsmanship and traditional art by machines. The intrusion of machines into the traditional system may well jeopardize this creative life. On the other hand, if it is properly adapted to the historical and artistic conditions of the community, it may enhance this wealth of experience and knowledge. Many examples of such interdependence between the economic and the cultural could be provided.

Change and the Perennial Nature of Culture

After this brief survey of the chief components in the cultural personality of Iran, we may assert that despite an apparent Westernization, this personality still preserves an authentic nature to its very roots. One example will suffice to demonstrate this cultural survival, that of the Persian language, which, through its poetry and means of expression, illustrates age-old values in a present-day context. As long as the Persian language remains true to itself, its spirit will be faithful to the country's history and memories—although, provided men continue to plan and act according to this spirit, our culture will assimilate new elements and enrich itself through contact with the outside world (in this event, the West), as it did at the time of the fullest flowering of its genius. But if, blinded to the trappings of a design that is foreign to us, men remain insensitive to this spirit, then it will simply revert to the path bequeathed to it by an esoteric tradition and wait its time. One of the hallmarks of our age is the determination displayed by the dominant forces of this world to impose their own options on other cultures. Why should we have to choose between an excessive modernism, leading society to the destruction of its very foundations, and a traditional attitude isolating it from all connection with the outside world?

Why should we have to choose between a frenzied individualism shattering all the links that bind a community together and exalting man's will to power, and a collectivism that, in the name of the general interest, crushes the human personality?

There is no doubt that, if only for our survival, we cannot do without science and technology in order to make the best possible use of our resources and enable our people to accede to material well-being in conditions of dignity and equity. However, this does not mean that we should regard this material well-being as the sole objective or bestow on it the same forms as it assumes in the West, particularly in view of the fact that different approaches to well-being and modernization are now becoming apparent. Thus, our principal concern might be to interrogate other societies on their various experiences.

The West must gradually become accustomed to interrogating other cultures and other societies, instead of seeking to make them like itself. On a historical scale there is a danger of this trend toward uniformity eventually impairing the human species and resulting, through deculturation, in a loss of identity for man; the progress to which we aspire would then no longer have any meaning. The West can vouchsafe us progress in only one dimension, but we must seek the other dimensions that, with it, and taken together, constitute the individual personality, in what our thinkers described and depicted as the image of "the perfect man" (Isan-e-Kamel) and so realize a dream that comes to us from the depth of our historical consciousness. Could this not be an inspiring task for our rising generations if they again wish to play an important role in the world?

Old and New Values in Changing Cultural Patterns

Hormoz Farhat

It goes without saying that all nations of the world, to a larger or lesser degree, are moving toward technological advancement. The universal goal is to achieve a better life through industrialization. Western countries of Europe, and particularly the United States of America, are being looked up to as the model. These countries, over the past two centuries, have gone through the so-called Industrial Revolution, which in most cases has been, in fact, not a revolution but a logical evolution that had its roots in the Renaissance.

Most Asian and African countries, due to separate sets of circumstances and foreign domination, were not placed in the course of this evolution. For them, industrialization has been truly a revolution. Viewing the material gains of the West, and presuming that the Western man has become a happier man by such gains, the East is struggling to catch up. Indeed, it may be justified to equate the industrialization of the West with her ability to exploit and dominate much of the world.

Emphasis on material values is an outcome of technological advancement. The Americans, who by all accounts are judged to be the most technologically advanced people in the world, are proverbial for their acute sense of materialism, something that has been the source of much criticism, by themselves among others. Yet, America has become more and more aware of her exaggerated reliance on material values. Conscious movements have been made, during the past 15 years, to refocus the aims of life to the spiritual. This consciousness has most prominently manifested itself in the attitude of the young people toward life, and is demonstrated in their behavioral patterns. The formation of hermit-like orders is a somewhat naive expression of this tendency.

Elsewhere, this reaction against materialism has not been as pronounced, and the high material standards of America are still the objective and the goal of most nations around the world. The East, in particular, has fallen prey to the lure of Western technology. The breakdown of feudal systems, the emergence of liberal thought and the growth of the bourgeoisie have all come to accentuate the desire for the possession of material goods and the ability to acquire them.

A consequence of the materialism imported into the countries of the East is the adoption of new values—values on goods and luxuries, on entertainment and general indulgence, on changing vogues and impermanence and eventually on materially established relationships, human and otherwise. Are such new values compatible with the traditional standards in old societies, and can traditional values also be supported? Experience has shown that there are inevitable conflicts between the two sets of values. The disruption of the old patterns in nearly every society where material values have taken hold is clearly witnessed. Respect for traditions is diminished, customs are forsaken, family ties are broken and loyalties are shaken.

While traditions are not necessarily always things of value or even beauty, there are, to be sure, elements of identity. And identity is what I believe we must have. Whereas all creatures of the same species instinctively flock together, it has been a singular manifestation of the nobility of man to strive to make his person recognized and distinguished from others of his race. In a broader view, dissimilarities between people and nations are indications of man's attempt to make himself expressed and recognized. Surely, the world would be a far less colorful place if all people behaved in the same manner and were governed by the same sets of values. However, if it should come to a choice between the old and the new, it would be quite futile to propose that the new should be sacrificed. That simply cannot be done, unless in societies under some form of a totalitarian regime where the course of social developments can be strictly controlled.

Is, therefore, the traditional culture doomed? Not necessarily. What may not be able to survive are the outward manifestations of a traditional culture. Its essence, when reduced to basic elements, can and must be salvaged; and these elements are the ethics and the poetics of a civilization.

Much has been said about the things that distinguish human beings from other creatures and about the attestations of what signifies the nobility of man. I tend to take as the most significant indicator man's sense of aesthetics, and with it his ability to create. It is by such virtues that order, proportion, refinement and beauty are created. These are the sublime qualities of man, and they are the ingredients of permanence and value in any culture. The ethics and the poetics of a civilization are the ultimate rewards of man's sense of aesthetics and his creativity.

If by the process of technological advancement we are losing our sense of aesthetics, it is then the ethics and the poetics of the society that suffer, and decadence sets in.

Let us now focus our attention on what has been happening in Iran in terms of the points just raised. The country is going through an enormous social upheaval. Westernization, which was begun in the 19th century, was accelerated during the first half of the 20th century. But it is the years since 1960 that comprise a transitional period of the utmost consequences. Industrialization and mechanization have been the supreme essays of this era. Raised standards of living have led to the emergence and the constant growth of a middle class that is, in the main, the by-product of this transitional period.

This middle class is displaying a gradual moral breakdown that is quite alarming. Respect for one's faith, for one's fellow-men, for decency, honesty and the law has been diminishing. The resultant spiritual bankruptcy is perhaps the most serious threat to the very fabric of the Iranian society.

In modern times, as is the case everywhere, the middle class in Iran is becoming the determinant force for the molding of social patterns. More and more, it is the taste, wants and traits of this group that are coming to be the governing factors. The traits that have been exhibited so far have been predominantly motivated by materialistic aims devoid of any commendable aesthetic values. The middle class' passionate zeal for material possessions has brought about a most distasteful development in architecture, furnishings, objects and other material goods.

It may be argued that such is the lot of all middle classes everywhere. But there are distinct differences in the cultural buildup of social groups where their emergence has been due to evolutionary and inner-directed processes, with those that have risen suddenly, whose main impulse has been outer-directed, that is, motivated by non-native elements.

Another dangerous development that has begun to be noticed in Iran is in the popularization of the arts. A dreadful kind of popular music, a cheap pulp literature, and a generally dreary cinematic output are among the most striking outcomes of this popularizing trend. Effects of this kind of a trend have long been detected in Europe and in America. But in this case, also, such a process in the West is a consequence of an evolutionary growth and receives its impetus mainly from within. In Iran, it is coming about swiftly and mostly as a result of blind imitations of what is happening in the West.

With the passage of time, the problems just referred to will become more acute unless well-defined objectives and policies are drawn and overall social consciousness is raised.

To begin with, it must be realized that no civilization can be maintained without a moral foundation. And it is futile to search for an ethical platform within any of the existing religious doctrines. The unequivocal fact is that no dogmatic religion can answer the questions of our times, and no religion can be genuinely endorsed by all strata of a society. In particular, it has been widely shown that as economic conditions improve, religious inclinations diminish. It stands to reason, then, that ultimately a different guideline must be followed.

I believe that the ethics of a society in today's world can be drawn only from truth and justice, which, in fact, is in accord with the germane elements in any religious doctrine. It is by the truth and through justice that people can come to have faith. Truth inevitably encompasses a social morality that is not abstract or absurd. And justice is the antidote for corruption.

Recent events in the U.S. are case studies in how immorality in a governing body can be fostered by lack of forthrightness. It has been clearly established that truthfulness in a social system is the foundation of morality. As for justice, it is all too clear that no system can long survive without it.

Referring back to the strength and identity that lie within traditions, I propose that in Iran the ancient code of "Good Thought, Good Words and Good Deeds" be revived. Its full implications and its application should be taught and made into a national discipline, so that it would not become a mere hollow motto. Also, the ancient Iranian love of the truth must be rekindled. I believe that the current revolutionary state of the nation, when important and far-reaching measures are effectively enacted, provides the right circumstances for a national resurgence in the direction of a moral uprising based upon truth and justice.

The ideal technologically based society cannot do with a principle of ethics alone; equally important are the poetics of a society. Those elements that give to life the dimension of beauty and grace, and the things that are expressions of the nonpragmatic gifts of men, the things that cannot be contained in predetermined and contractual shapes and orders, the things that say different things to different people and in all arouse some inexplicable sense of joy and desire and goodness, those sublime and mysterious things we call the fine arts, poetry and, above all, music—these are the poetics of a people and of a society.

To be sure, no form of human society, primitive or advanced, large or small, is without varying forms of artistic expression. What is important is the extent of the society's involvement with the arts, the role they play in the lives of the people and their relative usefulness toward the purification and the elation of men's minds and souls.

It is through the arts that the noblest and the most lasting of man's expressions are made. No civilization of any merit can be conceived in which artistic creativity is not a major endeavor. It would be a sorry state for humanity if through technological advancement it should become reticent in its artistic expressivity; or, as is evidenced in some Western cultures, if this expression should become a mere reflection of a mechanized society.

In this connection, it is absolutely essential for Iran to come forth with a national objective and a national policy. We must come to realize that the arts are immensely important for the future development of our society, and that a civilization in which people have little appreciation and involvement in the arts cannot become great, the realization of which is our goal.

Fortunately, in certain areas, the artistic traditions of the Iranian people are extremely strong and are still fully vital. This is particularly true of the folk arts, applied and decorative. Yet in this very domain, the migration to cities and the impact of urban centers on the character of the rural people are posing serious threats.

Literature and poetry are powerful traditions that must be preserved and strengthened. It is not enough to make everyone literate; it is the love of reading that must be instituted among our people.

As for music, our society is sadly deficient. The great significance of music as a moral and social force is completely overlooked. It is only the cheap, the playful and the entertaining kinds of music that are understood. In this regard, very serious thought must be given to the ways in which music can be used as an important element to refine and sensitize the temperaments of our people, especially those who, in the grips of the present turmoil of materialistic growth, are becoming markedly coarse and callous.

Both the highly humanistic tradition of Persian music and the immense treasury of Western, as well as Eastern, music can be utilized to serve the purpose. Let us not forget that music is the one truly universal expression.

Comments and Discussion

In "Cultural Development in Iran," Ehsan Yarshater attempted to define the chief characteristics of Persian culture as it has developed over the ages. This was not easy since the totality of human culture does not reflect simple chronological progress; rather, cultures, as units of human history, are separate entities, rarely deriving from each other. Defining a culture may be done by assessing the value system, the directions it takes, the areas of concern and the contributions it has made. His paper sets forth the chief features of Persian culture, with special reference to the spiritual culture (achievements of religious thought) and the aesthetic culture (Persian art and art forms).

In the absence of author Ehsan Naraghi, Mohammad Moghadam presented "Iran's Cultural Identity and the Present Day World." The essay identifies the principal elements of Iranian culture as being religion, language and the pre-Islamic past. Although Iran's religion is Shiite Islam, a religion that is true to the basic principles of Islam, it has some special dimensions. Iran's language (modern Persian or Farsi) has changed very little in

1,000 years. It expresses Iran's national identity and philosophy of existence, which includes mysticism. As for Iran's pre-Islamic past, it remains alive and is a distinctive aspect of Iranian culture and thought. Poetry has a special place in Persian culture, the essay suggests. ("If culture is memory, then memory in Iran is chiefly poetry.") Reasons for long Western ignorance of Persian culture and thought are identified, and the possible effects on Iranian culture of Westernization and "developmentism" are discussed. The author questions whether Iran must follow the path of the West and measure its own degree of civilization by referring to the ills of Western civilization. Iranian culture is a deep and daily reality for the mass of Iranian people. It can assimilate new elements and enrich itself through contact with the outside world while retaining its own basic special features.

In introducing "Old and New Values in Changing Cultural Patterns," Hormoz Farhat observed that Iran is advancing its technology and that emphasis on material values is a common outcome of technological advancement. Iran has a strong cultural heritage, but it is being subjected to new values, especially the importance attached to goods and luxuries, entertainment, changing modes, etc. Experience shows that such new values inevitably conflict with traditional values and threaten a nation's cultural identity. But Iran's traditional culture is not necessarily doomed. Its essence—ethics and the poetics of a civilization—can and must be salvaged. (In Mr. Farhat's view, ethics and the poetics of a civilization are the "ultimate rewards of a man's sense of aesthetics and his creativity.") In the author's judgment, Iran's ethics are threatened by a gradual moral breakdown in the middle class and its poetics are jeopardized by popularization of the arts, including bad popular music, cheap literature and poor films. In his view, problems will become worse unless a moral foundation is retained, with the ethics of society based on truth and justice. But a principle of ethics alone is not enough. Poetics are also needed: elements that give life beauty and grace, the fine arts, poetry and, above all, music. Mr. Farhat appealed for a "national objective and a national policy" regarding the role of the arts in Iranian life. Given the degree of interest and dedication that The Shabanou has shown in these matters, he thought that, under her patronage, the formulation and implementation of such a national policy might become a reality.

Iran's Cultural History

Differing interpretations of Iran's history were offered at a plenary session and special discussion group, with one Iranian scholar challenging many of the precepts in "Cultural Development in Iran," which he felt reflected Western scholarship and views rather than indigenous research. [Among the issues debated at these sessions were the questions of whether the Aryans were "always" in Iran or came to Iran from elsewhere; the geographic origins—internal or external—of the Arabs who occupied Iran; whether the Mithra who lived in the 3rd century B.C. was responsible for the subsequent "legend" of Jesus; and whether Alexander (so-called "the Great") ever reached Persia, as held by Western and other scholars.] Others commented on the emphasis given to Iran's sense of national identity and to continuity of traditions and values, despite the fact that Iran has been invaded many times and subjected to many different cultures.

Role of Culture in National Life

A number of participants from within and outside Iran stressed the importance of culture in national life. An Asian observed that Iran, a relatively wealthy country, will become a society "consumed by envy" unless its people find a way of preserving and enjoying their culture. In his view, social discipline may be a less important goal than enjoyment of culture, especially in poor countries that cannot hope to "catch up." An Iranian urged the importance of bringing high-quality art into the lives of people who are being taken away from art by technological involvements. If the quality of life in Iran is to be bearable, art must become an increasing part of the public sphere, it was suggested. To make art a concern of government is a possible alternative to leaving peasants in remote villages so that they may continue to enjoy their traditional folk culture, a participant observed.

Problems Arising from Impacts on Culture of Modernization and Westernization

An Asian commented on the plight of young people and especially villagers who become alienated from their cultural heritage In his country, where many imitate the West, some are appealing for increased attention to traditional and folk culture. But a European questioned whether "nostalgia is in order." In his view, there may be no real possibility of simultaneously modernizing and retaining old values. At the same time, he observed, Westernization does not necessarily mean accepting foreign hegemony; it means being equal to the people who would impose such hegemony. Modernization doesn't necessarily destroy ethics, although it may change them. Philosophy, as well as art, is flourishing in the West. Although Europeans may seem Americanized in their dress and drink, they have retained their national identities; despite the universality of culture today, there is room for individual differences. Various participants expressed the view that Iran should not try to build fortresses for the protection of its culture, observing that Iranian culture has survived many previous inputs. In these participants' view, what is good about Iranian culture will survive poor influences from outside. An American suggested that, although the present state of affairs may appear dismal, Iran has a long tradition of being able to assimilate; it may not be in real danger. Others concurred that the deep cultural traits in Iran will find a way to express themselves; they may assume somewhat different forms, but their basic characteristics will be preserved.

Others differed with this view, expressing the opinion that, unless Persian culture is protected, it may not survive the present "invasion," since it is very different from past invasions and so all-embracing. A specialist observed that in former times Iranians held the material world in some contempt and that they offset the "horrors" of the material world by poetry, grace in social inter-course, charity and similar values. But Iran's rich values, includ-ing its special religious genius, may be endangered by a Western concern for material things. This could adversely affect Iranian skills and workmanship. It would be a great loss to the world if Iran were no longer a source of art, taste, delicacy and imagery.

An Asian, whose own country has experienced Westerniza-tion, urged that Iran accept the good elements of foreign culture, suggesting that "If they fit your mind, they won't corrupt you." Another outside participant, who felt that Iran was probably unin-tentionally adopting the worst features of Western culture—bad architecture and bad music—concurred that there may be no harm in adopting good culture from the West.

Possible Approaches to the Problem

Various suggestions were offered relative to preservation of Iran's culture, traditional values and the place of art in the national life. A non-Iranian suggested that education can play an important role: first, educated citizens who know what is going on in the outside world can relate these developments to local leaders, serving as a kind of bridge; second, higher education and other institutions can offer study programs relating to the nation's cultural heritage, bringing students into contact with traditional culture and sending teachers of traditional culture to the villages. Institutions of artistic excellence should be concerned with relating art to social de-velopment. Several persons noted that Iran's developing TV and radio network is already beginning to play a role in communicat-ing traditional culture to schools, *e.g.,* radio broadcasts of classi-cal Persian music. [But an estimated 30 percent of National Ira-nian Radio and Television (NIRT) TV broadcasts are purchased from abroad and dubbed in Persian; programs like *Marcus Welby, M.D.* are instruments for communicating non-Iranian culture and values to Iran. An American urged that Iranian TV officials avoid the Western commercial approach to TV and that they experiment with ways of using TV for two-way exchanges between the villages and the center.] Reaching Iranian young people is especially important, it was held, since many go abroad for study and return home with little knowledge of Persian language, literature or history. Several participants suggested that greater emphasis be given to Iranian culture in the school curriculum. An Iranian acknowledged that the curriculum is deficient in this regard.

The possibility of discussing these kinds of concerns at future conferences and symposia was mentioned. It was also suggested that the government form a council to consider national policy on the role of art in national life. An American urged that a national committee of public and private sector representatives could be established to review broadcasting operations with reference to desired cultural values.

Culture in International Relations

An American wondered whether culture, as well as economics and politics, can bear on Iran's relations with the Western world and asked what cultural contacts Iran is contemplating with other nations. An Iranian observed that it takes time for Western businessmen coming to Iran to understand Persians; we need to work together to understand each other better.

7.   The Future of Iran

The Future of Iran*

Amir Abbas Hoveyda, the Prime Minister of Iran

I shall attempt in this essay to make a sketch of some of Iran's aims and aspirations in this last quarter of the 20th century, and the ideals and values on whose basis our nation is determined to meet the challenge of the year 2000.

The task is admittedly not an easy one. Any forecast of the course of events over so long a period must allow for contingencies whose cause or impact cannot be foreknown. Yet, contrary to the thinking of some seers, whose portrayals depict an immovable future at which we shall arrive with predestined certitude, I believe that, given a sufficient body of pertinent data, and an estimate of the vigor of the human will, the future can not only be predicted, but indeed, created. For the past 13 years, this has been the basis on which we in Iran have proceeded and, if I may add with modesty, succeeded.

It is our firm belief and cherished hope that Iran will become the first of the world's ancient civilizations to utilize fully the immense opportunities for material and moral advancement provided by the technological revolution of the past few decades. In wishing to do so, and in working toward that goal, we are determined to preserve our cultural identity, while upholding the everlasting moral and human values formulated and defended by our forefathers over thousands of years of our recorded history.

Our record for the past 13 years, since the launching of The Shah and People's Revolution, gives us the hope and the assurance that Iran is poised for further successes in transforming itself within its traditions. It is not by discarding our past that we mean to create our future. On the contrary, we see our future as a deepening of the great experiences of our past, and the application of our traditional cultural and moral values to the problems and potentials of today and tomorrow.

In a world dominated by materialism, where philosophy often becomes an exercise in the presentation of abstract models shaped by marketplace realism, we have chosen the path of idealism. In a world conceiving of state-craft as the art of the possible, meaning the subjuga-

---

*The Aspen Institute/Persepolis Symposium concluded with a public session at which the Prime Minister delivered this major address on the future of Iran.

tion of the human spirit by shortsighted designs and stratagems, we have chosen vision and the courage to dare. We believe that the world as a whole is beginning to cast a fresh and critical glance at the basically monistic views of human development that have dominated international thinking for the past century.

During the past 100 years, we have seen man reduced to the level of a blind and elemental force, locked in perpetual conflict with his fellow-men because of different functions within a certain economic system. The advocates of this brand of monism have presented what we believe were the particular characteristics of specific societies at specific times, as universal rules for understanding the course of human development for all eternity.

We have seen the conception of man that has been held by these societies leading to the building of Utopias that crumble before they are fully shaped. We have seen how the most meticulously organized stages of history have failed to turn man into an actor in the monistic farce that often becomes a tragedy.

We have also witnessed the virtuoso performance of social engineers of all descriptions, leading to the creation of societies in which man is no more than a consumer of often useless and dehumanizing objects. We are all aware of the abuses of technology that to some have been the New God and to others the New Venus.

In the plethora of philosophical models and political experiences of others, there is thus much that has to be examined if our quest for a future of greater hope and promise is to succeed. We have witnessed the emergence of great bureaucratic empires, in which political power becomes a self-motivating and self-perpetuating quantum, representing human alienation on almost cosmic scales. We have also studied societies that, beginning with a democratic consensus, are facing the danger of modern tribalization—societies that subsidize sloth and indolence and are divided against themselves.

I do not believe that in our quest for the modernization of the material and technological basis of life in our country we need to pass through the storms and stresses of either brand of society I have briefly described. Just as we do not have to re-invent the steam engine in order to acquire present-day industries, we need not pass through the sweatshops of the Industrial Revolution, the class struggles of the 19th century and the moral crises of modern industrial nations.

Nor do we have to go through the furnace of colonialism that melted not only the colonized but also the colonizer. The catastrophes unleashed upon the world by chauvinism, presented in the attractive wrappings of nationalism, are still fresh in memory. We have witnessed the explosion of the myth of universally applicable models inspired by this or that "ism." At a time when both the ideological man and the technological man can be seen vacillating between unrelieved gloom and

Panglossian optimism, we believe we are not only entitled but duty-bound to seek our own path to the future.

This path has been charted, thanks to the endeavors of our people and the leadership of our sovereign, during the past 13 years. It shall lead us to what we have felt courageous enough to call the Great Civilization. It is neither out of unjustified pride nor self-delusion that we speak of the Great Civilization. The achievements of our nation through its long history, the resilience of our culture under the most adverse conditions, and Iran's almost unique regenerative abilities entitle us to such an aspiration.

Our starting point is a national unity and concord that has few parallels in the contemporary world. This unity, which is without uniformity, has enabled us to work out a social contract, the first article of which is human dignity. We conceive of economic development as a means not only of satisfying human needs but also of anticipating them. By developing our economy, maximizing the rational use of our natural resources, extending the options open to all of our people and creating national wealth, we do not mean to create only a powerful state, as so many others have done. Far more important to us is ensuring the material well-being of our people while offering them full opportunities to develop and utilize their intellectual abilities and creative powers.

It was with such an objective in view that Iran adopted the system of public planning to organize and guide its economy nearly three decades ago. During the past 13 years, as we have gained in experience, we have been able to improve our planning tools and methods. Without making a fetish of planning, we have utilized it as a means of mobilizing and allocating our national resources, while allowing ample scope for private enterprise and individual initiative. Iran's investment in its development projects during the past five years was probably larger than the total investments made in this country in the preceding two centuries. Far more important, however, was the orientation of Iranian investment policies. More than 60 percent of total public investments were aimed at giving the nation a modern socioeconomic infrastructure, with education, public health, communication networks, hydroelectric projects and resource development plans receiving the lion's share.

It is not my intention to present an exhaustive statistical exposé of Iran's performance during the past 13 years, or the targets we mean to achieve by the year 2000. But a few figures will help illustrate the dramatic changes that have taken place in this country, and that we expect to see during the next 25 years. In 1963, the year The Shah and People's Revolution was launched, Iran's GNP per capita was estimated to be around $100 per annum. By 1977, this figure will be $2,069. The projected figure for the year 2000 is $6,052 at constant 1972 prices. By the year 2000, Iran's total population is expected to top the 65 million mark, while a GNP of $441 billion will be attained.

Far more important than those broad figures, however, are the social statistics we are able to present. In 1963, there were only 10 centers of higher education in this country with a total student population of less than 20,000. The number of universities and centers of higher education in this country has now reached 184, with a total student body of 149,000. When the academic year 1975–76 begins in late September, more than 7 million Iranians of all ages will be attending some institution of learning, from the kindergarten to the most advanced centers of higher studies and research. That figure is well over one-fifth of our entire population.

At the same time, a major item in our foreign expenditure bills has been investment in the education of our young people in a large number of foreign countries. At the moment, over 40,000 Iranians are attending universities and technical schools in Europe, North America and elsewhere. The total eradication of illiteracy and the improvement of the quality of education at all levels remain our primary objectives. We expect to achieve full literacy within the next 12 years.

We consider material and social investment in education as the single most important guarantor of our success in achieving the goals of the Great Civilization. We are conscious of the fact that we still have a very long way to go before achieving the kind of qualitative transformation that our entire educational system must experience. The first basic steps in that direction have already been taken. With the Iranian people's natural propensity to learn, and with determination to make our entire education system meet the needs and aspirations of our nation, for today as well as for tomorrow, we will not cease in our efforts to make education the mainspring of all our future endeavors.

Iran's cultural life has never been the preserve of a privileged elite, and we mean to help retain this. Ferdowsi, Hafez and Saadi have been and remain loved and understood by people from all walks of life. Unlike certain stratified societies, one did not have to belong to any special economic or social class to make our literature, our music and our philosophical traditions. The fact that we have never had plebeians or patricians demonstrates our nation's basic cultural unity. This unity is indeed our chief asset. It gives shape to our aspirations for the Great Civilization.

Our experience during the past 13 years has proved our people to be among the most diligent in the world. For thousands of years, the people of this land have measured the strength of their will against a harsh nature that offers but meager opportunities for agriculture. The development of our underground water canals, the *qanats* that are still considered marvels of engineering, provides an example of human ingenuity in the struggle to survive. Our architecture, book illuminations, carpets and a whole range of other cultural products demonstrate not only our people's aesthetic endeavors, but their love of precision, of balance and of intellectual discipline. In insisting that creative work, social responsibility and social discipline should remain major values, we reflect the most deeply felt traditions of our people. It is through creative work and a sense of the past that the Iranian people have succeeded in safeguarding their national identity. And it is on the basis of these values that we are determined to define and shape our future. We mean to make economic development and technological change a means to furthering social justice, social cohesion and fraternity.

The choice of technology remains a critical question for Iran and all other developing countries. In developing our national technology, we have our country's specific needs, potentials and abilities in mind. There are certain areas in which we believe we have the natural and human resources needed for the development of a technology of the most advanced order. I mean to refer here to the development of those technologies that are not only theoretically possible but are indeed applicable.

First among those is mass education. Mass education in Iran started at a time when we had not only the means to prevent stratification, but also the determination to ensure equal opportunities. To eliminate illiteracy and to offer free education, as we have done, to all Iranians, we shall have to make use of the most advanced educational techniques and methods. It is my belief that in 25 years' time, Iran will be able to offer the world a rich experience as well as a high level of technological advances in the field of mass education. Necessity is not only the mother of invention; it can also be the basis for the creation of new technologies.

Another field in which I believe we shall be developing our own national technology is energy. Apart from its oil resources, Iran has vast deposits of natural gas, perhaps the largest in the world, We also mean to exploit the opportunities offered to us by solar energy. We are already beginning the development of nuclear energy for peaceful purposes. With the vast and uninhabited open spaces that our country provides, we hope that in building and making use of nuclear power we shall not face the problems of pollution that threaten the overcrowded areas of Europe and Japan.

In the field of energy, it is not only the necessities but also the possibilities open to us that provide the basis for Iran's technological development. In petroleum-based industries such as petrochemicals and pharmaceuticals, we are bound to develop technologies of our own within the next 25 years.

Another area in which Iran has the means and the need for developing its own technology is related to the use of water. I have already mentioned our ancient *qanats*. But the development of our agriculture, the expansion of our industries and the growth of our urban centers dictate the need for the use of methods of an entirely different nature and on entirely different scales. The use of desalination plants and their adoption to Iranian conditions, the development of new modes of organizing the use and distribution of water, including the system of drip irrigation and the employment of snow pack and cloud-seeding techniques for agriculture are among the fields in which Iran will have a technology of its own before the turn of the century.

Public health, medicine and health care measures provide another field in which distinctly Iranian technologies could be developed. Through massive infusions of funds into public health and proper development and distribution of health care manpower resources, given the climatic and demographic characteristics of Iran, I believe we would be in a position to present our experiences as something original by the year 2000.

Construction is another field in which necessity will impel Iran to develop technologies of its own. Housing is a national priority, and our people neither wish nor are expected to wait as long as their counterparts in traditional industrial states for economic development to give them better housing conditions. The variety of building materials available in Iran, and the fantastic diversity in climate in our country, offer ample scope for innovation and the development of new techniques of construction. The public sector's unparalleled investment in vast construction projects offers the economic impetus needed.

I have spoken of Iran's main options in developing its own technology in order to stress our belief that science and technology can be positive forces in human development, if they are based on concrete realities and aimed at meeting specific needs. In other words, we shall not allow ourselves the luxury of aimless technological curiosity, symbolized by prestige projects.

Equally important for our future is the rejuvenation of our agriculture. Land reform has removed the political and social barriers to the revival of agriculture in Iran. Industrial development has created a vast potential market for farm products and raw materials. Yet it is true that agriculture has been something of a Cinderella in our economy during the past few years. The standard of living of the free farmers has increased dramatically, but total agricultural production has failed to match rates of growth achieved in other sectors of the economy. With younger people leaving the countryside for urban regions, with the maintenance of many farming units that fall below their regional optimum size; with our irrigated lands around hydroelectric units under-utilized, Iranian agriculture has done little more than hold its own in an era of rapid change. But the importance of agriculture for the future, not only of our economy but also of our very life style, is now being realized once again. This is why our Fifth Development Plan, to be completed in two years' time, has given investment in agricultural development a privileged position. Millions of Iranian farmers will have to leave their economically unviable villages during the next decade. Yet we do not mean to achieve this through coercion. Using the techniques of persuasion to achieve this mass transfer of productive ability to more promising and better equipped agricultural regions will certainly slow down the process of change. But we believe in changes brought about through the exercise of human will, and not imposed through the dictates of either the planner or the economist.

The next two decades will, therefore, witness a basic transformation of Iranian agriculture—a transformation that we hope will enable us not only to meet local demand for food and raw materials, but also to make a contribution toward fighting hunger and scarcity on a global scale.

Before leaving the subject of Iran's future technologies, I do want to refer to the climate of industrial relations in which Iran's industries will be owned and operated by the turn of the century.

Other essays presented at this symposium have already referred to the new legislation pertaining to the workers' ownership of private and public industries; therefore, I shall limit myself to a brief reference of its essentials.

Under this law, which has now been incorporated in the charter of our revolution, 49 percent of the shares of privately owned industries, and 99 percent of the shares of most government-owned industries, will be sold, in the first place, to the workers, and then offered to the farmers and the public at large. The government will provide the workers with long-term loans at concessionary interests, to facilitate the transaction. By 1978, the program will have been completely realized.

In my opinion, this is one of the most progressive pieces of social legislation ever enacted anywhere, ensuring not only the workers' sense of psychological and actual participation in the prosperity of their country, but a just and fair distribution of income as well.

In reviewing our path to the Great Civilization, I have already referred to our belief in the necessity of unity without uniformity. It was in that context that earlier this year Iran developed a new political organization embracing the entire nation. This new organization is the Iran Resurgence Party. It represents the revival and modernization of a long-established tradition of political solidarity and unity of action in our country. It came after many decades of experimenting with basically imported political party models. Those who have sought to study our new political organization, through terms of reference that have nothing to do with Iran's characteristics at the present stage of our development, have failed to understand our political institution. The Iran Resurgence Party, which we believe will be the vehicle for our nation's political development towards the Great Civilization, symbolizes our people's unity on three principles: the monarchy, the constitution and The Shah and People's Revolution.

The minimum condition for any nation's progress, indeed of survival, is agreement on a body of tenets and a set of definitions. Almost all nations have sought to define their basic points of unity in one way or another. In many cases these basic points have been imposed by minorities representing particular tribes, socioeconomic strata or self-perpetuating cliques. This often assumes the form of a one-party system in which membership in the party is an exclusive privilege. We all know of the philosophies and organizational styles of unique parties in totalitarian states. We also know the way in which the *de facto* one-party system operates in the whole or in certain parts of countries that supposedly have a multiparty national system. We have also, not long ago, witnessed how political extremists, at times using semi-conspiratorial techniques of organization, have tried to secure control of different parties and thus gain power and influence far beyond their original numerical strength or political influence.

Equally recently, we have heard the leaders of certain nations in whose countries the multiparty system had been introduced as an imported ideology declare that system a threat to their national survival, after years of experimenting with it.

It would indeed be difficult to find many countries with a multiparty system in which the government in power enjoys even numerical majority. A wide range of coalitions and majorities made possible through the indifference of millions of voters appears to be the rule. At the same time, many people who could make major contributions to their country's material and moral development are automatically excluded from the decision making process because of the so-called "democratic process of selection."

There are people who have been asking, in all sincerity, how could people with different political views belong to a single party. But we need go no further than the United States to answer that. Am I not right in thinking that Professor Galbraith and Governor Wallace both belong to the same party?

The Iran Resurgence Party is not an exclusive organization designed to set one section of the society against others. Apart from its three basic principles, it does not demand any kind of intellectual conformity. On the contrary, by eliminating artificial party barriers, it opens the way to the full and active participation of the entire nation in all stages of decision making. Our party's three basic principles are not products of a few ideologues or political prophets. Monarchy has been the focal point of Iranian unity through 25 centuries. It provides the basis of our nation's political life, and has always been accepted and revered by our people, despite the traumatic experience of many centuries.

The Iranian constitution, the second basic principle in the charter of the Iran Resurgence Party, was achieved by generations of struggle. Our forefathers voted for it with their lives. In its defense rose not only Iran's literate and enlightened urban groups, but also poor serfs from the deepest recesses of our old society and nomadic tribes that were hardly integrated in the country's political and economic system in the early 20th century. It was the first constitution to be won by the masses in an Asian country, and it was won through a revolution that embraced the whole of the nation, with the exception of a few small cliques backed by the imperialist forces of the day.

The Shah and People's Revolution, whose charter was ratified by the overwhelming majority of Iranians in a national referendum, provides the nation with a vital force for progress and regeneration. The charter of the revolution safeguards the interests of all sections of the society, thus unifying them in defense of interests that go beyond parochial limitations to assume national dimensions. Protecting the just interests of farmers, for example, becomes as important a goal to an urban intellectual as it is to the many millions of men and women working the land. The Iranian revolution, by rejecting the notion that sectoral interests are necessarily in conflict with each other, succeeds in turning them all into national interests.

Beyond these three principles, which I hope I have shown to be qualitatively different from traditional "credos" imposed by minorities on whole nations in so many countries, the Iran Resurgence Party not only provides for, but strongly demands, variety and versatility within a comprehensive system of dialogue, debate and, even, dissent. The aim is man, his dignity, happiness and prosperity; the means could be as diverse as men are capable of conceiving them.

More than 800 years ago, the great Iranian philosopher and saint Abu Sa'id spoke of "looking in the same direction without looking alike" as the system of thought coming most naturally to Iranians. The fact that the very word "class" did not have a Persian equivalent until one was borrowed from the Arabic demonstrates the fact that the Iranian people never allowed themselves to be regimented in social groups, locked in internecine feuds of an economic-ideological nature. Even at times of great stress in our history, when divisive forces were strong, the Iranian people were constantly able to maintain their national unity, thanks to their ability to transcend factional conflicts. Thus the borrowed model I referred to proved unable to strike roots here, essentially because it worked toward uniformity while ignoring unity.

I have attempted briefly to review the natural, technological, economic and political factors which, I believe, will play key roles in shaping our future society. We have achieved our revolution on the basis of our traditions and not against them. This, I believe, shall continue to chart our path to the Great Civilization. The Shahanshah has said: "The best way for me to describe the soul and the philosophy of our revolution is to stress the fact that it is not an imported commodity but a purely Iranian movement completely adapted to our traditions. It would have been undignified on the part of a country, which, during millennia, had so much enriched thought, philosophy and logic, to borrow ideas emanating from foreign quarters."

By remaining Iranian we do not only preserve our cultural identity, of which we are justly proud, but will, I believe, also contribute to world peace and international concord. Whenever the world was dominated by but a few "ways of life," with only a few options open to all nations, conflict and war became inevitable. World peace and international economic and cultural development are conditional on the achievement and maintenance of full freedom of choice for all nations. Attempts at imposing certain ways of life and certain options on any nation, whether through direct war or via cultural invasion and economic pressure, constitute direct threats to world peace and understanding. If we are all going to live in peace and benefit from sharing each other's experiences, if we are to meet together the great challenges of the third millennium, we ought not only to accept but also to endorse and support each and every nation's freedom to shape its own destiny. It would be a dull and dangerous world without an Iranian way of life, an American way of life, a Vietnamese way of life, a Peruvian way of life and so on. Cultural and technological imperialism could be as dangerous as economic and political imperialism proved to be in the 19th century. The sharing of experiences, exchanges of views, debate and dialogue and the comparing of notes on an international scale ought to proceed on the basis of equality and mutual respect.

Iran, because of its historic role, its geographic location and its diverse cultural contacts, is in a privileged position for advocating cultural and political diversity within a framework of international unity and solidarity. We mean to assume our responsibilities in this domain with greater vigor and dedication. Certainly, we do not presume to teach the world how to overcome its problems and how to utilize its resources for the betterment of the human condition. But we are fully prepared to play our part in the common quest for future peace and prosperity. In this respect, I am certain that the association between your organization and our country could prove beneficial to mankind as a whole. The very name of your Institute, the Aspen Institute for Humanistic Studies, gives you all an essential, perhaps even a vital, role in encouraging and fostering the kind of inquiry the contemporary world requires, if we are all to progress in freedom and peace.

Comments and Discussion

When Prime Minister Hoveyda had concluded his remarks, he responded to questions from participants along the following lines:

Commenting on the prospect of joint policy between Iran and Western Europe, in light of détente, and on Iran's relations with the EEC, the Prime Minister suggested that, given time, the Helsinki agreement may yield results. Iran is not opposed to détente—talking about peace is preferable to talking about war—but it is important to think globally. *Everyone* should work for détente in an interdependent world, where even a small country can make trouble. A two-way arrangement mutually beneficial to the East and West is needed. If economic colonialism disappears and a new world order is established, with a just division of labor in the world, this can contribute to understanding. As for the EEC, Iran has had difficulties. Agreement on the basis of terms set forth by the EEC is no longer possible; new terms must be discussed.

Commenting on how to stimulate a sense of social responsibility among Iranian intellectuals, the Prime Minister observed that intellectuals should meet the masses, visit farms and experience the life of the nation. Intellectuals who do not know their society cannot occupy their proper place in a nation. (Future symposia might include some Iranian farmers and U.S. workers—people without high social status.) Small groups may concern themselves with theoretical knowledge and not its application, but persons who apply knowledge must serve the larger public.

On the question of whether Iran's new elite and the centralization of oil revenues may be contributing to increasing centralization of political power in Iran, the Prime Minister indicated that Iran's policy of decentralization holds the answer. People in the rural areas should make decisions affecting their lives. Ministers are traveling to the regions; the system of provincial, district, city and village councils is also expected to help. Strong central planning by U.S.-trained officials is being modified to include decentralized and regional planning. Experiments are needed to see what methods are best.

To questions about when, and how much, oil prices will be increased and about the possibility of a joint OPEC-OECD fund to aid the Third World, the Prime Minister indicated, first, that oil prices may fluctuate. Second, he recalled that His Imperial Majesty The Shah has proposed a joint OPEC-OECD fund to aid developing countries; a majority of the 12 OPEC countries favored such a fund but some were opposed. Very poor countries will suffer from a new price increase, but oil may be a relatively unimportant factor among all the factors that determine their economies. Figures have been requested from the World Bank on the 25 poorest nations.

Commenting on whether decentralization can help to achieve more equitable income distribution, the Prime Minister indicated that bringing industries to rural areas; gradually increasing taxes, with tax revenues to be spent in rural areas; and reduced population in rural areas should contribute to more equitable income distribution.

Responding to a question about possible joint regional security arrangements in the Persian Gulf area, the Prime Minister noted that the Shah has proposed collective security for the Gulf by all states, large or small. If achieved, this could reduce the risks of war and subversion. Such a plan might also work for the

Indian Ocean; the Shah has proposed collective economic arrangements for the Indian Ocean, and these might lead later to a defense arrangement.

An Iranian added, on the question of whether Iran is trying to expand its economic growth too rapidly, that as the era of Iran's oil power declines, the era of gas power will begin. It is not impossible that Iran's gas reserves—estimated and not yet discovered—are worth $2 trillion. If this is true, Iran can achieve all its development goals without exhausting its resources.

8. A Humanistic Approach to Development

Address by Her Imperial Majesty The Shahbanou of Iran*

I feel deeply honored to be the recipient of the special award of the Aspen Institute for Humanistic Studies, which I accept with the utmost pleasure. I also wish to express my sincere joy at meeting you once again at the culmination of what I hope has been a sucessful Symposium. In thus honoring me with your special award, I consider this a tribute to the Iranian people as a whole. For whatever this country has achieved during the past few years is the fruit of dedicated and imaginative endeavors of our people as a whole, under enlightened leadership.

Your gathering at Persepolis bears testimony to growing interest in international dialogue, aimed at achieving deeper comprehension not only of thoughts and ideas but also of hopes and common endeavors. It is my hope that the contents of the essays presented here and the ensuing dialogue have served to provide you with a more intimate knowledge of the Iran of today and her prospects for the future.

I would like to extend my warmest appreciation to the Institute for its efforts in making this a creative gathering. Fortunately for all of us who inhabit what Buckminster Fuller called "Spaceship Earth," there exist organizations that concern themselves with the value content of research, of ideas, of those activities that ultimately aim to promote the quality of life.

---

*As the Symposium's final act, Aspen Institute Chairman Robert O. Anderson and President Joseph E. Slater, on behalf of the Institute's trustees, presented the Aspen Institute's Special Humanistic Award to Her Imperial Majesty Farah Pahlavi The Shahbanou of Iran. The citation read:

"Special Award of the Aspen Institute for Humanistic Studies
to
Her Imperial Majesty Farah Pahlavi The Shahbanou
of Iran

In recognition of Her Majesty's extensive commitment to social, cultural, and humanistic development; personal demonstration of the contribution that dedicated, sustained leadership can make in society; and Her Majesty's services towards improving the quality of life and in the mobilization of those cultural traditions, the richness of which provide individuals with the means of recovering their identity as well as their capacity for creation and expression."

The Shahbanou accepted the Special Humanistic Award with the above address:

During my brief visit to Aspen in early July of this year, I was very much impressed with both the content of the seminars and the setting in which they were conducted. I had the opportunity to attend the Institute's annual meeting of the board of trustees and discuss many issues I consider relevant to the plight of modern man. I realized how important it was for the active individual—whether his activity be business, politics, science, medicine, etc.—to be able to break away from the socially conditioning and partially imprisoning routine of daily life in order to come to a place like Aspen, where the Institute can help put him in touch with the social value of his work.

Too often we fail to question the roots and the ethics of the businessman's urge for profits and the politician's quest for power. Medicine begins as a lofty pursuit in the tradition of Hippocrates and winds up as a commercial proposition. Even science, which has been heralded as man's savior in the 20th century, fails to instill in people the need to question the value of what they are doing. There are many other examples on which I shall not dwell. Yet, I want to emphasize that although we live in a world of specialization, with tremendous forces attempting to shape us into technocrats, it would be to the benefit of man and society to question the values that lie behind our behavior. We must begin to think of ourselves as Renaissance men and women, rather than technocrats blindly doing a job; to place the individual again in the center of things and to remind ourselves that the ultimate aim of human activity should be geared toward the achievement of a creative humanistic world free from material want.

The Renaissance man may indeed be what we are all after. Otherwise, why bother to arrange for business managers to attend executive seminars that concentrate on Plato, Dostoevsky, Locke and Machiavelli, to name just a few. Wouldn't a series of lectures on business or economics be more appropriate? As seen from our vantage point, we would say no. For we share the Institute's desire to widen the horizons of man in the hope that he will recognize—more profoundly than the technocrat—the interdependence of social phenomena.

In Iran, we are not oblivious to the chasm that exists between the Renaissance man and the technocrat, between overall knowledge and excessive specialization. We are trying as rapidly as possible to achieve the goals of what His Imperial Majesty The Shahanshah has termed the Great Civilization. While the process of the economic transition and social transformation toward that goal seems clear, some ambiguity surrounds the cultural and psychological elements of this civilization.

Progress is not simply a quantitative economic phenomenon. It is above all a human process. Failure to work this significant factor into any calculus of development is an invitation to social and human catastrophe. Progress requires and creates new cultural values, norms and concepts while redefining the traditional ones.

In Iran, while we are proudly committed to our rich heritage and traditions, we shall not hesitate to create an environment conducive to achieving the human aspects of our aspired goals. This may well entail a new set of values under which a greater balance will be achieved between the material and the spiritual needs of man.

It is our hope in Iran that the end result of our unified approach to development will eliminate the alienation of man from man, of man from nature, and of man from society. In our schemes for development and our aspirations for a new economic, social and political order, man is the end and not simply the means. The cultural and sociopsychological changes that must—of necessity—accompany the economic transformation of our society will hopefully be a synthesis of our traditions and the social requisites for modernization. If the requirements of specialization have taken man away from the focal point of human endeavors, our hope is that through awareness, good leadership and good planning, we will reach the era that will restore the individual to his proper position. While the task is difficult and success by no means guaranteed, we should not be dismayed. And we must not forget that the spiritual balance we wish can be achieved only after the attainment of a material balance whereby all individuals are able to satisfy their basic human needs.

In the transition period to affluence, rather sophisticated indicators for the precise measurement of economic progress, in terms of its psychological, social and cultural effects, need to be emphasized. We are indeed in great need to develop human and humanitarian indicators to measure the effect that any social program has on the psyche of man and the extent to which it contributes to his happiness or alienation. In the battle of indicators, man must prevail, and it is my hope that all men and women of goodwill throughout the world will contribute their share to this endeavor.

Aspen Institute/Persepolis Symposium Participants

Non-Iranian Participants

Graham Allison
John Fitzgerald Kennedy
School of Government
Harvard University

Robert O. Anderson
Chairman, Aspen Institute
for Humanistic Studies
Aspen/New York

Les Aspin
Democratic Congressman
Wisconsin

Maureen Aspin
National Center for
Voluntary Actions
Washington, D.C.

Peter W. Avery
King's College
Cambridge University, England

Claudine Rulleau Balta
Journalist
Paris

Paul Balta
Specialist, Middle
Eastern Affairs
Le Monde, Paris

Catherine Bateson
Dean of Graduate Studies
Damavand College, Tehran

Iran: Past, Present and Future

Marion Countess Doenhoff
Publisher, Die Zeit
Hamburg, The Federal
Republic of Germany

Francois Duchene
Director, Center for
Contemporary European Studies
University of Sussex, England

Alvin C. Eurich
President, Academy for
Educational Development
New York

Nell P. Eurich
Consultant to International Counci
for Educational Development
New York

Georges Fischer
Director of Research,
National Center for Scientific
Research,
Paris

Jacques Freymond
Director, Graduate Institute of
International Studies
Geneva

Antoinette Freymond

John W. Gardner
Chairman, Common Cause
Washington, D.C.

Aida Gardner

Richard N. Gardner
School of Law
Columbia University, New York

Danielle Gardner

Robert F. Goheen
Chairman, Council on
Foundations, Inc.
New York

Margaret Goheen

William C. Greenough
Chairman, Teachers Insurance
and Annuity Association
New York

Doris Greenough

Anthony G. S. Griffin
Chairman, Home Oil
Company Limited
Toronto

Kathleen L. Griffin

Najeeb E. Halaby
Halaby International Corporation
New York

William L. Hanaway, Jr.
University of Pennsylvania
Philadelphia

Lorraine Hanaway

Alan Hart
Director of World Film
Maidstone, Kent, England

Nicole Hart

Bohdan Hawrylyshyn
Centre d'Etudes Industrielles (CEI)
Geneva

Lennie Hawrylyshyn

James F. Henry
President
The Edna McConnell
Clark Foundation
New York

Susan Henry

Philip E. Hoffman
U.S. Representative to
U.N. Commission on Human Rights;
Chairman, Executive Committee,
U.S. Realty & Investment Co.
Newark, New Jersey

Bertha Hoffman

Evelyn Linowitz

John H. Lorentz
Middle East Studies Center
Portland State University
Oregon

Golriz Lorentz

Mochtar Lubis
Journalist
Jakarta, Indonesia

Hallie Lubis

Roy MacLaren
Senior Advisor, Department of
Industry, Trade and Commerce
Ottawa, Canada

Alethea MacLaren

Yoichi Maeda
Managing Director
International House of Japan, Inc.
Tokyo

Yu Maeda

Lucy Rowan Mann
Executive Secretary and
Assistant Treasurer
The Walter W.
Naumburg Foundation
New York

Robert Mann
Musician/Composer
New York

Marya Mannes
Author/Lecturer
New York

Paul E. Martin
President and Chief
Operating Officer
Canada Steamship Lines, Ltd.
Montreal

Sheila Martin

Robert B. McKay
Director, Aspen Institute
Program on Justice, Society
and the Individual
New York

Kate McKay

Donald C. McKinlay
Attorney
Denver, Colorado

Helen McKinlay

Cesare Merlini
Director, Istituto Affari
Internazionali (I.A.I.)
Rome

Luciana Merlini

Arjay Miller
Dean, Graduate School
of Business
Stanford University

Frances Miller

Mollie Moon (Mrs. Henry Lee)
Member, National Advisory
Food and Drug Committee,
U.S. Department of Health,
Education and Welfare
New York

Jose Antonio Munoz-Rojas
Secretary General of
the Banco Urquijo;
Director, Society of Economic
and Social Development
Madrid

Marilu Munoz-Rojas

John M. Musser
President, General
Service Foundation
St. Paul, Minnesota

Elizabeth W. Musser

Kenneth D. Naden
President
National Council of
Farmer Cooperatives
Washington, D.C.

Elizabeth M. Naden

Zygmunt Nagorski, Jr.
Director, The Thomas J. Watson
Meetings Council on
Foreign Relations
New York

Waldemar A. Nielsen
Director, Aspen Institute Program
on Pluralism and
the Commonweal
New York

John B. Oakes
Editor of the Editorial Page
The New York Times, New York

Margery Oakes

Andrew Peacock
Member of Parliament
and Foreign Minister
Melbourne (Victoria), Australia

Susan Peacock

Aurelio Peccei
Vice Chairman,
Olivetti & Company,
Rome

James A. Perkins
Chairman, International Council for
Educational Development
New York

Ruth Perkins

Howard Petersen
Chairman, Fidelity Bank
Philadelphia

Elizabeth Petersen

Aronelle S. Pines
Psychiatric Social Worker
Urbana (Illinois) School System

David Pines
Professor of Physics,
University of Illinois, Urbana;
and Chairman, Board on
International Scientific Exchange,
National Academy of Sciences
Washington, D.C.

John Powers
Academy for
Educational Development
New York

Kimiko Powers

Donald S. Rickerd
President, Donner Canadian Foundation
Toronto

Julie Rickerd

Jacquelin Robertson
Architect, Llewelyn-Davies,
V. A. Shoraka
Tehran

Marianna Robertson

William Roth
Roth Real Estate
San Francisco, California

Joan Roth

Timothy Rothermel
Special Assistant to
the Secretary General
United Nations, New York

Joan Ebert Rothermel

Dankwart Rustow
Graduate Center (Political Science)
City University of New York

Teodore Shanin
Department of Sociology
University of Manchester
Manchester, England

Colette Shulman
Leader in International
Women's Affairs
New York

Iran: Past, Present and Future

Marshall D. Shulman
Russian Institute
Columbia University

J. E. Slater
President, Aspen Institute for
Humanistic Studies
Aspen/New York

Anne Slater

Soedjatmoko
Diplomat
Jakarta, Indonesia

Mini Soedjatmoko

Theo Sommer
Editor-in-Chief, Die Zeit
Hamburg, The Federal
Republic of Germany

Stephen Stamas
Vice President, Public Affairs
Exxon Corporation
New York

Elaine Stamas

Murray E. Stewart
Executive Vice-President
International Agribusiness
Alexander & Baldwin, Inc.
Honolulu

Muriel A. Stewart

Shepard Stone
Director, Aspen Institute Berlin
West Germany

Mildred Talbot
President, National Council of Women
New York

Phillips Talbot
President, The Asia Society
New York

William J. vanden Heuvel
Partner, Stroock & Stroock & Lavan
New York

Arthur J. Vidich
Graduate Faculty, Sociology
and Anthropology, New School
for Social Research
New York

Mary R. Vidich

Adam Watson
Director-General, International
Association for Cultural Freedom
London/Paris

Katherine Watson

Harold M. Williams
Dean, Graduate School
of Management
University of California
at Los Angeles

Estelle Williams

Shirley Williams
Secretary of State, Department of
Prices and Consumer Protection
London

Page H. Wilson
Advisor, Women, Food and
Population Program
Population
Crisis Committee
Washington, D.C.

Thomas W. Wilson, Jr.
Director, Aspen Institute Program on
Environment and the Quality of Life
Washington, D.C.

Hans Wuttke
Managing Director
Dressner Bank, A.G.
Frankfurt am Main, Federal
Republic of Germany

Tadashi Yamamoto
Director, Japan Center for
International Exchange
Tokyo

Chiyoko Yamamoto

Daniel Yankelovich
Yankelovich & Associates
New York

Hasmieg Yankelovich

Masamoto Yashiro
Esso Standard Sekiyu
Kabushiki Kaisha
Tokyo

Yoko Yashiro

Charles W. Yost
Chairman, National Committee on U.S.
–China Relations; Senior Fellow,
Brookings Institution
Washington, D.C.

Irena Yost

Dorothy S. Zinberg
Program for Science and
International Affairs
Harvard University

Norman Zinberg, M.D.
Cambridge, Mass.

Marvin Zonis
Center for Middle Eastern Studies
University of Chicago

Lucy Salinger Zonis

Iranian Participants

Gholam Reza Afkhami
Deputy Minister for
Social Affairs
Ministry of Interior

Nader Afsharnaderi
Professor of Sociology
Tehran University

Ismail Ajami
Professor of Sociology
Pahlavi University, Tehran

Amin Alimard
Deputy Minister
Ministry of Interior

Bahman Amini
President
Ghazali College, Ghazvin

Parvin Amini
Director for Coordination
Private and Public Sector
Plan and Budget Organization

Farokh Aminzadeh
Director, Population and
Manpower Plan and
Budget Organization

Lily Amir-Arjomand
Director
Institute for the Intellectual
Development of Children and
Young Adults

Abbas Amiri
Executive Director
International Institute
for Political and
Economic Studies

Mohamad Ali Amiri
Director, Bureau of Education
Plan and Budget Organization

Ahmad Ashraf
Director, Division of Planning
for Social Development; Professor of
Sociology, National University, Tehran

Mehran Assadi
Deputy Director, Planometrics
and General
Economy Bureau
Plan and Budget Organization

Firouz Bagher-Zadeh
Director General of Iran Center
for Archeological Research

Hamıd Baghshomali
Professor of Economics
National University of Iran,
Tehran

Shaul Bakhash
Journalist
Keyhan newspaper

Jaffar Boushehri
Professor of Law,
University of Tehran; Attorney-at-Law

Reza Doroudian
Undersecretary for Economic
Affairs Ministry of
Cooperatives and Rural Affairs

Cyrus Elahi
Professor of Political Science
National University of Iran,
Tehran

Hadi Entekhabi
Alternate Member of the Board
and Deputy Director of
International Affairs
The National Iranian Oil Company

Reza Fallah
Deputy Chairman and Managing
Director of International Affairs
The National Iranian Oil Company

Mohsen Fardi
Director of International
Economic Bureau
Plan and Budget Organization

Bahere Farhang
Principal,
Anoushiravan Dadgar High School

Hormaz Farhat
Vice Chancellor, University
of Farabi, Tehran;
Chairman, Department of
Music, Tehran University

Khodadad Farmanfarmaian
Chairman of the Board
Industrial Bank of Iran

Mansoor Farsad
Director, Bureau of Financial
Resources Plan and
Budget Organization

Mohamad Ali Fekrat
Professor of Economics
Georgetown University
Washington, D.C.

Fereydoun Fesharaki
Visiting Fellow, Center
for Middle Eastern Studies
Harvard University

Mahmood Foroughi
Ambassador; Director, Institute for
International Affairs, Tehran

Manouchehr Ganji
Special Advisor to
the Prime Minister;
Professor of International Law,
Tehran University

Ahmad Ghoreyshi
Dean, Faculty of Economics
and Political Science
National University, Tehran

Gholam H. Kazemian
Minister Counsellor for
Cultural Affairs
Imperial Embassy of Iran
Washington, D.C.

Shirin Mahdavi
Analyst, Bureau of Planning
Plan and Budget Organization

Abdolmajid Majidi
Minister of State in
Charge of Plan and
Budget Organization

Symposium Participants

475

Farhang Mehr
President
Pahlavi University, Shiraz

Hassan Ali Mehran
Deputy Minister
Ministry of Economic
Affairs and Finance

Abbas Milani
Professor of Political Science
National University
of Iran, Tehran

Ismail Mofidi
Researcher
The Institute of International
Relations

Mohammad Moghadam
University Professor;
Consultant to the
Imperial Organization for
Social Services

Habib Momayez
Professor of Political Science
National University
of Iran, Tehran

Farokh Najmabadi
Minister of State in Charge
of Industries

Bagher Namazi
Undersecretary of State
for Regional Affairs
Plan and Budget Organization

Fereydoun Naseri
Deputy Minister
Ministry of Labor
and Social Affairs

Nosratollah Khatibi Noori
Chief of the Office of Research
Ministry of Cooperatives
and Rural Affairs

Hassah Parnianpoor
University Professor; Consultant, Agency
for Atomic Energy

Parviz Parsa
Official at the
Imperial Inspectorate

Hashem Pessaran
Acting Director, Economic
Research Department
Central Bank of Iran

Rouhollah Ramazani
Visiting Professor
University of Virginia
Charlottesville, Virginia

Nosratollah Rassekh
Chairman, History Department
Lewis and Clark College
Portland, Oregon

Keyvan Saleh
Director Iranian National
Bank Hospital

Hamideh Sedghi
Analyst
Plan and
Budget Organization

Shapoor Shahbazi
Director
Achaemanid Institute,
Persepolis

Iraj Tabibzedeh, M.D.
World Health Organization

Amir Taheri
Journalist
Kayhan newspaper

Mahmood Tajdar
Director General in Charge of
Economic Statistics Affairs
Central Bank of Iran

Abdollah Tamadon
Deputy Minister
Ministry of Agriculture

Gholam-Ali Tavassoli
Sociologist; University lecturer;
Official of the
Imperial Inspectorate

Firouz Tofigh
Professor of Sociology,
Tehran University;
Deputy Minister of State
and Director of Iran's
Statistical Order

Firouz Vakil
Director, Planometrics and
Central Economy Bureau
Plan and
Budget Organization

Ehsan Yarshater
Director, Middle Eastern Center
Columbia University
New York

Symposium Staff

Jill Davis
Assistant Secretary to
Board of Trustees
Aspen Institute for
Humanistic Studies
New York

Robert Dalrymple
Assistant to Forrest Murden
New York

Hassan Ghorbani
Managing Director
Iranian Center for
International Conferences
Tehran

Jane W. Jacqz
Symposium Rapporteur
New York

Moselle Kimbler
Coordinator for Iran Program
Aspen Institute for
Humanistic Studies
New York

Loic Mirabaud
Assistant to Forrest Murden
New York

Gena Moezzi
Assistant to Manouchehr Ganji
Special Advisor to
the Prime Minister
Tehran

Forrest D. Murden
Consultant
New York

Index

socioeconomic development in Iran, 57 ff.
Soedjatmoko, Mr., 4
special regional projects (SRPs), 251
Statistical Center of Iran (SCI) Surveys, 268 ff.
systemic power, 228

technology, choice of, 451
The White Revolution (book), 40
Tofigh, Firouz, 57, 69

United Nations, 21 ff.
　—General Assembly, 25
　—Group of Experts, 25
　—Security Council, 27
Universal Education Act, 244

Vakil, F., 83, 122
values in Iran, 433
Voluntary Corps, 212
Vossough-ed-Dowleh, 36

westernization of Iran, 428
White Revolution Charter of Iran, 247
women's condition in Iran, 201 ff.
Women's Organization of Iran (WOI), 213,
　239
World Food Conference, 18

Yankelovich, Daniel, 1, 3
Yarshater, Ehsan, 407, 438

Zoroastrianism, 409

Aspen Institute for Humanistic Studies

717 Fifth Avenue
New York, New York 10022

Post Office Box 219
Aspen, Colorado 81611

Robert O. Anderson, Chairman
Joseph E. Slater, President
John Hunt, Vice President

The Aspen Institute for Humanistic Studies, a private, non-profit organization founded in 1949, is a unique national and international institution concerned with the problems of contemporary life. It has a thought-leading-to-action approach to major societal issues. It brings to contemporary problems an act of faith in the humanistic tradition: that one must both reflect and act in order to ensure that all human enterprise—political, scientific, economic, intellectual, and artistic—will serve the needs of human beings and their institutions.

Directors, Thought-Leading-To-Action Programs

Douglass Cater, Communications and Society
Harlan Cleveland, International Affairs
Francis Keppel, Education for a Changing Society
Robert B. McKay, Justice, Society and the Individual
Waldemar Nielsen, Pluralism and the Commonweal
Walter Orr Roberts, Science, Technology and Humanism
Shepard Stone, Aspen Institute Berlin
Thomas W. Wilson, Jr., Environment and the Quality of Life

Aspen Institute Berlin
Inselstrasse 10
1 Berlin 38
WEST GERMANY

Aspen Institute in Japan
A cooperative program with
The International House in Japan, Inc.
Tokyo 107 JAPAN

Special Advisors

Antonio Carillo-Flores
Secretary General, World Population Council
Special Consultant for Latin American Affairs

Alvin C. Eurich
President, Academy for Educational Development
Special Advisor to the Institute

Fereydoun Hoveyda
Special Advisor for Middle Eastern
and United Nations Affairs

Teddy Kollek
Mayor, Jerusalem
Special Advisor on Public Affairs and
the Quality of Life

John G. Powers
Academy for Educational Development
Special Advisor to the President

Mostafa Tolba
Executive Director, United Nations
Environment Program
Special Advisor to the Institute

Charles W. Yost
Special Advisor and Coordinator
of Aspen Institute/Iran Program